Security Architecture: Design, Deployment and Operations

Christopher M. King
Curtis E. Dalton
T. Ertem Osmanoglu

Osborne/**McGraw-Hill**
New York Chicago San Francisco
Lisbon London Madrid Mexico City
Milan New Delhi San Juan
Seoul Singapore Sydney Toronto

Osborne/**McGraw-Hill**
2600 Tenth Street
Berkeley, California 94710
U.S.A.

To arrange bulk purchase discounts for sales promotions, premiums, or fund-raisers, please contact Osborne/**McGraw-Hill** at the above address. For information on translations or book distributors outside the U.S.A., please see the International Contact Information page immediately following the index of this book.

Security Architecture: Design, Deployment and Operations

234567890 FGR FGR 01987654321

ISBN 0-07-213385-6

Publisher
Brandon A. Nordin

Vice President & Associate Publisher
Scott Rogers

Executive Editor
Steven Elliot

Project Manager
Dave Nash

Acquisitions Coordinator
Alex Corona

RSA Press Project Manager
Mark Luna

Technical Editor
Stephen Beck, RSA Security

Cover Design
Greg Scott

Production
MacAllister Publishing Services, LLC

Contents

Acknowledgments

To Shannon, my lovely and supportive wife, whom this book would not be possible without, may you always dream with me.
To my sons Michael and Nicholas, dreams can come true if you work hard and take the time to follow them through.
To Doreen for her support and to Connie my biggest fan.

—Christopher M. King

To God, without whose blessings, nothing is possible.
To my wife Kelly, whose boundless love and support replenishes and enriches my soul.
To my daughters Kaylee and McKenzie; if all that I could ever be is your dad—that would be enough.
To my mom, who is so loving and giving of herself—and so proud, but still asks what I do for a living.
To my dad, who introduced me to adventure, challenges, and taught me to dream.
And to CMK for guiding my career in this direction.

—Curtis E. Dalton

To Mom & Dad for their continuous support.
To Cathy Watson for being there for me during the long hours of writing.

—T. Ertem Osmanoglu

About the Authors

Christopher M. King, CISSP—Security Practice Leader

Chapter 1: Business and Application Drivers (Case Study)
Chapter 11: Application Security
Chapter 15: Validation and Maturity
Christopher M. King is the Practice Leader of Information Security group at Greenwich Technology Partners. He has over 16 years experience in the information security field with particular expertise in quantifying security risks, vulnerabilities, and applying emerging security technologies such as VPN, PKI, and Web access controls to large-scale business applications. He is a regular contributor to *Information Security* Magazine and *Business Communications Review*.
You can reach Chris King at cking.rsapress@rsasecurity.com.

Curtis E. Dalton, CISSP—Regional Practice Leader

Chapter 5: Security Infrastructure Design Principles
Curtis E. Dalton is a Regional Practice Leader with Greenwich Technology Partners. He has more than 13 years experience designing and deploying large-scale information security and network-based solutions in industries ranging from finance to telecommunications, manufacturing, R&D, and has published numerous works in *Network* Magazine, *Information Security* Magazine, and *Business Communications Review*.
You can reach Curtis Dalton at cdalton.rsapress@rsasecurity.com.

T. Ertem Osmanoglu, CISSP, MCSE, CCNA—Managing Consultant

Chapter 4: Applying the Policies to Derive the Requirements
T. Ertem Osmanoglu is a Managing Consultant in the Security Practice of Greenwich Technology Partners. Mr. Osmanoglu has experience in the review, design, and implementation of secure electronic commerce infrastructures including certificate authorities, PKIs, and general network and host security. Mr. Osmanoglu regularly provides e-business strategy, risk management, and infrastructure consulting to Global 2000 companies, focused primarily upon Financial Services (FSIP) clients.
You can reach Ertem Osmanoglu at eosmanoglu.rsapress@rsasecurity.com.

About the Contributing Authors

Michael J. Santarcangelo, II, CISSP—Security Regional Practice Leader

Chapter 2: Security Polices, Standards, and Guidelines
Michael J. Santarcangelo, II, is a security regional practice leader in the information security practice of Greenwich Technology Partners. Prior to joining GTP, Mr. Santarcangelo worked as a consultant in the information security practice at Andersen Consulting. While at Andersen Consulting, he worked with several large clients to design and implement secure policy development solutions, user management systems, web platforms, and network architectures. Michael holds a Bachelor of Science Degree in Policy Analysis from Cornell University.

Keith E. Strassberg, CPA, CISSP—Senior Network Engineer

Chapter 3: Information Classification and Access Control Plan
Mr. Strassberg is an experienced information systems security consultant who holds a B.S. in Accounting from Binghamton University. Mr. Strassberg earned his CPA by working in the Computer Risk Management Group of Arthur Andersen, LLP where he aided clients by identifying and minimizing operational, technological and business-related risks present in their IT systems. Mr. Strassberg joined Greenwich Technology Partners ("GTP") in June of 1999. Working in their computer security practice, Mr. Strassberg has assisted numerous clients in developing risk assessment methodologies and information classification systems.

Thomas B. DeFelice, CISSP, MCSE, MCP, MCP +I—Senior Network Engineer

Chapter 6: Network Partitioning
Tom DeFelice is an experienced information systems security consultant with over 13 years in providing network and systems security design services. Most of his experience has been spent in many large multi vendor environments addressing interoperability and security concerns. Mr. DeFelice joined Greenwich Technology Partners ("GTP") in July of 1998. Working in their information security practice, Mr. DeFelice has assisted numerous clients in design and deployment of network security devices and reporting tools.

Brian Beckwith—Senior Network Engineer

Chapter 7: Virtual Private Networks
Brian Beckwith is a Consulting Engineer in the Security Practice of Greenwich Technology Partners. Mr. Beckwith is an experienced technology consultant with over 9 years of professional information systems experience, encompassing internetworking, open systems, information security practices, and methodologies. He

has an extensive background working in large corporate environments focusing on detailed designs and analysis for securing perimeter networks and corporate data communications. Brian holds a Bachelors Degree in Mathematics and Economics from Rutgers University.

Richard J. Gondek, CCIE (#5941), CISSP—Senior Network Engineer

Chapter 8: Wireless Security
Mr. Gondek is a security and internetworking consultant with a B.S. in Business Administration from Fordham University, and an M.A. in Computer Resource Management from Webster University. His areas of expertise include large scale network design, perimeter systems and network hardening, and emerging technologies, to include network traffic management and local and wide area wireless networking. Mr. Gondek joined Greenwich Technology Partners in October, 1999, and has focused on assisting clients with the process of securing and increasing the availability of their existing environments, while introducing new technologies and methods of communicating.

David E. Stern, CISSP—Network Engineer

Chapter 9: Platform Hardening
David E. Stern is a Senior Network Security Engineer at Greenwich Technology Partners in NYC. He was immersed into the UNIX and networking world in college after joining a startup ISP/security appliance developer. He has experience in systems, network, and security architecture and focuses on penetration tests, platform hardening, and system security analysis. David is also a volunteer Fireman/EMT and is currently Lieutenant of the EMS Company.

Carlos Macedo Gomes, CISSP—Senior Network Engineer

Chapter 10: Intrusion Detection Systems
Mr. Gomes achieved his B.S. in Computer Engineering from Texas A&M University in 1996. His entry into information systems security occurred in the early 1990's as an undergraduate and as one of several campus wide UNIX consultants during the campus security incident, which gave rise to the TAMU Tiger package. In 1996 Mr. Gomes joined NetSolve in Austin, TX which in close partnership with the WheelGroup of San Antonio jointly developed a NOC for monitoring WheelGroup NetRangers Intrusion Detection Systems (WheelGroup was bought by Cisco Systems in the 1998) and later Cisco PIXs. Mr. Gomes joined Greenwich Technology Partners ("GTP") in February of 2000 and has continued to use detailed TCP/IP forensics and analysis to solve problems and mitigate risks during clients engagements involving a wide variety of security and internetworking tools and systems.

J.R. Carlucci—Network Engineer

Chapter 10: PKI: Components and Applications

Mr. Carlucci has been employed as a consultant for over five years. He has helped design and deploy large NetWare and NT rollouts on both the client and server side. More recently, Mr. Carlucci has performed extensive research and design of PKI systems. Mr. Carlucci joined Greenwich Technology Partners ("GTP") in February 2000 in their computer security practice is currently designing a PKI system to support a large-scale VPN implementation.

Gene Berkinsky—Senior Network Engineer

Chapter 10: PKI: Components and Applications

Gene has been consulting for financial and pharmaceutical firms for the past seven years. Gene brings a well rounded background to the technology industry. He has a Sociology degree coupled with project management, operations, systems, and security work experience. He joined Greenwich Technology Partners in April of 2000 and has been heading up the testing, design, and implementation of Smart Cards and PKI at a major financial institution.

Gabriel Ioan—Consulting Engineer

Chapter 13: Security Event Management

Mr. Ioan has been involved in various computer projects since the early 1990's. Although he has been a consultant for a number of industries, his primary focus is on data communications and TCP/IP security for corporate and eCommerce projects in Banking and Brokerage, as a technical analyst and project lead responsible for architecture design and risk management. Mr. Ioan joined GTP in November of 2000, after serving as Technical Architect for an Internet systems management and deployment company, and continues to work with clients designing, deploying, and managing secure IP-based systems.

Steve A. Rodgers, CISSP—Principal Engineer

Chapter 14: Administration and Management

Mr. Rodgers is an experienced security consultant with a B.S. in Computer Information Systems from Southwest Missouri State University. Mr. Rodgers earned his CISSP while working as a senior consultant at International Network Services. Mr. Rodgers joined Greenwich Technology Partners ("GTP") in July of 2000 and has provided leadership and support to their security practice. In addition, he has assisted numerous clients in attack and penetration tests, high-level security architectures, as well as security policy and standards development.

About Greenwich Technology Partners

Greenwich Technology Partners (GTP) designs, builds and manages complex networks that utilize advanced Internet protocol, electro/optical, and other sophisticated technologies. Service offerings in the seven key technology areas that comprise integrated infrastructure services, including internetworking, security, directory services, convergence, systems engineering, performance management and network management. GTP's clients are large service providers and Global 2000 enterprises.

Through a proprietary GTP NetValue methodology, GTP's consultants and engineers provide a framework of best practices and procedures for managing and delivering professional services. The key distinguishing elements of GTP's solution include:

An objective approach that provides clients with vendor-neutral recommendations that enable optimal technology alternatives within the context of each clients' strategic business objectives, technology requirements and existing network infrastructures. Strategic relationships with industry-leading developers of network equipment and software. Technology expertise in the complex network technologies required in enterprise and service provider networks. A commitment to attracting and retaining experienced, highly skilled professionals who possess in-depth knowledge in a variety of advanced networking technologies, extensive field experience, and the leading industry certifications and credentials.

GREENWICH TECHNOLOGY PARTNERS

www.greenwichtech.com

About the Reviewer

As the leading publisher of technical books for more than 100 years, McGraw-Hill prides itself on bringing you the most authoritative and up-to-date information available. To ensure that our books meet the highest standards of accuracy, we have asked a number of top professionals and technical experts to review the accuracy of the material you are about to read.

Stephen Beck is the Director of Worldwide Consulting Services for RSA Security's BSAFE product line. In the more than two years since Stephen joined RSA in 1999, he has built a team of some of the most talented security professionals in the world. Stephen has more than 18 years of experience in the information systems industry, architecting, designing, implementing, and managing the development and delivery of complex information systems. He is a featured speaker at security industry conferences and seminars and is engaged with clients all over the world. Stephen received his B.S. in Computer Science from Brown University and his M.S. in Computer Science from the University of Michigan in Ann Arbor.

We take great pleasure in thanking Mr. Stephen Beck for his insights.

Preface

Chapter Organization

The intent of this book is to discuss the proper application of security technology to an applications life cycle. The security centric solution composed of security technology and its configuration is referred to as a security architecture. The purpose of the three case studies is to bring a sense of reality to this book. All of the case studies are taken from typical fortune 500 organizations; one is the corporate site and the other two are specific vertical applications (financial and healthcare).

The book is broken down into 3 distinct sections: 1) Planning and design; 2) applying the appropriate security technology to the case study; and 3) the operational and support process of the deployed system. If the reader is interested in a more in-depth study of the technology sections, they are many vertically focused texts on these subjects. See Figure 0-1.

Figure 0-1

Chapter Organization Pyramid

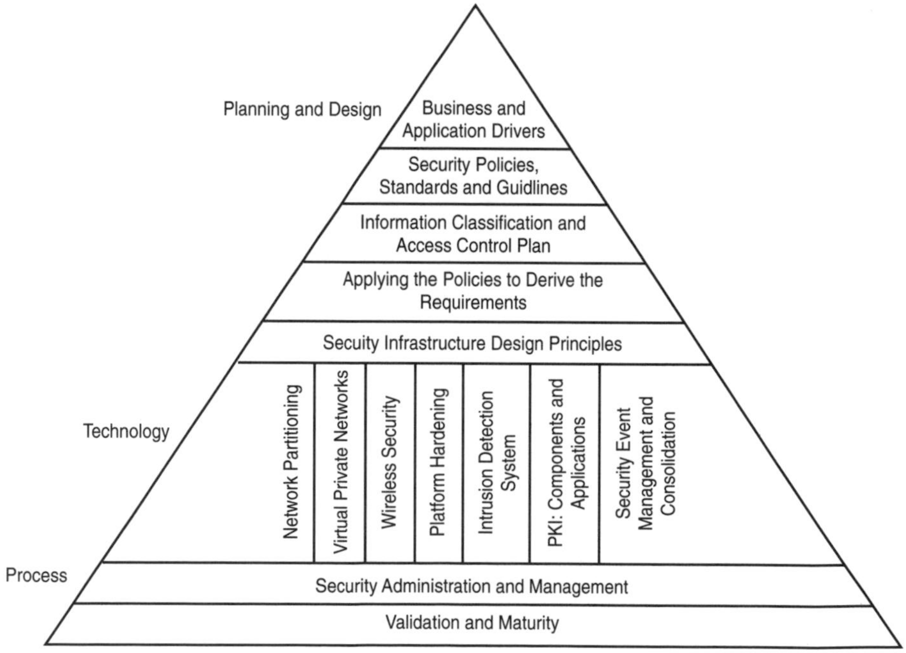

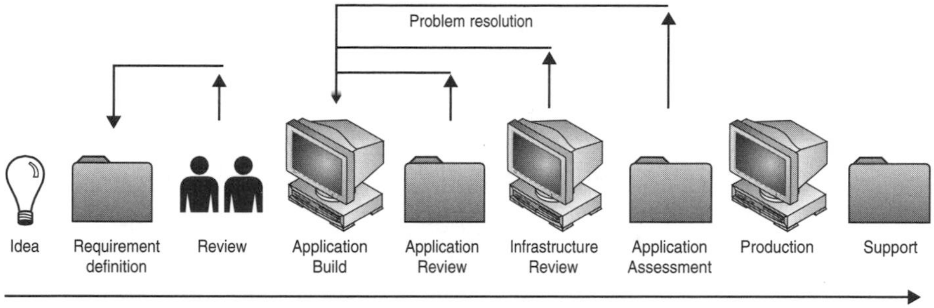

Figure 0-2

The Solutions Lifecycle

Figure 0-2 depicts a typical application lifecycle. All applications start with an idea to address a particular problem. The idea is captured in written form into a requirements definition document that is reviewed by senior management for approval. The application is then designed and built. This can be a one step or two step process (design, then get approval, then build). Once the application is reviewed, it must be placed within the infrastructure. Any changes to the infrastructure must be reviewed. After the application is place within the infrastructure, an security assessment can be performed to validate the changes do not present and insecurities. If no security exploits are found, then the application will bo movod in thc production environment, after which it will just require support.

Planning and Design

The best solution starts with a thorough plan and design phase. It also facilitates an less complex build and testing phases. In today's fast pace industry, many times this part of the lifecycle is cut short to make the "time to market" constraints.

Chapter 1—Business and Application Drivers

This chapter defines the business and the applications that solve the specific business problems. Each of the three case studies will be referenced in each chapter of the book. This will provide a common theme that each phase of the book organizational pyramid will address.

Chapter 2—Security Policies, Standards and Guidelines

Security policies form a foundation for all good security architectures. The differences between a policy, standard, and guideline are covered, as well as, applicable regulatory requirements depending on the vertical business (financial or health related).

Chapter 3—Information Classification and Access Control Plan

To justify the adequate security controls, the data needs to be valued from a quantitative and qualitative aspect. The data must be classified into certain levels depending on the risks of loss, reputation, competition, loss of data, and availability. The roles and responsibilities of the user base must be defined with the proper access control plan.

Chapter 4—Applying the Policies to Derive the Security Requirements

This chapter maps the security polices and regulatory specifications to the specific security requirements for the three case studies. The security requirements are categorized by security service (confidentiality, integrity, and availability). Depending on the types of processing required on the data, a specific access control mechanism will be employing (for example, authentication, authorization, auditing, and administration).

Chapter 5—Security Infrastructure Design Principles

The ability to develop a secure infrastructure that meets all the security requirements and can safeguard against any future attacks is a mixture of art and science. This chapter introduces basic design principles that are common throughout security deployments.

Security Technology

The security technology should never interrupt the business processes. Each technology section consists of a background section that provides the required background; a methodology section that shows how to use the technology; and lastly, an applications section that relates it to the case studies.

Chapter 6—Network Partitioning

The first line of defense to protect sensitive applications is a separate network. The only traffic on that network should be from trusted platforms. Direct connectivity from untrusted platforms and networks (for example, Internet and Extranet partners) is too risky. High availability techniques, multiple network interfaces, and host-based versus appliance platforms will all be covered.

Chapter 7—Virtual Private Networks

Faster edges and more access points to the Internet have propelled VPN technology. The ability to securely share a public network significantly lowers the cost of leased lines and increases the speed of traditional dial-up access. This relatively new technology does not come without challenges.

Chapter 8—Wireless Security

The ability to access information anytime, anywhere, in any manner, without a hardwire connection is the appeal of wireless networking. Wireless networks have more security challenges than wired networks (for example, eavesdropping, spoofing, and denial of service).

Chapter 9—Platform Hardening

The second line of defense to protect sensitive applications is a hardened platform. Poorly written applications or weak network controls could expose the platform to an unauthorized user. Cellophane unwrapped operating systems have many default user accounts and unnecessary network services. The only method to harden a platform is to test it with the application (for example, Web server, Database, or application server).

Chapter 10—Intrusion Detection Systems

To adequately monitor a network, host or application, an intrusion detection system must be employed. Firewall, platform, and application logging creates reams of information that is worthless to a human observer. IDSs vary between attack signature matching to anomaly recognition.

Chapter 11—Application Security

With multiple connections to the Internet, external business partners, and remote access traffic, traditional network and platform security controls do not provide the necessary granularity of access controls to sensitive resources. The infrastructure is not well suited to protect the inner application functionality and its data. Applications need to be able to ensure that they are used only for their intended purposes and only by the appropriate users. Application layer security is the enforcement of access control principles within the application to prevent and detect unauthorized access.

Chapter 12—Public Key Infrastructure: Components and Applications

Public Key Infrastructure (PKI) is a collection of components and procedures that support the management of cryptographic keys through the use of digital certificates. PKI-enabled applications provide authentication, integrity of data, confidentiality, and non-repudiation security services. This technology has been called the solution to many problems in the information security field. This chapter exposes the advantages, disadvantages, and applications to the case studies.

Operations and Support

The security architecture planning, deployment, and configuration are complete. In practice, security architecture components do not fail exposed (open). The main cause of exposures is due to human error (component misconfigurations). Managing the security components, administration of users, and security events. Lastly, a measure methodology that allows an organization to measure their security architecture against the best business practices is covered.

Chapter 13—Security Event Management and Consolidation

Security components are capable of generating very granular security events logs. The more devices located at strategic places in the architecture and the more detail per device will provide a clearing picture of the environment. Collaboration and correlation of all of these security events in real-time provides irrefutable proof that an attack is underway.

Chapter 14—Security Administration and Management

Security administrators manage network, platform, and application security configurations. User administration is generally outside a security administrator's purview. It is relegated to the business that owns the application or to a corporate help desk. This chapter covers all the aspects associated with managing a corporate environment, as well as, application management.

Chapter 15—Validation and Maturity

The security architecture planning, deployment, and operational processes are at the end of their life cycle. The security controls in any system should be commensurate with the business risks. A security assessment validates that the security architecture meets or exceeds the security policies and the best business practices. A security maturity model allows an organization to measure a security architecture based on the best business practices in the industry and tie it back to the business.

Foreword

The need to protect information is as old as information itself. The first documented mathematical "cipher" used to encode and decode messages was the Caesar cipher, attributed to Julius Caesar himself. Herodotus, the ancient Greek historian wrote in 479 BC:

"...as soon as news reached him at Susa that Xerxes had decided upon the invasion of Greece, he felt that he must pass on the information to Sparta. As the danger of discovery was great, there was only one way in which he could contrive to get the message through: this was by scraping the wax off a pair of wooden folding tablets, writing on the wood underneath what Xerxes intended to do, and then covering the message over with wax again.

"In this way the tablets, being apparently blank, would cause no trouble with the guards along the road. When the message reached its destination, no one was able to guess the secret until, as I understand, Cleomenes' daughter Gorgo (who was the wife of Leonidas) discovered it and told the others...This was done, the message was revealed and read, and afterwards passed on to the other Greeks..."

Ironically, in the world of information technology (IT), which has been in existence for around one hundred years, information privacy, integrity, authenticity, and reliability have, with the exception of government use, been largely an afterthought. It should therefore come as no surprise that in this modern age of interconnected computers, telephones, laptops, palmtops, and PDAs, the need to protect information has (re)emerged as one of the top priorities for the providers and consumers of information technology alike. As evidenced by the almost daily accounts of intrusion and mischief into corporate and government IT systems, and with the ongoing perception in the consumer community that the Internet can be a dangerous place, the demand for information security has never been greater.

The challenge to those of us in the information security industry is threefold: 1) to help our customers navigate and keep pace with the dizzying array of available security technologies while 2) simultaneously staying fluent in how to integrate security into the exponentially increasing combinations and permutations of IT devices, systems, applications, and infrastructures, and 3) affecting large scale behavioral changes in order to combat "social engineering" threats that exploit weaknesses in human nature (such as the use of passwords that are easy to remember and thus easily guessable by a potential intruder).

This book provides an excellent cross-section of the information security marketplace in terms of all three areas. It presents a comprehensive top-down view of the best practices involved in establishing and enforcing security policies, standards, and guidelines as well as processes for classifying information and users in order to assign access rights. Using business case studies as examples, it provides specific, practical information on how to design a security infrastructure and provides numerous examples of available security technologies (including exciting new capabilities in wireless security) and how and where these technologies integrate into an IT infrastructure.

Based on their cumulative years of experience implementing secure solutions for customers, the authors provide sensible, proven ideas for designing and implementing a security infrastructure as well as a menu of technology choices in each of several key areas. The result is a comprehensive, common sense guide to the field of information security that should provide technology consumers with actionable solutions to meet their information security requirements, now and in the future.

Stephen H. Beck
Director of Worldwide Professional Services
RSA Security, Inc.

Foreword

Information security has received unheralded attention of late, given the fact that the vast majority of commercial organizations are now connected to the Internet and the World Wide Web. These days, for most senior corporate executives, security is not just "on the radar screen": it's directly in their sights. A security breach can utterly deflate a company's market valuation and threaten the organization's very existence. Even minor breaches can place the organization's reputation, customer privacy information, and intellectual property at risk. As if that weren't enough, successful attacks can inflict major personal damage on individual corporate officers. The National Information Infrastructure Protection Act of 1996 makes corporate officers liable to stock-holders for gross negligence; according to the law, the company must show a due diligence for the protection of corporate assets.

With these kinds of risks, therefore, one would think that the deployment of effective security infrastructures would be a "no brainer" in most large organizations. Unfortunately, one would be wrong. Many organizations lack effective security measures for good (though not sufficient) reasons. Deploying a reliable security infrastructure is both complex and potentially costly, since security is fundamentally both a horizontal as well as vertical (pervasive) practice. There is much overlap with internetworking, systems, and network management. Worse still, the security environment is constantly changing. Security disciplines must keep pace with fast-moving application development technology. Web-based application environments are getting more loosely coupled (with processes distributed across Web servers, application servers, enterprise JAVA beans, and databases). Providing access control into these forms of distributed architecture is a major challenge. These problems will not go away with time. As new networks, applications, and platforms are developed (with ever-increasing speed and features), security defenses will consistently lag behind the rapid evolution of this technology.

Furthermore, delineating the return on investment (ROI) for the costs of deploying security can be a major challenge. When it comes to assessing the ROI, the security risk (and cost) has to be put into context with the business risk (and cost); an exercise that requires a major effort at many companies. Despite the widespread publicity around major security exploits, therefore, many organizations respond slowly or not at all: unless the impact of vulnerability can be mapped to a particular risk within the business, companies will continue to be reluctant to fund the safeguards, and to support extensive (and expensive) staffs of security experts.

In such an environment, how can organizations effectively address these issues? One alternative is to deploy outsourced solutions such as managed firewall services, remote access offerings, and remote security event monitoring. However, outsourcing the protection of an organization's assets to a third party can be risky, since outsourcers can typically protect only a company's outer shell (or perimeter). Once that perimeter has been compromised, hackers have a clear path to resources and sensitive data. So while outsourcing can be helpful, it will not address all the challenges.

Happily, there are tried and true approaches that have helped many organizations build secure and flexible infrastructures and protect even the most complex applications and resources. By applying the proper security techniques discussed in this book (planning, deploying access control mechanisms at various levels, and monitoring, to name a few), organizations can effectively (and cost-effectively) protect themselves in the face of unknown adversaries.

Johna Till Johnson
Senior Vice President
Chief Technology Officer
Greenwich Technology Partners
June, 2001

CHAPTER 1

Business and Application Drivers (Case Study)

Applying the information security discipline to real-life business applications is the goal of this book. Information security controls reduce the risk of potential exposures by restricting unauthorized individuals from an organization's computing resources. The information security field has evolved recently since the advent of the World Wide Web over the Internet, as the new computing paradigm of mainframes moved toward distributed systems. Prior to this, most of the information security research and development was done for the government to protect information affecting national security. For this reason, a majority of the present-day commercial security technology and the individuals whose career is information security have their roots in previous U.S. government work. Also, Internet Protocol Security (IPSec) and public key cryptography have their roots in the U.S. government. Public key cryptography is over 30 years old.

Mainframes historically have enjoyed the most mature access-control capabilities of all computing platforms. This is partly because they have been in existence since the beginning of the computing age and have fairly successfully resisted the pull to the open Internet. Mainframes also utilize inherent centralized controls to restrict access. This level of maturation in security required many years of refinement. This monolithic system has many layers of security with fine grain access to resources under its control. As distributed computing (for example, divide and conquer) was ushered into being during the 1980s, these protected resources were scattered among computing platforms with less stringent controls. In fact, subsequent distributed systems that were developed (for example, UNIX and Microsoft NT) were—contrastingly—inherently open. Application deployment (for example, Web server, application server, database server, content server, and directory server) has increased in complexity over the last five years. Multithreaded object-oriented applications take advantage of technologically improved hardware resources almost as fast as they are developed. This fact, coupled with the security weaknesses of the predominant network transport (TCP/IP), causes information security to become a moving target.

The information security discipline is worthless without something to protect. All applications in existence are developed for a specific purpose, typically to solve a business problem or improve productivity. With the associated cost of developing large-scale applications in today's market, senior management must give its approval to incur the cost of such an effort. Decision makers must weigh the monetary risk of security spending with the risk of doing nothing. This chapter details the background necessary to get an enterprise-class application functionally secure and operational within your environment without sacrificing stated business requirements.

Because the Y2K budget freezes have dissipated, information security now has the opportunity for critical financial backing enabling it to become an important and viable requirement in today's business model.

The Multi-National Conglomerate Corporation (MCC)

The MCC is analogous to a General Electric Company or Siemens Corporation. Companies of this magnitude are typically separated into business and consumer products and services divisions. Their lines of business are within each division (for example, consumer electronics, financial services, healthcare, insurance, plastics, and manufacturing). See Figure 1-1.

Three case studies are covered in this text. The first case study, entitled "Corporate," is modeled after typical corporate business and application requirements (for example, remote access, electronic mail, access to sensitive corporate applications, wide area network connectivity, Internet access, and so on).

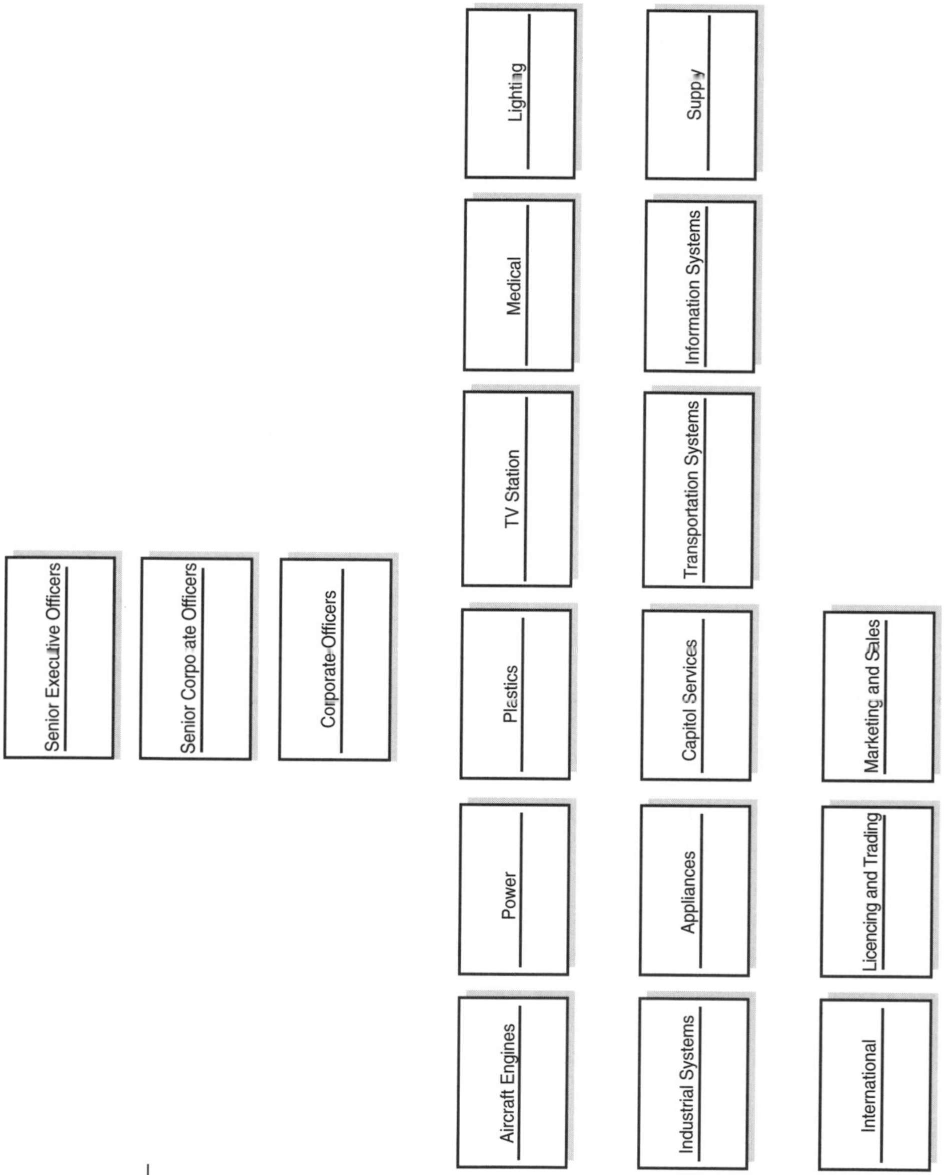

Figure 1-1 MCC high-level organization chart

The second case study, entitled "FinApp," is a typical business-to-business financial services application (for example, position calculations from trade and settlement activities, foreign exchange service, and trade capture). FinApp is a non-Web application.

The third case study, entitled "HealthApp," is a healthcare insurance Web-based application (posting electronic claims and billing inquires, physician office/hospital posting, and checking on posted claims).

Case Study #1—Corporate

The MCC corporate case exemplifies most of the typical applications and functions required by a large corporation. See Figure 1-2 for an MCC high-level organization chart.

MCC desktops and laptops are based on Microsoft Windows NT workstation. They are planning to migrate to Windows 2000 before the end of the fiscal year. The file and print services are based on Novell. A majority of their application servers run on UNIX variants (Sun Solaris and IBM-AIX); however, some application servers require Windows NT server platform.

Electronic mail (e-mail) is the main form of communication inside and outside of the corporation. E-mail utilizes an MCC address book to find any corporate user e-mail address (white pages) or a local address book of external or most frequent recipients of messages. E-mail attachments are used to send documents, presentations, spreadsheets, and Web links to an individual or a list of recipients. In many instances, the e-mail client is combined with a calendaring or scheduling function. Many of these closed and proprietary e-mail address books are the basis of an MCC directory. MCC is in the process of transitioning its users to Microsoft Exchange from an unsupported package.

MCC has many Internet access connections mainly for redundancy. The MCC Intranet is protected by a series of firewalls and access routers. All the user's network addresses are dynamically assigned and hidden by the firewall. Incoming connections from the Internet are allowed to the MCC Web servers, e-mail, domain name servers, and remote access using virtual private network (VPN) technology.

Internet traffic is not allowed directly to the MCC network; instead the public facing network (Demilitarized Zone) platforms communicate with the MCC Intranet. These DMZ platform operating systems and applications have been built securely to safeguard against software exploits.

The MCC sales and marketing Lines of Businesses (LODs) need to collaborate on the existing client base and prospective customers. The accounting information associated with each existing client (for example, number of units sold, discount, current product inventory) is separated. The MCC marketing group is also responsible for the content on the public facing Web server. They use a content management software package to ensure that content is accurate and to upload changes to their Web sites.

MCC is constantly updating and searching for new products to complement its business. The MCC marketing group champions this function. The MCC marketing database houses all the research analytics, proposed product upgrades, additions, and product release schedules.

All the product developments occur on the MCC Engineering network and platforms. Many of the engineers develop the necessary product hardware and software using their workstations. A majority of the engineers have portable computers to enable them to work outside of the office.

The MCC Legal and HR systems process all the personal information about the employees, customer contracts, and external partner agreements. With the recent legal and regularity awareness to personal information, these systems require more robust security controls.

MCC has over 5,000 UNIX variants, 10,000 Windows NT servers, and over 100,000 Windows NT workstations. Platform administration is still one of the most challenging security problems. Most platform and application administrators (NT administrator, UNIX superuser, database administrators) have unrestricted access to all of the sensitive resources residing on the systems that they administer.

The MCC information technology group (help desk) is responsible for supporting the internal (remote access, file and print, e-mail) and external (Web, VPN) users. The primary method of contact for this corporation is by voice and e-mail messages.

The MCC Enterprise Resource Planning (ERP) systems consist of SAP, Oracle Financial, and PeopleSoft. Access to these systems is tightly controlled using the security mechanisms provided by each product. See Table 1-1 for a list of MCC corporate application by function.

The ability to access the MCC network and its applications remotely is one of our biggest corporate initiatives. Remote users are executing sensitive applications, storing corporate data, and accessing non-corporate

Table 1-1

Corporate Application and Functional Breakdown

Corporate Function	Purpose	Components
Electronic mail, Calendaring	Collaboration	Mail gateway, LOB mail servers
Corporate directory	Locate users contact information	Series of directory servers tied to the LOBs
Internet connectivity	Research	Firewall, DMZ networks, Desktop browsers
Sales contact information (existing customer base and prospective clients)	Sales forecasting, accounting, legal departments	A client/server application with a DBMS backend
Marketing database	Repository for marketing research and engineering requests	A client/server application with a DBMS backend
Engineering network and systems	Repository for hardware and software designs of MCC products	Software configuration management system, CAD DBMS, home-grown repositories
Legal and HR network systems	Hold and process employee and legal information	PeopleSoft and HR Workstations
Technical support (help desk)	Support the internal MCC staff	Workstations accessing the authentication and ERP systems
ERP systems	Supports many LOBs	Three-tier architecture
Remote access and control (Citrix)	All users to connect securely to the Intranet	Modem servers, VPN gateways, Citrix servers
Intranet applications	Supports many LOBs	Three-tier architecture

information. Some of the MCC users are issued portable computers and the rest use their personal PCs.

A myriad of Web development tools is available to MCC developers; these tools enable transparent access to MCC database management systems (DBMS) and mainframes. Many of the MCC antiquated client/server applications are in the process of being retooled with a Web front-end.

MCC is hard pressed to find and keep software developers. Many MCC LOBs are outsourcing application development. The external developers need remote access to corporate resources to develop and test the software.

Figure 1-2
MCC perimeter picture

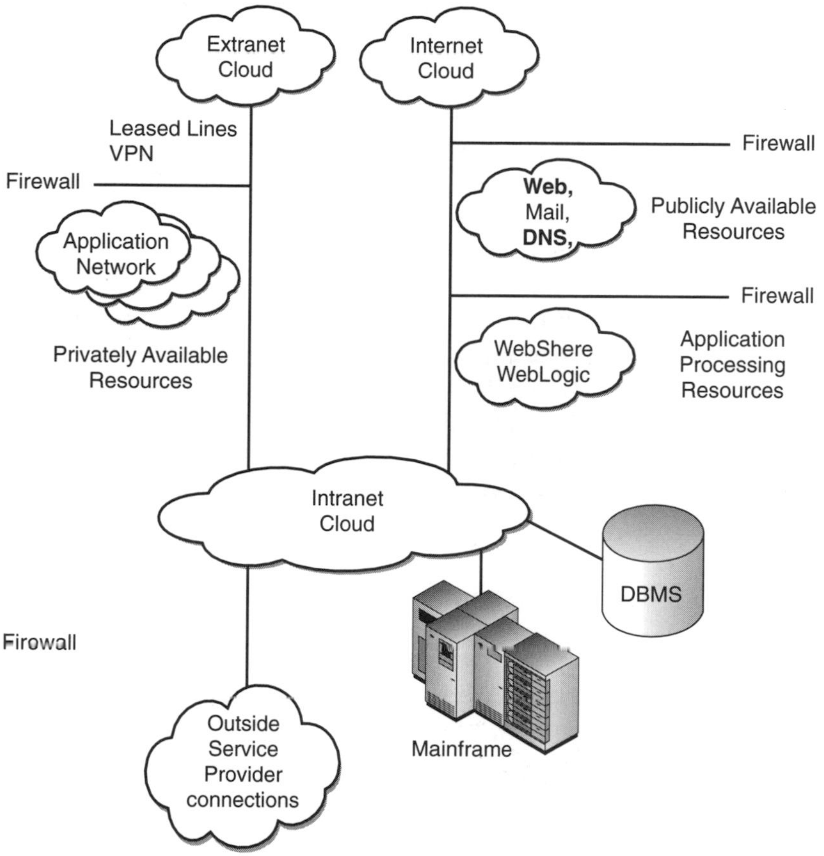

As systems become more complex and costly, the support required goes beyond the capabilities of MCC staff members. MCC has begun to transition some of its mission critical applications (Web-based e-commerce, ERP) to application service providers (ASP). This is predominantly due to the shrinking talent pool within the industry, lack of expertise in MCC's technical staff, and time to market constraints defined by the LOB's.

Case Study #2—FinApp

MCC has an investment-banking LOB that is responsible for issuing new securities in the commodities market. This MCC LOB must protect its investors by upholding the rules and regulations put forth by the Securities and Exchange Commission.

FinApp is a new business-to-business investment banking application that provides future and option clients with post trade statement information and basic account management information. The majority of users of this system are other financial institution's commodity trading advisors.

FinApp is capable of processing one million trades per day. FinApp requires transaction level protection, which relies on online transaction processing integrity and accuracy (for example, two phase commits—the ability to rollback activities of a transaction). System down time is estimated at $500,000 dollars per minute. A redundant network and application system utilizing messaging middleware has been deployed. All trades are recorded for regulatory and security purposes. Because the futures markets are very volatile, each transaction is considered binding and legitimate.

Access to the system is done via a proprietary set of application programming interface (API) calls that run over the TCP protocol suite. The agreed upon data format uses the extensible markup language (XML). The FinApp systems are hosted at a co-location facility in three regions around the globe. A private line from each of the co-location facilities runs back to the MCC financial data center. Many external trading institutions have dedicated lines into the MCC financial data center using private lines, frame relay, and VPNs that form the FinApp Extranet. See Figure 1-3.

Figure 1-3
FinApp logical diagram

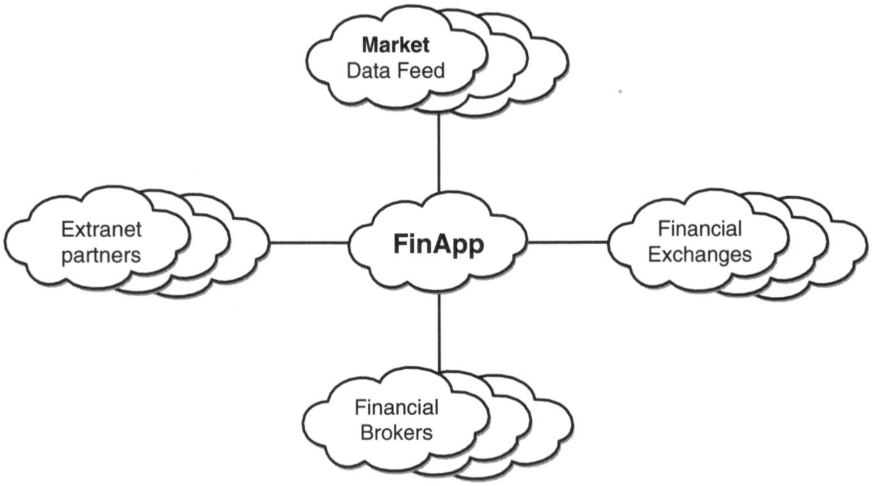

Application development is performed 50 percent inside MCC; third party developers perform the remaining 50 percent. Below is a list of external connections that support the FinApp.

- Financial exchanges (for example, Chicago Board of Trade)
- Financial information feeds (Reuters, Bloomberg, and Standard and Poors)
- Financial brokers (for example, Autex)

Case Study #3—HealthApp

MCC has a health insurance LOB that is responsible for providing nationwide health care services. There is an initiative this year to automate claims processing and broker quotes, and to provide MCC members with online access to their statements. The HealthApp "portal" provides its users with a content aggregation and delivery from a centralized point (one entry point for all the user base).

Claims processing requires access to patient's medical records, a detailed description of the service performed within the claim, account, and billing information. Once an insurance claim is submitted, the physician's office or hospital needs the ability to check the progress and clear any submission errors. Because most medial office computer systems are antiquated, MCC has chosen a Web browser for the interface.

The current method of quoting MCC insurance products is done over a dial-up system. MCC is spending $250,000 a month managing a dial-in solution for third-party brokers. This system is being decommissioned very shortly. The new system will be accessed via the Internet. The broker quoting system will pay for itself within two months time.

Currently, HealthApp members are billed monthly. All the claim disputes are performed over the telephone. In an effort to save on the cost of supporting a large call center, there is an initiative to utilize the Web to automate the disputes. Users will be able to access their statements and correlate the payment with the user's policy coverage. This will reduce the amount of time spent on the dispute call and the amount of claims support staff. See Figure 1-4.

Figure 1-4
HealthApp logical diagram

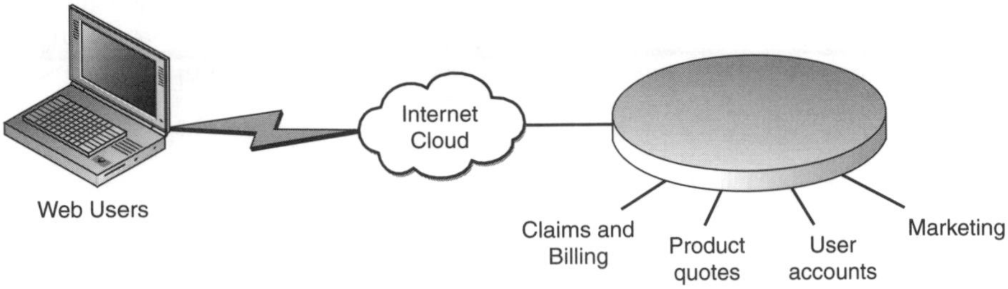

Implementation Considerations

Most technology disciplines have theorists and practitioners. Many security professionals understand the theory behind information security (communications and computer security), but unless the security controls can be inserted in the proper places within an application (for example, data flows, storage, and processing), the solution will be not be effective. In addition, if the inserted security solution is not managed with the proper processes in place (for example, change management, separation of duties, notification, escalation), the level of security provided will degrade with time until the inserted control is ineffective and thereby provides a less effective overall solution.

The two biggest challenges that a security professional faces are to keep up with the current changing application development technology (for example, Corba, XML, EJB), computing platform changes (for example, operating systems, storage area networks, and application servers), and internetworking (for example, high-speed devices, convergence, and so on). The second, and potentially most dangerous, is user apathy. If the security is not a priority at the senior management level, then the entire organization is at risk. Assigning the proper importance to security-minded architecture design will reduce the number of security flaws uncovered in deloyment.

As these technologies evolve, so should the security solutions (for example, intrusion detection systems are less effective in switched and high-speed environments) that have been implemented to protect them. The hardest and most versatile element of these systems to comprehend—as well as to understand and plan for—is the human factor. Locks are used to keep honest people honest. Effective security planning must include thinking outside of the box. This thinking outside of the box might include a line of what the system response will be to unanticipated occurrences (both malicious or accidental) and how will the system respond to these threats? Will it blow up and offer up the keys to the kingdom or will it crash and be unavailable to legitimate users, costing millions of dollars and public relations nightmares? As you attempt to secure your corporation from the hacking hordes of the planet, be prepared to think as they do. As Sun Tzu once phrased it, "Know thine enemy as thyself."

CHAPTER 2

Security Polices, Standards, and Guidelines

Corporations need to protect the assets vital to the health of the company. These assets range from people to location to the physical computers and the electronic information the computers hold and process. An information security program protects these items. Before the information security program can be formulated, a set of policies, procedures, and guidelines needs to be developed. The specifics of the security program should align with the policies of the corporation.

Without strong management policies, corporate security programs will be less effective and not necessarily align with management objectives and desires. Policies, standards, and guidelines form the foundation of a corporation's security program. Effective policies are a sign of due diligence, often necessary in the event of an audit or litigation. More than the foundation, policies also serve as the blueprints that help the corporation create the security program. The combination enables the corporation to implement the specific controls, processes, and awareness programs necessary to increase the security posture and awareness within the corporate entity, which ultimately protects the corporation.

An effective information security policy is as necessary to a good information security program as a solid foundation is to a house. A reputable builder would not build a house without the proper foundation. Once the foundation has been constructed, tested, and certified as strong, then the builder can start to build the house, one floor at a time. Similarly, in the corporation, once the information security policy has been created, reviewed, and published, the corporation can start to move forward and build the information security program.

Although it may be understood that policies are important, "policy" tends to be a confusing word. According to *Webster's* (*Webster's Revised Unabridged Dictionary*, © 1996, 1998 MICRA, Inc.), policy is defined as

1. A plan or course of action, as of a government, political party, or business, intended to influence and determine decisions, actions, and other matters: American foreign policy; the company's personnel policy.

2. a. A course of action, guiding principle, or procedure considered expedient, prudent, or advantageous: Honesty is the best policy.

b. Prudence, shrewdness, or sagacity in practical matters.

These definitions help illustrate the fact that a well-constructed policy serves the organization as the course of action—for the security program and decisions—in the most prudent and advantageous manner possible. But what does a policy look like to a company? Is a policy one sheet of paper, a book, or several books? The answer is "yes." A policy can be all of these, depending on the corporation and the needs of the corporation. More important than the physical manifestation of the policy is the direction it sets for the corporation, and the way it is embraced and used to carry the security goals of the corporation forward.

Many different people in the corporation play a key role in the development, implementation, and usage of the policies that drive the information security program. Because the security policies provide the course of action for the business, they must be communicated and supported by the executive management of the corporation. Once the support of the management has been obtained, the policies need to be written and approved by the management team. Approved policies need to be implemented by various technical and operations teams in the corporation. And everyone in the company, including the executives, needs to abide by the policies that apply to their job functions and actions on the corporate network.

Corporations also create policies so the employees and others who work with the corporation understand how to act. Policies enable management to communicate what is and is not acceptable to the corporation. Policies have consequences for a breach. Failure to comply with the corporation's policies can result in disciplinary action, suspension, or even termination. Policies also define expectations, such as an email policy that says "All email is the property of the corporation and is monitored. Employees should have no expectation of privacy within the corporate mail system." This statement sets the expectations that the corporation may choose to monitor the email. Further, in the event someone has misused the email, it can be used as grounds for disciplinary action.

While creating the policies, standards, and guidelines, a careful balance between security and the ability to conduct business must be weighed. This also includes the dollars spent to protect the assets. The specific decisions about what to spend and how are made at the information security program level. It is the role of the policies, procedures, and guidelines to dictate that the level of control over an asset (any asset) must be commensurate with the value of the asset to the business.

Security in general and therefore the policies, standards, and guidelines that shape the information security practice are dynamic in nature. They need to be reviewed on a regular basis and modified to reflect changes in technology, workforce demography, the competitive landscape, corporate leadership, and operating procedures.

It is also important to understand the differences between policies, standards, and guidelines. Policies are higher level documents that do not specify technologies but focus on addressing a complete picture. Policies cover large amounts of information in a more general way. Effective policies are succinct and easy to understand (and communicated by the executives). A policy that not only explains the how, but also the why, provides a stronger baseline for people to follow, and through this simple education it enables people to understand the goal of the security program. Policies set direction and provide information, but they do not suggest the technical controls and programs necessary to achieve compliance. A policy establishes the control direction for the corporation and identifies the compliance requirements for all users of corporate information. An example of a policy statement is, "All communications must be protected from eavesdropping." The policy does not specifically state how this is to be accomplished, or the technology that should be deployed. It is the function of the standard to define such information.

Standards are derived from policies but deal with specific components and technologies. A standard describes what is allowed in terms of configuration and specific steps that need to be followed. Standards are the processes and procedures required to implement the policies across the various technologies that support corporate information. Standards provide the detail and specifications that can be audited. To follow the previous example, the corresponding standard would be, "All network-based communications must be encrypted using 3DES (Triple Data Encryption Standard)." This statement clearly defines the technology that must be in place, 3DES, and is something that can be checked against. Note that a standard, while specifying the solution, does not necessarily dictate how the solution must be implemented. That provides limited flexibility to choose the manner best suited to the specific situation and as technology changes, the standard is not necessarily outdated.

Different from policies and standards, guidelines are created and used to help organizations, departments, and individuals bring corporate systems and other areas of responsibility into conformance (necessary steps for compliance) with the stated policies and standards. Guidelines are sometimes also referred to as handbooks. Guidelines provide recommended approaches that are intended to complement Information Technology Control Policies and Standards. While not policy requirements, they are intended to be the best practices to assist all corporate business and technical areas in complying with policy requirements. A guideline is not something that *must* be followed, but it provides users with a method of meeting the standard in compliance with the policy. In our example, the guideline would provide details about how to configure the network elements to encrypt the information as per the standard. However, the engineers responsible for deploying the solution are able to choose another method, provided the standard is met within the guidelines of the policy.

Once the policies, standards, and guidelines have been approved, the employees—and sometimes clients—of the corporation need to be aware of them and understand them well enough to be able to abide by them. This is when the awareness and training aspect of policy management is introduced to the corporation. The objective of awareness and training is to properly educate each user as to the policies, standards, and guidelines they need to be familiar with and what is expected of them to be in compliance. Another important policy idea is that employees should be required to acknowledge that they have read corporate policies and sign off on them. HR should do this annually and a record of that sign-off is maintained.

Once the policies have been created and the entire corporation made aware of their existence, it is important for each of these policies to have the continued support of the executive team. Without the support of the executives, a policy isn't worth the paper it is written on. People who more clearly understand the goals of the security program, as well as some methods to achieve those goals, are more likely to support the efforts. This directly improves the security posture of the organization.

Different Types of Policies, Standards, and Guidelines

There is not a one-size-fits-all policy for all corporations. Similarly, most corporations cannot have a one-policy-fits-all approach. Smaller corporations may be able to create an Information Security Policy that covers the basics of what they need with some smaller policies covering specific areas (such as network security or remote access). However, larger corporations like MCC typically need to have an information security policy augmented with one or all of the policies outlined in this chapter.

Just as no one-size-fits-all policy exists, policy development has different inputs and influences. Just as important as the different influences in the development of a policy is the development of program policies. Figure 2-1 shows the different inputs as well as a common chain of policy development. Typically, the program policy is developed first, and the subsequent policies need to abide by the program policy as well as incorporate the Business Impact Analysis (BIA) results and direction of the company.

Figure 2-1

Different inputs in the development of a policy

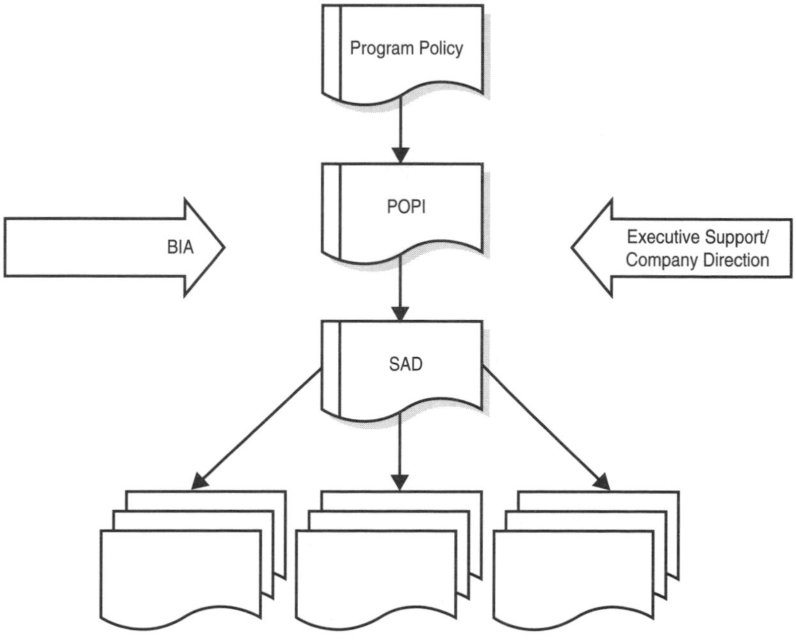

Common Elements

This section will take an introductory look into the more common and typical elements of policies, standards, and guidelines. Although the following elements tend to be more common, they are not necessarily included in all policies, standards, and guidelines. Policies, by their nature, must be customized to the corporation. As such, some corporations may opt for different elements or a different structure. More important than the exact structure and format of the policies, standards, and guidelines is the fact that a corporation has taken on the effort of clearly defining what is and is not acceptable and has attempted to communicate that throughout the corporation.

That said, the more successful policy implementations usually include the following elements. Where applicable, some examples have been provided to help reinforce the spirit of the policy, standard, or guideline.

Elements of a Policy

Some elements of a policy are common, even necessary, to all policies. In order for a policy, standard, or guideline to be applied effectively, it needs to be understood and constructed in a way that is easy to follow, even if it requires work to achieve. Some of the key elements of an information security policy are as follows:

- **Scope** The scope statement outlines the purpose of the policy, statement, or guideline and includes links to the companion documents. Scope statements should be brief and included in the beginning of the document.
- **High-Level Policy Statements** Also included in the beginning of the document, the high-level policy statement is usually a single paragraph stating the goal of the overall policy.
- **Accountability** This is often a section that identifies the personnel involved in enforcing the policy, standard, or guideline.
- **Non-compliance** A statement pertaining to the loss that could occur if the policy is not fulfilled.
- **Monitoring** This is a section that covers how the policy, standard, or guideline will be kept validated and up to date. It is often necessary as part of a compliance function in the organization.

- **Exceptions** In the event that an aspect of the organization cannot be compliant with policy, this section lays out the mechanism by which variances are granted. This is typically a case-by-case basis and for a limited amount of time.

Elements of a Standard

As with policies, some elements to a standard are common to all standards. The common elements tend to make it easier to understand and therefore easier to comply with. Some of the key elements of an information security standard are

- **Purpose and Scope** This section provides a description of the standard's intent (building an Apache Web server on a Solaris 8 platform).
- **Roles and Responsibilities** This section defines the corporate roles and responsibilities for defining, executing, and supporting the standard.
- **Guidance** This section references the overriding policy statements.
- **Baseline Standards** This section articulates high-level statements that apply to platform and application.
- **Technology Standards** These include statements and the associated descriptions (configuration or unnecessary system services).
- **Administration Standards** These include the initial and ongoing administration of the platform and application.

Elements of a Guideline

Guidelines also have elements common to all guidelines. Given the fact that guidelines often vary significantly from corporation to corporation, the elements in common are useful to convey the purpose of the guideline and enable the corporation to efficiently meet the standard and policy requirements. Some of the key elements of an information security guideline are

- **Purpose and Scope** This section provides a description of the guideline's intent (Checkpoint Firewall-1 change management guidelines).

- **Roles and Responsibilities** This section defines the corporate roles and responsibilities for defining, executing, and supporting the guidelines.
- **Guidelines Statements** The step-by-step process associated with supporting the technology in a secure fashion.
- **Operational Statements** These statements define daily, weekly, and monthly duties required to operate the given technology.

Policy Examples

No two corporate security policies look identical. The following is an abstraction of many different corporate policies, designed to provide a closer look at some of the most common policy essentials.

Program Policy

The program policy is the security policy that initiates an information security program within the corporation. It is the overall umbrella-like policy that sets the general direction for and is supplemented by the more technical policies, standards, and guidelines. It also commonly establishes a corporate Information Security Services Group and a corporate-wide information security awareness program, and it selects a senior management champion who supports issues to the corporate officers. This policy needs to clearly state the overall policy statement for the corporation and define responsibilities (security is everyone's responsibility). As the basis for the security program, the security policy has to explain the five main goals:

- **Avoidance** The ability to prevent unauthorized access to corporate information assets.
- **Assurance** The compliance with policies, standards, and guidelines with regard to the protection of the corporate information assets.
- **Detection** The ability to identify intrusions and launch the appropriate countermeasures.
- **Investigation** The ability to apply forensic techniques to extract information about the intrusion and the intruder.
- **Continuity** The ability to guarantee that disaster recovery plans have been developed and tested.

The establishment of a security program includes the following:

- Governance of the security policies, standards, and guidelines
- Members of the team
  - Security manager
  - Corporate and business unit members
  - Links to security operations and business continuity
- Senior management champion
- Security awareness program
- Security integration
- Security operations

Information/Resource Classification Policy

This policy establishes corporate expectations and requirements for the protection of proprietary information. This policy serves to define the protection strategy for all information that is sensitive or critical to corporate business as well as that which requires protection by law or regulatory standards by establishing uniform corporate-wide standards regarding the treatment of all information owned by or entrusted to the corporation. Some of the major points are to protect the value of the information to the corporation, to prevent and monitor against loss or compromise, and to provide legal support to defend against unauthorized use.

Information classifications are a critical component to building new applications. The classification helps ensure that we understand which information is being processed and any potential risks to the business due to a compromise of the information/system. Once we understand why we need to protect the information, we will be able to build in the appropriate security controls to address the risk.

Standard Access Definition Policy

This policy defines the methods and procedures used to enable access to computer resources (data, applications, transactions, functions, and so on). This is done using a tabular form with the organization's information assets on the X-axis and the employee responsibility/function (role) on the Y-axis. The intersection of these two points means the role has access to the resource. The three following principles need to be adhered to when one is assigning access:

- **Individual accountability** Consists of holding someone responsible for his or her actions. Accountability is normally accomplished by identifying and authenticating users of the system and subsequently tracing actions on the system to the user who initiated them.
- **Least privilege** Tthe practice of restricting a user's access (DBMS updates, student's names and addresses, or remote administration) or by the type of access (read, write, execute, delete) to the minimum necessary to perform the job.
- **Separation of duties** The practice of dividing the steps in a critical function (direct DBMS access or Java applet updates) among different individuals.

Password Management Policy

A password management policy is often at the core of most corporations' policies. It typically includes password expiration as well as length and strength checks. The following password management list is typical of the best business practices:

- The minimum length of passwords must be seven or more characters.
- The password must not be a word in the dictionary.
- It must be a combination of letters and non-alphabetic symbols.
- The password must expire after a pre-determined time period.
- The network administrator's passwords must expire more frequently and should be longer.
- Passwords to access mail and Web servers must differ from system-based passwords.
- Corporate passwords must differ from passwords used on non-corporate systems (such as ISP).
- A password history list must be kept to prevent password reuse (it saves up to six old passwords).
- Newly assigned or reset passwords must be unique to the user and not be easily guessed.

The following are the best business practices for account administration:

- Newly created accounts must expire if not used within a pre-determined time period.

- Only one simultaneous login must be permitted unless a specific business reason exists.
- The login process must disconnect the session if three or more authentication failures occur.
- The account must be deactivated (locked) after a specified number of failed login attempts.
- Requests for a password reset must be authenticated and verified. In general, this is a very weakly enforced part of a corporate security policy (that is, a social engineering threat).
  - **Activation** Passwords are typically part of the human resource function. A contractor/part-time employee's activation period must be limited to his or her contract dates.
  - **Usage** The usage policy must be signed off before the user is issued the password.
  - **Termination** Immediately after the user is terminated, their user account must be disabled.

Internet Usage Policy

An Internet Usage Policy, sometimes referred to as an Internet Acceptable Use Policy (I-AUP), is the document that details how any user on the corporate network should use the public Internet. This policy would describe any filtering or blocking software that is in use to protect the corporation as well as the specific tasks that are allowed and those that are not allowed. It would even be appropriate to cover the methods of authentication before accessing the Internet outbound to prevent people from using the corporate network for illegal purposes.

Specific protocols covered in an Internet usage policy include the following:

- **Electronic Mail** This covers all forms of email in use by the corporation. This section of the policy defines acceptable use and declares any filtering and scanning software in use. The policy clearly states any expectation of privacy or lack thereof. It must also outline any specific requirements as to the type of data that should not be sent through the email system and recommend procedures for handling such messages if a user receives them. These sections are important to a company should they need to take disciplinary action.

- **Web** This section of the policy defines specific requirements as to the type of Web traffic that is acceptable. Since the World Wide Web (WWW) uses HTTP (HyperText Transport Protocol) to move information, this typically covers the types of Web sites that would be strictly forbidden (pornography, gambling, and so on).
- **FTP** Many companies choose to block file transfer protocol (FTP) access at the firewall. Allowing users access to FTP provides an easy way to download exploits and viruses into the company as well as distribute company confidential information to outside servers. However, technical support personnel usually need some level of access to FTP to download patches and updates. This policy should therefore discuss the authorized uses of FTP.
- **Chat/IRC** Internet Relay Chat (IRC) is less commonplace in the corporate environment than other chat programs such as Yahoo!, ICQ, and AOL Instant Messenger (AIM). These programs create risks because the information is being sent through servers external to the company and little or no protections exist for the information while in transit. However, this section of the policy needs to balance the appeal of these products/services with the interests of the company.

Some of the following are included in the Internet usage policy:

- Acceptable use of (or compliance with)
  - Downloading files
  - Newsgroups
  - Transmitting sensitive data
  - Types of attachments
  - Size of messages
  - Non-licensed software
  - Unapproved software application packages
  - Exporting sensitive information
  - File protections
  - Virus protection
- Change management
- Data storage practices
- Reliability and availability

- Information protection, based upon classification
- Access controls
- Email and corporate data retention
- Monitoring
- Exceptions and modifications to this policy

Network Security Policy

This policy covers network access to all the computing and information resources. This policy does not apply to computers that use modems to make outgoing dial-up calls, provided these systems do not receive unattended incoming dial-up calls.

This area of policy, standards, and guidelines specifically addresses the network elements of security. Specific sections will be devoted to cover the following:

- Internet and Extranet firewalls
- Network intrusion detection
- Security event monitoring

This section also details the physical security measures that must be taken to ensure that network elements are not easily tampered with.

The standards will outline the specific equipment types that are supported and the procedures for configuring, updating, and maintaining different types of equipment. Guidelines for network security will include suggested best practices for network element maintenance and operation. Following the guidelines should result in a network that meets the security standards and policy.

Remote Access Policy

A remote access policy and the supporting documents should clearly state the allowed/approved methods of achieving remote access to the internal network from outside. It should also clearly state what is not accepted. For example, using the company-owned dial-up modems would be acceptable, but allowing users to install and operate modems in their workstations would not be acceptable.

Any computers that can be reached through a third party (such as dial-up over Plain Old Telephone Service [POTS] or ISDN, a Value Added Network [VAN], a private direct WAN or leased line, or the Internet) must be protected by a privilege access control system approved by the information security department. This may require the encryption of data in transit to protect against eavesdropping.

The remote access policy should also detail vendor access and the administration of remote access user IDs and passwords.

Desktop Policy

Enterprise organizations often invest copious amounts of time and money into effectively supporting the needs of the users through desktop and server administration. Companies often experience a cost savings by defining a "common operating environment" that details the specific hardware and software that is supported.

Similarly, secure desktop guidelines clearly outline for users and support staff alike what is expected and necessary to maintain a security posture appropriate to the organization. This set of documents should outline desktop and server access controls, ID administration, anti-virus software and updates, server and desktop encryption, and other compensating controls. Here are some examples:

- Inactivity (screen saver locks)
- Virus protection
- Executing non-corporate applications
- Opening e-mail attachments, FTP, and Active content (ActiveX or Java Applets)

Server Platform Policy

In the age of distributed networks, it is often necessary to address the security of the various servers and workstations by creating a separate policy. A secure platform build and administration policy details how a platform should be built securely as well as the administration efforts, which are necessary given the voluminous number of patches and updates that are routinely available for the various operating systems.

Application Security Policy

This policy describes how the application(s) can meet specific policy controls mandated, for example, by regulatory requirements.

Policy, Standard, and Guideline Development

As the focus of this book is on how to apply the various concepts, it may seem out of place to devote a section of the chapter on policy on how to actually construct the policy. However, in being able to effectively develop and apply policies, it is important to understand the steps necessary to develop them. By understanding the various elements that go into policy, standard, and guideline development, it is easier to comprehend the trade-offs that can be made in applying the policy. It also allows for better decision-making.

Policy Creation

Policy creation is a process. Several steps are necessary for creating any information security policy, as shown in Figure 2-2:

1. Determine the scope of the policy.
2. Obtain executive/management-level support.
3. Conduct a Business Impact Analysis (BIA).
4. Interview key employees.
5. Draft initial policies.
6. Stakeholder policy review.
7. Distribute policies.
8. Review and revise policies.

Determine the Scope of the Policy

The determination must be made as to whether the policy will be company-wide or apply only to the department or business unit level. For example, the MCC will be using some policies tailored specifically to the application.

Obtain Executive/Management-Level Support

It is important to ensure that management supports the development of the policies. Without this support, enforcing the policies becomes an arduous, if not impossible, task.

Figure 2-2
Information security policy creation cycle

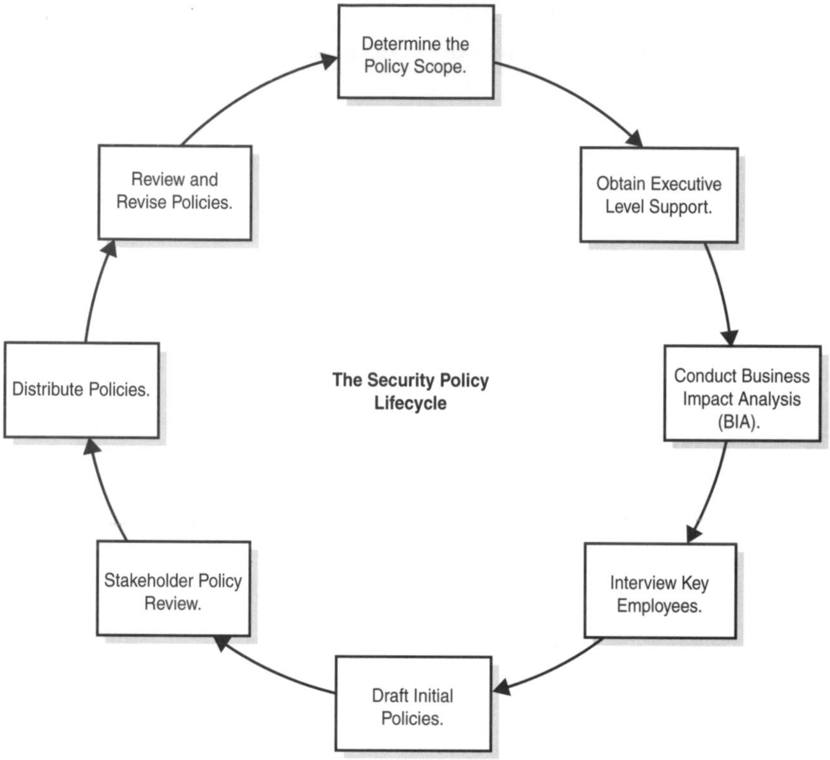

Conduct a Business Impact Analysis (BIA)

In order to develop effective policies, it is important to determine the assets that are to be protected and their relative and absolute values to the company. The information gathered and analyzed in the BIA is used to determine the appropriate controls (technical and administrative) described in the policy. This information also helps determine the focus given to each area developed in the policy.

Although often skipped, this is a vital aspect to policy creation, because it really is at the heart of the motivation for defining and implementing the security policy. Even if a formal analysis is not conducted due to time or another problem, an informal assessment of the various "potential targets" and (minimally) their relative value to the company should be considered.

Some of the key questions to be asked and considered in a BIA are

- What are you trying to protect (*assets* your organization possesses)?
- Who do you want to protect it from (potential *threats* to those assets)?
- What is the *probability* of threat and organizational vulnerability?
- How important is the resource (*cost estimates* of losses, should a potential threat be realized)?
- What *measures* can you implement? Are they cost- and time-effective? Will they seriously hinder the progress of work for your users?
- What should be done in the case of policy *non-compliance*?
- Re-examine the policy you have developed on a *regular* basis to see how your needs and circumstances have changed.

Interview Key Employees

Be sure to interview technical and business team members alike (each has various perspectives). In order to build support and determine the current practices, the interviews enable the opportunity to gather information on the processes and practices in use today. This may be of tremendous benefit to the organization in and of itself. Once the information is collected, try to gauge if current practices are documented and if documented practices are followed. This will lend valuable insight to the policy creation process.

Draft Initial Policies

Once the scope has been agreed to, the executives have committed their support, and the business impact analysis has been completed, the initial policies must be drafted to address the threats to the vital assets.

Stakeholder Review

This is a critical step in the success of the policies. In order for the policies to be applied effectively, the key stakeholders have to support the stated goal of the policies. The opportunity to review the policies provides necessary input in order to have a more complete document. It also enables the various reviewers to have the opportunity to affect the final document. Participation in the creation process builds the support of the policies when released.

In order for the review to be productive, it needs to be structured. The timeframes and anticipated process should be stated early in the process. It is usually beneficial to also set the expectations of the reviewers by explaining clearly who has final edit control of the policy. As feedback is received, it is important to incorporate the relevant comments into the document and then circulate drafts as appropriate.

Keep in mind that full consensus is not necessary for effective policies, but management, and sometimes legal, approval is necessary.

Policy Distribution

Once the policies have been finalized, they must be read and understood in order to be applied effectively. The process by which the policies are distributed and updated is of critical importance. It is quite common in many organizations today to prominently post the policies on the company Intranet.

Review and Revise Policies

As technology and the business environment evolve, so must the various information security policies. To ensure the policies are kept up to date, they must, at a minimum, be reviewed quarterly and updated yearly.

Regulatory Considerations

Although most corporations have the ability to create a set of policies, standards, and guidelines that reflect the best practices of the industry they are in, combined with a clear understanding of their business, some corporations also need to understand and incorporate regulatory requirements.

The specific examples and information contained in this section are heavily U.S.-centric. However, the process of reviewing, understanding, and incorporating regulations into the policies, standards, and guidelines of a corporation are common to all organizations.

Depending on the industry, corporations have different regulations with which to comply. Regulations can be federal, state, or local. Some regulations are heavily enforced, while others are self-enforced, where the corporation has to certify itself. Two main areas where U.S. corporations are currently working to comply with regulations are financial services and health care.

Financial organizations and banking institutions have to comply with the U.S. Security and Exchange Commission (SEC) and the Federal Deposit Insurance Corporation (FDIC). For example, the Federal Financial Institutions Examination Council (FFIEC) Information Systems Examination Handbook's Chapter 14 covers physical and data security. The FDIC also has Financial Institution Letters (FIL), which have been published since 1995. Table 2-1 displays some pertinent information-security-related letters.

The SEC has similar regulatory statutes. The SEC Final Rules document entitled "Record Keeping and Reporting Requirements for Trading Systems Operated by Broker-Dealers" (Release No. 34-35124, File No. S7-3-94) stipulates that all broker-dealer communications (voice, email, and Web transactions) must be recorded and archived for three years.

Corporations that deal with health information have to comply with the Health Insurance Portability and Accountability Act (HIPAA) and Administrative Simplification (AS). HIPAA lays out specific requirements that are published as part of the federal register. Others, like privacy, are more difficult for people outside the legal community to understand, as the requirements can come from court cases or other sources, like the EU and the data privacy requirements that have led to the safe harbor agreements.

The MCC FinApp and HealthApp have different regulations and considerations to handle. Although it would be possible for some companies to create one information security policy that addresses regulatory requirements, the MCC in our example has already decided that the most effective way to handle the various policies is to create more specialized policies. This enables more specialization in developing the policies, standards, and guidelines. At the same time, it enables the collective set of

Table 2-1

Financial Institution Letters

Financial Institution Letters	Titles
FIL 124-97	Suspicious Activity Reporting
FIL-131-97	Security Risks Associated with the Internet
FIL-68-99	Risk Assessment Tools and Practices for Information System Security
FIL-67-2000	Security Monitoring of Computer Networks

policies, standards, and guidelines to be referenced more easily and, more importantly, to be updated more easily.

Another option available to the company, and even the MCC in this example, would be to create an application security policy that covered the regulations for both applications (as well as other policy guidelines). The benefit to that approach is having one policy that addresses all application development work.

In the case of MCC, different divisions within the company handle the FinApp and HealthApp applications. As a result, having one policy is awkward for the company. MCC is able to more effectively utilize specialized application security policies for each application. But as with all policies, it is important that the specialized application security policies for FinApp and HealthApp are in harmony with all other policies created for MCC.

Privacy Regulations

Organizations lacking adequate privacy practices have to face challenges from the legal and regulatory dimension of privacy. On the other hand, organizations that manage privacy risks effectively not only minimize the risk of drawing the attention of the local privacy regulator, but may also enhance their customer confidence and wider reputation. The following regulations have significant impact on how MCC should design and implement its privacy policies:

- The Gramm-Leach-Bliley Act (November 12, 1999)
- Privacy of Consumer Financial Information (Regulation S-P), June 22, 2000. Effective date: November 13, 2000. [Release Nos. 34-42974, IC-24543, IA-1883; File No. S7-6-00]
- Amendments to the Commission's Freedom of Information and Privacy Act Rules and Confidential Treatment Rule 83, September 1, 2000. Effective Date: October 13, 2000. [Release Nos. 34-43239; FOIA-191; PA-30; File No. S7-14-99]
- Directive 95/46/EC of the European Parliament and of the Council of the European Union (24 October 1995).
- Standards for Privacy of Individually Identifiable Health Information. The Administrative Simplification subtitle of the Health Insurance Portability and Accountability Act of 1996 (HIPPA).

The Gramm-Leach-Bliley Act, which became Public Law 106-102 with President Clinton's signature on November 12, 1999, requires that a financial institution (including a broker-dealer, fund, or registered adviser) must provide its customers with a notice of its privacy policies and practices like the one shown in Figure 2-3. Additionally, the financial institution must not disclose nonpublic information about a consumer to

Figure 2-3

The U.S. Department of Justice Web Site Privacy Notice at www.usdoj.gov

PRIVACY AND SECURITY NOTICE

This is how we handle information we learn about you from your visit to our website. The information we receive depends upon what you do when visiting our site.

If you visit our site to read or download information, such as career opportunities or press releases, we collect and store ***only*** the following information about you:

¥ The name of the domain from which you access the Internet (for example, aol.com, if you are connecting from America Online account).
¥ The date and time you access our site.
¥ The Internet address of the web site from which you linked directly to our site.

If you identify yourself by sending an E-mail containing personal information:

You also may decide to send us personally-identifying information, for example your mailing address, in an electronic mail message requesting that information or records be mailed to you. Information collected in this manner is used solely for responding to request for information or records.

For **SITE MANAGEMENT,** information from both categories is collected for statistical purposes. This Government computer system uses software programs to create summary statistics, which are used for such purposes as assessing the number of visitors to the different sections of our site, what information is of most and least interest, determining technical design specifications, and identifying system performance or problem areas.

For **SITE SECURITY** purposes and to ensure that this service remains available to all users, this Government computer system employs software programs to monitor network traffic to identify unauthorized attempts to upload or change information, or otherwise cause damage.

NOTICE: We will not obtain personally-identifying information about you when you visit our site, unless you choose to provide such information to us.

nonaffiliated third parties unless the consumer permission has been obtained.

Regulation S-P (Privacy of Consumer Financial Information) consists of privacy rules published under section 504 of the Gramm-Leach-Bliley Act. Section 504 authorizes the U.S. Securities and Exchange Commission (SEC) and other federal agencies to issue regulations as may be necessary to implement notice requirements and restrictions on a financial institution's ability to disclose nonpublic personal information about consumers to nonaffiliated third parties. This regulation is effective November 13, 2000. Compliance is mandatory as of July 1, 2001. According to the SEC, joint marketing and service agreements in effect as of July 1, 2000 must be brought into compliance with section 248.13 of Regulation S-P by July 1, 2002.

The Freedom of Information and Privacy Act of September 1, 2000 deals with making public bodies more accountable to the public and to protect personal privacy by

- Giving the public a right of access to records
- Giving individuals a right of access to, and a right to request correction of, personal information about themselves
- Specifying limited exceptions to the rights of access
- Preventing the unauthorized collection, use, or disclosure of personal information by public bodies
- Providing for an independent review of decisions made under this Act

The Privacy section of this Act covers the collection, protection, and retention of personal information by public bodies. It specifically talks about the following areas:

- The purpose for which personal information may be collected
- How personal information is to be collected
- The accuracy of personal information
- The right to request the correction of personal information
- The protection of personal information
- The retention of personal information

Another privacy regulation that affects MCC is the Directive 95/46/EC of the European Parliament and of the Council of the European Union on the protection of individuals with regard to the processing of personal data and on the free movement of such data. The Directive 95/46/EC of

October 24, 1995 deals with the difference in levels of protection of the rights and freedoms of individuals, notably the right to privacy, with regard to the processing of personal data in the European member states. The difference in levels of protection may prevent the transmission of such data from the territory of one member state to that of another member state.

The Health Insurance Portability and Accountability Act of 1996, HIPAA, is best known as the means of enabling patients to maintain insurance when they switch jobs and as the force behind crackdowns on Medicare coding. But it also involves rules proposed by the U.S. Department of Health and Human Services (DHHS) establishing national electronic transaction standards and governing the security and confidentiality of all electronic health data and all paper-based data created from any electronic media (under the heading of Administrative Simplification). These rules require all providers, health insurers, and claims clearinghouses to use national transaction formats and data content for nine electronic transactions if they already transmit electronic transactions or plan to do so. The rules require entities to develop and implement administrative, technical, and physical safeguards to ensure the security, integrity, availability, and confidentiality of individually identifiable electronic health data.

Failure to comply with HIPAA can result in civil fines of up to $25,000 a year for each violation of a standard. Because HIPAA encompasses dozens of standards, the fines can add up quickly, and wrongful disclosure of health information carries a criminal fine of up to $250,000, 10 years imprisonment, or both.

Analysis of Case Study #1—Corporate

The first and most basic of policies would simply be considered the information security policy. In many small organizations, this policy is suitable to cover the array of information security needs. However, in our MCC example, an information security policy is only the start.

The MCC has the need for multiple policies to support the security programs and needs of the company. Separate policies have been created in accordance with the information security policy to address the remote access needs of the corporation as well as the unique needs of the financial and health care applications.

Even as the MCC needs several policies, it is important that they be created in a manner that enables them to share a similar theme and meet the broader goals of the information security program. This method to creating policies is akin to using a roadmap to guide yourself on a journey, in this case, a journey to better security at your company.

In the ideal situation, the information security policy is created first. It typically states the goals of the information security program at the company as well as high-level goals, objectives, and direction for specific areas, which typically include the following:

- Acceptable use
- Incident response
- Anti-virus policy

Once that policy is in place, the organization needs to assess areas that need more direction. A corporation with the size and diversity of MCC needs to separately address network security, remote access, incident response, and application level security: the FinApp and HealthApp.

In the case of network security, the policy would be created to comply with the information security policy, which could be considered the master-level policy document. However, it is often difficult to apply a policy, so once the network security policy has been created, a standard would be created. The standard document addresses the specific technology in use by the corporation and sets forth the criteria by which compliance with the policy can be measured.

However, although standards provide a clear understanding of what needs to be done in order to comply with a policy, there may still be some confusion on how to best achieve the standard. This is when a guideline is a necessary document. A guideline provides people with a set of best practices and suggested processes and procedures to help them meet specific standards and policies.

As each document is created, it is important to ensure that they all conform to the information security policy and do not contradict each other. Table 2-2 outlines the different functions in the corporation and suggests the specific policy that would address the concerns.

Table 2-2

Policies, Guidelines, and Standards by MCC Function

MCC Function	Policies, Standards, and Guidelines that Apply	Justification
E-mail, calendaring	Internet usage, password management	Sensitive email over insecure mediums is part of the MCC Internet usage policy. All email systems require passwords, and this password must be different than your remote access or domain one.
Corporate directory	Information/resource classification policy	MCC contact information is not public information and could have high value to competitors.
Internet connectivity	Network security, Internet usage	A connection between trusted MCC and untrusted entities (Internet or Extranet partners) must meet the network security and Internet usage policies.
Sales contact information (existing customer base and prospective clients)	Information/resource classification policy	Sales contact information is one of MCC's most valued assets.
Marketing database	Information/resource classification policy	Sales contact information is one of MCC's most valued assets.
Engineering network and systems	Secure workstation and build	Intellectual Property (IP) is one of MCC's most valued assets.
Legal and HR network and systems	Information/resource classification policy	Highly sensitive legal and personnel data must be protected to avoid liability and to comply with regulations
Technical support (help desk)	Remote access	Social engineering is still a major threat to MCC.
ERP systems	Application security	Highly sensitive personnel data must be protected to avoid liability and to comply with regulations.
Remote access and control	Remote access	This is typically the backdoor of most organizations.

Analysis of Case Study #2—FinApp

MCC has an investment-banking line of business (LOB) that is responsible for issuing new securities in the commodities market. This MCC LOB must protect its investors by upholding the rules and regulations. The FinApp application policies must follow the MCC corporate policies and the applicable FDIC and SEC regulatory. These policies must communicate security requirements for each of the areas listed in Table 2-3.

Table 2-3

The FinApp Policies, Standards, and Guidelines' Areas of Requirements

Category	Areas of Requirements
Business Data	• Data Classification
Security Objectives	• Confidentiality • Availability • Integrity
Security Services	• Accountability • Identification and Authentication • Access Control and Authorization • Auditing and Monitoring

Regulations	• FDIC Laws and Regulations www.fdic.gov/regulations/laws/index.html
	• SEC Regulations www.sec.gov/rules/final.shtml
	• Privacy Regulations
	  • The Gramm-Leach-Bliley Act
	  • Privacy of Consumer Financial Information (Regulation S-P)
	  • Directive 95/46/EC of the European Parliament and of the Council of the European Union
	• Compliance Monitoring

Analysis of Case Study #3—HealthApp

MCC's health insurance LOB is responsible for providing nationwide health care services. The LOB intends to automate claims processing and broker quotes as well as to provide MCC members with online access to their statements. The HealthApp application policies must follow the MCC corporate policies and the health care regulatory that applies to individually identifiable health information. These policies must communicate security requirements for each of the areas listed in Table 2-4.

Table 2-4

The HealthApp Policies, Standards, and Guidelines' Areas of Requirements

Category	**Areas of Requirements**
Business Data	• Data Classification
Security Objectives	• Confidentiality • Availability • Integrity
Security Services	• Accountability • Identification and Authentication • Access Control and Authorization • Auditing and Monitoring
Regulations	• Standards for Privacy of Individually Identifiable Health Information. The Administrative Simplification subtitle of the Health Insurance Portability and Accountability Act of 1996 (HIPPA) • SEC Regulations www.sec.gov/rules/final.shtml • Privacy Regulations • Directive 95/46 /EC of the European Parliament and of the Council of the European Union • Compliance Monitoring

References

www.usdoj.gov/oip/foi-upd.htm

www.oipcbc.org/BCLAW.html

http://europa.eu.int/eur-lex/en/lif/dat/1995/en_395L0046.html

www.sec.gov/rules/final/34-42974.htm, Final Rule: Privacy of Consumer Financial Information (Regulation S-P)

CHAPTER 3

Information Classification and Access Control Plan

The ability to use information has become a competitive advantage in today's fast-moving marketplace. In a rush to capitalize, corporations have created a multitude of Internet-enabled applications including Intranets, Extranets, Customer Service Applications, Order Entry Systems, Video Streaming Applications, e-marketplaces, and so on. Although these applications have lowered costs and opened new markets, most corporations have not thoroughly considered and controlled the risks these applications pose to their business and data. By assessing and addressing these risks through an Information Classification process, corporations can develop efficient and effective controls to mitigate these risks to acceptable levels. A robust Information Classification (IC) process will become even more valuable to corporations as technology becomes more pervasive and the process of protecting it becomes an increasingly complex task. More people are accessing sensitive information from more locations, leaving security staffers an obligation to play catch-up in the race to be connected.

The starting point for establishing an effective IC process is the corporate information security policy. The corporate information security policy is the foundation that establishes corporate information as an asset that must be protected. It defines the corporation's sensitivity to risk and consequences for breach for each classification of data. The corporate security policy also defines how data should be protected, again according to its assigned classification. To be most effective, the IC should have the sponsorship and support of senior management. This will be an important asset in both the funding and the acceptance and support within the corporation of an IC process. This chapter details a methodology for identifying and classifying the various risks to information. At the close of this chapter, we will finish with an analysis of the three case studies described in Chapter 1.

Background

An Information Classification (IC) system, in its simplest form, is a set of guidelines and requirements for protecting corporate confidential information. It is also the embodiment of management's tolerance of information risk (is the corporation risk averse by nature, or a risk taker?). The goal of an effective Information Classification system is to consistently develop well-controlled applications with information risk appropriately mitigated.

The classification system is developed to support business practices and is broader in focus than a given application. The IC is best applied to each application during various phases of the application development life cycle to identify risk and ensure that the controls being developed adequately address those risks. In addition, once developed, it can be retroactively applied to existing applications via an audit. This will enable you to tailor the IC to best suit your business and the present application.

A robust control environment can mitigate information risk to levels where an application's benefits far outweigh its potential for loss. Corporations must understand that all information has a level of risk associated with it. This form of risk is referred to as inherent risk. Certain pieces of information have higher levels of inherent risk than others (for example, someone can do more damage impersonating you with knowledge of your social security number than with only your name). Some examples of risk include a malicious individual gaining unauthorized access to sensitive data of a personal or financial nature, disruption of service resulting from denial of service attacks, system downtime or system failures, and a corporation's mishandling and/or processing data. These risks can have a serious competitive as well as financial impact on a corporation, resulting in lost sales, disenchanted customers, and negative publicity causing damaging to the corporate brand name.

With proper controls, inherent risk can be mitigated and managed. An Information Classification system ensures that the application development process consistently identifies and adequately addresses risks inherent in information. In addition, the classifications guide the actions of personnel when handling data on a daily basis. One important caveat is that the IC is not a panacea, meaning that not all risk can be mitigated. A residual risk will always be present. Residual risk is the remaining risk when all available and cost-effective controls have been applied. This residual risk is typically permissible given that the cost to eradicate it far outweighs the threat associated with the risk.

Creating Classifications

The initial purpose of the Information Classification is to assign data into groupings and appropriate classes. By defining classes, corporations will know how to treat that data throughout its life cycle of creation, usage, and storage. The various classes defined are based on the relative importance and sensitivity of the data to the corporation. Most corporations will find that a four-level schema is sufficiently robust for grouping data based on its business sensitivity. Although the schema is a guideline and establishes a minimum level of classification for given data, it should be the information owners' responsibility and discretion to apply a higher label if warranted.

The various classification levels that a corporation defines will be driven by a number of elements. The driving focus will be risk balanced against the corporation's tolerance of risk. Remember that the IC is a business decision that drives technological solutions. The less tolerant a corporation is to risk, the more stringent each classification level may be. Typical information related risks include

- **Risk to confidentiality** The risk that sensitive data will be accessed by an unauthorized party and/or prematurely disclosed.
- **Risk to data integrity** The risk of unauthorized modification to data such as financial information or product specifications.
- **Risk to availability** The risk that critical systems cannot be accessed timely, resulting in missed sales or diminished worker productivity as well as negative public relations.

- **Risk to repudiation** The risk that an individual can deny sending or receiving a message (for example, the ability to deny executing a stock trade). This can also be referred to as accountability.
- **Risk to privacy** A risk related to a corporation's unauthorized use, disclosure, or gathering of user personal information.

An Information Classification scheme targets the application layer data. Application development and operational procedures, rather than firewalls and proxy servers, are best suited to protect data at the application layer. Although firewalls are highly effective at protecting the infrastructure on which the applications exist, they are typically not capable of the complex logic that would be required to guard different classifications of data by their assigned classification.

Table 3-1 shows a typical IC classification schema.

Risk Assessment

After establishing classifications, the IC methodology should address the various types of controls that are required. A control is essentially a safeguard that is applied to an action whose purpose is to restrict or govern that action as desired. Controls should attempt to mitigate damages when unauthorized actions are detected, and alert appropriate staff members when they occur. Additionally, controls should provide an audit trail of activity to support the reconstruction of events leading up to and including the unauthorized action.

When developing controls, it is important to avoid single points of failure within the control architecture. In addition, it is often good practice to implement redundant controls to limit or prevent system damage in the event that a control fails (like having a steering wheel lock for your car even though a lock is on the door).

What do controls have to do with an Information Classification? Controls attempt to reduce risk by affording the proper protection to defined groupings of data. An IC defines those data groupings into logical sets that can be adequately protected in a similar manner. For these reasons, different data groupings should not be mixed with one another. However, when this is unavoidable, the classification that is assigned to this informal group should equal the classification of the highest data component in that group. This is necessary to provide adequate protection to your most sensitive data.

Table 3-1

Sample Classification Scheme

Classification Level	Classification Definition	Examples
Public	The MCC considers information public if it has been expressly authorized for public disclosure. Public information is disseminated to the public via authorized channels including press releases, magazine articles, and the MCC corporate home page.	■ Released marketing and advertising materials ■ Press releases ■ Magazine and newspaper articles about MCC ■ Retail pricing information ■ Commercially procured computer hardware, software, and manuals
Internal	The MCC considers all information internal that has not been expressly authorized for public disclosure. For purposes of protection and handling, MCC Corporate Internal Information is classified according to the most sensitive data or material it contains. In addition, data must receive the same classification and therefore similar levels of protection regardless of the format it is stored in (that is, electronic or paper). The examples cited in this policy represent the minimum classification that should normally be assigned to these types of information. The data owner may elect to apply a higher classification if it is deemed appropriate.	■ Trade secrets, proprietary concepts ■ Research and development data ■ Customer information ■ Human Resources information ■ Pricing information ■ Organizational charts ■ Disaster recovery and business resumption plans ■ Security policies, procedures, and standards ■ MCC corporate telephone directories ■ Corporate training materials ■ Corporate e-mail systems (please reference corporate e-mail policy for more information)

continued

Table 3-1 (cont.) Sample Classification Scheme

Classification Level	Classification Definition	Examples
Confidential	The MCC considers all information confidential such that, if compromised, it would likely result in an *adverse* impact on MCC Corporate, its customers, vendors, and/or employees. This includes information that may be widely available to employees in the normal course of business, but is to be kept within the control of MCC Corporate and may not be disclosed to the public without authorization. The protection and handling requirements for MCC Corporate Confidential data exceeds that for MCC Internal data.	■ Non-public corporate financial reports (for example, cost center reports) ■ Internal audit reports (may be *highly confidential*, depending upon subject matter) ■ Materials and production costing data ■ Short-term business plans ■ Competitive analysis with other industry vendors ■ MCC individual product line software source-code and documentation ■ Purchasing contracts and bid information (for example, vendor names and addresses) ■ Building and emergency equipment plans ■ Other material of such a sensitive nature that the originator believes it warrants this degree of classification

continued

Table 3-1 (cont.) Sample Classification Scheme

Classification Level	Classification Definition	Examples
Restricted	The MCC considers all information restricted when and if compromised the result would likely be cause for *severe* financial, legal, regulatory, or reputation damage to MCC Corporate, its customers, vendors, and/or employees. This category of information is extremely sensitive in nature and requires specific, individual "need to know" verification prior to access. Recipients of MCC Restricted data are designated by name. Protection methods include ensuring that all copies of such information are specifically accounted for and destroyed prior to disposal. Protection and handling requirements for this classification exceeds that of MCC Confidential data.	■ Financial and customer order base (contact, type, channel, # licenses, product serial #, credit information, order history) ■ Corporate payroll information ■ Pre-release product information (for example, schedule, new product information, unreleased advertisements) ■ Long-term strategic business plans ■ Business unit's financial information and staffing requirements ■ Reports of significant exposures or risks ■ Security investigations and analyses ■ Trade secrets and proprietary concepts ■ Root/operator passwords and PINS ■ Firewall configurations and rule sets ■ Other material of such a sensitive nature that the originator believes it warrants this degree of classification

Corporations need to balance information risk and their controls in order to achieve the greatest efficiency. In addition, a proper understanding of the risks to an application will help ensure that the controls developed address the risks pertinent to the application. There is little value in developing a complex authentication system for public data while ignoring controls to protect the integrity of that data.

Risk, in the broadest sense of the term, is any condition and or situation, whether direct or indirect, with the potential to cause harm. An Information Classification scheme facilitates the understanding of risk and the creation of proper controls to minimize that risk. By creating an Information Classification scheme, corporations can begin to quantify the information risks associated with new applications and then make cost-effective decisions that work to protect them.

The projected benefits of an application should always exceed the residual risk to justify its implementation. In addition, the cost of implementing a control should not exceed the value of the data it is attempting to protect. To help corporations establish appropriate expenditure levels for controlling identified risk, it is beneficial to translate risk into quantifiable terms (that is, dollar values). One way to do this is to determine the likelihood and the effects of exposure. Determining exposure levels requires the creation of a number of loss scenarios where various controls fail and a risk is realized. For each scenario, establish a frequency that it may occur (for example, weekly, monthly, yearly) and the cost incurred by the corporation for each occurrence. When considering costs, be sure to include direct items, such as lost sales, reduced productivity, and replacement costs as well as indirect items such as reputation, brand name damage, and the resultant loss of customer confidence. Armed with an approximation of expected loss, corporations can implement an appropriate control for that risk. For example, spending $500,000 to upgrade a trading system to achieve 99.999 percent availability may seem overly expensive on the surface, when in actuality it is a trivial expense considering system downtime can cost the corporation $250,000 per hour of outage.

Controls are designed to govern the following actions:

Authentication/Identification

Identification is the process of providing personal or assigned credentials via a challenge response mechanism (for example, a login screen). Authentication is the validation of those credentials proving that you are who you say you are. Authentication can be used to verify people and data elements involved in a transaction as well as authenticate the origins of all transmissions. The failure to properly authenticate and identify users reduces system integrity and accountability by creating confidentiality and integrity issues. Privacy issues also arise because unidentified individuals are now accessing or altering data potentially not intended for them.

Authentication mechanisms generally fall into three categories: something known (a password), something you are (physiological traits such as fingerprints), or something possessed (a token, Smart card, and/or certificate).

Authentication is performed to ensure that only the appropriate or "authorized" individuals are accessing protected systems or resident data. The level of authentication that will be required will be dictated by the sensitivity assigned to that data. However, authentication is only the front door to the application. Once users are properly authenticated, a system must ensure that they are permitted to access the information contained within an application.

Authorization

The failure to perform authorization checking creates similar risks as with the failure to properly authenticate users. Not all users will have access to every piece of functionality and data within a system. Therefore, after a user has been authenticated to a system, the application must ensure that they have sufficient rights, or are authorized, to perform the requested operation and deny any requests they shouldn't be allowed to perform.

The authorization mechanism should be implemented in such a way that it cannot be bypassed. The authorization mechanism should also be invoked each and every time a system access request is received. In addition, the closer the authorization decision is to the protected resource, the harder it is to bypass, and the more granular control that can be exerted. To demonstrate, say you keep valuables inside your house; to prevent theft, every entrance to the house (doors, windows, and so on) must be secured. However, if the valuables are inside a safe within the house, access control over that safe can be exerted to prevent theft of the valuables. This enables you to differentiate people who need access to the house but not the valuables.

Authorization is the granting of rights based upon one's identity, such as read, read-write, read-write-delete, or any combination thereof to protected resources within a system. For example, certain users may be authorized to view and update their own profiles but not the profiles of other users. Authorization is often based on access control lists (ACLs). An ACL is a list of actions (such as the above mentioned authority to read, write, and delete) that can or cannot be performed on a resource given the source or destination of those actions. For example, a user should be able to see the inventory availability for a particular item, but not be able to update that inventory.

When implementing access control policies, it is important to follow the principle of least privilege. Least privilege dictates that processes and/or users should only be granted the minimum set of rights and privileges necessary to do their work. People who only need to read reports do not need update access to customer databases and accounts payable personnel should not be permitted to make purchases (that is, in effect creating a bill that they would be able to pay).

In larger systems, keeping track of user rights can quickly become a daunting task. Access control systems can be classified as discretionary or mandatory. Discretionary access control systems enable users to set the access control settings for their data. One of the most popular discretionary access control systems is a role-based access control system. Within the application, a number of different profiles or "roles" are created. Each role is assigned rights within the system. The rights assigned mimic those of a typical user of that role. Users are granted rights to the system by their role assignment. This access control solution can significantly reduce management overhead, and permit the roles to be periodically audited to ensure that they not only contain appropriate users, but also provide the proper functionality.

Mandatory access control systems require that all elements of the system have a label, and the governing system controls access based on that label. Mandatory access control systems are best suited for military purposes, as they tend to be extremely expensive to implement and maintain.

Confidentiality

Confidentiality requires the protection of private and/or personal information, such as corporate data, social security numbers, and financial transactions. Confidentiality is achieved through proper access control over information in storage and the use of encryption when data is transmitted over untrusted and/or non-secured networks. The higher the sensitivity (for example, assigned classification) of the data, the stronger the encryption should be to protect that data.

When determining the confidentiality requirements for data, consider the length of time it needs to stay private. For stock pricing information, it may only need to stay private for 10 or 20 minutes before the value in its confidentiality is gone. Proprietary processes or formulas, on the other hand, may need to stay private for many years. The encryption system therefore needs to ensure privacy of information for as long as keeping it a secret is valuable.

Understand that all encryption schemes can be broken given enough time and money. Many of today's encryption schemes work by encrypting data with a piece of secret information referred to as a key. The more values the key can have, the stronger the encryption system can be considered. This is referred to as the applicable key space. Someone who wishes to decrypt a piece of information will, at a maximum, need to try all the possible keys within the key space via a brute-force attack. This is commonly the attack of last resort and is also the most time, and resource-intensive. Brute-force attacks can be performed by either a very powerful special purpose computer or by harnessing the processing power of many smaller computers. Although the likely entities with the resources for the former are predominantly large governments, the Internet has been used to mount successful attacks via the latter. This is not to say that encryption is useless. By current methods, finding the correct key in today's strongest encryption systems may take many billions of years. This is very likely much longer than the amount of time the information needs to remain secret.

Additional uses of encryption include the ability to verify the identity of the senders and receivers of a communication. Encryption can also be used to detect when information has been altered while in transit (either maliciously or accidentally). Finally, encryption can be used to ensure that the parties to the transaction cannot deny later that they sent or received a message.

Confidentiality is far larger than just the encrypting of data. Confidentiality also encompasses how a corporation uses certain types of information. One of today's hottest issues is customer personal privacy. Although the Internet has created tremendous opportunities for communication, it can be used to violate and abuse one's right to privacy. Unprecedented amounts of personal information can be regularly captured and analyzed without the knowledge of the user. Privacy is widely understood as the right of individuals to control the collection, use, and dissemination of their personal information that is held by others. The Information Classification process should clearly identify all applications that will contain or collect personal information about its users. For example, the average Web application is able to build a sophisticated behavior profile of visitors to its site by recording the pages they viewed and how long they viewed them. This information can be collected over multiple sessions and over any desired period of time one's actions can be tracked and analyzed. The more interesting aspect here, however, is who owns these details, and what is done with this information.

Privacy protection is the ethical obligation associated with the collection and use of personal information. When organizations collect information about individuals, they should make the individual aware of the information that is collected and how it will be used. Corporations should also ensure that they comply with local legal regulations as well as offer consumers the ability to opt-out of data collection efforts. The single biggest item is to manage expectations effectively; deceptive practices can cause enormous public relations nightmares and even consumer backlash. Consult with popular consumer privacy groups such as the Electronic Privacy Information Center (EPIC) for information on current privacy regulations, information, and best practices. Finally, be sensitive to the local climate and existing legislation. Europe, for example, is far more strict on personal privacy than the United States.

Authenticity and Integrity

Just as it is important to maintain data confidentiality, data integrity should be protected to ensure that it has not been illegitimately modified in transit or storage. The accuracy of data faces numerous threats, including data entry errors, malicious users, transmission errors, and application processing errors. As noted above, encryption can be used to verify that information was not altered in transit, whereas strong authentication and authorization controls ensure that only authorized users can input data into systems.

However, maintaining systems with high integrity goes well beyond authenticating and authorizing users. The information produced by an application will only be as useful as what was put in. Good application systems will perform exhaustive input validation checking. This means ensuring that the dates entered are correctly formatted and reasonable (for example, the application should not allow orders from several months ago or 10 years in the future).

Authenticity lends itself directly to authentication and authorization controls. All users should be accountable for actions performed within the system. Accountability requires that all system actions including system transactions, access violations, and attempted accesses are associated with an individual user who can then be held responsible for their actions.

Authenticity also has an important function when communicating with remote systems. Applications will sometimes need to verify the origin of the message to ensure that a malicious individual was unable to insert data into the transaction stream. Cryptography lends itself nicely to verifying the authenticity of a message.

Availability

System availability ensures that systems are appropriately resilient and available to users on a timely basis (such as when users require them). The opposite of availability is denial of service, where users cannot access the resources they need on a timely basis. Denial of service can be intentional (the product of malicious individuals) or accidental (hardware or software failures). Unavailable systems cost corporation's real dollars in lost revenue and employee productivity, as well as in intangible ways through lost consumer confidence and negative publicity.

The best practice solution for availability is to avoid single points of failure within the architecture. This includes redundant and fail-over configurations at the hardware, network, and application layers. An assessment of the application availability requirements should be performed to understand the financial impact when systems are unavailable to appropriately determine application resiliency requirements. It is also important to monitor systems for utilization and increase system capacity accordingly.

No system is bulletproof. Unanticipated occurrences and events that cannot be planned for will always be present. Corporations should create detailed plans for responding to system failures and restoring services quickly. This planning is often referred to as Disaster Recovery/Business Resumption (DRP) planning. A good DRP is a detailed plan and procedure that enables critical systems to be recovered relatively quickly and efficiently in the event of a disaster. The plan covers system backups, documenting important contacts and their assigned roles, preparing detailed procedures for recovering systems, and maintaining alternate hardware and facilities to house the recovery. These plans should be tested and updated on a regular basis.

Non-Repudiation

Non-repudiation controls are controls that are designed to prevent an individual from being able to deny receipt or transmission of a message. Non-repudiation can also be used to verify the time of the communications. They should be implemented in applications where simply authenticating a user is insufficient. The key to non-repudiation is the ability to uniquely identify an entity without question.

How does one decide whether to implement non-repudiation controls? The question to ask is what are the consequences and costs associated with a customer being able to deny a specific action? Let's create a fictitious individual named Alice. Alice has an online brokerage account through Bob's Brokerage. Alice isn't a particularly risky or active trader and has a portfolio consisting of relatively low-risk investments (New York Stock Exchange [NYSE] blue chip stocks). One day, Alice gets a big stock tip on a biotech firm that's about to get FDA approval and it's going to triple overnight. So she logs into her brokerage account, sells the blue chip stocks, and buys this biotech stock. Alice reluctantly realizes she has been misinformed, and instead of skyrocketing, the biotech stock implodes and her entire portfolio becomes worthless. Alice tries to liquidate her biotech position, but Bob's systems are overloaded and the order isn't processed immediately, adding to Alice's losses. A host of factors influence the outcome of the resulting lawsuit. What if Alice claims it wasn't her using her account that day? Can Bob prove it was Alice or that the order was executed timely and that he has no culpability for Alice's losses? A repudiation system could have been used to ensure that Alice was in control of her account and have provided timestamps on all messages to verify when they were transmitted.

Non-repudiation can be used to avoid protracted and costly legal disputes such as those that might ensue in this example. It may be worthwhile to consult an attorney to determine if a non-repudiation scheme is warranted for a particular application you are reviewing.

Audit/Monitoring

Systems do not operate in a vacuum and people will attempt to use applications in ways never anticipated (intentionally and unintentionally). Therefore, it is extremely important to monitor system activity. Applications should record system events that are both successful and unsuccessful. Verbose logging and diligent reviews of those logs can alert administrators to suspicious activity before a serious security breach occurs.

An audit trail is the chronological set of records that provides evidence of system activity. These records should be sufficiently detailed to reconstruct, review, and examine system transactions from inception to output of final results. The records can also be reviewed to track system usage and detect and identify intruders.

Applying the IC

We have defined risk as well as control, but a consistent method for applying the Information Classification must also be discussed. A highly effective method for applying the Information Classification is via a questionnaire. A good questionnaire has relatively open-ended questions that facilitate discussion and analysis of the proposed application. The questionnaire should identify the types of information that will be processed as well as ask the business unit to identify risk to the applications data. Once the various data elements have been identified, a risk rating can be assigned. The rating assigned is akin to the perceived inherent risk of the data. In addition, the data's classification level should also be factored in when assigning a rating. The higher the data's risk rating, the more stringent the level of controls should be that are required. Table 3-2 provides a sample questionnaire.

The IC and the Application Development Process

The Information Classification questionnaire is best applied at the start of the application development life cycle. It should then be revisited during the various stages of the application development life cycle to ensure that the necessary levels of control are being implemented. The initial completion of the IC is primarily the responsibility of the business process owner and the individuals most directly responsible for the information. These individuals have the most intimate understanding of the information and the risks to it. Once completed, the application developers can reference the completed IC to understand the areas of risk that will need to be controlled.

Table 3-2

Sample IC Questionnaire

	MCC Corporations Information Classification Questionnaire
Confidentiality	1. Provide an overview of the types of information processed by this application; please indicate its data classification levels. 2. Who will be accessing this information and where will access be available from? 3. Provide a description of the impact if the above indicated information is disclosed, manipulated, or destroyed by an unauthorized individual. Include a description of the following: ■ Potential financial impact including direct losses (lost business, fines, lawsuits) and indirect losses (for example, competitive disadvantages) ■ Reputation damage that could occur as a result of disclosure ■ Legal, contractual, or regulatory restrictions that apply to disseminating this information ■ How much of an unfair advantage could a client or competitor gain from unauthorized disclosure? 4. Data privacy is becoming an increasing concern. Please indicate the following: ■ What kind of personally identifiable information will be collected by this application? ■ Will this information be used internally or made available to third parties? ■ Will the users be notified of what information is collected and how it will be used?
Integrity	1. What kinds of interaction will the users of this application be capable of? (View only, update?) 2. What would be the impact to the business if data were inappropriately modified, erroneous, or deleted? Consider the following: ■ To what degree could inaccurate information in this system, (that is, as a result of tampering or processing errors) affect operations? ■ To what degree could the inaccuracy of this information, if made public, result in damage to the firm's reputation? ■ To what degree may unauthorized modification to this information result in fraud? ■ To what extent would legal, regulatory, or contractual obligations be breached if unauthorized changes were made to information?

continued

Table 3-2 (cont.)
Sample IC Questionnaire

	MCC Corporations Information Classification Questionnaire
	3. Is the information used for business decision support? Explain. 4. Is the information used to update the firm's official financial records? Indicate any dependencies or interfaces with other departments, locations, or vendors.
Repudiation	1. How much concern is there over an individual denying responsibility for initiating a transaction or message through this system? 2. How much concern is there over an individual denying receipt of a transaction or message from this system?
Availability	1. How time-sensitive is the information provided by this application? 2. What is the estimated cost in dollars (in lost revenue) to the corporation in the event of a system outage (in terms of minutes, hours, days)? 3. What kinds of potential loss could our customers suffer if this application was not available? 4. How long can the business operate efficiently without this application? 5. What is our customers' tolerance of system outages?

The completion of the IC should not be a static event. The requirements and application functionality may change during the design and implementation phases of the project that impact the control requirements. The IC should be revisited during the application development life cycle to ensure that risks and controls are being adequately addressed and implemented.

Analysis of Case Study #1—Corporate

MCC is a large company with many thousands of employees and offices around the globe. MCC is a prime candidate for an Information Classification schema to ensure that sensitive corporate information is afforded the same protection across the company. Based on the example schema presented earlier in the chapter, we can assign the various classifications to data handled in Case Study #1, as shown in Table 3-3.

Table 3-3

Sample Classification

Classification Level	Examples
Public	MCC Corporate Web Server
Internal	Corporate e-mail
Confidential	Accounting information MCC Marketing Database ERP systems HR systems
Restricted	MCC Marketing Database Legal system Payroll information within the HR systems

Note that some of the applications and processes described in the case study contain multiple kinds of data in different classifications.

Analysis of Case Study #2—FinApp

Stepping into the role of the data owner for the FinApp application, we complete the IC questionnaire and identify the risk areas within the application (marked by italics) in Table 3-4.

Analyzing the questionnaire, we can identify the following risk areas within FinApp:

- Confidentiality responses indicate that FinApp will require certain elements of information (such as customer) to remain private for indefinite periods, while other communications have less stringent timeframes (pricing and trading data).
- Integrity responses indicate that FinApp will not tolerate input and/or processing errors.
- Repudiation response indicates that repudiation controls should be implemented as part of this application.
- Availability responses indicate that FinApp will be highly utilized and downtime will result in significant lost business. This can be translated into a requirement for a highly available system.

Table 3-4

FinApp IC Questionnaire

	MCC Corporations Information Classification Questionnaire
Confidentiality	1. Provide an overview of the types of information processed by this application; please indicate its data classification levels. *This application is a business-to-business investment banking application that provides futures and options clients with post trade statement information and basic account management information. The FinApp application will also be processing one million trades per day from institutional and non-institutional clients. To support the trading activity, the application will provide pricing information.* *The customer account and balance information contained is considered MCC Proprietary Information. The pricing information can be considered public information but will only be provided to certain customers.* 2. Who will be accessing this information and where will access be available from? *The majority of users of this system are other financial institution's commodity trading advisors who will be accessing FinApp over the Internet. In addition, we will have institutional and personal traders executing single stock trades for NYSE and Nasdaq Stocks. The application will be accessing financial exchanges for pricing and executing orders. Finally, market data feeds will supply additional pricing information.* *It is important to note that this application will be hosted at a third party. Although this facility will provide 24x7 monitoring and support, this does create physical security issues over the data and equipment, which will need to be addressed.* 3. Provide a description of the impact if the above indicated information is disclosed, manipulated, or destroyed by an unauthorized individual. Include a description of the following: ■ Potential financial impact including direct losses (lost business, fines, lawsuits) and indirect losses (for example, competitive disadvantages) ■ Reputation damage that could occur as a result of disclosure ■ Legal, contractual, or regulatory restrictions that apply to disseminating this information ■ How much of an unfair advantage could a client or competitor gain from unauthorized disclosure?

continued

Table 3-4 (cont.)

FinApp IC Questionnaire

	MCC Corporations Information Classification Questionnaire
	Unauthorized disclosure of the information contained within this application could have serious negative impacts on MCC operations. Knowledge of our institutional investors' activity can at times be considered insider information violating SEC disclosure laws. An individual could use this information to "front-run" the market for financial gain. In addition, this could have a negative impact on our customers' execution activity (they could end up getting worse prices in the market). 4. Data privacy is becoming an increasing concern; please indicate the following: ■ What kind of personally identifiable information will be collected by this application? ■ Will this information be used internally or made available to third parties? ■ Will the users be notified of what information is collected and how it will be used? *The application will contain personally identifiable information such as names, addresses, and social security numbers for a number of reasons. This information will be disclosed only to those third parties directly responsible for settling trades (settlement operations are outsourced).*
Integrity	1. What kinds of interaction will the users of this application be capable of? (View only, update?) *Users will be able to view account information as well as post trade statement information. Certain users will be able to execute trades through FinApp; we will have restrictions on the dollar amounts of the trades they can execute (depending on preauthorized trading limit and the value of assets in the account). In addition, users will be able to view market pricing information, and qualified and paying customers will be able to view pricing information in real-time, whereas others will be provided data on a 15-minute delay. Database administrators will only be able to access the database for maintenance. We plan on maintaining a helpdesk that can reset passwords, operations personnel who can perform back-up operations, and full system administrators with access to all functionality.*

continued

Table 3-4 (cont.)

FinApp IC Questionnaire

	MCC Corporations Information Classification Questionnaire
	2. What would be the impact to the business if data was inappropriately modified, erroneous, or deleted? Consider the following: ■ To what degree could inaccurate information in this system (that is, as a result of tampering or processing errors) affect operations? ■ To what degree could the inaccuracy of this information, if made public, result in damage to the firm's reputation? ■ To what degree could unauthorized modification to this information result in fraud? ■ To what extent would legal, regulatory, or contractual obligations be breached if unauthorized changes were made to information? *This system will have zero tolerance for processing errors.* 3. Is the information used for business decision support? Explain. *Our customers will use the pricing information to make financial decisions. We can also anticipate that MCC business decisions will be made based on the revenue generated by the application.* 4. Is the information used to update the firm's official financial records? Indicate any dependencies or interfaces with other departments, locations, or vendors. *This application has multiple financial impacts as follows:* ■ *The corporation will collect a commission for each transaction performed.* ■ *The corporation will have a number of investors trading on margin; we will charge an interest rate for all equities owned on margin (this interest rate will vary depending on market conditions).* ■ *In addition, customers will also accrue interest for cash in their accounts.*
Repudiation	1. How much concern is there over an individual denying responsibility for initiating a transaction or message through this system? 2. How much concern is there over an individual denying receipt of a transaction or message from this system? *Customers may try to deny executing trades or may claim that FinApp did not execute the order timely, resulting in losses.*

continued

Table 3-4 (cont.)

FinApp IC Questionnaire

	MCC Corporations Information Classification Questionnaire
Availability	1. How time-sensitive is the information provided by this application? 2. What is the estimated cost in dollars (in lost revenue) to the corporation of a system outage (in terms of minutes, hours, days)? 3. What kinds of potential loss could our customers suffer if this application was not available? 4. How long can the business operate efficiently without this application? 5. What is our customers' tolerance of system outages? *During market hours, there is zero tolerance for system downtime. Unavailable systems will result in lost customers and revenue for the corporation. In addition, customers will expect to have marketable orders executed almost immediately upon placement; the inability to execute orders may result in losses for our customers, which MCC could potentially be held liable for.* *During off-market hours, account information should not be unavailable for an extended period and must be available before the market opens the following day. To maintain customer confidence, the FinApp application should be up 99.999 percent of the time during off-hours and 100 percent of the time during market hours.*

Based on the information provided, FinApp has significant confidentiality, integrity, and availability requirements. FinApp has less stringent requirements for privacy and repudiation controls. Translating those security requirements will be detailed in the following chapter. In addition to determining the inherent risk of the application data, we can begin to formulate an access control plan.

In addition to completing the Information Classification, the application development community can begin to develop an access control plan. The questionnaire identified a number of different types of system users as well as proposed system functionality. It is useful to create a table to identify the most efficient set of roles for this application. Table 3-5 is an analysis of the expected users of the FinApp; a separate chart should be compiled for system administrative functions.

Table 3-5 FinApp Role-Based Access Control

Role	Public Data	Account Information	Pricing Information	Perform Trades	Up to Equity in Account	Margin Available	Line of Credit
Public/Anonymous Access	✓						
Customers	✓	✓					
Trader	✓	✓	✓	✓	✓	✓	
Institutional Trader	✓		✓	✓		✓	✓
Margin Trader	✓		✓			✓	
Institutional Salesperson	✓		✓				

At this stage, we can see that the application will require a public access role for accessing any public data such as an opening screen and so on. All other access must be authenticated and will require an authorization system to control access. FinApp will provide access to basic customers to look at their accounts as well as various levels of traders for trading activities. Finally, a sales role has been identified that will not require trading access.

Analysis of Case Study #3—HealthApp

Without repeating the IC questionnaire here, we can see that the proposed healthcare application has the following risk areas:

- **Confidentiality** The healthcare application is going to contain personal information, including medical records; therefore, strong privacy and confidentiality controls will be required. Finally, customer policy information that is also going to be accessible through this application should be properly protected.
- **Integrity** The accuracy of those records will also need to be important but probably not as much as with FinApp. MCC should follow-up on the integrity requirements of the quote processing system before proceeding with development.
- **Repudiation** Controls do not appear to be paramount in this application.
- **Availability** Downtime for this application could affect claims processing, new policy quoting, and customers attempting to access their records and dispute claims. Availability requirements for this application are high because of the policy quoting system that drives business.

Again, without repeating the Access Control Matrix, we can determine that the healthcare application will require the following roles: a public role, a customer role, a claims processor role, and a physician role.

The Information Classification process is most effective when supported by management and the Corporate Security Policy. An effective Information Classification requires corporations to develop and disseminate a classification schema that groups information according to perceived sensitivity. Once developed, the schema is used as a basis for identifying information risk during the application development life cycle and assists in the identification of control requirements to mitigate and manage those risks. The IC can be an effective tool and when used consistently, it will continually produce well-controlled applications.

References

Handbook of Information Security Management 1999. Micki Krause, Harold F. Tipton editors. CRC Press LLC, 1999.

Computer Security Basics. Deborah Russell and G.T. Gangemi Sr. O-Reilly and Associates, U.S., 1992.

CHAPTER 4

Applying the Policies to Derive the Requirements

This chapter depicts the information security requirements as they are derived from corporate policies, standards, and guidelines. Organizations that fail to address security requirements will not have the sufficient controls in place to minimize risks. These risks could lead to significant financial predicaments. Appropriate management, operational, and technical controls are required to minimize the risks associated with the confidentiality, integrity, and availability of information assets. In this chapter, we define the information security requirements based on three interrelated functional levels of control: management, operational, and technical controls.

A *requirement* can be defined as a condition or capability to which a system must conform. The term *system* may include business operations and processes, operating systems, applications, database platforms, networking components, business units and responsibilities relating to systems, and personnel practices regarding addition, transfer, and termination procedures.

The main goal of information security is to protect the confidentiality, integrity, and availability of an organization's information assets. Defining and managing your information technology security requirements is crucial in meeting your corporate business objectives while minimizing risks associated with the confidentiality, integrity, and availability of information assets.

This chapter contains baseline information security requirements that are driven by the corporate business strategies and objectives of our case studies. However, every organization is different and should not just follow these security requirements. Rather, an organization should use these generalized requirements as a foundation to build its own unique security requirements. The terminology used within this chapter to indicate the status of a security requirement is the following:

- The words *must* and *shall* are used to indicate mandatory security requirements.
- The word *should* is used to indicate preferred and higher level security measures than the mandatory security requirements.

Before we can accurately define the security requirements for our case studies, it is important to understand various threats and risks that exist in our digital world.

Threats

In today's business environment, more and more companies are leveraging the networked nature of the Internet. Many companies want to take full advantage of the Internet and distributed computing to serve their customers and help their employees work more productively. With the explosive growth in information sharing, increased Internet use, and the rapid deployment of electronic commerce infrastructures, companies are facing an increased number of vulnerabilities and threats. Companies have more systems to worry about, such as Intranets, Extranets, and value-chain networks (supply chain networks).

Basically, threats are conditions with a potential to cause harm to company resources (people or network resources). Threats may come from your systems' vulnerability to unauthorized use by hackers as well as from employees performing non-business activities, the exposure of internal information, data destruction including customer records and confidential business information, the corruption of your products and the information your business supplies, natural disasters, and so forth.

According to the Computer Security Institute (CSI) and Federal Bureau of Investigations' (FBI) "2000 Computer Crime and Security Survey," 90 percent of survey respondents detected cyber attacks in 2000, and 273 of those organizations reported $265,589,940 in financial losses. This amount is significantly higher than the average annual total of financial loses over 1997, 1998, and 1999, which was $120,240,180. According to the study, the most serious financial losses occurred through the theft of internal information, as shown in Figure 4-1.

Typically, an organization incurs two types of loss as a result of these threats: direct loss or consequential loss. Direct loss is when a system or a related component of it is damaged or destroyed. Consequential loss might occur as a result of a direct loss. It can occur in many ways:

- Loss of customer
- Loss of supplier
- Public embarrassment
- Loss of competitive advantage and information
- Loss of tangible assets and decreased cash flow

Consequential loss usually accounts for a significant portion (90 to 95 percent) of total losses arising from a breakdown in a system's security. Therefore, protecting an organization from consequential loss needs to be the main focus of system security.

Threats may originate from various sources in this constantly changing digital economy. Threats can be categorized in many ways. We group threats under two categories: external threats and internal threats. The attacks discussed in the following sections may fall under both external and internal threats. However, the attacks are clearly placed under one of

Figure 4-1

Financial losses by type of attack or misuse

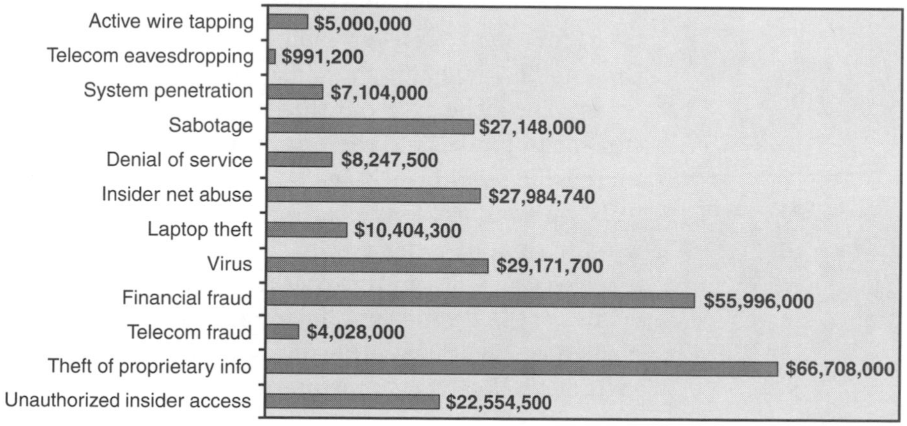

Source: CSI/FBI 2000 Computer Crime and Security Survey

the two categories depending on where they originate from and who commits them. It should be noted that we are simply outlining the various types of attacks that you are more likely to see so that you have some familiarity with these when we introduce the security requirements that, when implemented, would reduce or eliminate the risk of these occurring.

External Security Threats

In January 2001, some employees of one of the world's major beverage companies and other people who browsed on its United Kingdom division Web site read the following words on the Web page rather than the usual main Web page:

> "multinational corporations
> genocide of the starving nations
> multinational corporations
> make their profit from the starving nations
> indigenous people become their slaves
> from their births to their grave
> multinational corporations
> take their profit from the starving
> making another product for you to buy
> you will keep on paying until you die"

That day the company found out that a hacker had defaced its Web site. Web site defacement is one of the most common methods that have been used by hackers to make others pay attention to a certain issue of importance for them. A hacker usually reaches a pretty decent size audience via this method depending upon the popularity of the targeted Web site. This is just one of the external threats that companies are facing today. As you can see in Figure 4-2, the total number of Web site defacements has been increasing significantly in recent years.

Have your systems been hacked? Have your computer systems been used to commit cyber crime? How would you know if they had? With the increased use of the Internet as part of day-to-day business, traditional crimes of theft and fraud have migrated from a paper-based world into an electronic one. Some other attacks that may originate from the Internet include the following: masquerading as another user, packet replay, denial

Figure 4-2

Total number of Web defacements that happened in 1999 and 2000

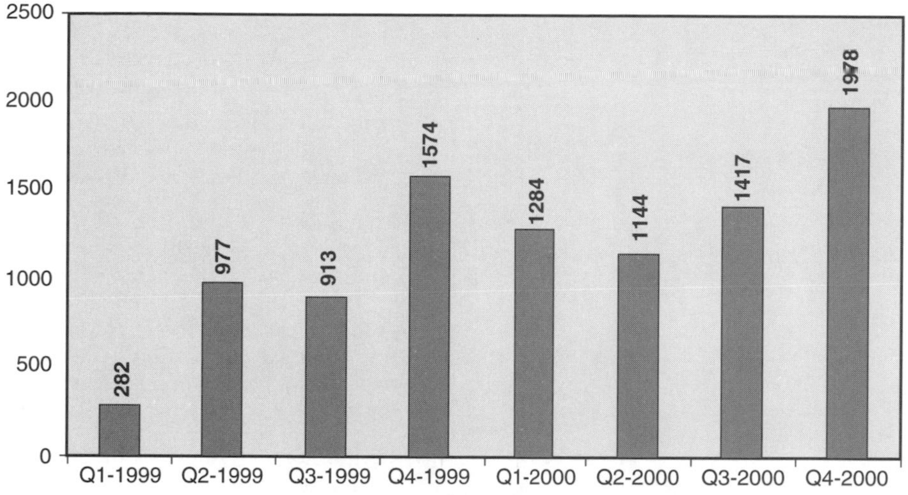

Source: Attrition (**http://www.attrition.org/mirror/attrition/annuals.html**)

of service (DoS) attacks, remote brute-force and dictionary attacks, system identity spoofing, eavesdropping on communications, Trojan horses, viruses, and worms. Table 4-1 provides quick definitions for each of these attacks.

All these attacks have one thing in common: they are a direct threat to the confidentiality, integrity, and availability of an organization's information assets. Figure 4-3 illustrates a good example of this. In all the crime cases listed in Figure 4-3, the attacker or attackers have threatened and harmed at least one of the three core information security objectives (confidentiality, integrity, and availability). They have been prosecuted under a computer crime statute and the information has been released to the public in regards to what security objectives these crimes have threatened and harmed.

Of course, physical and environmental threats still exist that would be considered external threats. These threats include events such as a power outage, natural disasters (storms, earthquakes, lightning, flooding, and tidal waves), sabotages, vandalism, arson, strikes, riots, and collisions from transportation utilities (such as, aircraft crashes) with the potential to disrupt mission critical business functions.

Table 4-1

Quick Definitions

Attack	Description
Packet replay	Packet replay is the recording and retransmission of packets in the network. It is a significant threat for programs that require authentication sequences because an intruder could replay legitimate authentication sequence messages to gain access to a system.
Denial of service	An attack that compromises all available system resources, making the system unusable for any users, resulting in a degradation or loss of service. An example for this is the Jolt/SSPING attack. Jolt/SSPING is a program that effectively freezes any Windows95 or Windows NT connection. It works basically by sending a series of spoofed and fragmented ICMP packets to the target.
Trojan horses	Trojan horses are programs that pretend to have a set of useful features, but actually perform an unauthorized and damaging function. SIMPSONS.EXE, a Trojan horse that deletes files on selected drives via an extracted .BAT file, is a good example. The SIMPSONS.EXE file appears to be an installer program on the user's computer.
Viruses and worms	A virus is usually designed to replicate itself on a user's computer without his/her knowledge. A worm is a type of virus that operates over a network and replicates itself to infect all the computers that may be attached to the same network. Yankee Doodle is an overwriting, memory resident, file-infecting virus. It infects .COM and .EXE files. LOVE-LETTER-FOR-YOU.TXT.vbs is a good example of a worm that uses built-in functions of VBScript in order to write itself to the local system and distribute itself via Outlook messaging. It will arrive in an e-mail message.

Internal Security Threats

On July 30, 1996, the Omega Engineering Corporation, a New Jersey-based manufacturer of high-tech measurement and control instruments used by NASA and the U.S. Navy, discovered that all its design and sophisticated production programs had been deleted. After a detailed investigation, the company officials found out that the company had been a victim of a *logic bomb* that had been planted by a former network administrator, Timothy Allen Lloyd. Lloyd had just been fired 20 days earlier on July 10,

					Target		Perpetrator Charged		
Colloquial Case Name (District)	**Press Release Date**	**Confidentiality**	**Integrity**	**Availability**	**Public**	**Private**	**Juvenile**	**Adult**	**Organized Group**
U.S. v. "HV2k" (VA local)	December 6, 2000	X	X	X		X	X	X	
U.S. v. Torricelli (S.D. NY)	December 1, 2000	X	X		X			X	
U.S. v. Diekman (C.D. CA)	September 21, 2000	X	X		X	X		X	
U.S. v. "cOmrade" (SD FL)	September 21, 2000	X			X		X		
U.S. v. Gregory (ND TX)	September 6, 2000	X				X			X
U.S. v. Zezov et. al. (SD NY)	August 14, 2000	X				X		X	X
U.S. v. Torricelli (SD NY)	July 12, 2000	X	X		X	X		X	
U.S. v. Lloyd (NJ)	May 9, 2000		X	X		X		X	
U.S. v. Dennis (AK)	April 19, 2000	X		X	X			X	
U.S. v. Davis (ED VVI)	March 1, 2000	X		X		X			X
U.S. v. ?? (MA)	February 23, 2000	X	X	X	X			X	
U.S. v. Miffleton	December 20, 1999	X	X			X		X	X
U.S. v. Smith (NJ)	December 9, 1999		X	X	X	X		X	
U.S. v. Alibris (MA)	November 22, 1999	X				X			X
U.S. v. Burns (ED VA)	November 19, 1999	X	X	X	X	X		X	
U.S. v. Lindsly (ND TX)	September 16, 1999	X				X		X	X
U.S. v. Mitnick (CD CA)	August 9, 1999	X	X			X		X	
U.S. v. Kashpureff (ED NY)	March 19, 1998			X		X		X	
U.S. v. Tenebaum (Israel)	March 18, 1998	X			X			X	
U.S. v. An Unnamed Juvenile (MA)	March 18, 1998	X		X	X	X	X		

Figure 4-3 A summary chart of recently prosecuted computer crime cases

1996. However, the court trial testimony indicated that Lloyd had been testing the computer program that destroyed Omega's most critical manufacturing programs since February 1996. According to court records, the total damage including lost contracts and lost productivity totaled more than $10 million.

Logic bombs are one of the most destructive internal threats. A logic bomb is a malicious code that is designed to execute a set of instructions at a certain date and time or under a certain specified condition. Some other internal attacks include the following: Trojan horses, unauthorized copying (theft) of confidential data, password sniffing, data diddling, unauthorized software modifications and trap doors, eavesdropping, viruses, worms, and so on.

Trojan horses are programs that pretend to have a set of useful features but actually perform an unauthorized and damaging function. Trojan horses provide a common technique for planting other attacks in computer systems including logic bombs, viruses, and worms. A virus is a program that modifies other programs in a system to replicate itself. A worm operates over a network and replicates itself to infect all the computers that may be attached to the same network. Data diddling is all about modifying data (falsifying) before or after it is entered into the computer. Password sniffers are programs that capture username and password information on networks used by systems that attackers are interested in penetrating. Many more attack types exist; however, we won't list or go into detail with every attack. What one thing do all these attacks have in common? They all have an initiator, an internal person such as a disgruntled employee.

According to the CSI and FBI's "2000 Computer Crime and Security Survey," disgruntled employees are still the most likely source of attack, as shown in Figure 4-4.

Management Security Requirements

The success and effectiveness of an information security program is largely dependent upon the support of senior management and the security function's location in the organizational hierarchy. Both financial and political support is needed from the senior management. To be effective,

Figure 4-4

Likely sources of attack

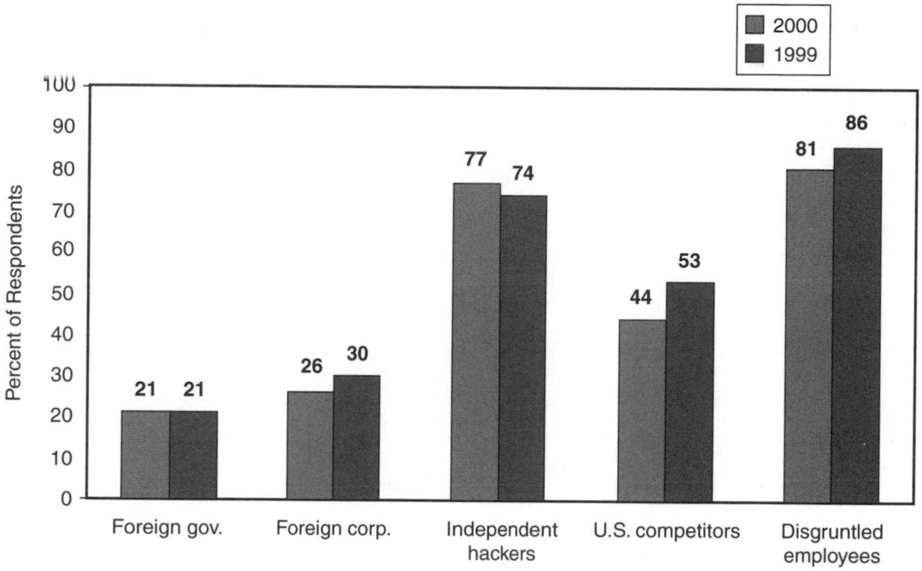

Source: CSI/FBI 2000 Computer Crime and Security Survey.

the information security function will need the senior management to clearly define the following elements:

- Management support
- Proper placement in the organization
- Clear responsibility and authority
- Resources needed to affect change

Information security must adapt as new technologies are introduced, business initiatives change, more people (employees, customers, vendors) interact with the company's systems, and the organization matures. Therefore, it is essential that the information security program follow a life cycle and modifications be made as it becomes necessary. Figure 4-5 illustrates the information security life cycle.

Management security requirements focus on the high-level management controls that would affect the entire organization's security architecture design and deployment. Operational and technical security requirements that are going to be explained later in this chapter should fully support the management security requirements.

Figure 4-5
Information security life cycle

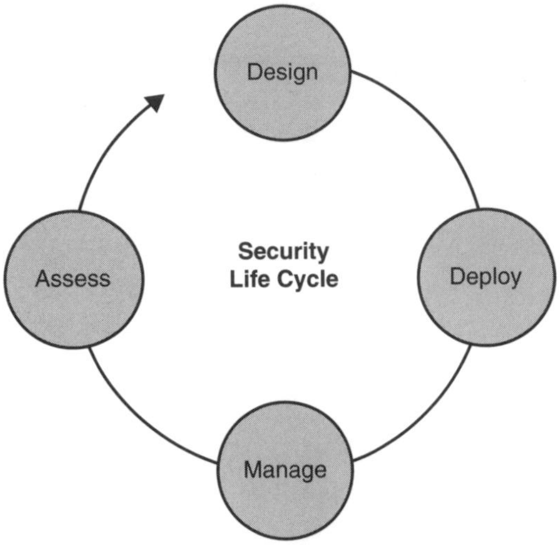

Defining the Security Model

The security model is composed of risk assessment and Information Classification processes as its core elements. Business data needs to be classified based on the corporate objectives and security needs of the organization. In Chapter 3, we defined the Information Classification levels for MCC, as shown in Table 4-2.

Business Impact Analysis and Risk Assessment

The Information Classification process, business impact analysis, and risk assessment process are interdependent upon each other. These processes play a significant role in defining security requirements for an organization. Requirements and controls are based on the extent of business dependency and business risk. Therefore, MCC's first security requirement is

- MCC must perform a Business Impact Analysis (BIA) to understand the impact of a loss or reduction of business functionality. MCC must identify its most critical assets.

The business impact assessment process can aid in lowering the overall cost of information security while still ensuring that the most critical data is adequately protected. The cost of protecting all corporate data is

Table 4-2

MCC Information Classification Levels

Information Classification Level	Definition
Public	Information that is expressly authorized for public disclosure. It is generally communicated to the public by proper channels (newspapers, magazines, WWW, and MCC anonymous server).
Internal	Information that is not generally known to the public at the time it is made known to the individual. This information has also not been expressly authorized for public disclosure.
Confidential	MCC corporate information, which if compromised, would be likely to have a material adverse impact on MCC, its customers, vendors, or employees. This includes information that may be widely available to employees in the normal course of business, but is to be kept within the control of MCC and may not be disclosed to the public without authorization.
Restricted	MCC corporate information, which if compromised, would be likely to cause severe financial, legal, regulatory, or reputation damage to MCC, its customers, vendors, or employees. This category of information is extremely sensitive in nature and requires specific, individual need-to-know permission prior to access.

extremely high. BIA helps identify the most critical resources and the threats against them in an organization. The risk assessment should start at the business level. Through an information-gathering process, the impact of a loss in business functionality should be measured (quantitatively and qualitatively) for each of the MCC business units. Each business unit at MCC should fill out a BIA form similar to the one shown in Figure 4-6. Business units should complete this form and document the impact of the unavailability of key components in their business units in relation to the attributes on the left column of the table. For instance, if the user account removal function of an organization's Information Security department becomes unavailable (that is, the only person who administers a certain system is sick), the department may not be able to remove a privileged user, who has just been terminated, from a sensitive system in a timely manner. This puts the integrity, confidentiality, and availability of data on that system at risk.

Figure 4-6

For each column, indicate the risk associated with the following key.

	Impact after 15 minutes	Impact after 1 hour	Impact after 2 hours	Impact after 1 day	Impact after 3 days	Impact after 1 week
Confidentiality						
Integrity						
Availability						

H: High Impact is critical to the operation of the business.

M: Medium Impact is very important to the continued operation of the business.

L: Low Impact is not vital to the continued operation of the business.

N: No impact No ramifications to the continued operation of the business.

Managing security is not straightforward, and it is difficult to determine the risks and costs associated with information technology processes in simple business terms. Additionally, as technology advances, information in the systems, the risks associated with the systems, and the security requirements are changing. Therefore, information security should be periodically reassessed and the following key questions should be answered periodically:

- What are we trying to protect?
- What are the critical assets that our organization possesses?
- How important are those assets?
- What are the threats to those assets?

- What is the probability of those threats occurring?
- What are the assumptions we are making when we answer these questions?

As shown in Figure 4-7, changes to the answers of any of these questions might impact the success and effectiveness of an information security program.

Personnel Security

Personnel security is one of the most critical areas of information security because employees are ultimately responsible for controlling the dissemination of sensitive MCC information. MCC personnel requirements are as follows:

- The MCC Human Resources department must subject prospective employees of MCC to pre-employment screening, which includes background investigations, as determined appropriate by the MCC Senior Management.
- All employees who are serving in a trusted role and have access to MCC-restricted data must be subject to a more detailed background

Figure 4-7
Defining security requirements

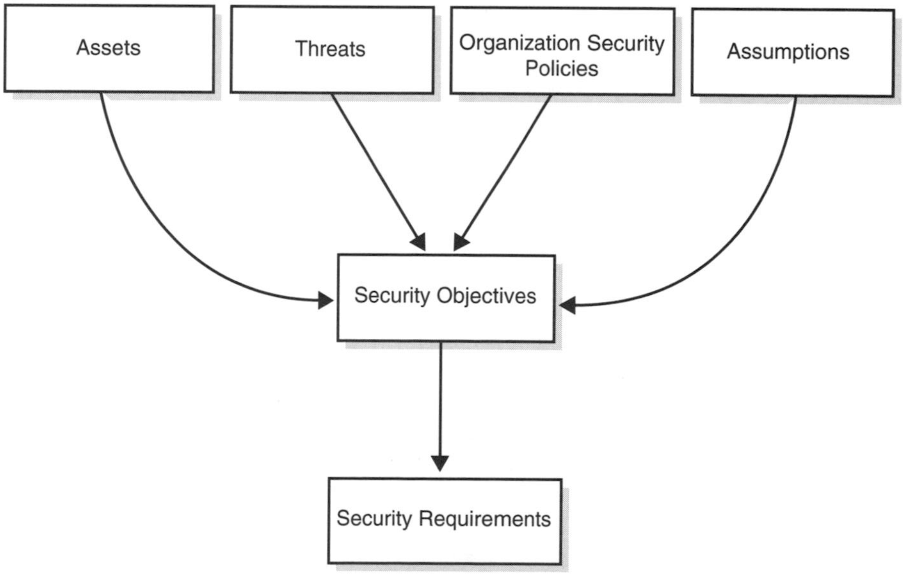

investigation prior to initial employment including a credit check, criminal record search, and testing for the use of illegal substances.

- MCC must have adequate supervisory practices in the organization to ensure that roles and responsibilities are properly exercised and to assess whether all personnel have sufficient authority and resources to execute their roles and responsibilities.
- MCC must ensure that all employees receive a copy of the MCC information security policies and acknowledge in writing that they understand their responsibilities as stated in this document.
- The Human Resources department must immediately notify the MCC security function upon the resignation or termination of employees. MCC must revoke all IDs and passwords upon termination or resignation of employees, and revoke or modify access upon the transfer of responsibilities.
- When users with access to restricted information are terminated, the employee's manager shall be responsible for directly coordinating with the system administrator or other appropriate supervisor to remove the user's access rights.

Security Awareness and Training Measures

Information security awareness is an integral part of a company's training program. To create and maintain an effective security awareness program, it is imperative that support is obtained from all levels of management. Without appropriate management support, a security awareness program will fail. Employees are the key elements of an effective information security program. Therefore, they must understand their role in the program.

Employees should receive regular training and reminders. Security reminders help ensure that the information security policies are not forgotten easily. Information security programs may take many different forms. However, the delivery method should have a clear message that "every one in the organization should care about security." The delivery methods that may be used include

- Briefings
- Discussions
- Custom video presentations

- Notices
- Posters
- Give-aways (that is, key-fobs)
- Newsletters

MCC security awareness requirements state that MCC employees must be provided with orientation upon hiring and ongoing training to maintain their knowledge, skills, abilities, and security awareness to the level required to perform effectively.

Change Management

Sufficient procedures should exist to ensure that changes to MCC resources are made and tested thoroughly and correctly. Documentation should be provided to ensure that the processes exist and are followed correctly. Non-conformance may result in loss of control over changes to MCC resources, resulting in unauthorized access into a resource and the potential for an unauthorized person to alter security configuration parameters. Personnel installing changes must be authorized to do so and be held accountable for the change. MCC change management requirements are as follows:

- Changes to MCC systems resources (hardware and software) and supporting systems must be documented, prioritized, tested on "test bed" systems, and authorized prior to being implemented.
- All requests for changes and system maintenance must be standardized and subject to formal change management procedures.
- All requests for changes must be assessed in a structured manner for possible impact on the resource functionality.
- System maintenance must be performed during non-peak times to minimize traffic impact. System maintenance procedures must include "roll back" procedures for use in the event that an upgrade or other maintenance task fails.
- Urgent processing problems must be documented and resolved by authorized individuals through the use of documented problem management procedures.
- The change management system must provide for an adequate audit trail facility that enables tracing from incident to underlying cause.

Password Selection and Change Requirements

Password selection and change requirements are two of the most important parts of an effective security program. Passwords are, in effect, the last line of defense before gaining system access. Therefore, MCC systems must meet the following password selection and change requirements:

- User passwords must consist of at least seven alphanumeric characters.
- System and administrative accounts' passwords must use a complex password. A complex password must consist of a mix of eight alphanumeric characters including uppercase and lowercase characters and at least one special character (#[]&%*).
- User passwords must not contain the user's name or ID.
- Passwords shall not be communicated in a manner other than from the security function to the user directly when it is assigned or changed.
- If a user is provided with an initial password (one-time password), this password must be changed the first time a user logs into a system.
- Users must log on in order to change password.
- Before a password change takes effect, users must be required to enter their new password multiple times (the user enters the new password twice for confirmation purposes).
- User password resets must only be performed when requested by the individual to whom the user ID is assigned. The relevant business unit should be responsible for verifying the identity of the user. The new password must be a one-time password.
- Passwords for user accounts must expire after a maximum of 60 days and a new password must be created. The same password must not be selected more than once in 90 days.
- Passwords for system and administrative accounts must expire after a maximum of 45 days and a new password must be created. A given password must not be used more than once in 90 days.
- Clear-text user ID and passwords must not be included in batch processing logon processes.
- Default passwords shipped with software and hardware must be disabled or changed immediately.

- Generic accounts and group passwords must not be allowed so that individual accountability can be maintained at all times.
- User account and password databases and files containing passwords that ship with various products (operating systems and network equipment) must be encrypted with the strongest encryption method available to that specific product.

Operational Security Requirements

Operational security requirements address the controls required to sustain normal business operations. The most common questions that operational security seeks to answer include the following:

- Have physical and environmental security controls been implemented to protect the MCC facilities that house system resources that support the company operations?
- Are there tested contingency plans and disaster recovery plans in place to allow the continuity of mission-critical functions?
- What are the application, hardware, and system maintenance controls?

Physical and Environmental Protection

Controls are necessary to protect the facilities that house MCC system resources against physical and environmental threats for continued operation. For instance, failures of electric power, air-conditioning, heating, water, and other utilities may have severe effects on electronic equipment. MCC requirements for physical and environmental protection are as follows:

- MCC must ensure that environmental protection measures and control devices exist to ensure the availability of the MCC global data centers, networks, systems, and continuity of operations. Sufficient measures must be put in place and maintained for protection against environmental factors (fire, dust, power, excessive heat, and humidity). MCC data centers must be protected against fire by using both smoke detectors and a fire suppression system. Water detectors must be installed within the raised floor areas.

- MCC must ensure that procedures exist for facilities management to monitor and test fire-suppression system equipment at least every six months and document test results.
- All MCC data center personnel must be trained in the use of any automatic fire-suppression systems, the use of portable fire extinguishers, and in the proper response to smoke and fire alarms.
- Health and safety practices must be in place and maintained in conformance with applicable national, regional, state, and local laws and regulations.
- MCC must ensure that MCC data centers are protected against a disruption in the power supply to the processing environment by utilizing both Uninterrupted Power Supplies (UPS) and Emergency Power Supplies (EPS). This equipment must be tested on a regular basis.
- MCC must prohibit food or drink in the data centers at anytime. Trash must be stored in appropriate containers and emptied periodically (at least daily). MCC must ensure that fluids, cleaning supplies, and other liquids are stored in containers away from equipment. MCC must ensure that exits and aisles will remain unobstructed at all times.

Physical Access Controls

All MCC information facilities should have appropriate physical access controls in place to protect information assets from unauthorized access. This section addresses requirements related to the protection of and physical access to MCC-distributed computing facilities. These facilities include data centers, computer rooms, network control centers, and other related areas. MCC requirements for physical access to distributed computing facilities are as follows:

- MCC must physically secure each component of the data processing equipment including computers, peripherals, terminals, controllers, and other related equipment and adhere to all local, state, and national electrical, fire, and other appropriate codes and insurance requirements. MCC must prevent unauthorized access to host computer equipment (servers, routers, switches, communications equipment, and so on) through the use of locked rooms and/or pass-code protection. Where technically possible, a log of successful and unsuccessful access attempts should be provided using access control devices.

- For MCC locations that have large computer centers (more than 10 servers), physical access to communications equipment must be further restricted within the computer room.
- A MCC liaison must be assigned to non-MCC employees who need access to the MCC data centers. These people may include vendors, service, and maintenance personnel. A written approval is required. These accesses must be logged and retained for at least one year.
- Combinations or key locks protecting doors shall be changed periodically and at the discretion of the MCC security function (for example, when an employee who has access is terminated).
- As part of a periodic third-party review of access controls, the MCC corporate audit department should commission a reviewer (either the corporate audit department or an external auditor) to review automated access control audit trails and visitor logs for appropriateness.
- MCC must provide adequate building security (such as, guards and/or alarmed doors) to protect the entire facility (in addition to computer room security) during off-hour periods. Alarms, close-circuit television monitoring, guards, badges, and biometrics (fingerprint or retinal scanners) should be employed to prevent unauthorized physical access to the building and controlled areas.
- All network facilities must have real-time monitoring of the access control system on site or must be connected to a 24-hour monitoring station that is manned seven days a week.
- All security systems must have a self-contained battery backup and should work in a networked environment or stand-alone as needed. Each system must have the capability to archive data for retrieval if an investigation is called for.

Business Continuity and Disaster Recovery Services

Business Continuity Planning (BCP) and Disaster Recovery Planning (DRP) enable companies to preserve the business in the event of major disruptions to normal business operations. BCP plays a significant role in averting potential contingencies and minimizing the damage these contingencies cause to organizations by taking early steps to control the event. The disaster recovery plan identifies the critical information technology application programs, operating systems, personnel, data files, and time frames needed for recovery after a disaster occurs. The disaster recovery plan incorporates an identification of alternatives regarding the backup site and hardware as well as a final alternative selection. MCC, BCP, and DRP requirements are as follows:

- Business continuity and disaster recovery plans must be in place and periodically tested to ensure the integrity and continuity of systems and minimize the impact to MCC in the event of a disaster.
- Management must implement a comprehensive strategy for backup and restoration to ensure that it includes a review of business requirements. Backup procedures for the data centers are documented and include incremental backups of each server, which are made daily, and complete backups of the entire week's changes, which are made on a weekly basis.
- The disaster recovery framework must define the roles and responsibilities, the approach to be adopted, and the structure of the plan. All critical personnel, both on-site and off-site, must have current versions of the disaster recovery plan. An electronic version should be stored off-site.
- The MCC disaster recovery plan must cover the planning and procedures to resume normal operations upon reconstruction of the information technology site after a disaster occurs, incorporate emergency procedures to ensure the safety of all affected staff members, and include procedures for reestablishing the telecommunications and network services used by the organization.

System and Application Maintenance

Application and system maintenance controls are used to monitor the installation of and updates to application and system software. These controls should provide reasonable assurance that selection and implementation or an upgrade of system and application software does not cause processing errors or undermine system software-based controls. Controls include the following:

- System software selection
- Version control
- Testing of new system software or upgrades to existing system software prior to the migration to the production environment
- Roll back to the prior release in the event an upgrade fails

MCC requirements are as follows:

- Products licensed to run on a specific computer or at a particular site shall not be copied onto another computer or another site without written authorization.
- Only authorized software, hardware, and devices that are owned or properly licensed and approved by MCC shall be used, installed, or brought into MCC production environment.
- MCC system and application software should be kept up-to-date in respect to vendor-recommended security patches. Current versions of the system and application software contain processing and security enhancements. Security patches correct bugs that have been communicated to the vendor.
- MCC data center system software problem records should identify the severity of the problem, record its assignment to a specific individual for analysis and resolution, and specify the timely resolution of the problem.

Disposal of Sensitive Materials

When MCC-restricted, confidential, and internal materials are disposed of, it is important to ensure that information is not improperly disclosed. MCC security requirements include the following:

- MCC-restricted, confidential, and internal classified information created or used by MCC must be securely stored, collected, and properly destroyed and disposed of when it is no longer needed.
- MCC-restricted, confidential, and internal information that is no longer needed must be shredded before discarding. Microfiche must be finely shredded to ensure that information cannot be recovered after it has been discarded.

- Magnetic media (floppy disks or magnetic tapes) that includes MCC-restricted, confidential, and internal classified information must be properly disposed of. The following steps must be followed: demagnetizing, reformatting, and cutting into pieces.
- MCC must place restrictions on the reproduction of hard copy, magnetic media, microfiche, and system-generated reports that contain restricted, confidential, and internal information.

Technical Security Requirements

Technical security requirements focus on controls that exist within the computer systems and applications as opposed to the employees or business processes. The main goal of technical security controls is to protect the confidentiality, integrity, and availability of an organization's information assets.

Data Integrity

Integrity is ensuring that information is protected from unauthorized alterations, unintentional modifications, or changes. Integrity deals with the quality or state of being complete; integrity requires soundness and completeness of information. It is the aspect of information that is complete, accurate, and valid. Meeting security requirements from the data integrity perspective reduces or eliminates the risk of critical information being accidentally or intentionally manipulated. The data integrity requirements for MCC are as follows:

- MCC must ensure the consistency of data values within a system (the operating system, hardware device, application systems, and databases) and also maintain the consistency between information internal to the system and information from outside systems.
- MCC must ensure that information can be recovered to a known consistent state in the event of a system failure.
- MCC must ensure that data is only modified by authorized means (authorized users and authorized systems).

Confidentiality

Confidentiality is the prevention of unauthorized disclosure of information. Information should be protected from unauthorized disclosure based upon the Information Classification (Restricted, Confidential, Internal, and Public) as defined in Chapter 3. The confidentiality requirement for MCC is listed in Table 4-3.

- MCC must ensure that information is disclosed only to authorized individuals, entities, and processes at authorized times.

Availability

Availability is ensuring that information and critical services are available when needed to meet business requirements. The availability objective requires that information systems function properly as scheduled, data is available for use, and data is easily recoverable in case of loss. Information availability can be affected in many ways, such as through natural disasters or human error, resulting in an interruption of the service provided by a system, in which the information becomes unobtainable or a degradation of the system's performance occurs such that

Table 4-3

Confidentiality Requirements Based on MCC Information Classification Policy

Information Classification	Confidentiality Requirement
Public	None
Internal	Encryption over public communications (Internet, dial-up) is required. Authentication credentials must be encrypted.
Confidential	All communications must be encrypted. Files must be encrypted on user workstations/laptops.
Restricted	All communications must be encrypted. Files must be encrypted on user workstations/laptops. Communications may only be made within MCC to named individuals having an authorized "need to know."

the information is not available in an acceptable amount of time. The availability requirements for MCC are

- Critical information must be available on a timely basis wherever it is needed to meet business requirements. Table 4-4 lists a sample of availability requirements based on the criticality of MCC systems. Table 4-5 shows the availability requirements based on the MCC Information Classification policy.

Table 4-4 Availability Requirements Based on Criticality of MCC Systems

System	Availability (High, Medium, Low)
Engineering network and systems	High
Electronic mail, calendaring	Medium
Corporate directory	Low
Internet connectivity	High
Human resources and payroll	High
Marketing	Medium
Remote access and control	Medium
Technical support	Medium
Intranet applications	High
Sales and distribution	High

Table 4-5 Availability Requirements Based on MCC Information Classification Policy

Information Classification	Availability Requirement
Public	Virus scanning and fail over backup site
Internal	Virus scanning and backup/restore
Confidential	Virus scanning, strong system configuration and change management, and backup/restore
Restricted	Virus scanning, strong system configuration and change management, and backup/restore

User Identification and Authentication

Authentication is the way of proving that you are who you say you are. Authentication within computing systems encompasses user identity verification, transmission origin authentication, content authentication, and detection of tampering. Identification is the means by which a user provides a claimed identity to a system. A user can be a human user, a computing system, or a process executing on another system. Three commonly known mechanisms verify a user's identity:

- Something a user knows (for example, a password or personal identification number)
- Something a user has (for example, a smart card)
- Something a user is (for example, fingerprints or a voice pattern)

Identification and authentication are the core components for most types of access control and for establishing user accountability.

The most commonly known authentication method is the password-based authentication, which is considered a single-factor scheme. The only thing an attacker has to guess in this method is the password. This single-factor scheme is also known as basic authentication. The ease of attacking a basic authentication scheme has been increasing significantly over the recent years with the help of readily available automated tools (password crackers, tools for dictionary, and brute-force attacks).

Today, more and more companies are using what is known as "two-factor" authentication for remote access to their critical assets. In a two-factor authentication scheme, the user must possess some item (that is, a smart card or time synchronous token) in addition to something only the user knows (that is, a PIN). The second factor can also be a unique identifying feature of the user (for example, biometric authentication schemes such as a fingerprint, retinal scan, or voice recognition). Some environments might need to have a highly secure authentication scheme that uses three factors of authentication (for example, a smart card and retinal scan). An authentication scheme that requires at least two factors is also referred to as "strong authentication." MCC identification and authentication requirements are as follows:

- All individuals must have unique user accounts. Every effort should be taken to not only avoid sharing accounts, but to avoid assigning a single individual multiple usernames for the same platform.

- In cases where administrators require general system utilization, they must be issued a non-administrative user account to ensure that administrative functions are segregated from normal operations.
- A user ID and password must be authenticated as a whole. Authentication failure must not provide an error-message to the user that indicates whether the user ID or password is correct (that is, "incorrect login" or "incorrect password.")
- All temporary employee accounts must have an expiration date that matches the end date for employment contract services and must use a different naming scheme than normal full-time employees.
- User accounts that have been inactive for more than 60 days must be disabled until the account owner requests that the account be enabled and provides proof of identity.

Table 4-6 lists the identification and authentication requirements based on the MCC Information Classification policy.

Table 4-6

Identification and Authentication Requirements Based on MCC Information Classification Policy

Information Classification	Identification and Authentication Requirements
Public	None
Internal	User IDs and passwords (encrypted username, password)
Confidential	Strong authentication (encrypted username, password, token, certificate)
Restricted	Strong authentication (encrypted username, password, token, certificate)

Non-repudiation

The non-repudiation security objective provides assurance that a specific action occurred. It comprises of the following components: non-repudiation of origin, non-repudiation of submission, and non-repudiation of delivery. Non-repudiation controls prevent an individual from being able to deny receipt, submission, or delivery of a message. The MCC non-repudiation requirements are listed in Table 4-7.

Table 4-7

MCC Non-repudiation Requirements

Information Classification	Non-repudiation
Public	Change control is required.
Internal	Change control is required. Minimal document change history must be maintained.
Confidential	Strict change controls are required. System-level file change history must be maintained. Digital signatures are required.
Restricted	Strict change controls are required. Field-level file change history must be maintained. Digital signatures for creator and the checker are required.

Authorization and Access Control

After a user has been authenticated to a system, the system must ensure that the user has sufficient rights to perform the requested operation. This is called authorization. Users have different levels of access to certain functionality or data within a system. These rights are granted to an individual by management to access information within a system based upon the individual's clearance. As explained in Chapter 3, authorization is often implemented through access control lists (ACLs) that exist within systems. ACLs contain a list of rights that a user can perform over an object such as read, write, and execute. Access controls can be implemented based on various criteria such as user identity-based, role-based, time-based, and transaction-based.

Role-based access controls can be very effective. Role-based access controls enable access to information based on the job function of the user who is requesting access. Some job examples include programmer, computer operator, and system administrator. The segregation of duties is the process of separating roles and responsibilities so that a single individual cannot subvert a critical function. This is to minimize the risk of negligent or deliberate system misuse and execution of certain duties to the extent that opportunities for unauthorized modification or misuse of data are at the acceptable risk level. MCC requirements for authorization and access controls are as follows:

- MCC least privilege principle: user privileges must be restricted to only those privileges minimally necessary to perform assigned duties.

Table 4-8

MCC Roles and Functions

Business users and application users (FinApp, HealthApp, and Corporate)
System administration
Computer operations
Application, system development, and maintenance
Network management
Change management
Security administration
Security audit

Table 4-8 shows the MCC roles and functions that shall not be carried out by the same employee.

- All restricted, confidential, and internal information as well as MCC resources must have system access controls to ensure that these resources are not improperly disclosed, modified, or deleted. Table 4-9 lists the authorization and access control requirements.

Table 4-9

Authorization and Access Control Requirement

Information Classification	Authorization and Access Control Requirement
Public	Access control for modification is required.
Internal	Authorization by business unit or function and access control are required.
Confidential	Authorization by business unit or function and detailed role-based access control are required.
Restricted	Authorization by business unit or function and detailed role-based access control are required.

Privacy

Privacy protection is one of the most significant business issues in today's information economy. Organizations lacking adequate privacy practices are facing challenges from both the legal and regulatory dimension of privacy and the ethical issues that are raised with the use of personal information. Privacy applies to the information handling practices of an organization including

- Information collected about a person (an employee or customer)
- The way information about a person is collected
- The way information about a person is used
- What information about a person is shared
- Implications of collecting and sharing information about a person
- The way a person can control the information collected about him or herself

All too often, the personally identifiable information (PII) is in the spotlight. This is because PII lets you identify and locate a person. If one can tie the identity and the location of a person with health, financial, and private communication information, this data becomes extremely sensitive and can run the risk of identity fraud. Examples of business activities that create privacy risks include human resource systems management, employee monitoring, e-mail, Internet-use, consumer transaction processes that collect personal data, direct marketing, data warehousing and data mining, and international data transfers.

Privacy is about trust. Organizations that fail to create a climate of trust for their consumers and/or employees will quickly compromise consumer and employee confidence. Many states and governments in the world are moving to enact some kind of privacy legislation. For instance, the European Union (EU) Data Protection Directive, which became effective on October 25, 1998, requires that transfers of personal data to non-EU countries should take place only to countries that provide an "adequate" level of privacy protection.

In the United States, the Federal Trade Commission (FTC) has made several declarations to Congress regarding consumer-oriented commercial Web sites. According to the May 2000 FTC report to Congress, consumer-oriented commercial Web sites that collect PII from or about consumers online are encouraged to comply with the four widely accepted fair information practices of notice, choice, access, and security. Table 4-10 provides a description of these four practices.

The Health Insurance Portability and Accountability Act (HIPAA) of 1996 also protects privacy. The HIPAA was enacted as part of a broad congressional attempt at incremental health care reform. All medical records and other individually identifiable health information held or disclosed by

Table 4-10

FTC Fair Information Practices in the Marketplace: A Report to Congress, May 2000

Category	FTC Fair Information Practices
(1) Notice	Web sites would be required to provide consumers clear and conspicuous notice of their information practices, including what information they collect, how they collect it (directly or through non-obvious means such as cookies), how they use it, how they provide choice, access, and security to consumers, whether they disclose the information collected to other entities, and whether other entities are collecting information through the site.
(2) Choice	Web sites would be required to offer consumers choices as to how their personal identifying information is used beyond the use for which the information was provided (for example, to consummate a transaction). Such choice would encompass both internal secondary uses (such as marketing back to consumers) and external secondary uses (such as disclosing data to other entities).
(3) Access	Web sites would be required to offer consumers reasonable access to the information a Web site has collected about them, including a reasonable opportunity to review information and to correct inaccuracies or delete information.
(4) Security	Web sites would be required to take reasonable steps to protect the security of the information they collect from consumers.

a covered entity in any form, whether communicated electronically, on paper or orally, is covered by the final regulation that was published in *Federal Register* on December 28, 2000. The final compliance date for large health care organizations is February 26, 2003. Table 4-11 lists the three purposes of HIPAA regulation.

Aforementioned privacy regulations affect companies like MCC significantly because MCC is a global company. The MCC privacy requirements are as follows:

- MCC must develop operational procedures within the organization to ensure that privacy issues are addressed on a daily basis.
- MCC must complete a tailored comprehensive privacy audit program in order to provide an opinion on the adequacy of its privacy compliance with regulations in the regions (North America and Europe) where MCC operates.

Table 4-11

Health Insurance Portability and Accountability Act of 1996 (HIPAA)

The HIPAA regulation has three major purposes:
(1) To protect and enhance the rights of consumers by providing them access to their health information and controlling the inappropriate use of that information.
(2) To improve the quality of health care in the U.S. by restoring trust in the health care system among consumers, health care professionals, and the multitude of organizations and individuals committed to the delivery of care.
(3) To improve the efficiency and effectiveness of health care delivery by creating a national framework for health privacy protection that builds on efforts by a state's health systems and individual organizations and individuals.

Source: The HIPAA DHHS Final Rule (**http://aspe.hhs.gov/admnsimp**)

- MCC health care-related business units must comply with the HIPAA legislation requirements.
- MCC must also comply with EU Data Protection Directive because significant portions of the operations take place in Europe.

Network Security Requirements

The MCC network infrastructure is the information superhighway of MCC. It includes all internal and external systems, where information is transferred between related and non-related MCC personnel and affiliates (business associates). In recent years, like many other corporations, MCC moved from central processing (mainframe) to distributed processing environments that provide users with Internet access and the ability to dial or VPN (Virtual Private Network) into the network when they are at home or on the road. Although these distributed systems have brought the ease of use and flexibility, they are also far more vulnerable to unauthorized penetration than legacy systems. The reasons are clear: the movement of data over an open system (the Internet), more points of access, decentralized controls, and the use of mixed network environments (such as, Novell, Windows NT, Unix and running SAP, Oracle, and PeopleSoft).

MCC should define the cost-effective protection of a network resource at a level that is appropriate to its value to MCC. This approach links network security to the value of the business processes the network supports. Network security must be commensurate with the exposure level and degree of risk associated with each application, database, or platform connected to the network. MCC network security requirements are as follows:

- MCC network security should provide centralized management controls over distributed systems (security administration performed from one network operations center for multiple data centers and company locations).
- MCC network entry points must provide a system banner to communicate that use of the system is restricted to authorized users only. In addition, the banner should list the actions that the company would take against unauthorized users. Considering past litigation cases where unauthorized users gained access to a company's computer resources, a computer crime cannot be proven unless there is evidence that the user knew that he or she was entering a restricted system. A system banner must be displayed to all users attempting to access MCC computer systems.
- All production network equipment including LAN servers, routers, and switches must be physically secured from unauthorized access by placing them in locked rooms or closets.
- All direct and dedicated network connections to parties outside MCC companies must be approved by the MCC information security function.
- All traffic from the Internet and Extranet partners to MCC networks must pass through a MCC firewall.

Firewalls

Internet and distributed computing have changed the way organizations do business and the way they approach network security. Corporate networks are no longer defined by physical boundaries, but instead by enterprise-wide security architectures. It is important to understand that firewalls are part of an overall security architecture that creates a perimeter defense designed to protect the information assets of the organization. A firewall is a dedicated device (hardware and software) that restricts access between two or more networks.

- MCC must control access between internal networks and external networks via perimeter firewalls. Access must also be controlled between publicly accessible servers and servers not directly accessible from the Internet via a demilitarized zone (DMZ) firewall. A DMZ is an untrusted network segment connected to usually two other networks through separate firewalls.
- MCC must control access between internal networks of differing security and access requirements (for example, accounting or payroll servers versus engineering development servers).
- Strict controls must put in place for access through the modem pools and private dial networks.
- Access to and from third-party managed networks must be controlled via the firewalls.
- Internal network addresses must be hidden from external networks.
- Firewall documentation must be in place and, as a minimum detail, the firewall policy and the rational for the inclusion of each individual rule should also be in place. Documentation should also justify the exclusion of specific rules, where the absence impacts the security of the firewall and the corporate network.
- Strong password controls must be utilized on the firewalls and all network devices (routers and switches). The firewalls and all network devices must provide adequate identification and authentication controls. Strong authentication must be utilized for remote administration of the firewalls.
- The configuration of firewalls and routers must promote security for the internal network that is in line with MCC's security policy. For instance, access control lists must be developed that specifically restrict access of incoming traffic that has an internal IP address. Source routing must be disabled in the routers and the firewall product to prevent IP address "spoofing." Sensitive services (FTP, TELNET, TFTP, RLOGIN, and so on) must be filtered on inbound traffic by the firewall and routers via the port number. All redundant and unnecessary processes must be removed from the firewall. For instance, all compilers must be removed from the firewall host.
- The firewall product selected must support *stateful inspection* rather than simple packet filtering solutions.

Remote Access

More and more companies are trying to leverage the Internet and the widely available dial-up Internet access of national service providers to provide mobile users with a way of accessing corporate network resources. Remote access via any mechanism through dial-up, frame relay, ISDN, cable modems, or Digital Subscriber Lines (DSLs) can potentially expose a corporation's internal network to the same threats as those posed by a public network. Therefore, sufficient controls must be in place to mitigate the risks.

The following requirements must be met in order for remote access to be an effective tool for users:

- For remote access to MCC resources from the Internet, data confidentiality and integrity must be maintained on the public network at all times.
- Both endpoints must determine the identity of the other endpoint by some strong means of authentication. Remote users who remotely access systems that contain information that is classified as confidential and restricted must use two-factor authentication.
- The use of remote control software (such as, pcAnywhere) with personal communications equipment attached directly to the personal computers must be strictly controlled.
- All the remote access traffic must go through a centralized control point (centralized modem pools and firewalls) to facilitate centralized security administration and logging.
- The remote access session must automatically terminate once the connection is broken or require re-authentication. The session must automatically terminate after 10 minutes of inactivity.
- The remote access session must be terminated after three invalid connection access attempts and must remain disabled until a security administrator resets it.

Security Monitoring and Auditing

Security monitoring is crucial to maintaining a secure computing environment. Activities related to the use of corporate systems should be monitored to ensure that company information on these systems is not disclosed to unauthorized individuals and that the integrity, confidentiality, and availability of data is maintained. Monitoring processes include the day-to-day or operational procedures that organizations employ to monitor security. These monitoring activities may include network and host-based intrusion systems, event-logging tools, log review procedures, security event reviews, periodic and real-time activity assessments, compliance assessments, and penetration testing.

All too often, system users and operators discover new ways to intentionally or unintentionally bypass security controls. The security audit logs support individual accountability by recording user actions. Without adequate audit mechanisms, users cannot be held accountable for their activity and security violations may go undetected.

Manually reviewing security features and interpreting audit logs can be a time-consuming task. Monitoring should be done via automated tools. In the MCC network environment, devices produce a range of events such as firewall logs, Intrusion Detection System (IDS) events, system vulnerabilities, and user audit and accounting trails on disparate systems. This makes it very difficult to differentiate between an anomalous event and a serious, coordinated attack.

The following are MCC monitoring requirements:

- A central monitoring solution that consolidates all security events into a single managed console is required. From this managed console, security events from the various data sources can be reviewed for detail, used to trigger external events based upon their analysis, and generate reports revealing an enterprise security profile and status.
- All MCC application, platform, database, and network systems or other systems that interface with these systems must provide logging capabilities. The type of information that must be logged includes
  - All changes to system security parameters, security profiles, and security account passwords
  - All changes performed by privileged accounts (system administrators)
  - All changes performed to security parameters by privileged processes, transactions, or programs
  - All attempts to modify and delete audit logs
  - All changes made to restricted and confidential production data and software
  - All security violations (logon attempts or password guessing activities)

  - The user ID of the person who conducted the activity, the date and time of the incident, the name of the resource affected, the action performed, and the location of the device (IP address or terminal ID) are also required at the minimum.

- All logs must be protected against unauthorized modification or deletion. All logs must be protected from unauthorized read access.
- All remote access (dial-up and Internet-based) to MCC resources must be logged including connections, disconnections, and violations.
- All logs must be maintained for a minimum of six months or in compliance with regulatory requirements.
- All security logs of critical data (restricted and confidential data) must be reviewed daily or weekly. All other logs must be reviewed at least every 60 days.
- Both network and host-based real-time intrusion detection systems (IDS) on critical application, platform, database, or network entry points must be used to detect attacks or system intrusions.
- A Computer Incident Response Team (CIRT) should be created consisting of system engineers, security, operations, and IT personnel. This team should develop a course of action in the event of an emergency situation (for example, disconnecting a virus-infected machine from the network), and should have the authority to carry out these actions immediately. The names and contact information (cell phones or beepers) of every team member should be distributed to all MCC employees.

Platform Security Requirements

Information resource protection is critical to effective business risk management. All hardware and software platforms are MCC corporate information resources that require protection based on their value to the organization and the potential impact of their loss. All data stored, processed on, or transmitted by an operating system platform should be fully protected from unauthorized disclosure, modification, and destruction. Access controls appropriate for protecting the nature of the data stored on platforms must be implemented. MCC operating system platforms are listed in Table 4-12.

Table 4-12

MCC Operating System Platforms

Category	Platform
Desktops and Laptops	Windows NT Workstation Migrating to Windows 2000
File and Print Services	Novell
Application Servers	Sun Solaris IBM-AIX Windows NT Server

The MCC requirements are as follows:

- MCC platform security must be commensurate with the exposure level of the most sensitive and valuable application running on the platform.
- The appropriate systems and information security management must approve all changes to security settings of MCC platforms.
- Only necessary services for system operations must run on a platform.
- Platforms must implement standard naming conventions that clearly distinguish between production and non-production resources.
- When a user gains authorized access to a system, the system should have the capability to display a banner containing the date and time of the user's last successful logon and the number of last unsuccessful logon attempts that have occurred recently. Users must be trained to observe this banner and report any anomalies to the security group.
- All MCC restricted and confidential data must be kept encrypted on user workstations and laptops.

Electronic Mail

In today's Internet world, electronic mail (e-mail) has become a critical and indispensable business tool for both external and internal communication. The scale of possible risk and damage is exponentially greater when dealing with a communications medium that is digital, globally internetworked, massive, and unregulated. Risks associated with e-mail use include

- Possible disclosure of trade secrets and other internal information
- Disclosure of confidential customer information
- Lawsuits revolving around sexual harassment or discrimination
- Liability for copyright infringement
- Misrepresentation of the company's position
- Loss of reputation through unauthorized comments
- Exposure of computer networks to infection by viruses and worms

MCC e-mail is the main form of communication inside and outside the corporation. E-mail is used to send documents, presentations, spreadsheets, and Web links to an individual or a list of recipients. MCC provides access to e-mail resources for authorized users and uses only. MCC has the following security requirements for e-mail communications. These requirements are listed in Table 4-13.

- E-mail message content confidentiality and integrity must be maintained on the internal and external network at all times. Information classified as restricted, confidential, and internal must be encrypted.

Table 4-13

E-mail Security Requirements

	E-Mail Security Requirements			
Security service	**Public**	**Internal**	**Confidential**	**Restricted**
Confidentiality	None	Required	Required	Required
Integrity	Required	Required	Required	Required
Availability	Availability of MCC e-mail services is crucial for the day-to-day operations. High-availability solutions must be applied to the MCC e-mail architecture (e-mail servers, storage space).			
Non-repudiation	Required	Required	Required	Required
Monitoring	Required	Required	Required	Required
Virus scanning	Required	Required	Required	Required

- Non-repudiation of origin, non-repudiation of submission, and non-repudiation of delivery must be provided as functionality in the MCC e-mail architecture. In other words, an individual shall not be able to deny receipt, submission, or delivery of a message.
- The availability of MCC e-mail services is crucial for the day-to-day operations. High-availability solutions must be applied to the MCC e-mail architecture (e-mail servers and storage space).
- E-mail monitoring for inappropriate content and virus scanning must be performed. For instance, e-mail resources must not be used for creating and transmitting insulting, offensive, and sexually explicit messages.

Analysis of Case Study #1—Corporate

Table 4-14 lists the MCC application-specific baseline requirements for the Corporate case study.

Analysis of Case Study #2—FinApp

Table 4-15 shows the MCC application-specific baseline requirements for the FinApp case study.

Analysis of Case Study #3—HealthApp

Table 4-16 lists the application-specific baseline requirements for the HealthApp case study.

Table 4-14 MCC Application-Specific Baseline Requirements—Corporate Case Study

	MCC Information Classification			
Security Service	**Public**	**Internal**	**Confidential**	**Restricted**
Confidentiality	None	Encryption required over public communications medium (Internet, ISP-based connections, dial-up).	Encryption required over all communications channels. Confidential data must be kept encrypted on user laptops and workstations.	Encryption required over all communications channels. Confidential data must be kept encrypted on user laptops and workstations. Such information is to be disclosed only to named individuals on a need-to-know basis.
Integrity	Business unit managed change control is required.	Business unit managed change control is required. Minimal document change history must be maintained.	Business unit managed change control is required. System-level file change history must be maintained.	Business unit managed change control is required. Field-level change history must be maintained. Rollback functionality is required.
Availability	Virus scanning is required.	Virus scanning and regular backups are required.	Virus scanning, regular backups, and redundant and high-availability solutions are required.	Virus scanning and redundant and high-availability solutions are required. Strong system configuration, change control, and regular backup/restore processes are required.
Identification and authentication	None	Basic authentication with encryption.	Strong authentication (encrypted username and password, token, and certificate)	Strong authentication (encrypted username and password, token, and certificate)
Authorization and access control	Access control for modification is required.	Authorization by business unit or function and access control is required.	Authorization by business unit or function and detailed role-based access control is required.	Authorization by business unit or function and detailed role-based access control is required.
Non-repudiation	Change control is required.	Minimal docoument change history must be maintained.	Strict change controls are required. System-level file change history must be maintained. Digital signatures are required.	Strict change controls are required. Field-level file change history must be maintained. Digital signatures for creator and the checker are required.
Auditing and monitoring	System-level for events and alarms	System-level for user-access, failed login attempts, alarms	System-level for user-access, file changes, failed login attempts, alarms	All events and alarms
Compliance with regulations	Compliance with the European Union Data Protection Directive is required.			

Table 4-15 MCC Application-Specific Baseline Requirements—FinApp Case Study

Security Service	MCC Information Classification: Public	Internal	Confidential	Restricted
Confidentiality	None	Encryption required over public communications medium (Internet, ISP-based connections, dial-up).	Encryption required over all communications channels. Confidential data must be kept encrypted on user laptops and workstations.	Encryption required over all communication channels. Confidential data must be kept encrypted on user laptops and workstations. Such information is to be disclosed only to named individuals on a need-to-know basis.
Integrity	Business unit managed change control is required.	Business unit managed change control is required. Minimal document change history must be maintained.	Business unit managed change control is required. System-level file change history must be maintained.	Business unit managed change control is required. Field-level change history must be maintained. Rollback functionality is required.
Availability	Virus scanning is required.	Virus scanning and regular backups are required.	Virus scanning, regular backups, redundant and high-availability solutions are required.	Virus scanning, redundant and high-availability solutions are required. Strong system configuration, change control, and regular backup/restore processes are required.
Identification and authentication	None	Basic authentication with encryption.	Strong authentication (encrypted username and password, token, and certificate)	Strong authentication (encrypted username and password, token, certificate)
Authorization and access control	Access control for modification is required.	Authorization by business unit or function and access control is required.	Authorization by business unit or function and detailed role-based access control is required.	Authorization by business unit or function and detailed role-based access control are required.
Non-repudiation	Change control is required.	Strict change controls are required. System-level file change history must be maintained. Digital signatures are required.	Strict change controls are required. System-level file change history must be maintained. Digital signatures are required.	Strict change controls are required. Field-level file change history must be maintained. Digital signatures for the creator and the checker are required.
Auditing and monitoring	System-level for events and alarms	System-level for user-access, failed login attempts, alarms	System-level for user-access, file changes, failed login attempts, alarms	All events and alarms
Compliance with regulations	Compliance with the European Union Data Protection Directive is required. Compliance with the Health Insurance Portability and Accountability Act of 1996 (HIPAA) is required.			

Table 4-16 MCC Application-Specific Baseline Requirements—HealthApp Case Study

	MCC Information Classification			
Security Service	**Public**	**Internal**	**Confidential**	**Restricted**
Confidentiality	None	Encryption is required over public communications medium (Internet, ISP-based connections, dial-up).	Encryption is required over all communications channels. Confidential data must be kept encrypted on user laptops and workstations.	Encryption is required over all communications channels. Confidential data must be kept encrypted on user laptops and workstations. Such information is to be disclosed only to named individuals on a need-to-know basis.
Integrity	Business unit managed change control is required.	Business unit managed change control is required. Minimal document change history must be maintained.	Business unit managed change control is required. System-level file change history must be maintained.	Business unit managed change control is required. Field-level change history must be maintained. Rollback fnctionality is required.
Availability	Virus scanning is required.	Virus scanning and regular backups are required.	Virus scanning, regular backups, and redundant and high-availability solutions are required.	Virus scanning and redundant and high-availability solutions are required. Strong system configuration, change control, and regular backup/restore processes are required.
Identification and authentication	None	Basic authentication with encryption	Strong authentication (encrypted username and password, token, and certificate)	Strong authentication (encrypted username and password, token, certificate)
Authorization and access control	Access control for modification is required.	Authorization by business unit or function and access control is required.	Authorization by business unit or function and detailed role-based access control is required.	Authorization by business unit or function and detailed role-based access control are required.
Non-repudiation	Change control is required.	Minimal document change history must be maintained.	Strict change controls are required. System-level file change history must be maintained. Digital signatures are required.	Strict change controls are required. Field-level file change history must be maintained. Digital signatures for creator and the checker are required.
Auditing and monitoring	System-level for events and alarms	System-level for user-access, failed login attempts, alarms	System-level for user-access, file changes, failed login attempts, alarms	All events and alarms
Compliance with regulations	Compliance with the European Union Data Protection Directive is required.			

References

The Computer Security Institute (CSI): **http://www.gocsi.com/homepage.shtml**

U.S. Department of Justice: **http://www.usdoj.gov/criminal/cybercrime/rolex.htm**

1998-02-17 Lloyd, Timothy Indictment-News Release **http://www.usdoj.gov/criminal/cybercrime/lloydpr.htm**

2000-05-09 Lloyd, Timothy Allen —Guilty Verdict — News Release

http://www.usdoj.gov/criminal/cybercrime/

Privacy Online: Fair Information Practices in the Electronic Marketplace. A Report to Congress. Federal Trade Commission. May 2000.

http://aspe.hhs.gov/admnsimp/

Secrets and Lies, Bruce Schneier

CHAPTER 5

Security Infrastructure Design Principles

Designing security is almost always a mixture of art and science as well as process. Not only must you completely understand the value of the assets that you are designing security to protect, but you must also anticipate mal-intent in the many forms it may take.

The art of security requires an intuitive mind and many years of experience in dealing with hackers to the point where you may anticipate many, yet not all, of their potential exploits. The science component of the design equation is much more tangible than this. To protect your corporation, arm yourself with knowledge. After you fully understand the corporate assets you need to protect and how they operate, your first duty as security architect is to consistently practice an examination of the industry. Staying abreast of current events, such as maintaining a cursory knowledge (at least) of the latest hacker tools and attack techniques, will be a key component in your ongoing struggle to remain ahead, or at least spot the wave as it crests.

Your second duty, as security architect, is to design and build a security infrastructure that most adequately suits your business practices at present, yet one that provides scalability and support in the coming years. The idea here is to first become aware of present-day threats and comprehend their direction prior to designing and integrating your security infrastructure. How you implement security technologies within your infrastructure represents the process sub-component. Process is the way in which you deploy your chosen security strategies (such as a tactical strategy) to protect your corporate assets. Process typically includes not only physical and logical device placement, but also the manner in which these devices are monitored and kept in operation.

This chapter explores the many components of security infrastructure design and incorporates industry-best practices to guide their deployment. In this chapter, the components of a security infrastructure such as authentication, authorization, accounting, physical and logical access controls, and the governing corporate security policies and procedures will be discussed and their correlation to one another illustrated.

Component or Infrastructure . . . ?

Before we dive into design principles, we must first understand some basic definitions and components of our security design. What is a security infrastructure? The response to that question may be many different things to many people, but let's try to boil its meaning down into one comprehensive thought. A security infrastructure should provide a synergistic use of the many components of its architecture, organized in such a manner as to improve the overall security posture beyond any single component. Using this definition, we can infer many things about the design and nature of a security infrastructure.

Employing a firewall, however excellent your security policy may be, does not constitute a security infrastructure if it does not work in conjunction with other components of your architecture. Because this firewall, for example, doesn't interact with other aspects of your security infrastructure, it is a security component and not part of the security infrastructure. The concept being alluded to is the synergy component of the previous definition. If we were to send alerts from this firewall to the corporate event management station (the accounting component, as referenced earlier) where events could be processed into alerts used to notify Network Operations Center (NOC) staff, then we are beginning to build an infrastructure. By itself, the firewall may do a wonderful job screening out most intruder traffic and collecting log entries, but with no one to notify, its value is not fully realized. Add to this firewall a cohesive mix of Intrusion Detection (ID), strong authentication, and encrypted tunneling (virtual private network [VPN]) components, and we are on our way to designing a basic security infrastructure.

Infrastructure Components

The major components of a security infrastructure can be defined as belonging to one of four categories. These categories are

- Network
- Platform
- Physical
- Process

The network category encompasses firewalls, routers and switches, remote access devices (such as VPNs and dial-up modem banks), and network-based ID systems that add some security features to the overall design. These components are used to monitor, filter, and/or restrict traffic as seen either by their network interfaces or as defined logic in software. The intent of these security components is the monitoring and/or protection of the data traversing the network, or the protection of data traversing or utilizing the application.

The platform category encompasses the server and client-side software (such as underlying operating system and security applications' controls). Devices that perform some electronic operation such as Smart cards and readers, hardware token-producing cards, and hardware-based encryption devices fit into this platform category. Application-level access controls, such as soft token-producing programs, digital certificates, host-based ID programs, virus scanning and eradication, and event collection agents and analysis software programs—to name a few—are also components of the platform category. The purpose of these application-level access controls is to provide functions like authentication, authorization, host-based intrusion detection and analysis, virus detection and eradication, and event accounting and analysis. These security functions are used to protect the application that resides within these major infrastructure boundaries.

The physical components of a security infrastructure include standard door keys and locks, key cards, identification badges, security cameras, motion sensors, audible and visual alarms, cages, fences, signage, security guards, and system or device labels. Biometric components fit into this category as well and include hand geometry readers, facial geometry cameras, and retinal-scan cameras. The typical intent of these biometric components is to identify and authenticate users via the nature and purpose of their hardware design. Network cabling and backup power devices such as UPS systems and diesel generators fit into this category as well. The primary goal of a physical security component is to keep unauthorized persons out and to keep infrastructure components supplied with power and network connectivity.

Another goal of physical security is to provide the least amount of information to untrusted parties as is feasible for the operation of your business. This secondary goal is typically not adhered to and encompasses building signage ("Welcome to our Data Center") as well as labels on important physical keys, servers, or systems (such as "Key to Safe" or "PKI Root CA").

The final category includes the process component of security design. This category includes corporate security policy and procedural documentation that governs the creation, use, storage, and disposal of corporate data, as well as the systems and networks on which that data resides. The purpose of a corporate security policy is to define the scope of protection for corporate assets and suggest or require a specific protection mechanism for those assets. Corporate security procedures, a component of the corporate security policies document, are utilized to guide employee actions in particular circumstances. Social engineering attacks, for example, are most often defeated by the instantiation of executed security policies and procedures.

Corporate security policies and procedures are the building blocks of your security infrastructure. With a comprehensive security policy and procedural document in hand, the security architect can understand which assets the corporation wants to protect and how stringently those assets should be protected.

Although the defined security policy document will provide data, system, and network protection strategies, it will not typically define the tactician details necessary for vendor selection, design, or implementation. The successful implementation of these components requires a thorough understanding of the goals of your security infrastructure. Without the proper understanding of your security infrastructure goals, crucial assets inevitably may be inappropriately protected or entirely overlooked.

Goals of a Security Infrastructure

The primary goal of a security infrastructure design is the protection of corporate assets. The way we protect these assets is by the proper deployment of security components into an organized and cohesive security infrastructure. Assets may include hardware, software, network components, and intellectual property. The controls applied in the protection of these assets should be in line with your corporate security goals as well as your corporate security policy documentation. Though only the protection of data is mentioned, it is implied that in protecting the data and ensuring its availability, the underlying systems and networks are also protected.

Depending upon your chosen data classification scheme, each of the following data protection goals should be appropriately represented and weighted accordingly:

- Data confidentiality
- Data integrity
- Data availability

When designing a security infrastructure, target your applications for the best results. Your applications are the closest things to your data as they process, exchange, and store your data. By deciding that your design goals will address data confidentiality, data integrity, and data availability, you will discover that you are securing not only your applications, but your enterprise as well. This concept is illustrated in Figure 5-1.

The premise behind data confidentiality is the prevention of the unauthorized viewing of one's data that is not intended for public (or anonymous) consumption. Data confidentiality, in this case, applies to any one

Figure 5-1

The bulls-eye of security design: target your application with your security policy

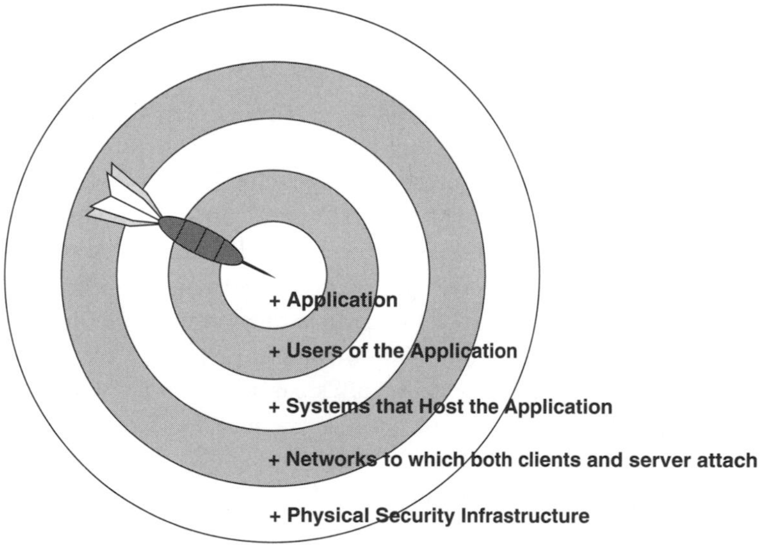

of the defined Internal, Confidential, or Restricted data classification labels used in this book. The protection of data confidentiality is provided for by secure data storage and transmittals. The typical techniques employed to satisfy data confidentiality requirements include encryption during the transmittal of data or safe online (authenticated access) or offline storage (locked safe or cage).

Data integrity must also be observed in the protection of corporate assets. Data integrity is concerned with the protection of any unauthorized alteration or destruction of data. The primary focus of this goal, then, is the accuracy and legitimacy of the data. Integrity is typically satisfied by programs that are capable of producing a checksum of the original data set that can be compared with its copies to determine authenticity.

A common solution for providing data integrity involves the use of common encryption strategies (such as Internet protocol security [IPSEC]) that use such a checksum strategy to ensure that the data sent equals the data that was received. In protecting data from corruption or destruction, the solution can be as simple as the use of anti-virus programs or as complicated as the deployment of critical path storage solutions, clustered highly available firewalls, and company-wide acceptance of change management practices.

Storage and change management procedures, defined in the corporate security policy, should also be put in place to protect both the data backup routines as well as provide for a thorough pre-cursor review of any suggested changes made to systems and networks or governing procedures that are followed by staff members. To prevent unauthorized usage or destruction, authentication and authorization controls are best suited to the task.

Lastly, data availability is also of great concern. Your goals for data availability will vary with the importance of the data made available. Although you may determine that some systems require Highly Available (HA) operations (99.999 percent uptime), some lesser systems and applications may require much less. Protection provided to HA systems, typically but not always, involves the use of redundant systems. Redundant power, data access and storage, network, and application server processes are common, not to mention expensive.

Redundancy does not satisfy all data availability concerns, however. Recent exploits of popular e-business Web sites have demonstrated the impact that Denial of Service (DoS) and Distributed Denial of Service (DDoS) programs can have on corporate revenues. According to the Computer Security Institute (CSI) and the Federal Bureau of Investigations's (FBI) "2000 Computer Crime and Security Survey," it is estimated that

$8,247,500 was lost in the U.S. alone during the 2000 calendar year due to DoS/DDoS exploits. Although a handful of vendors claim to have solutions for offering varying degrees of protection against this form of risk to data availability, this will more than likely remain a game of catch-up as vendors scramble to write detection and prevention routines intelligent enough to identify and stop the latest batch of Dos/DDoS attacks.

Design Guidelines

The first and arguably most important design guideline to follow is to ensure that your corporate security policies and procedures are in line with your present business objectives. If they are not, then steps should be taken to implement the necessary changes to these policies and procedures prior to designing and building a security infrastructure. Without the full acceptance and support of such corporate guidelines from executive management, your security design cannot fully reach its potential and in fact may fail due to the lack of both written guidelines and managerial support.

Following the appropriate reformation of your corporate security policies with business objectives, the next step is the development of a Computer Incident Response Team (CIRT). These team members are basically the worker bees behind the corporate security policies and procedures. It is the responsibility of these team members to carry out the necessary actions or precautions in the event of a security alert. In order for team members to be well-versed in event handling (such as a security breach or disaster recovery), they should train as realistically as possible. In many cases, this equates to unsolicited test scenarios where the actions of CIRT members can be measured as to their response, efficiency, completeness, and eradication of a given security event. The goal of such test scenarios is always the improvement of the communication and procedural steps followed by CIRT members, and not retribution.

When policies and procedures are in line with present business practices, and after CIRT members have been defined, it is time to design the infrastructure security services that will directly support the stated guidelines and requirements. These services include

- Authentication
- Authorization
- Accounting

- Physical access controls
- Logical access controls

The design, deployment, and operation of these services in your enterprise should follow a specific methodology. This methodology should be used to guide every aspect of security introduction and augmentation within your organization. This lifecycle of security design, deployment, and its operation is illustrated in Figure 5-2 as well as previously in Chapter 4.

The steps defined in this methodology include Assessment, Design, Deployment, and Management. During the Assessment phase of this lifecycle, existing business and security requirements are analyzed to determine if the most practical and effective security solution is either presently available or must be designed and built. Next in the lifecycle is the Design phase. Here a security solution is designed that directly addresses the Assessment findings uncovered in the previous phase. Once the design has been drafted, it is time to build the solution. The Deployment phase includes the building and installation of the security solution. Lastly, the installed solution must be validated and managed to ensure that the solution you have built functions properly and addresses the security concerns uncovered in the assessment phase. This is the very purpose of the Manage phase. Including this concept of a security lifecycle within your design methodology will improve every aspect of your security solution.

Figure 5-2
Security lifecycle

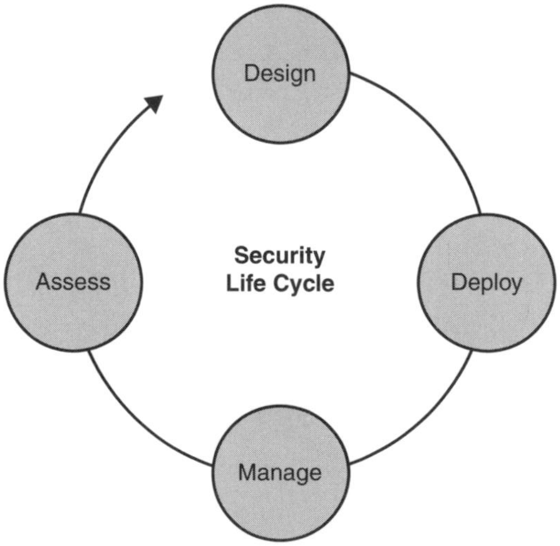

Authentication

Authentication will service users of Internet resources, Extranet resources, and Intranet resources, so be sure to delineate between these as they are likely to require different levels of security pertinent to their inherent risks. Intranet users may enjoy automated authentication based upon their domain logon ID, while Internet and Extranet users, for example, may be required to logon using an assigned hard or soft token and a PIN.

The popular methods for authenticating users include static usernames (UID) and passwords, two-factor (strong) authentication, One Time Password (OTP) authentication, and Single Sign-On (SSO) authentication. In all likelihood, you will deploy a combination of at least two of these methods in your corporation. The reason being that you will have different classifications of data requiring differing levels of protection. Choosing the most appropriate authentication method for a given data classification set will represent the most important decision you make here.

The most common form of authentication is the static UID/password combination. Because static passwords don't change very often, if at all, the protection these afford the data set is minimal. Static UID/password combinations can be successfully subjected to many forms of attack including replay attacks and brute force attacks. In a replay attack, the UID/password combination is captured from a previous authentication session and replayed to the authentication server to gain access by impersonating the stolen UID/password. Brute force attackers, on the other hand, typically know only the UID (or use a default system account) and attempt to logon by trying numerous password combinations with the known UID to gain access. Both forms of attack are in widespread use and can severely diminish the integrity of static methods. For this reason, only data classified as either Public or Internal (as identified in this book) should rely upon static methods for authentication.

Higher classifications of data may require more stringent solutions, such as the use of strong authentication methods and OTPs. Strong authentication, otherwise known as two-factor authentication, requires you as the user to possess two disparate components: something you know and something you have. The something you know is typically an assigned PIN or PASSPHRASE, while the something you have is most commonly a token-producing card, a software program, or a Smart card. Token cards or programs utilize an algorithm to produce, typically, a six-digit number.

The resultant PASSCODE then becomes the combination of this six-digit number suffixed by the users assigned PIN. Smart cards, however, typically contain a piece of information within identifying its rightful owner. This piece of data is most often either a digital ID or a private key.

Although this form of authentication is superior to the static method, the OTP component is not necessarily a feature of this solution. The nature of the OTP component is that, once used, a password is no longer valid. Most token-producing cards and token software programs utilize this OTP feature to further improve upon their authentication integrity.

Because OTP is not a default feature of some authentication solutions, it is recommended that this be made a requirement when searching for a vendor. The combined strength of both strong authentication and OTP is then obviously far superior to static UID/password combinations in that it is impervious to replay attacks and is virtually unaffected by brute force attacks. Many devices such as Smart cards and two-way pagers will self-destruct after a number of invalid access attempts. For this reason, even if many of these portable devices are lost or stolen, their susceptibility to attack is muted.

To improve upon your use of static authentication methods, institute a password-aging procedure where user passwords must be changed after a certain interval of days (typically on a monthly basis). You can also enforce password strength by dictating password strength requirements in your security policy documentation as well as by requiring a predetermined level of password strength on authentication servers (most operating systems will support this natively).

Another aspect to be concerned with when designing your authentication scheme is the choice of distributed or centralized authentication. Distributed authentication is represented by the most commonly prevalent scenario in the industry, which is when users have a separate UID and password for each system they access, sometimes even for each application they access on a given system.

The inverse to this solution is Single Sign-On (SSO). SSO empowers users to utilize a single account and password combination to access many of the resources available to them within the corporation, yet typically not all of them. The security benefits of SSO become apparent in their use. Users of SSO solutions are far less likely to store UID/password combinations on their file systems or on sticky notes stuck to their monitors. Ease of administration is also a relieved burden such that administrators now have far fewer accounts to track and passwords to reset when forgotten by their owners.

SSO, however, is not without a few headaches of its own. Introducing an SSO solution into your environment and getting it to operate effectively in heterogeneous environments may simply present new struggles for administrators. These new struggles may include any number of compatibility issues, issues with either its deployment or functional operation, as well as administrative learning curves that will become evident in the management of such a solution. As with most things, if the appropriate talent and resources can be applied to introduce a SSO solution, it can be made to successfully address most corporate-wide authentication requirements. The fruits of this technology, however, will not come without both a price and an adequate measure of diligence.

Authorization

Authorization is the act of permitting or denying prescribed privileges based upon one's identity or group involvement. Authorization should be handled from the application outwards. By focusing first on the control of authorization at the application level, you will find that you are inadvertently securing the lower protocol levels. Application security, after all, is what we are all striving for. Strive to understand your applications and how they communicate with clients, databases, and other server processes.

Applications will typically use a static set of ports and protocols to communicate with other entities. Often times, ranges of ports are used to handle the sending and receipt of communications. Determine what these ports are and the protocols used. With this information, you will understand which forms of application sessions are in use (such as TCP sessions) or whether your application communicates through bursting its session-less data (such as UDP or HTTP). Understanding how and what your applications communicate will help you design authorization controls that are effective and appropriate.

Once you feel that you have a good understanding of how your applications function, next determine who should have access to which data and at which times of the day. You will also need to determine who should be granted physical access to application servers, their databases, or the network segment they reside on. Having access to any one of these could allow an intruder to circumvent your authorization controls. By limiting application access to specified groups during specific times of the day, you reduce the attacker's window of opportunity.

Groups should be utilized to segregate users into separate bins based upon their assigned resource privileges. By grouping users by resource, you can apply authorization controls at the application level to control group member activities by their assigned group tag. Such strategies are commonly referred to as Role Based Access Controls (RBAC).

Although RBAC controls are well suited to service large data sources classified as either Public or Internal with large populations of users, more stringent controls are needed to protect data labeled as either Confidential or Restricted (as referenced in this book). User Based Access Controls (UBAC) are based upon individual authorization privileges rather than by the assignment of roles. UBAC requires that each individual be authenticated and authorized individually. UBAC controls, by nature, provide more granularity of control because they apply directly to an individual or single entity rather than a group of individuals or entities.

An example of both RBAC and UBAC control schemes is best exemplified by a typical user account such as jdoe. User jdoe authenticates and is granted authorization privileges based upon his/her group affiliation. Because jdoe belongs to the sales group, he/she has access to sales files located on the sales department file server (RBAC control). Because user jdoe also belongs to the sales task force, he/she also is granted access, on an individual basis, to the directory on the file server that contains task force-developed proposals and other materials that were developed solely for specific task force members (UBAC control). By implementing the appropriate mixture of RBAC and UBAC, you'll be able to apply individual and group-level access control granularity where it best suits the data being protected by these controls.

Accounting

Accounting refers to the logging and monitoring of actions, events, and subsequent alerts that result from a satisfied condition. Most operating systems can be configured to produce accounting logs used to alert administrators of various system-generated events. The most prevalent operating system log utilities are Syslog (used on UNIX-based systems) and NT Event Log (used on Microsoft NT-based systems). The satisfied condition may simply be a UNIX Syslog or Microsoft NT Event Log setting of WARNING that produces WARNING-level messages (or of a higher significance) in its log file. However, the condition may be as complex as correlating and collaborating several non-contiguous events from different agent sources across the corporation such that the resultant alert means something of importance. Regardless of complexity, accounting results can (and should) provide us with the following:

- Operating system usage details
- Application usage details
- Internet, Extranet, or Intranet network activity
- Data for forensic analysis
- Data for trending analysis
- Data for report generation

Each of these results is valuable to a corporation for many reasons. In addition to providing performance forecasts and trending analysis, events can be used to ascertain one's security profile and to identify existent or potential threats. Operating system events can be used to notify security staff members of failed logon attempts, attempts to gain root or administrator access, and whether file systems have been mounted for export to name a few.

The timeliness of events is just as important as the scope that the events cover. What value is there in monitoring security events from your operating system, key applications, and the traffic on the segment when an administrator only manually reviews these event logs once per week? Chances are that by the time your administrator gets around to reviewing these event logs, he or she will be looking at a piece of history. Both the hacker, and any traces of their exploits, may be long gone, possibly except for a Trojan or two they left behind to siphon critical data out at will.

In this Internet age of point and click, everything happens quickly. Even novice hackers are well prepared to target your corporate assets with potentially dozens of hacker tools. By reaping the benefits of expert hackers, these novices (or script kiddies) with their tailored hacker tool sets can wreak havoc like the best of them.

To combat your opposition, you'll need to arm yourself with not only solid access and authentication controls, but also real-time event management and Intrusion Detection (ID) solutions. ID solutions will be discussed as part of the accounting solution here because its nature is that of event detection, analysis, and sometimes prevention—very similar to the purpose of event management. Event management has been historically discussed as a statistic-gathering tool. The intention here is to discuss the benefits of event management as a real-time security alert mechanism.

With that said, let's first discuss ID solutions. Two forms of ID exist: host-based and network-based. The job of host-based ID solutions is to monitor actions taken on the resident host system, such as failed logon attempts, attempts to access files for which no such privilege exists, attempts to export additional file systems, and the starting and stopping of application processes to name a few. Although host-based ID solutions do a good job of tracking possible attacks on systems, they will not alert you to network-based attacks.

Network-based ID systems fulfill their security role by monitoring traffic on the segment to which they are attached. With their built-in attack signature recognition, these devices are able to identify, log, and even thwart many forms of network-based attacks. The capability to thwart an attack that is underway is a key feature of a network-based ID system and can only be accomplished by a real-time inspection and analysis of network-based data. Particular thresholds or conditions, for example, can be configured to instruct the ID system to either intercept or drop undesired packet traffic, reset the communication stream (if the offending traffic is TCP-based), and even rewrite the access control policy on access routers and firewalls to prevent further attacks.

Because many times attackers will first probe the network to discover attached devices and then follow up with a port scan aimed at these discovered devices, it is a good idea to employ network-based ID solutions as well as the host-based models. Very little overlap takes place between these two forms of defense, and hence they should be considered complementary to one another rather than mutually exclusive. For additional coverage, apply host-based ID solutions to your key servers and apply network-based ID solutions to their attached segments.

A popular mechanism for monitoring multiple switched segments via a network-based ID is a Shomiti tap. A Shomiti tap is simply an Ethernet wiring scheme (a specifically designed cable) that enables the tapped device to extract all of the traffic traversing the switch, not just the port traffic and switch-wide broadcasts.

We need to be familiar with two forms of network traffic to understand this concept. Broadcast traffic is analogous to several people talking loudly in a crowded room. Although possibly no one is speaking to you directly, you still hear them and their conversations distract you and possibly prevent you from holding your own conversation. Unicast traffic, on the other hand, is analogous to your one-on-one conversation with another individual. The purpose of a switch is to reduce the amount of device-wide traffic seen on each port. The way it accomplishes this is by sending only broadcast traffic between ports (device-wide), but it restricts unicast traffic to only the sender and recipient of a particular communication. A Shomiti tap enables your network-based ID system to retrieve both of these forms of communications (broadcast as well as unicast), in essence circumventing switching restrictions on this tapped port.

An alternative would be to simply enable port mirroring on a particular port of the switch and plug your network ID into this designated port. This alternative, however, is slightly more intrusive than the Shomiti solution.

A security event management solution should be instituted as part of your security infrastructure to garnish further details as to the health and well-being of key components. Security events typically will be retrieved from well-known security devices. Examples of security event sources would include firewalls, authentication servers, dial-in modem servers, VPN gateways, ID systems, routers, switches, application servers, and dB servers. Events can be retrieved from these devices using any one or more of the following techniques:

- **Syslog** A UNIX-based operating system log utility.
- **SNMP** Events that satisfy a pre-configured condition.
- **Application logs** Events produced by the operation of the application.
- **LEA (Check Point)** Events produced by Check Point and selected OPSEC-compliant devices.
- **Other (Proprietary)** These include proprietary protocols and event content.

It is the job of the Security Event Management Server (SEMS) to act on these events by performing some logic operation and, as a result, present a hopefully meaningful and valuable alert to support staff. It is far better to permit this generation of alerts from your centralized SEMS rather than spawn alerts from each non-contiguous source. Spawning alerts from your individual devices (firewalls, ID systems, gateways, and so on) can be equated to the quick, inexpensive, and dirty technique to event management. What any medium to large-sized corporation should strive for is a controlled flow of events from distributed sources to centralized management stations.

By forwarding events (which become alerts after logic is applied by the management console) from these distributed sources to a central management station, you enable both event correlation and collaboration.

Event correlation is the capability to find the similarities between two or more events and use these similarities to derive a more broad-reaching understanding of what is actually happening. Event collaboration, somewhat the inverse of correlation, can be defined as the capability to find the differences between two or more events and use these differences to derive a more broad-reaching understanding of what is actually happening. The basic concept behind both event correlation and collaboration is illustrated in Figure 5-3.

Figure 5-3

Example of event correlation and collaboration

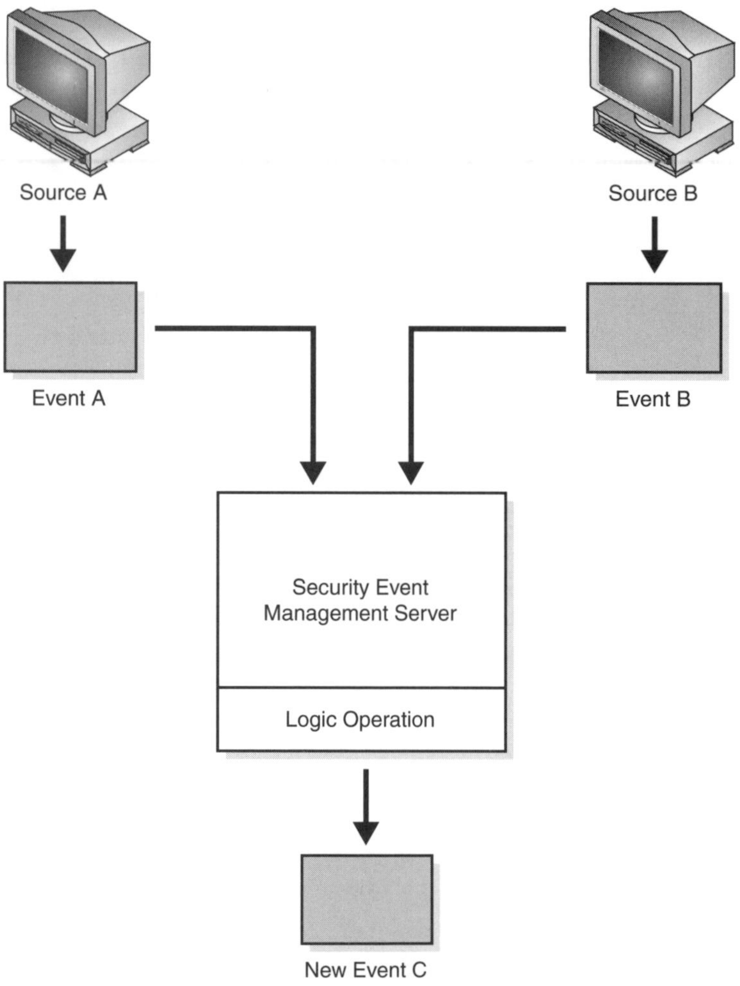

This concept is illustrated in the following example. Event A is received by the SEMS at 11:12 P.M. and is identified as a Denial of Service (DoS) attack underway on the perimeter firewall in Atlanta. Moments later, similar events arrive at the SEMS, indicating that the perimeter firewalls in Boston and New York are experiencing the same form of attempted disruption. The SEMS makes use of predefined logic to infer that a corporate-wide DoS strike is underway (event correlation).

In a second example, Event B is received by the SEMS at 12:30 A.M. and is identified as a port-scan emanating from the Atlanta perimeter firewall. At the same time, Event C arrives at the SEMS, indicating that the homegrown healthcare application has begun its nightly processing. During this nightly processing cycle, several sequences of ports are attempted as server processes attempt to synchronize their databases from within the perimeter. The SEMS applies its pre-configured logic to interpret this port scan, detected as Event B, as actually belonging to the nightly healthcare application processing (event collaboration).

Both event correlation and collaboration will only be possible if your SEMS is capable of the previous logic comparisons. In most cases, proprietary agents must be installed on monitored systems. These lightweight pieces of agent code (sometimes referred to as probes) are tailored to the operating system and/or application for which they were intended such that events collected from these systems have special meaning. Just because you allow full auditing on a system you want to monitor doesn't mean the event will be accurately interpreted, by default, when it arrives at your SEMS. It is the job of these agents to interpret collected system and application events prior to sending them to the SEMS for further logic operations.

Complex event management solutions are, however, not for everyone. These solutions are relatively expensive and will require a good deal of expertise to integrate into your enterprise. If this sort of solution is an option for your corporation, you should also consider the tiered approach to event management.

To build upon the concepts of event correlation and collaboration, medium to large-sized corporations may find it necessary to introduce a tiered approach to manage events. A tiered solution infers multiple, special purpose layers. Each tier in this model performs a specific logical operation, sometimes on specific event sources and other times on specific event categories. By defining special purposes for the different SEMS tier levels, you can build a higher degree of granularity into your event management solution. Higher degrees of granularity can mean fewer misdirected alerts.

Together with event correlation and collaboration, which can result in fewer false positives, the end result will be a powerful and robust event management solution. The tiered approach to event management is illustrated in Figure 5-4.

Utilizing the tiered approach to event management includes the incorporation of multiple SEMSs, each with its own specific correlative and collaborative purpose. Events would be categorized as to both context and severity, and forwarded to the appropriate SEMS device where further logic can be applied to derive a more robust conclusion.

The receipt of Events A and B, for example, can be used to illustrate this concept. Event A represents a file system capacity alert, and Event B represents an application error. To ensure that these alerts are processed by the proper logic operations, security staffers have designed a series of

Figure 5-4
SEMS hierarchical tiers

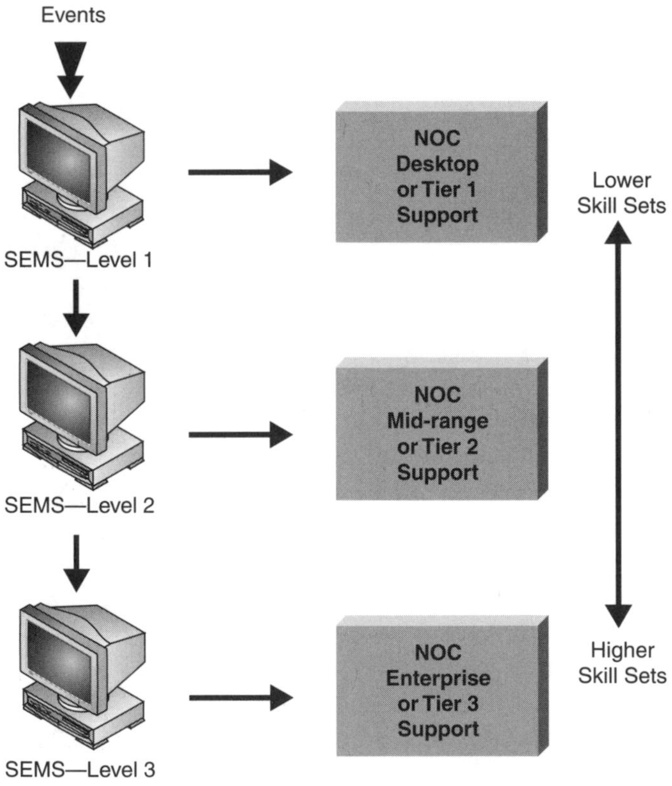

Standard Management system (SMS) tiers that have been tailored to handle specific categories of events. Event A represents a system alert, and as such will be forwarded to SEMS1 where logic has been applied (and is maintained by the system support group) to accurately process system alerts. Event B represents an application alert, and as such will be forwarded to SEMS2 where logic has been applied (and is maintained by the application support group) to accurately process application alerts.

Neither SEMS1 nor SEMS2, however, will be responsible for notifying support staff (NOC staff). Instead, both SEMS1 and SEMS2 will forward their alerts to a third management station (SEMS3) where event correlation and collaboration logic can be applied to derive the cause of the event, rather than begin with addressing the symptoms. In this example, the logic programmed on SEMS3 determined that the FinApp application was generating large amounts of application log errors that were filling up the file system. The correct response taken by SEMS3 to address this action is to notify the FinApp application support group.

Regardless of the event management strategy you choose to implement, real-time events are the key. By getting the processed alerts to your support staff quickly and efficiently in some meaningful context, you greatly improve your chances of thwarting an attack and reducing its effect on your corporate assets.

Physical Access Controls

Physical access controls pertain to the elements of your security infrastructure that typically work in conjunction with one another to reduce the effects of abuses by humans and acts of God. Physical controls are as much operational as they are physical.

Common physical access controls include standard keys, key cards, Smart cards, identification badges, security cameras, motion sensors, audible and visual alarms, doors, locks, cages, fences, signage, security guards, and system or device labels. The way these elements are put into use determines the quality of your physical access control strategy. Operational procedures, as defined in your corporate security policies and procedures documentation, should define how specific classifications of data and underlying systems are protected. These procedures should also state which actions are taken to notify appropriate personnel in the event of a disaster, define appropriate forensic procedures as they apply to the importance of the data affected, and state how associated risks may be mitigated.

In addition to reducing the risk, or effects, of a security breach, disruption of service must also be factored into your physical protection strategy. Disruption of service strategies typically includes a mixture of proper component placement and redundancy. The placement of physical security infrastructure components is as important as redundancy for several reasons. The primary reason is best explained in an example.

Company A, an ASP, decides that it requires highly available systems (data) to satisfy its customer expectations. In addressing this issue, Company A installs redundant T-1 connections into its data center where applications are hosted on clustered systems. Redundant power is also supplied from a pair of Uninterruptible Power Supply (UPS) devices in the basement of the facility. During a relatively small construction operation on the corporate parking lot, the construction team determines that they will not need to contact the local DIG SAFE office to identify underground cabling. A backhoe inadvertently uproots and severs the pair (redundant) of T-1 connections to the facility that had been incorrectly installed in the same conduit and on the same egress point from the facility.

In addition, a construction worker steps inside the facility to use the first floor restroom (above the UPS devices in the basement) and unintentionally floods the room with water from an overflowing toilet. The water, acted upon by forces of nature such as gravity, proceeds to flow into the basement just below where it shorts out the in-line UPS devices, shunting power to the data center. As this example illustrates, disasters such as this can easily be prevented with a little forethought invested in the placement of your physical infrastructure components.

Logical Access Controls

Logical access controls probably receive the most limelight of all the security infrastructure controls available. These controls consist of firewalls, routers, switches, VPNs, and application-level controls put in place to restrict both system and network use. Building upon previously discussed concepts, logical access controls sometimes utilize authentication and authorization information to make a determination as to whether access will be granted or denied. Other times, these decisions are made based upon either the port or protocol being used. As stated earlier in this chapter, it is best to focus first on applying controls to your applications, followed by controls to restrict the lower level protocols.

For illustrative purposes, let's assume a HealthApp application utilizes TCP on port 8111 to communicate with HealthApp clients and TCP 8104 to conduct server-to-server communications. Rather than begin applying access controls to known undesired ports and protocols, first understand how your application functions. In this example, the HealthApp server communicates with other servers by first performing a Domain Name System (DNS) lookup to find the IP address of the server it wants to communicate with. For this reason, DNS queries will have to be permitted between each HealthApp server and its respective DNS server(s).

In this basic example, the next steps are to deny all traffic on the access control devices (such as firewalls, routers, and switches) that is not associated with the operation of the HealthApp application and test the application for proper operation. In this way, you are targeting the application to derive the most secure logical access control set available to you. You'll find that using this strategy is the most efficient means of protecting your application data as well as the underlying systems.

Logical access controls can be applied in a variety of ways to restrict system or network use. In the protection of application access, logical access controls are typically applied within the application itself. These can be designed to explicitly restrict or permit certain users, or groups of users, based upon their authentication and authorization criteria. Network access controls typically make the determination to permit or deny traffic based upon the port number and/or protocol attempting to traverse a network segment. Many firewalls, routers, switches, VPN gateways, and ID systems can be configured to restrict traffic based upon its type (TCP, UDP, or IPX), source, destination, or even payload. ID systems are mentioned here because many are capable of both identifying and preventing specific packet traffic from traversing a segment.

Common methods that ID systems use to this end include the sending of a TCP RESET (RST) packet to the originator of the unauthorized network communication. This RST packet informs the originating (offending) host that the data session has not been received. Though the offending host may continue to retry its unauthorized communication across the given network segment, the ID system will continue to reset this session, thereby preventing the traffic from reaching its destination.

Best-practice design strategies for the implementation of logical access controls involve the establishment of a perimeter, as well as internal application and network-based controls, to protect the infrastructure. The establishment of multiple perimeters (zones of trust) will determine which systems and networks can be trusted the most (internal), which can be somewhat trusted (DMZ), and which cannot be trusted at all (external). The common model for such a design is illustrated in Figure 5-5.

By designing separate zones of trust, you enable the capability to apply access controls that best fit the business purpose of the systems and networks within that zone. For example, Internet-facing systems will require a different level of access control than Extranet or Intranet systems will. Not only must the appropriate access control technologies be chosen and inserted into your design, but they must also be included in the proper locations of your infrastructure. Installing your ID systems inside your perimeter firewalls will net a much different result than if placed outside of your firewalls. Not only will the resultant events differ in focus and content, but differing data confidentiality, integrity, and availability requirements will apply, altering the focus of these devices considerably.

Figure 5-5

Perimeter security: Establish zones of trust.

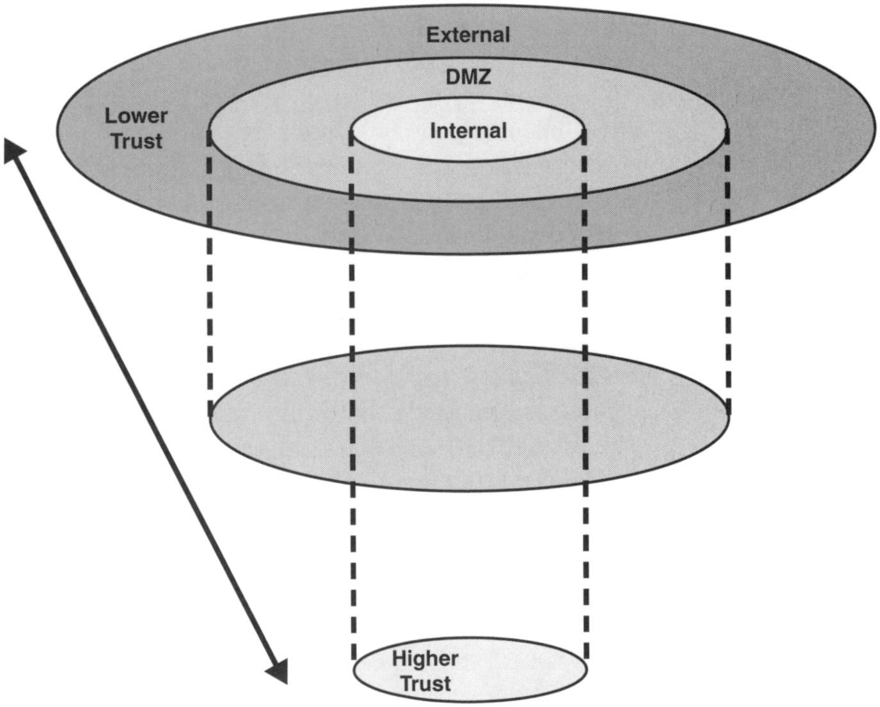

When implementing controls, the best fit for your corporation should involve restriction without sacrificing much in the way of productivity. This is typically a fine line and must be given much thought. Each corporation, non-profit organizations exempt, is in business for one primary purpose—to make money. Executives will not likely allow you to cut off the lifeblood of the corporation simply because it makes the most sense from a security perspective. It has been said that the only safe computer is a computer that is buried in concrete, with the power turned off, and its network cable cut, but what good is that computer to your business? The answer is simply, no use at all.

Case Study Overview

The objectives of the following case study analyses are to apply the technologies discussed in this chapter and offer a valid strategy for their deployment based upon industry-best practices. Although each of the following case study analyses provides a summary of the issues pertaining to that case study, it is advised that the reader review the case studies originally detailed in Chapter 1 prior to continuing.

Analysis of Case Study #1—Corporate

MCC primarily employs Microsoft Windows NT Workstation as the predominant desktop operating system among its user population. File and print sharing is based upon Novell, and most application servers are operated on either Sun Microsystems' Solaris platform or IBM's AIX UNIX operating system. Management has tagged e-mail as a critical application as both its messaging and attachments are key forms of communication within the company. Redundant Internet connections service access to the Web for both office-based and mobile employees who connect to the company by VPN access. Internet-facing systems have been segregated from Intranet-based systems by the establishment of a Demilitarized Zone (DMZ). Enterprise Resource Planning (ERP) applications such as SAP, Oracle, and PeopleSoft are in use. Web application development has become more popular over the recent years, but often times MCC has not been able to hire the necessary high-priced talent to accommodate both the expertise and the workload that they regularly experience. Hence, some 50 percent of the present Web developer population at MCC is comprised of outsourced staff. MCC doesn't see the need for Web expertise diminishing either. With this in mind, the future use of Application Service Providers (ASPs) is also being discussed.

To address data confidentiality, MCC will employ the use of strong authentication, encryption technology, and strict application controls. Strong authentication will be required for mobile workers to gain access to the corporate VPN gateways. This requirement will be satisfied by the use of soft tokens distributed to staff members upon direct managerial approval. It has been determined that the logistics as well as the cost associated with the programming and distribution of hard tokens is inhibitive. All remote access systems (VPN gateways and dial-in modem servers) will need to support this technology to permit authenticated user access. Specific client-side hardware and configuration parameters must be adhered to.

Prior to the granting of secured VPN access, mobile worker systems will be required to have disabled split tunneling. User systems will be queried by an internal Microsoft SMS system that will report the number of active network adapters in use by the client. If either split tunneling or multiple adapters is in use, the connection will not be permitted. Permitting such a connection could extend the boundary of the corporate network to untrusted systems if the remote worker simply enabled IP forwarding between interfaces. This is true because split tunneling permits a VPN client to send and receive traffic with other (untrusted) destinations while also talking with you within the *secured* tunnel.

By the simple application of a Trojan horse program on your client, which could siphon data from your client system to the attacker's system after the data is decrypted at the protected interface, the protection afforded by your VPN could be circumvented. A second concern here is that the complete compromise of your VPN security is just a client configuration away. If a client has more than one active network interface and the client system were to be configured to forward traffic between these two interfaces, all traffic within your secured connection could now be sent unencrypted to untrusted destinations.

To further protect these remote systems, the institution of password aging and complexity restrictions could enhance the authentication of internal systems. To guard against unauthorized authentication, passwords will be aged after a period of 45 days. After 30 days, users will be warned that they need to change their passwords but will be granted a 15-day grace period in which to do so. Accounts that have not been changed after the 45-day cycle will be disabled and managerial approval will be required to reinstate such accounts.

To protect data in transit that is classified as either Confidential or Restricted, VPN technologies employing IPSec and IKE for key management will be required. Encryption strength must equal 128-bit 3DES or greater for such data payloads and will be used to provide access to internal PeopleSoft application servers and financial Oracle servers as well as to grant access to mobile workers. Application controls on these servers will restrict access based upon both username and group assignment. Data centers that house these application and database servers will also employ strict physical access controls that monitor and restrict human access to these servers.

To address data integrity concerns, MCC will employ this same VPN technology to this end. The protection of data integrity will be protected natively by IPSec, which performs a checksum on the data sent and compares it with the checksum on the data that is received. Provided that these checksums match, integrity is guaranteed by the secured protocol.

Encrypted File System (EFS) will also be used to protect both Confidential and Restricted data that is stored to either disk or backup media. Access to EFS-protected files will require complex passwords that consist of a combination of at least eight alphanumeric characters. Data corruption concerns (a component of data integrity) will be satisfied by the use of well-documented backup procedures and by the use of anti-virus software at both the desktop and Microsoft Exchange servers. Backup procedures will include nightly full backups and weekly off-site tape storage. Wherever possible, application use will be terminated at a predetermined off-hours time so that Confidential and Restricted data resources can be encrypted and backed up to media securely. Data of these classification levels must be encrypted; otherwise, off-site tape storage will not be permitted.

Backup media will only leave the premises of MCC by requiring the media courier to present a valid vendor's identification badge with photo. Media couriers will also be required to sign backup media out using a property pass identifying time, date, location, tape or set ID, and its destination. In addition, backup procedures will clearly state that any backup media containing two or more separate classifications of data will necessitate the labeling of that media to the highest classification in use. This means that a backup tape containing data labeled as Public, Internal, and Confidential will be labeled as Confidential.

Data availability concerns will be alleviated through the use of redundant communications links, redundant network devices, redundant power components, and redundant application servers. Communications links into the data centers will arrive at differing ingress points at different sides of the building housing the particular data center. In addition, two separate carriers will be utilized in a load-sharing configuration using the BGPv4 routing protocol. Data availability will also be monitored by means of event notification from RAS servers and in-line network devices to the MCC NOC where corporate policies and procedures identify operations and security staff of the appropriate steps to follow in event notification, security breach containment, and its eradication.

Analysis of Case Study #2—FinApp

MCC issues new securities in the commodities market and consequently must protect investors by upholding rules and regulations enforced and set forth by the Security Exchange Commission (SEC). MCC has developed a financial application (FinApp) that provides futures to clients as well as post-trade statements and personal account information. The primary users of FinApp are institutional trading advisors that are not employees of MCC. FinApp has been designed to process up to 1M (million) trades per day. System downtime is reported to equal 500K per minute; hence, redundant network and application services have been deployed in its protection. All trades are recorded and each transaction requires non-repudiation to ensure the identification for trading requests is accurate. Systems that host the FinApp application are co-located in three separate regions around the globe with private WAN links servicing their connection back to MCC's global access data center.

To address data confidentiality, MCC employs the use of strong authentication, Secure Sockets Layer (SSL) technology, and strict application controls. SSL is by far the most commonly used method for securing Web-based transactions. SSL secures transactions by encrypting all data between the source and destination systems.

Much the same as required in Case Study #1, strong authentication, for purposes of non-repudiation, will be required for users that access this system by both dial-up and VPN access. For this purpose, soft tokens will be put to use by both employees and brokerages. The Confidential nature of the data requires such a stringent stance on authentication in this case.

SSL (128-bit or better) technology will be used to encrypt authenticated sessions using the Web user interface to the FinApp application, and application controls will restrict user access by both user account and group assignment, creating separate containers of data for different access levels (employees and institutional brokerage firms). Access to the FinApp Web servers will traverse a firewall with tested rule sets and a network-based ID system that will identify any forms of known attack sequences.

In addition, a host-based ID program will be installed and configured on all FinApp Web servers and backend database servers to monitor suspicious activity. Data integrity concerns will also be satisfied by the use of both SSL and Web server certificates, which will identify itself uniquely as the MCC FinApp server and securely transfer data to the user's desktop. Web server certificates are used to uniquely identify the Web server by the digital signature applied to its certificate. Signature authorities can be either public (such as Verisign, Entrust, or Baltimore) or private (your own). The authenticity of these digital signatures is verified by the client system.

Data corruption concerns will be eased by the use of the same backup measures defined in Case Study #1. Data availability concerns will be addressed by employing redundant network links, devices, servers, and power supplies (both service-based and via in-line battery backup). Data availability will be monitored by means of event notification from FinApp servers and in-line network devices to the MCC NOC where corporate policies and procedures identify operations and the security staff of the appropriate steps to follow in event notification, security breach containment, and its eradication.

Analysis of Case Study #3—HealthApp

MCC maintains a line of business (LOB) that has initiated a directive to provide the necessary application automation to healthcare claims processing and brokerage quotations. Through the use of this new application, HealthApp, MCC also plans to provide MCC employees with online access to personal statements. The HealthApp portal provides such user services worldwide from a single centralized location. MCC will offer this online access to both patients and physicians through the use of a Web-based user interface. Currently, similar service is available via dial-up modem access, but future plans include making HealthApp available from the Internet.

To address data confidentiality, MCC will employ the use of complex passwords, SSL technology, file system encryption, and strict application controls. Strong authentication is not logically feasible, given the fact that several health care providers utilize this service. To increase this otherwise lacking authentication scheme, complex passwords that are aged on a 45-day cycle will be required by all users of the system. These passwords must contain a combination of at least eight alphanumeric characters. SSL (128-bit) will be used to encrypt data in transit between the Web application server and the user as well as ensure the integrity of the data delivered to the user's desktop. Access to the HealthApp Web servers will traverse a firewall with tested rule sets and a network-based ID system that will identify any forms of known attack sequences.

In addition, a host-based ID program will be installed and configured on all HealthApp Web servers and backend database servers to monitor suspicious activity. Data stored on a hard disk will also be encrypted, and any data backed up to media will be encrypted prior to archival and be released to third-party media storage and retrieval companies. Backup media will only leave the premises of MCC by requiring the media courier to present a valid vendor's identification badge with photo. Media couriers will also be required to sign backup media out using a property pass identifying time, date, location, tape or set ID, and its destination. Data corruption concerns will be addressed by the use of anti-virus software that actively scans contents in memory and by maintaining up-to-date operating system and application patches on the Web and database servers.

Availability concerns will be addressed in the same means as mentioned in the previous case studies, by way of redundant network links, network devices, power, and application servers. Data availability will be monitored by means of event notification from HealthApp servers and in-line network devices to the MCC NOC where corporate policies and procedures identify operations and security staff of the appropriate steps to follow in event notification, security breach containment, and eradication.

Conclusion

In conclusion, for your security infrastructure design to offer you the most benefit, you should recall several concepts from this chapter. First and foremost, stay in touch with current events going on in the industry. Performing a constant examination of the information security industry accomplishes this well. This sounds daunting, but you can streamline this process in a few different ways.

Plug yourself into the latest technology updates, hacking exploits, and product vulnerabilities and countermeasures. Some of this will require time on your part to actively browse popular Web sites like **www.securityfocus.com**. Other steps you can take can be more automated, such as actively subscribing to **www.cert.org**, Carnegie Mellon University's Computer Emergency Response Team, as well as any vendor mailing lists that may be available to alert you to vulnerabilities and patches associated with their wares. By keeping abreast of the security landscape, you'll be able to offer more thoughtful insight into both the design and augmentation of your security infrastructure.

Secondly, and prior to solution design and deployment, spend time with senior management and project leaders to fully understand business objectives. The best application of security is neither frugal nor frivolous. Both diligence and practicality should ring out as your design strategy. By diligently understanding the objectives of your organization, you'll be better equipped to apply the available technology in a practical manner.

When you have made your decisions on which technology and vendor solutions to implement as infrastructure components, it is time to apply these controls. Furthering the concept of practicality, apply access controls that are appropriate to the data that they protect. It makes little sense to spend valuable time and resources protecting data that has been assigned a Public information classification (as described in Chapter 3). Conversely, it also makes little sense to disregard the protection mechanisms that should be instituted to protect higher classifications of data (Internal, Confidential, and Restricted).

As a best-practice strategy for applying access controls, target your applications first. As stated earlier in this chapter, you'll discover that by focusing on protecting your applications first, by default you will be securing the underlying protocols and access pathways into your network and on your servers.

Unfortunately, regardless of your security prowess, without senior management support, your security infrastructure design will only fly at half-mast. Corporate security policies and procedures form the foundation of any good security practice. The aim of such policies and procedures are to guide the corporation through the proper course of action (whether addressing business requirements, the containment of breaches, the conducting of forensics, or the eradication of security issues) and may even protect the organization from costly litigation and other forms of liability. Without senior management support for such policies, any protection mechanisms and procedures you put into place will not perform as they should.

Lastly, to facilitate these best-practice recommendations, create a Computer Incident Response Team (CIRT, as referenced in Chapter 4). Your CIRT members should be versed in the technology that you employ within your corporation. It will be the responsibility of these CIRT members to maintain your security infrastructure as well as to respond to security events.

CIRT member responsibilities should include security event identification, containment, and eradication. The better trained these CIRT members are, the more fluid the response and eradication of security events within your enterprise will be. These CIRT members should also be assigned the task of designing safe builds of computer systems that can act as templates for large-scale deployments of computer hardware or software solutions to your users.

To this end, CIRT members must continually monitor the latest attacker strategies, hacking techniques, and vulnerabilities. It will be the responsibility of CIRT members to ensure that the latest patches and revisions of computer software and hardware are employed. The CIRT is the oil of your security infrastructure. Without such a well-trained team, your security engine could easily seize up.

CHAPTER 6

Network Partitioning

Computer networks have evolved considerably over the last 30 years. In the beginning, computer systems were stand-alone entities. Access to mainframes was provided via a dumb terminal over a serial line. All security and control was managed centrally. Early computer networks were usually comprised of private connections using propriety network media and protocols. Specific communication methods varied from vendor to vendor. This model started to change with the advent of local area networks (LANs) in the early 1980s and the introduction of TCP/IP. As the TCP/IP protocol gained momentum, distributed computing started to replace the mainframe/dumb terminal model. Interoperability between different platforms and standardization of network protocols stripped away the insulation of proprietary communication mechanisms. As this transformation took place, security challenges arose in its wake. However, TCP/IP and its network-based applications (Telnet, FTP, and HTTP) were *not* designed with security in mind.

As Internet accessibility became a method of communication for commercial entities, pockets of security weaknesses were created. Companies were now able to directly communicate with their customers and business partners over lower-cost public networks. Not only was data shared between these people, but it was also unwittingly shared with third parties on the Internet.

To counter these new challenges, many companies explored ways of segregating their networks from the public Internet. This practice came to be known as network partitioning. The method of network partitioning provided companies with the ability to shield important resources from unauthorized access. Within this new paradigm, the network was comprised of several segments as opposed to one large centralized network. By implementing these network partitions, companies achieved the ability to control what traffic flowed to and from a given network to any other. In the process of creating partitions for these networks, the corporate information technology assets that would reside on these networks could now be made to serve specific security purposes. Each with its own level of trust, these systems could now be designed and configured with specific security requirements based upon their level of trust. An example of basic network partitioning is illustrated in Figure 6-1.

Examples of the three most common security zones are

- **The Internet** A global network that connects computers worldwide. This is a public network that anyone can access.
- **The Intranet** A private network maintained by an individual company or organization, where access is typically limited to the company itself.
- **Extranet** An extension of the corporate Intranet that enables communication between itself and partner organizations.

Figure 6-1

An example of basic network partitioning

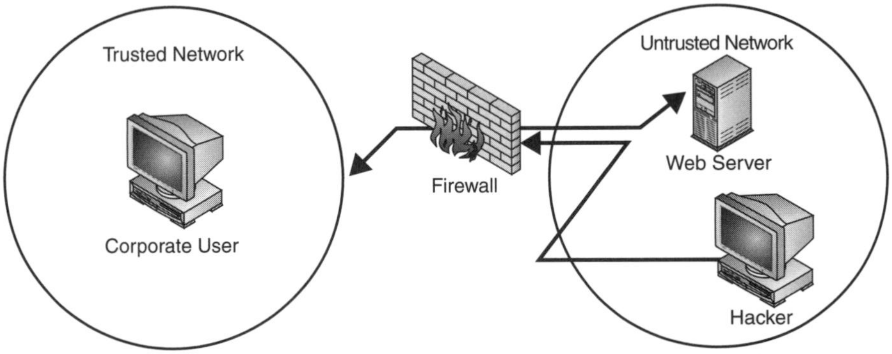

Overview of Network Partitioning

Network partitioning can be achieved by a number of different technologies or in a combination of those technologies, which is the common practice in most modern security schemes. Common methods include the use of packet filters, stateful inspection, application proxy, and layer 4 (L4) switching.

Virtual local area network (VLAN) partitioning A VLAN permits the creation of logical groups of users and/or systems for the purpose of network segmentation. Although it was originally designed to cut down on broadcast traffic to enhance performance, this technology enables certain assets such as servers to be isolated from the general user traffic.

New classes of switches are emerging that make switching decisions at layers above the network layer (layer 3 of the Open System Interconnection [OSI] model). The OSI model consists of seven layers that govern the way computers communicate with one another, as referenced in Figure 6-2.

This capability enables a greater level of control in directing which traffic can go where. Eventually, this type of functionality could open the possibility of on-wire content inspection. As more and more attacks/exploits occur at the application layer, this could be essential in protecting information assets. Current generation switches can work at the network layer or higher and can provide routing and filtering services. Given the point-to-point nature of this communication, the likelihood of interception (known as sniffing) of a given conversation between two hosts (while entirely foolproof) is less possible. Sniffing is a common method of attack

Figure 6-2
OSI model

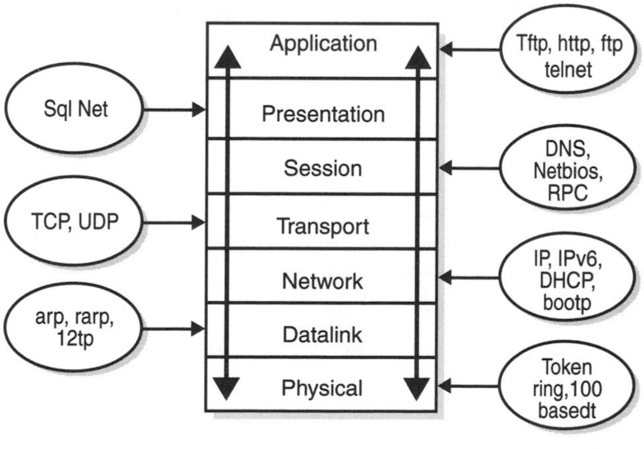

used to steal passwords and hijack application sessions within the shared environment.

Do's and Don'ts: *VLANs are good for containment.*

Packet filters This was the mechanism used by the first-generation firewalls. Essentially, this model acts as a traffic cop between two or more networks. Packet filters look at each packet that enters or leaves a given network and accepts or rejects it based on a user-defined rule. Packet filters work at the network layer of the OSI model and look specifically at the source, destination address, and protocol used. This type of security control tends to be fairly inexpensive, but it suffers from a few disadvantages. Packet filters are subject to spoofing and do not provide any protection beyond the network layer. Most modern switches, routers, and operating systems (that support TCP/IP) are capable of providing this type of service.

As the complexity of network applications has grown, so have the exploits. Given that packet filters are only concerned with what goes on at the network layer, they are not well suited to thwarting the newest generation of attacks. However, they still have their place in a comprehensive security design. Access lists on routers (a form of packet filtering) can be used as a first line of defense prior to a firewall processing traffic. By blocking all but the approved protocols as defined by a company's security policy, unwanted traffic is kept off the network.

Do's and Don'ts: *Certain types of information-gathering tools such as ping or trace route can be blocked at the perimeter, limiting an attacker's ability to map the network. In addition, administrative access to the routers themselves can be limited to the trusted network only.*

Circuit-level gateway This model acts as a relay at the session level. It creates a circuit between trusted clients or servers to trusted hosts and vice versa. A circuit-level gateway relies on data contained in the packet headers for the Internet's TCP session-layer protocol. A circuit-level gateway filters packets at the session layer of the OSI model. Because no direct connection is allowed from one end to another, this model is fairly secure; however, the drawback is that your applications must be designed to support this type of proxy mechanism. SOCKS-compliant applications are an example of this type of support.

Application proxy This model acts as a relay at the application level. It passes requests to and from a service on behalf of the requester. No direct routing takes place between the requester and provider. Most proxies support caching, which can be used to speed access to frequently visited destinations (specifically in HTTP applications) and limit the use of bandwidth and load on Internet connections.

User-level authentication is another key feature that most proxies support. Although this solution provides good security, this type of firewall can be subject to scalability and performance issues. Proxies can be limited in the number of applications supported, depending on the vendor. Some applications cannot work through proxies. They tend to be vulnerable to operating system and application-level bugs.

Pure proxies are best suited to provide content acceleration/filtering (HTTP traffic); they also can provide user authentication, thus helping to reduce the load on internal Web servers, perimeter firewalls, and outbound Internet connection(s). By utilizing content-filtering plug-ins, specific content such as pornography, gambling, and so on can be blocked. This functionality is usually provided by the use of a third-party product, but most proxies can be configured to filter specific sites. Another common benefit with proxies is their capability to control issues with HTTP tunneling (using port 80 to enable unauthorized applications to penetrate or exit the network). This is a common weakness with stateful firewalls.

Most firewalls do not provide adequate logging functions to discern the identity of the requestor. Usually only the IP address is listed in the log. As companies have moved toward dynamic IP addressing (DHCP), the ability to track a particular user's activities has become more difficult. Most proxies support logging and authentication, which enables administrators to track access based on username. Of course, this may require an additional authentication process when the user enters a browser so loss of transparency may occur.

Stateful inspection This model combines aspects of a packet-filtering firewall, a circuit-level gateway, and an application-level gateway essentially working at all seven layers of the OSI model. Application and communication state information is derived from all seven layers of a given session. The firewall keeps a table of this information so it can compare it to requests and responses to verify that the issuer and responder are genuine. This is designed to thwart common attacks such as IP spoofing and TCP session hijacking. Most of the commercial firewalls available today utilize this architecture.

The stateful firewall model has become the de facto standard based on the performance advantage, scalability, and transparency in which it can

Figure 6-3
Comprehensive partitioning

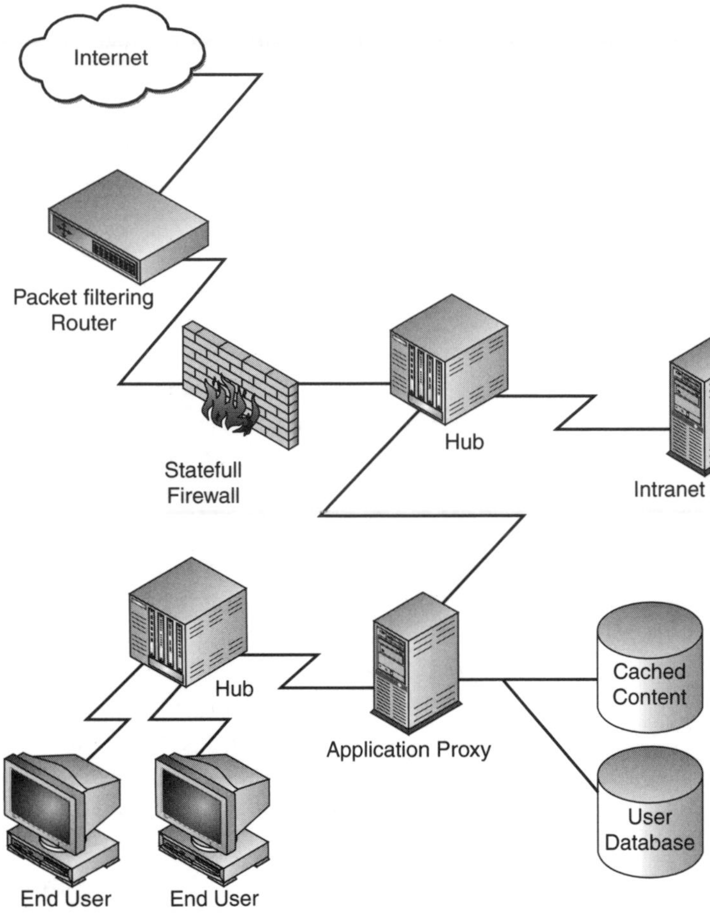

be deployed. Figure 6-3 depicts a common scenario where each of these architectures could be deployed in concert to provide a comprehensive solution.

Firewall Platforms

As with the various logical architectures, firewalls come in one of two hardware platforms: host- or appliance-based. Traditionally, firewalls were implemented as a host-based solution. Host-based firewalls are installed on a general-purpose platform such as an NT, Linux, or UNIX server. In addition to adding firewall services onto the system, additional work is required to harden the platform to make it suitable for providing firewall services. Most operating systems' out-of-the-box configuration is less than suitable for supporting a firewall function. This additional work requires a fair degree of understanding about the vulnerabilities that exist with a given operating system platform, and it can lengthen the deployment cycle of such solutions.

Appliances, on the other hand, tend to be black boxes built upon specific, special-purpose hardware and software components. Most appliances utilize a pre-hardened or proprietary operating system kernel that has been specifically designed to support firewall services. Usually, no additional platform hardening is required.

In recent years, vendors such as Cobalt (**www.cobaltnetworks.com**), NetScreen (**www.netscreen.com**), Cisco (**www.cisco.com**), and Nokia (**www.nokia.com**) have been producing specialized appliances that provide higher performance levels and lower administrative requirements in their deployment and operation.

Host-based firewalls tend to be less expensive than appliances, but appliances tend to outperform host-based solutions due to their specialized design. Appliances also tend to be more secure as they have less built-in vulnerabilities due to their pre-hardened operating systems. Host-based solutions offer some advantages within a high-availability solution such as load balancing, a feature which is absent in most appliances.

Many players are within the firewall market. Table 6-1 provides a quick look at some of the top vendors and where they fall in the architecture models.

Anatomy of the High-Availability Firewall

What does high availability really mean? That's a question many people ask when they first hear this term as it applies to firewalls. The response to this question will differ depending on the vendor. Simply put, high availability means that a given session is maintained through a failed condition or a set of failed conditions. Also, policy enforcement is not interrupted during this failed condition and therefore no security weakness is created by such an event. Given the previous two statements, not all solutions are created equal.

High availability, as it were, is offered in two distinct solutions: load balancing and standby. In the case of a load-balancing model, traffic is

Table 6-1 Sample Vendor Matrix

Vendor	Product	Application Proxy	Circuit-Level Gateway	Packet Filter	Stateful Inspection	Host-Based	Appliance-Based
Axent Technologies	Raptor	Yes	Yes	Yes	Yes	Sun, Windows NT	Cobalt Velociraptor
Cache Flow Inc.	Cache flow	Yes					Cache flow 600, 6000, 700,7000
Checkpoint Technologies Inc.	Firewall-1	Yes	Yes	Yes	Yes	Sun HPUX, IBM AIX, Linux, Windows NT	Nokia IP 110, 330, 440, and 650 routers, Instrusion.com PDS 2100
Cisco Systems Inc.	PIX, IOS firewall feature set		Yes	Yes	Yes		PIX 506, 515, 520, and 535 firewalls, firewall feature set for Cisco routers.
Net Screen	NetScreen	Yes	Yes	Yes	Yes		NetScreen 5, 10, 100, 1000
Network Associates	Gauntlet	Yes		Yes		HPUX, SUN, and Windows NT	WebShield E-ppliance 300
Microsoft	Microsoft Proxy Server	Yes					

aggregated across a firewall cluster. Any number of primary and standby devices can be used to form these active-standby relationships, and it typically appears as one logical firewall to users. During a fail-over, transition from the primary to standby device is generally transparent to users.

In the case of the standby model, one firewall acts as a primary device by shouldering the burden of traffic inspection and delivery. A second device, known as the backup node, becomes active only when a failure condition is met on the primary device. Furthermore, the primary and standby device relationship can exist in two formats: active-active or active-passive. In an active-active configuration, all firewall nodes are online, but only one firewall is processing traffic; the fail-over is automatic and does not require human intervention. Active-active fail-over is generally transparent to end users. In an active-passive configuration, a standby (backup) node is promoted when the primary node fails. This is typically achieved by a manual process that requires human intervention.

Licensing cost can play a big role in selecting the approach to take in regard to high availability. Most solutions, with the exception of an active-passive configuration, require a licensing cost for each firewall node. In addition, specific high-availability licensing may be required to enable the proper operation of fault tolerance. This will vary with each vendor.

Most high-availability solutions rely on maintaining a heartbeat signal between the nodes. This signal is used to communicate the health status of a given firewall. It is transmitted on one or more of the network interfaces of the firewall or in certain products via a propriety hardware connection.

Certain high-availability solutions have the capability to preserve existing sessions during a fail-over. In order for this to work, state information on all current sessions must be transmitted between each firewall. This is key to preserving transactions through a failed condition on a stateful firewall. State synchronization methods are platform-dependent and generally proprietary in nature.

Do's and Don'ts: *Given the chatty nature of the state synchronization, it is generally recommended that state information traffic be transmitted over a dedicated link as not to impact production traffic.*

Host-based solutions and appliances differ in the way that they handle high availability. Most host-based firewalls require a third-party solution to provide the underlying fault tolerance, which is separate from the firewall component. This function is provided via either a hardware or software solution or a combination of both. Some appliances may also require an underlying mechanism, whereas others provide the function as part of the operating system. Currently, clustering, or load balancing, is only available on host-based solutions or as a function outside the firewall (hardware load-balancing solution), although appliance vendors should be offering this capability shortly.

Checkpoint Firewall-1 Appliance

The Nokia is an appliance specifically designed for use as a router and/or firewall. The system comes preinstalled with Checkpoint. Fault tolerance is handled via the virtual router redundant protocol (VRRP) RFC 2338, 2787. The Nokia communicates state over a dedicated interface. Heartbeat, however, can be transmitted over several interfaces. A separate console is required for management and logging. VRRP can be implemented in one of two modes.

The VRRPv2 mode consists of a primary system and one or more secondary machines. This model provides an active-passive configuration, where the secondary machine(s) backs up the IP addresses of the primary. Two virtual routers are created for each segment in which the firewalls will provide fault tolerance. Each firewall node requires a unique virtual router ID (VRID) for each segment. If a particular adapter fails, that address is picked up via the backup system. This can create an asymmetric routing issue (a problem with stateful firewalls) so a routing protocol is required to run between firewalls.

In a monitored circuit mode, each system has a unique IP address and a shared address for fault tolerance. A single virtual router is created on each segment. Firewalls share a VRID, but if multiple segments are set up for fail-over, then a unique VRID must be defined for each one. If a particular adapter fails, all addresses get passed to the backup system. No asymmetric routes are created in this situation so a routing protocol is not needed between the firewalls.

Checkpoint Host-Based

Stone Beat is a third-party fault tolerance solution that runs on Sun or Windows NT and provides host-to-host fail-over. State and heartbeat are provided via a dedicated interface on each firewall node. A separate console is required to manage and provide logging for the cluster. Each node appears as the same machine and can provide load balancing over two or more nodes. The solution requires two or more identical servers and a management console; this solution works in conjunction with the Checkpoint High Availability module, which is a new feature of version 4.1. Typically, a NT box can support up to eight interfaces and the Sun platform can support 32 utilizing quad Ethernet cards.

Cisco PIX

The PIX firewall has been gaining popularity due to its performance and price. Where it lacks in ease of management, it excels in speed. The PIX firewall is an Intel-based stateful firewall appliance running Cisco's propriety internetworking operating system (IOS) and firewall feature set. Currently, the PIX firewall provides two-node fail-over, where one node is primary and the secondary is backup. Fail-over is comprised of a dedicated hardware link via a specialized cable and port from box to box. Several models are available, which vary in scalability. The higher end platforms support hardware redundancy in the form of multiple power supplies and teaming network adapters.

Network Associates Gauntlet

Gauntlet is a host-based firewall that runs on NT and various flavors of UNIX. It is essentially a combination of a packet-filtering application and a proxy-based firewall. Fail-over requires an underlying third-party solution such as Legato's Full Time Cluster or Stone Software's Stone Beat Full Cluster. In the case of Legato, the configuration is fail-over essentially with a primary and hot backup model where only one node is active at any time. Heartbeat is transmitted via the internal interfaces and users point to a virtual IP address shared by the nodes. State is not preserved through fail-over so connections must be reestablished after transition. This can cause problems for connection-oriented applications such as Telnet and FTP. Stone Beat, on the other hand, provides full cluster and load-balancing capabilities. Each firewall node needs a dedicated interface for heartbeat. All nodes share the same IP addresses and appear as one firewall. State is preserved through fail-over and should be transparent to end users. Hardware redundancy is platform-dependant.

Axent Raptor

Raptor is a host-based firewall that runs on NT and various flavors of UNIX. Traditionally an application proxy, the later versions provide stateful inspection. As with the Gauntlet, fail-over requires an underlying third-party solution. Stone Software's Stone Beat Full Cluster offers a version for Raptor and provides the same capability as the Gauntlet version. Hardware redundancy is platform-dependant.

Air Gap Firewall Strategies

Many security professionals say (usually tongue in cheek) that the best way to secure a system is to disconnect from the network. Although this would certainly protect a system from network intrusion, this is not a realistic option. However, if you could somehow create a logical disconnection between one or two networks and allow the right information to pass, it would make for a strong solution. Air gaps essentially provide this functionality. They come in several models, which are discussed in the following section.

Network switch This model works by creating virtual systems within a single host. Separate network interfaces connect to two distinct networks. System resources such as memory and disk storage are allotted to each interface. Information stored in one virtual machine cannot transverse to the other side.

One-way link This model is placed between two distinct networks. It works by allowing traffic to flow in only one direction, sort of like a network drop box. No information can pass back to the source. Obviously, this configuration has some drawbacks. Communication must be completed without response from the target.

Real-time switch This model is placed between two distinct networks. It works by connecting to one network reading in data that is destined for the other network, then disconnecting from the source network, and reconnecting to the target network. At this point, it forwards the information to its intended recipient. During the transfer, TCP header information is stripped from packets prior to delivering data. This can help to eliminate many vulnerabilities that exist with common protocols; content inspection efforts can also be done during this transition to provide further validation.

Partitioning Models and Methods

Network security can be deployed in many different ways, but it generally falls into one of three categories. These categories, again, include the Intranet (private network), Internet (public network), and Extranet (public/private). When determining how to deploy network security for any of the categories, a number of factors need to be assessed. First, you should start by identifying the following:

- **Support for your security policy** As with any security technology, defining and adhering to a network security policy is a must—specifically in the area of public or partner access to private data. This should be the foundation that your design is built on.
- **Physical layout of the network** It is essential to have a clear and concise diagram of your network, routing flow, and entrance points.
- **Logical layout of the network** Next, you need to identify the makeup of your network traffic. Understanding the nature of the applications deployed will help to determine which control methods will be effective within your network. It will also help define where to effectively place your security control points. During this process, you should identify how application/protocols will be handled through your access points. This could include defining whether authentication is required for certain application/protocols or governing who may use certain protocols such as HTTP or custom applications.
- **Identify and locate critical resources** Review your information assets to determine where your sensitive or critical information is stored. This is helpful in determining when host partitioning is necessary. Host partitioning is the practice of isolating servers onto separate networks and carefully controlling access to the resources through the use of a firewall or router access control lists (ACLs).
- **External or untrusted connections** Understand your connection to the outside world. Internet access, vendor access, and extranet requirements should be outlined clearly.

As with any security technology, careful consideration needs to be taken as to when and where network access points should be deployed. The following are some important points to consider when creating a design:

- **Fault tolerance** Any good design takes fault tolerance into consideration, especially for critical resources. In situations where this is cost-prohibitive, a clear recovery or work-around plan needs to be defined. At no times should access be allowed if a governing control is unavailable (such as bypassing a failed firewall to allow continued connectivity).

- **Performance** Security is important, but it has to be deployed in such a way that it is not a hindrance to business and it is not so open when it creates exposure. Careful thought must be taken when determining where security control points should be placed. If possible, you should get a baseline of your current traffic patterns prior to implementing a control.
- **Complexity** When possible, keep it simple. Elaborate design for the sake of design can only lead to failure down the road. Remember the general rule: That which is not explicitly allowed is denied by default.
- **Risk** Identify your areas of risk, location of data, access controls, and ability to audit. A multi-tiered security design provides depth of defense, but proper logging and audit are essential to gauging the effectiveness of controls.

Do's and Don'ts: *That which is not explicitly permitted is prohibited. This is a simple rule that is most often not followed and results in problems.*

Do's and Don'ts: *Use reverse logic rules (do not allow Telnet).*

Do's and Don'ts: *Log all the rejected (or catchall last rules). Any firewall rule set should have a clean-up rule essentially dropping any packets that do not meet the criteria of the previous rules. In addition, logging these rejected packets can help to identify suspicious activity.*

Perimeter Security Models

Perimeter security models benefit companies that have access to the public Internet or to external partners. Traditionally, the models that we will discuss in the following section pertain to providing public access to internal resources, such as e-mail, the Web, or application servers.

Single-tier or publishing model A public server is placed within an area that is known as a Demilitarized Zone (DMZ). This is generally the same segment as the access router to the Internet/Extranet. Internal systems push information to these public servers. Obviously, this provides little protection outside the controls of the operating system or application(s) hosted therein and screening functions of the access router. In addition, the added effort in maintaining duplicate information is cumbersome. Given the shortcomings of this model, most companies are moving away from it.

Pass through Another approach commonly taken is to place resources in the private network behind the perimeter security and create a conduit that enables access to flow through. Although this eliminates the issue of maintaining duplicate information, it also presents a couple of new issues. Due to the limitation in IP address availability, most companies have moved to private addressing (RFC 1918 non-publicly routable addresses). Because of this move, some type of network address translation (NAT) must take place. Most modern routers and firewalls can provide translation services.

Within NAT, a host has a public (routable to the outside world) and a private IP, a one-to-one relationship, also referred to as a static translation. The firewall/router maintains a translation table and is tasked with converting inbound and outbound traffic. For outbound-user traffic, the NAT is usually a many-to-one translation, where all users appear as the firewall's outside address; this is sometimes referred to as dynamic or global translation. The firewall/router maintains a connection table to keep these many-to-one translations straight. Certain types of protocols do not handle translation well, such as IPSec (a protocol used in virtual private networking [VPN] and secure IP transmissions). So when considering translation in your security model, you need to take application compatibility into account. This is where application proxies can come into play.

The second issue with this approach is the fact that the systems potentially have open access to the internal network. If the system can be compromised, an attacker might gain access to other internal systems and your data.

Two-tier The next common approach taken is to create a secondary private or public network that is separate from the main production network. In cases where this new network is public, the customer needs to either subnet his or her public IP address space or acquire additional IP addresses. For applications that do not support translation, this maybe is the best route to take. In the case when the decision is to make this a private segment (non-routable to the outside world), NAT will be utilized. Although this design provides a greater level of security and granularity of control, routing and policy configuration become more complex. This model is also used to provide greater control over access to back-end systems from the publicly hosted ones, such as a database server.

Three-tier/N-tier Resources (Web, transaction, and database servers) are separated between different perimeter security devices. One device provides access to the external public network, whereas the second device provides access to the middle-tier private network. Finally, a third layer provides access from the middle tier to the back-end database components. Although this design provides an even higher level of security, the routing configurations and security policies become more complex than the two previous designs. Additionally, this design usually involves the added cost and maintenance of operating more than one network access control point. This particular design is best suited to a public application where sensitive information is maintained. Figure 6-4 depicts a logical representation of each of these DMZ models.

Internal Partitioning Models and Methods

Internal network security is beneficial to everyone, but it is especially beneficial when sensitive data needs to be shared within the corporate network. When people think about internal security, host and application security controls usually come to mind, but what about the placement of those systems as a method of security? The concept of host partitioning, although not entirely new, is becoming more common.

For example, a software development company may want to segregate its development environments from the business production network, keeping source code from prying eyes and keeping potentially unstable code off of the production network.

In the case of a Human Resource department, servers maintaining private information about employees may be kept on a separate secure LAN with strict access controls to the data therein.

Internal networks are often segregated by means of VLANs and layer 3 switching, but it is not uncommon to see a firewall providing access between virtual LANs in place of a traditional router. Application proxies are another method that can be used to control access between segments generally by the use of authentication; here users gain access for certain applications or protocols by authenticating.

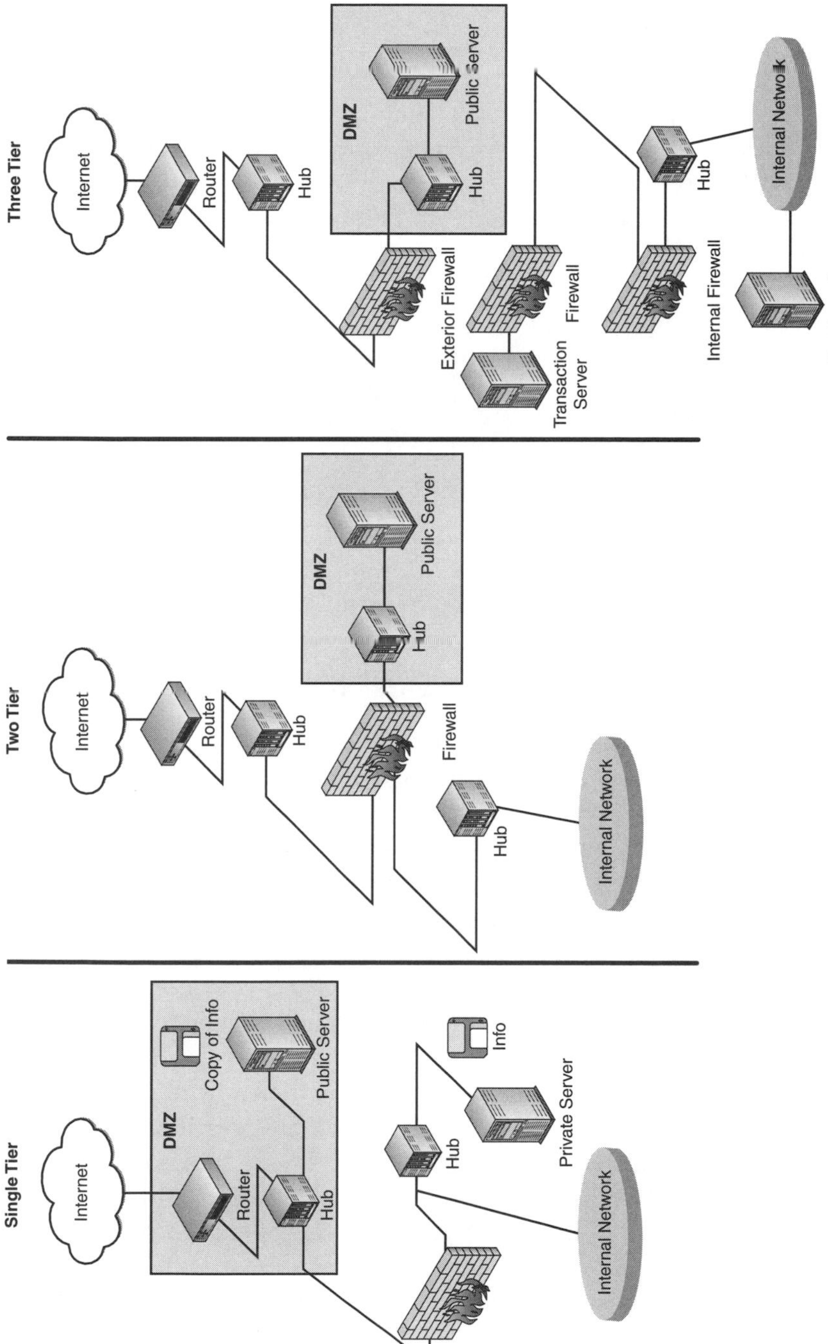

Figure 6-4 DMZ models

Analysis of Case Study #1—Corporate

MCC network is distributed across physical and geographic boundaries. This network serves thousands of employees in several offices around the globe. It provides the transport for communication and business activities between MCC, its partners, and customers. The underlying infrastructure is comprised of a fully meshed and redundant network. The following section outlines the proper approach to designing a workable security framework that adheres to company security requirements and does not present an impediment to business.

MCC Network Security Policy

MCC network security framework started by reviewing the requirements as set forth by the governing network security policy outlined in Chapter 2. From this analysis, MCC was able to create a matrix of requirements and compensating controls, which are listed in Table 6-2.

Physical layout of network MCC will maintain a private leased line network between its corporate headquarters and each of the satellite offices. This network will be fully meshed and redundant. All external Internet and Extranet access will be handled through communication links within the corporate and secondary backup data centers. MCC utilizes two separate providers for external Internet access. MCC utilizes BGPv4 to provide the necessary communication redundancy. To ensure the consistency and integrity of data replication between data centers, it is maintained over redundant private leased lines. Figure 6-5 depicts the physical layout of MCC's global network.

Remote, Extranet, and Internet access will be provided by separate wide area connections. In the case of extranet connections, a private leased line will be maintained for each business partner. Remote, Internet, and Extranet connections will pass through a firewall prior to being allowed access to a corporate network. This configuration provides the requirement that all public connections must be controlled via the perimeter firewall prior to accessing the private network. Internet access for corporate and satellite offices will be provided through proxy servers maintained at corporate and secondary data centers.

MCC utilizes private addressing internally. In the case of Extranet connectivity, all traffic will be translated to a private address space shared by

Table 6-2

Requirements and Compensating Controls

Requirement	Safeguard
MCC must control access between internal and external networks via perimeter firewalls. Access must also be controlled between publicly accessible servers and servers not directly accessible from the Internet via a DMZ firewall.	MCC will maintain perimeter firewalls for inbound and outbound traffic. User access to the Internet will be handled via proxy. This will enable MCC to provide authentication and content-filtering mechanisms to outbound Web traffic. Publicly accessible hosts will be accessible through the perimeter firewalls. Back office access from the Web server farm will pass through interior firewalls when required. Strict rules will enable access from specific Web servers to specific backend systems by protocol reducing the risk of unauthorized public access.
MCC must control access between internal networks of differing security and access requirements (accounting, payroll servers versus engineering development servers).	MCC will segregate its network by function and location.
Strict controls must be put in place for access through the modem pools and private dial networks.	Remote access devices will reside on separate networks from internal servers. All communication from these remote access LANs will pass through the perimeter firewall prior to being allowed to the production server networks.
Access to and from third-party managed networks must be controlled via the firewalls.	Each Extranet connection will terminate at a separate port on the perimeter firewall. Authentication is required at the firewall for all inbound connections from partner sites. Strict access controls will enable communication to specific production servers.
Internal network addresses must be hidden from external networks.	MCC will utilize RFC 1918 private address space internally. Perimeter and interior firewalls will provide translation services. Direct routing will not be allowed to the internal production servers.
Firewall documentation must be in place and as a minimum detail, the firewall policy and the rational for the inclusion of each individual rule should also be in place.	All rules will be documented and included within the configuration book for each firewall, proxy, or filtering router. Proper change management processes will be instituted for all production systems.

(continued)

Table 6-2

Requirements and Compensating Controls *(continued)*

Requirement	Safeguard
Strong password controls must be utilized on the firewalls and all routers. The firewalls and routers must provide adequate identification and authentication controls. Strong authentication must be utilized for remote administration of the firewalls.	Strong authentication must be utilized for remote administration of the firewalls. Firewall management will utilize a combination of Secure Shell (SSH) for secure console access, 128-bit secure socket layer (SSL) ,and proprietary encryption schemes (Checkpoint). Firewall administrators will use unique login accounts and will be required to change the passwords on a monthly basis.
The configuration of firewalls and routers must promote security for the internal network that is in line with MCC's security policy. For instance, access control lists must be developed that specifically restrict the access of incoming traffic that has an internal IP address. Source routing must be disabled in the routers and the firewall product to prevent IP address spoofing. Sensitive services (FTP, Telnet, TFTP, RLOGIN, and so on) must be filtered on inbound traffic by the firewall and routers via the port number. All redundant and unnecessary processes must be removed from the firewall. For instance, all compilers must be removed from the firewall host.	MCC will follow strict guidelines for firewall policy development. All rule changes will require a formal change request and must be reviewed by the MCC security analyst and business risk manager prior to implementation. No direct routing will be allowed inbound to the interior network. All inbound traffic will be directed to specific resources. MCC will utilize stateful firewall and anti-spoof filtering technology. MCC firewall services will be provided via hardened appliance solutions.
The firewall product selected must support stateful inspection rather than simple packet filtering solutions.	MCC will utilize stateful firewalls at the perimeter and interior junctions.

MCC and the particular Extranet partner. This method will be used to eliminate routing issues with Extranet partners, which utilize the same private addressing space currently in use by MCC. This also fulfills the requirement that MCC internal networks should be hidden from the public.

Each office will maintain a minimum of three distinct networks. Networks are to be segregated into specific functions. Traffic flow is carefully

Figure 6-5

MCC global network architecture

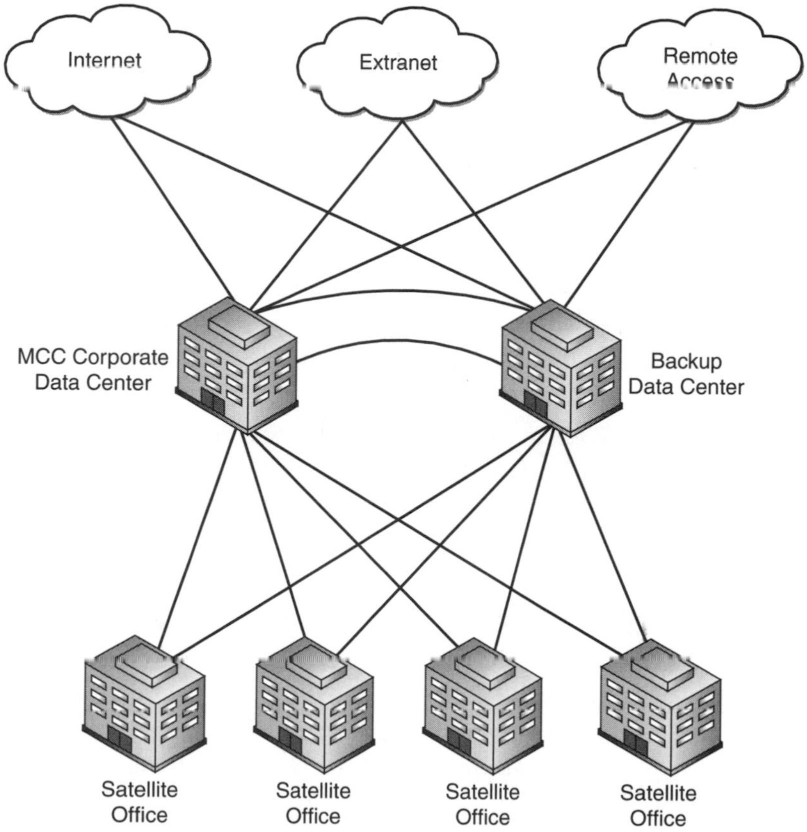

controlled between all network segments. In the case of communication between satellite offices and the corporate data centers, access control lists (ACLs) control traffic flow. For external connections (Remote access, Internet, and Extranet), this access control is provided by firewalls. The following outlines the common network segments deployed at the satellite and/or main data center locations

- **User** This network will contain user workstations and printer peripherals. (Public and private data will be stored on the servers.)
- **Servers** This network will maintain the corporate production servers for the specific locale. Each location will maintain e-mail, file, and application servers.

- **Vendor** This network will be used to provide access for visiting vendors. Vendor access will be restricted to the Internet only.

Naming conventions for network segments are as follows: location-network function. For example, in the New York office, the network on which user workstations are connected would be referred to NY-user. Although all sites will maintain the aforementioned network segments, specific locales may contain special purpose segments for specific functions.

- **Extranet** These networks will be maintained at MCC Corporate as well as a secondary backup facility and govern access to and from MCC partners and/or customers where applicable.
- **Web farm** This network will contain MCC public Internet servers and will be located at MCC Corporate and a secondary backup facility.
- **Remote access** This network will contain MCC VPN and remote access server (RAS) devices and provide an entrance point for employees and vendors to gain access remotely. This network will be maintained at MCC Corporate and a secondary backup facility.
- **Global network** This network will maintain MCC global, proxy, application, file, Intranet, and database servers and will be located at MCC Corporate and the secondary backup facility.
- **Corp-HR** This network will contain the human resource application and database servers and will be located at MCC Corporate and the secondary backup facility.
- **Development** These networks will contain the development and source control servers for MCC development departments. These networks will exist at several MCC offices. They are to be completely separated from the production networks and will utilize a separate private network for intra-network connectivity.
- **SANS** These networks will be comprised of MCC network-attached storage and will be maintained on isolated networks. These networks will exist within the corporate data centers in several MCC offices.

Logical Layout of Network

MCC network will be comprised of a mixture of Novell file and print, Windows NT and 2000, and UNIX servers. Network application/protocol makeup will consist of SAP, PeopleSoft, Oracle, Novell NCP, Windows SMB, custom applications, and standard TCP/IP such as SSH, HTTP, HTTPS, and FTP. Table 6-3 outlines the location and definition of MCC's critical resources and safeguards that will ensure their security.

MCC maintains several external connections. Table 6-4 outlines each of these connections, their locations, and specifics about how they fit within the security safeguards.

The following section lists the network security definitions for the terms used in Table 6-5, which shows the MCC Corporate network security definitions.

- **Source** Source network or user group
- **Destination** Destination network or user group
- **Application/protocol** Application or protocol governed by this security control
- **Action** Method of security control
- **Accept** Enable communication between source and destination
- **Authentication** Enable communication between source and destination once the source has been properly authenticated

Table 6-3

Critical Resources

Resource	Location	Comment
E-mail	Corporate global network and MCC satellite offices within the server networks	Public e-mail access will come into the MCC Corporate root e-mail servers and be delivered appropriately.
Human resources applications	Corp-HR network within the MCC Corporate and a secondary backup facility	Access by HR personnel only due to the sensitive nature of this information.
Development	Development networks	Will be completely isolated from production network and public access. A private Intranet will connect development offices.

Table 6-4

External Connections

Connection	Location	Comment
Internet	MCC Corporate and a secondary backup facility	All outbound Web access will be handled via application proxies and filtered for content. MCC will maintain separate proxy farms for internal staff and vendors. This will provide for concise reporting on Internet activity for employees and vendors.
Mega Financial Corp(MFC)	MCC Corporate and a secondary backup facility	MFC will require access to certain servers within the global network. Outbound traffic will consist of custom application traffic from finance and accounting servers to MFC.
World suppliers (WS)	MCC Corporate and a secondary backup facility	MCC requires access to WS ordering systems. This is custom application. MCC maintains a site-to-site VPN connection from the perimeter firewall cluster to WS firewall.
Web farm	Web farm network within the MCC Corporate and a secondary backup facility	Public access is required to MCC Web servers.
Remote access	These networks are maintained within the MCC Corporate and a secondary backup facility.	Remote access for employees and third-parties (non-extranet access, third-party Web developers) will be provided from the Internet. Users must authenticate to the remote access device, and then authenticate through the firewall prior to accessing the internal network. Firewall authentication utilizes a soft token system.

- **Encrypt** Encrypt the communication channel between the source and destination
- **Filter** Communication from the source and destination is filtered for content. (Web browsing is allowed to approved sites only.)
- **Inspect** Communication is allowed once the connection meets acceptance criteria (virus scan or malicious code check).

Table 6-5

Network Security Definitions for MCC Corporate

Source	Destination	Application/ Protocol	Action	Comment
Internet	Web farm	HTTP, HTTPS	Accept	Public access will be granted to MCC public Internet servers.
MCC-users	Global network	File sharing, application access	Accept	MCC users will be granted access to global resources.
MCC-HR	Corp-HR	SAP, PeopleSoft	Authenticate	HR personnel will be allowed access to corporate human resources once they authenticate to firewall(s).
Global network	HR satellite-servers	Exchange	Accept	E-mail connectivity will be allowed from central e-mail to satellite office's e-mail servers.
MCC-vendors	Corp-proxy	HTTP, HTTPS	Accept/Filter	Vendors will be allowed external access to the Internet. Content will be filtered.
MCC-vendors	Internet	SMTP, POP3, IMAP	Accept	Vendor will be allowed access to external e-mail.
Corp-proxy	Internet	HTTP, HTTPS	Accept/Filter	MCC employee will be allowed access to Internet. Content will be filtered.
MFC	Global network	HTTP, HTTPS, Application traffic	Authenticate	Extranet partners will be given access to specific servers once they have authenticated at the firewall.

Table 6-6 outlines network security for a typical satellite office.

Table 6-6

Network Security for a Typical MCC Satellite Office

Source	Destination	Application/ Protocol	Action	Comment
NY-user	NY-server	File, e-mail, and application access	Accept	User access will be allowed to local resources
NY-user	Global network	Application access	Accept	User access to will be allowed to global resources.
Corporate adminis-trators	NY-server	Remote access	Authenti-cate	Corporate access will be allowed to local resources for administration once authenti-cated through firewall(s).
NY-server	Global network	E-mail	Accept	E-mail connec-tivity will be granted from satellite e-mail servers to corporate e-mail servers.
NY-vendors	Corp-proxy	HTTP, HTTPS	Accept/ Filter	Vendors will be allowed access to the Internet via proxy servers at Corporate. Content will be filtered.
NY-vendors	Internet	SMTP, POP3, IMAP	Accept	Vendors will be allowed access to external e-mail.
NY-HR	Corp-HR	SAP, PeopleSoft	Authenti-cate	Local HR person-nel will be allowed access to corporate HR servers once they have authenti-cated at the firewall(s).

Analysis of Case Study #2—FinApp

MCC Financial must ensure investor protection and comply with the Security Exchange Commissions (SEC) regulations. The network security design has to be fault-tolerant and provide strong access and authentication controls. MCC chose to address the fault-tolerance issue by engaging a co-location vendor. The application resides in three separate data centers located strategically around the globe. A network of private leased lines provides redundant paths from center to center for application replication and from each center back to the MCC Financial corporate data center for administration, trader access, and central audit.

Authentication controls are provided via a number of mechanisms; in the case of trader authentication, a combination of soft token on the client side and digital certificate on the server side ensures the identity of each party. Authorization servers are located at the MCC Financial and co-location facilities. Time synchronization is required between MCC and the end users for soft token access. Application sessions are encrypted between client and server through 128-bit SSL. MCC has developed its applications to take advantage of soft token authentication; access controls are tied to the end-user soft token. Table 6-7 lists the requirements and compensating controls for the MCC FinApp security policy.

Physical Layout of Network

FinApp is hosted in three co-location facilities around the globe. These locations include New York City, London, and Hong Kong. Private wide area network (WAN) links connect these centers back to the MCC Financial data center.

In addition, each trading partner maintains at least one Extranet connection to the MCC Financial data center. These Extranet connections are facilitated over private WAN lines and VPN tunnels over the public Internet.

Each co-location facility is segregated into four separate networks:

- **Presentation** This network houses the front-end application server. These networks facilitate trading partner access to FinApp servers.

Table 6-7 MCC FinApp Security Policy: Requirements and Compensating Controls

Requirement	Safeguard
MCC security guidelines state that all communication channels for the application must be encrypted and strong authentication schemes must be implemented.	Trader access is allowed to the front-end application only. Each tier of the application is separated with a security control point between each communication tier (presentation, transaction, and backend data repository). All control points will be comprised of redundant stateful firewall pairs.
All trades are recorded and each transaction requires non-repudiation to ensure that identification for trading requests is accurate. Transaction information must be protected from tampering.	Audit servers are separated from production servers. Gap technology is used to provide isolation and one-way communication from production systems to local audit servers and local audit servers to central audit servers.
The system must be highly available in design.	Three separate co-location facilities house the application components. MCC utilizes multiple communication links, load balancers, and firewall and router pairs. All firewall pairs/clusters perform state synchronization to ensure session preservation in the event of fail-over and fail-back transition.

- **Middle tier** This network houses the transaction and business logic servers, which communicate between the front-end and the back-end processing systems.
- **Audit** This network houses the transaction logging and audit servers.
- **Data** This network houses the back-end databases.

Application development is handled at a fourth facility. Third-party developers use a combination of private WAN links and VPN technology to communicate to this fourth facility. This network is isolated from the main production networks. Application development consists of three networks. These include

- **Source** This network houses the source repositories.
- **Development** This network houses the production development environment.

- **Remote access** This network houses the VPN and remote access servers that enable telecommuting access into the Extranet for third-party developers.

The MCC Financial data center maintains connections to all trading partners and market feeds, as well as three co-location facilities. The network layout for the MCC Financial data center consists of the following:

- **Primary audit** This network houses the main audit repository.
- **Administration** This network houses the administrative users for the data center.
- **Server farm** This network houses the e-mail, domain name servers (DNSs), and file servers.
- **Trading partners** These networks service the trading partners.

Logical Layout of Network

FinApp is a distributed client-server application. The application is comprised of three tiers: presentation, transaction, and data.

The FinApp system is provided via a proprietary set of APIs that use TCP/IP protocols. Transaction components provide business logic and transaction services, utilizing HTTPS, structured query language (SQL), and custom TCP/IP ports. SQL database servers provide a data repository. A number of market feeds provide data services to the middle-tier application servers. The market services use propriety protocols. Figure 6-6 depicts the logical layout of MCC Financials network.

Table 6-8 outlines the location and definition of MCC Financials' critical resources and safeguards that will ensure their security.

MCC maintains several external connections. Table 6-9 outlines each of these connections, their locations, and specifics about how they fit within the security safeguards.

Table 6-10 defines MCC Financials' network security policies.

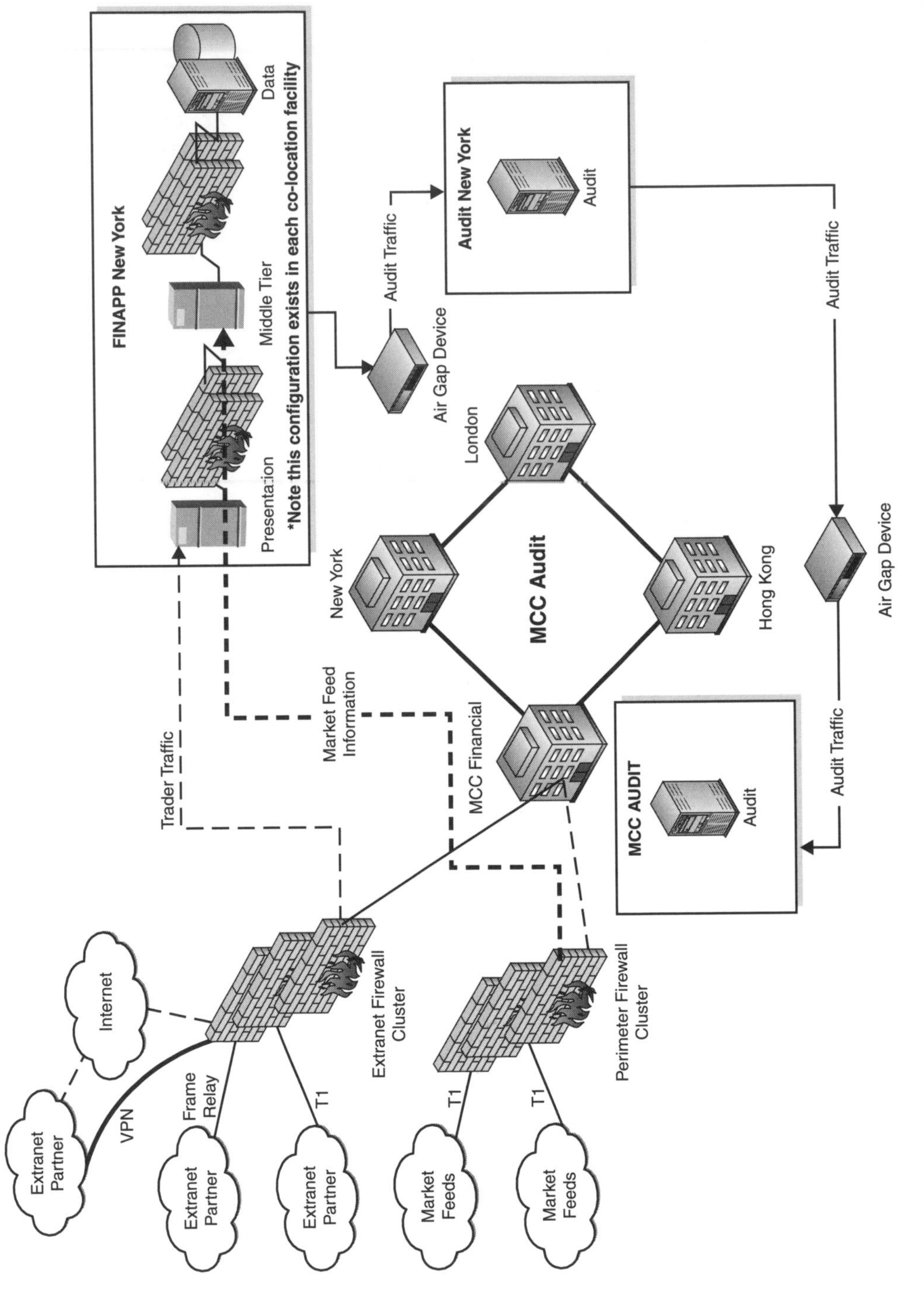

Figure 6-6 MCC financial network

Table 6-8

Critical Resources

Resource	Location	Comment
MCC databases	MCC co-location facilities	Database servers reside on a separate network. Only transaction servers have access into the database segment.
Market feeds	MCC Financial data center	Traffic passes through content inspection engines after being filtered through an exterior firewall.
Audit servers	Hosting facilities and MCC Financial data center	One-way air gap technology exists between server farms (all tiers) and the back end audit systems at co-location facilities, which communicate back to the primary audit server through additional one-way air gap links.

Table 6-9

External Connections

Connection	Location	Comment
Trading partners	MCC Financial data center	All Extranet connections terminate on separate firewall ports. All access into the data center will pass through an Extranet firewall(s).
Co-location facilities	MCC application service provider (ASP) provider	Each connection terminates at a dedicated firewall pair.
Market feeds	MCC Financial data center	Each connection comes in over a private network through a separate port on the perimeter firewall(s).

Analysis of Case Study #3—HealthApp

The MCC health care line of business (LOB) provides claims processing and brokerage quotation services. The current application architecture relies on maintaining a costly dial-up solution and closed application architecture. Claim disputes are currently processed via telephone only.

In an attempt to reduce cost and improve customer service, MCC is redesigning the health care claims-processing structure. The new solution will utilize Web technology and the Internet to facilitate claims and dispute processing. In addition, new features will give users access to such things as statements and payment and policy information.

Table 6-10 Network Security for FinApp

Source	Destination	Application/ Protocol	Action	Comment
Trading partners	Presentation segments	HTTP, HTTPS, custom protocols	Authenticate and encrypt	Access to front-end application servers will be allowed to traders once they have been successfully authenticated. All session traffic is encrypted.
Market feeds	Middle tier	Custom protocols	Inspect and accept	Access to market feed information from middle tier servers will be allowed. Traffic is always initiated out from the middle tier. No unsolicited traffic is allowed through the exterior firewall. All traffic is inspected for anomalies prior to being forwarded to servers.
Presentation	Middle tier	Custom protocols	Inspect and accept	Trader requests and processing are passed from the presentation servers to the middle tier servers. Information is directed from trusted host to trusted host by specific firewall rules. No outside initiated access is allowed to the middle tier.
Middle tier	Data	SQL	Accept	Access is allowed from the middle tier (transaction business logic) to the data segment (backend databases).
MCC data center	Co-location facilities	HTTP, HTTPS, custom protocols	Accept	Extranet traffic is allowed to the the co-location facilities. All traffic is authenticated prior to being routed.

Like the network security model, which supported the old system, this will need to be redesigned to provide the necessary safeguards for a publicly accessible application.

MCC HealthApp Security Policy

The health care industry is currently going through an overhaul to meet government-mandated regulations stemming from the Health Insurance Portability and Accountability Act of 1996 (HIPAA). MCC HealthApp will need to be in compliance with the regulation and certain controls will need to be implemented to ensure patient confidentiality, privacy, and efficiency. Table 6-11 outlines the security requirements as defined within the security policy and outlines the associated compensating controls.

Physical Layout of Network

HealthApp is hosted in the MCC and backup data centers. A disaster recovery site is also planned at a co-location provider. Data centers are connected via private leased lines. Each data center is segregated into four separate networks:

- **Public** This network houses the public Web servers, which comprise the user interface.
- **Application** This network houses the application and data servers.

Table 6-11 Requirements and Compensating Controls

Requirement	Safeguard
Confidentially of patient information	Application servers are not accessible from the public Internet. All data is stored encrypted within database tables. Communication between application servers and database servers takes place within the private network.
High availability	MCC utilizes redundant systems, communication paths, and data center facilities to ensure uptime. Network security integrity is maintained by the uses of redundant hardened access routers and firewall clusters.

- **Administration** This network houses the data center system administration's servers and consoles.
- **Development** This network houses application developers and systems.

Logical Layout of Network

HealthApp is a Web-based application. The front application is written in HTML and JavaScript. User access to the systems takes place over a 128-bit SSL (secure socket layer) session. Server and client side certificates are required to provide non-repudiation, where both parties (MCC and the end user) must instantiate their identity (through certificate presentation). MCC will issue and maintain both the server side and client certificates.

Application and data components use a combination of open database connectivity (OBDC) and SQL to communicate with each other. All private information is stored in encrypted format natively within the databases.

Table 6-12 identifies the critical resources that exist within the HealthApp architecture.

Table 6-13 depicts the various external connections present within the HealthApp network architecture.

Table 6-12

Critical Resources

Resource	Location	Comment
Internet and intra data center communication lines	MCC and backup data centers	MCC will maintain redundant communication and access control platforms to ensure connectivity in the event of a component failure. This will include multiple ISP connections through separate carriers, fault-tolerant firewalls, and networking infrastructure.
Databases	MCC and backup data centers	Back-end data repository for application and private data.
Development	MCC and backup data centers	Source code repository and development area.

Table 6-13

External Connections in the HealthApp Network Architecture

Connection	Location	Comment
Intra-data center	MCC and backup data centers	All communication between data centers is encrypted and carried over private leased lines.
Internet	MCC and backup data centers	Only the Web farm is accessible from the public Internet.

Table 6-14 outlines the overall network security for HealthApp.

Conclusion

Network security has come a long way since the days of the centralized mainframe model. The emergence of the Internet as a viable communication medium for businesses has introduced a multitude of security challenges. With industrial espionage and cyber-terrorism on the rise, security practitioners need functional solutions that address network security now more than ever. Deploying security policies and procedures ahead of the deployment of technology is key to providing an effective and functional network security design that protects your assets and enables you to conduct business in the face of these challenges.

Moving forward with a solid stance on policy and business requirements as a foundation, you can assess your particular environment to derive the necessary security solution. This involves the identification of your mission-critical resources, which types of traffic will exist on your network, and where network controls will be placed on your network to address these needs. From this knowledge, you can start to build a security framework that makes sense for your business and risk requirements. Once your framework has been defined, you can research which products and design strategies will work best for you.

References

Bobbitt, Michael. "(Un)bridging The Gap." *Information Security Magazine*, July 2000.

Gartner Group, Inc., "Firewall Market Magic Quadrant Update 2000."

Table 6-14

Network Security Definitions for HealthApp

Source	Destination	Application/ Protocol	Action	Comment
HealthApp users	Public	HTTPS	Authenticate and encrypt	Users will be allowed to access front-end Web servers once authenticated. All session communication including logon sequence is encrypted.
Public	Application		Inspect and accept	Communication is allowed from the Web servers to the application servers once sessions are inspected.
Adminis-tration	Application public	Web, maintenance traffic	Authenticate and accept	Administrative access is allowed to production systems once administrators successfully authenticate at the firewall.
Adminis-tration	Development	Maintenance traffic	Accept	Allows administrative access to development systems.

CHAPTER 7

Virtual Private Networks

Over recent years, the term virtual private network (VPN) has become a household name. With businesses realizing the fruits of secured private networking over otherwise public (unsecured) wires and airwaves, the demand for VPNs has grown tremendously. To meet this demand, numerous companies have been spawned, each with their own blend of functionality and protocol support. Although the basic premise of VPN technology is to secure data in transit, this is far from a complete security solution in and of itself. First, the security of the tunnel requires that its endpoints are authentic. This implies accuracy within the authentication mechanism employed. Secondly, we must ensure that data has not been modified while in transit from one location to the next. This implies a need for data integrity. Thirdly, we must be able to manage both the establishment and operation of our VPN tunnels. The likelihood that your corporation will employ more than one VPN-vendor solution is high. Enabling communication between these heterogeneous solutions will require the selection of appropriate authentication criteria, encryption, and tunnel properties. Although much attention is typically given to the election of the appropriate vendor solution to suit your business requirements, this will undoubtedly represent only a small piece of the puzzle. It is the configuration and management of your VPN solution that will affect your business operations on a daily basis. Understanding these concerns and the technology will enable you to deploy an effective solution.

What Is a VPN?

It is a widely accepted fact that Internet technologies have changed the way that companies do business in today's marketplace. The growing necessity for secure access to business-critical information and enterprise resources from various remote locations has brought virtual private network (VPN) technology to the forefront of IT initiatives. VPNs offer secure communications between network applications using a public or unsecured medium such as the Internet through the use of various technologies offering user authentication, data integrity, and access control. A VPN is not a single technology, but a complex interaction of different technologies. Systems, as advocated by industry renowned cryptographer Bruce Schneier, have several properties. They are complex, interact with each other, have emergent properties, and have bugs. "No system is perfect, and no technology is The Answer."[1] For companies to successfully utilize VPNs, it is critical that they obtain a complete understanding of the business's needs for virtual private networking as well as the knowledge of the current technology and effective implementations of these technologies. Let's take a closer look at the acronym to get a complete definition.

The virtual network in VPN means that the network is dynamic and the logical structure of the network is formed only of the network devices regardless of the physical structure of the underlying network (the Internet).[2] All service provider networking equipment is, in a sense, hidden from devices and users in the virtual network. What is of concern in building the secure virtual connection are the endpoints of the data transmission that establish and terminate the tunnel. These endpoint systems can be either hosts operating on underlying operating systems or special purpose appliances. Tunneling enables data streams to traverse the shared public network securely in a virtual pipe that is created between the two endpoints. An additional benefit that tunneling offers in hiding the under-

[1]Schneier, B. *Secrets & Lies: Digital Security in a Networked World*. New York: John Wiley & Sons, 2000.

[2]Kosiur, Dave. *Building and Managing Virtual Private Networks*: John Wiley & Sons, 1998.

lying network structure between the two endpoints is that companies can use private IP network addressing schemes for their internal networks without the concern of routing conflicts over the Internet.

Companies that use the RFC 1918 private IP addresses for internal network -addressing schemes would not be able to connect offices over the Internet, as these private addresses are not routable on the Internet. Encapsulating these packets at the entry point of the tunnel relieves this problem. Part of the packet encapsulation process performed by a tunnel endpoint includes adding a new official address in the IP header of the packet that corresponds to the other endpoint and is also routable over the public network. This functionality is available within a VPN solution, which we will address in some detail in the VPN Technology section of this chapter.

Another technology that addresses the issue of routing conflicts over the public Internet when connecting sites together is Multiprotocol Label Switching (MPLS). The MPLS solution is a scalable, service provider-focused technology that enables service providers to plan, provision, and manage IP VPN services according to a customer's service level agreement. MPLS is an involved technology that brings many benefits in addition to VPNs to IP-based networks; however, we will not cover MPLS. It is only mentioned because it is a technology used in service provider VPN offerings, sometimes in conjunction with the IP Security (IPsec) protocol for data privacy. For more complete information, see the Internet Drafts and RFCs from the Internet Engineering Task Force's (IETF's) MPLS Working Group at **http://www.ietf.org/html.charters/mpls-charter.html**. The issues of building virtual tunnels and handling IP address conflicts over the Internet are addressed through the use of these encapsulation and MPLS services.

The private portion of the VPN acronym is the foundation of this security solution. Private ensures that not only must a tunnel between two endpoints be established, but the communication must also include the provisioning for securing the data against eavesdropping and tampering by unauthorized parties. The primary purpose of VPNs is to secure the data in transmission. Four critical functions must be in place to ensure this:

- **Authentication** The source of the data transmission is who he or she claims to be and the destination is where you want the data to go.
- **Access control** Restricts unauthorized access to your networks.

- **Confidentiality** Prevents the viewing or copying of data as it traverses the network.
- **Data integrity** Prevents any tampering of the data in transmission.

Security services are a must in creating a VPN solution. Without the private portion of VPN, no VPN can exist. This may seem to be a simple statement, but it is critical. Some service providers and vendors market VPN offerings that are not true VPN solutions to customers. A provider may offer a VPN solution that provides a dedicated, switched path over the Internet in which only those companies that subscribe to this service would use this protected network. This is, in basic terms, referred to as a virtual circuit and offers no data security. Without any security services and cryptographic functions to secure the data privacy and confidentiality, this solution is not a VPN. Some people also consider traditional leased line connections or permanent virtual circuits, such as T1/T3 links or frame relay links, as Layer 2 VPNs. These data transmissions are also encoded (not encrypted) circuits that traverse unsecured service-provider equipment. Without the technologies in place to secure the data, these services are not true VPNs.

When deciding what VPN solution is right for your business, it is important to understand what each technology offers. A VPN system that offers only virtual circuits without encryption technologies is not a VPN solution. If your organization has to protect highly sensitive data, then the privacy of the data is undoubtedly one of the primary purposes for considering the deployment of a VPN system; this means that cryptographic processes will be required in the solution you choose. Almost all services and vendors today offer cryptography in the VPN solutions they provide, but it is important to realize that a VPN without cryptographic processes for data privacy is not a true VPN by definition.

A VPN is not intended to offer complete company-wide information security for all your data. Remember that a VPN system is only part of the overall security infrastructure. VPNs are designed to protect data streams while in transmission from one endpoint of the tunnel to the other endpoint—typically over a public-shared network. By restating this fact, it is clear that VPNs do not offer any data-packet security before or after the endpoints of the tunnel. These endpoints may be remote hosts, internal trusted networks, or un-trusted networks belonging to business partners. In any event, VPN technology does not address these issues; therefore, other areas of your overall security program will need to focus on these concerns.

Why VPNs?

Traditional networks that connect company sites or remote access users together to create a cohesive corporate-wide network typically run on T-1 links, frame relay, ISDN, xDSL, ATM, or simple dial-up over a PSTN. These technologies serve well in this process, but they lack many of the requirements that businesses have today. VPNs give us an answer to these requirements, offering direct-cost savings over other communications methods (such as leased lines and long-distance calls), as well as offering other advantages, including security, indirect cost savings as a result of reduced training requirements and equipment, increased flexibility, and scalability. These areas of focus are important to companies looking to stay competitive and profitable in a continually growing and dynamically-changing business environment.

Eighty-seven percent of network managers and managing directors think the security threat to corporate networks will grow during the next five years, according to a report commissioned by Siemens Network Systems. These types of statistics are borne out of the continuous number of high-profile security breaches realized by major global organizations, some costing millions of dollars, and a serious loss in customer confidence —all of which affect the bottom line. The high value and complexity of e-business initiatives today has made information security one of the hottest topics in the industry. VPNs are one of the many countermeasures against the infinite possibilities of threats in today's ever-changing network environment.

Data threats can present themselves in the form of network intrusions, IP address spoofing, packet sniffing, session hijacking, man-in-the-middle attacks, or a number of other attacks. The Internet has made tools freely available to anyone interested in engaging in an attack on any target of his or her choice. It is critical to identify the resources you are protecting and the methods by which you will protect these resources in your company security policy. Categorize all the private data that traverses the networks inside and outside the company, such as human resources (employee data, taxes, bonuses), databases (financial records, customer records), security information (user passwords, user accounts, network diagrams, network configuration files), business organization charts, and product-development information. To reap the many benefits of a VPN deployment, your company must be focused on the concerns of data security. In order to understand why security is critical in VPNs, we should first take a look at the driving forces deploying these technologies.

First and foremost are the cost savings of Internet VPNs as compared to the traditional private networks built using leased lines (T1/T3) that must deal with tariffs that are structured to include an installation fee, a monthly fixed cost, and a mileage charge, adding up to monthly fees that are greater than typical fees for leased Internet connections of the same speed. Additional savings come from the consolidation of network infrastructure. A company can reduce wide area network (WAN) connection setup and maintenance by replacing modem banks and multiple site-to-site circuits with single wide-area links at each location that carries remote user, site-to-site, and Internet traffic at the same time. Simplifying the overall network design and standardizing remote-client configurations to meet security requirements for remote-client access can also reduce the demand for technical-support resources. A company can even go a step further and outsource the VPN solution to one of the many service providers offering managed IP VPNs, which can further reduce support demands and costs. In addition to the cost savings of VPNs, there are benefits in the flexibility and scalability that VPNs offer are beneficial in an ever-changing corporate network.

As an organization grows, it may add new corporate sites or even new business-to-business (B2B) relationships that can increase business revenues through added services or operational efficiencies. VPNs offer a dynamically re-configurable solution to this need by allowing new connections to be added in a modular manner. This design also enables the uninterrupted provisioning of the local Internet links at each site if increased bandwidth at any one point is required. VPNs are also important due to the increase in mobile workers and the increase in residential broadband Internet services being deployed (xDSL and cable modems). Using a VPN connection, a mobile worker should be able to connect to any local service provider anywhere in the world and still successfully and securely access the corporate network. This type of anywhere access to corporate-networked resources is required to do business in today's world. Secure access to these resources is not only required, but is critical for the continued success of any business.

With the integration of a variety of technologies offering security and guaranteed Internet network performance via service provider agreements, VPN technology can be rightfully viewed as an enabling technology that enhances the organization's ability to achieve its goals and objectives.

Types of VPNs

Each type of VPN not only has specific requirements and priorities, but also comes with different possibilities in the way that it is implemented. VPNs have three different uses in today's business environment:

- Remote access for the mobile workforce
- Intranet connectivity or site-to-site
- Extranet connectivity or business-to-business (B2B)

Remote access VPNs between a corporate network and remote and/or mobile employees have specific requirements. Strong authentication is critical to verify remote and mobile users' identities in the most accurate and efficient manner possible. On the management side, remote-access VPNs require centralized management and a high degree of scalability to handle the vast number of users accessing the VPN. Remote access has become increasingly more important in the development of VPN solutions. Increased bandwidth for remote-access workers using VPNs with broadband technologies (xDSL and cable modems) is the number one driver for remote-access VPN deployment.

With Intranet VPNs that facilitate secure communications between a company's internal departments and its branch offices, the primary technology requirements are strong data encryption to protect sensitive information, reliability to ensure the prioritization of mission-critical applications, and scalable management to accommodate the rapidly growing number of new users, offices, and applications. These site-to-site tunnels are generally easier to deploy and manage with the exception of vendor interoperability issues. However, in developing a company-wide VPN solution, corporations should decide generally on a single-vendor platform. Vendors offer many scalable solutions to support a number of simultaneous encrypted tunnels, offer granular access-control capabilities, robust logging, and management, and even offer highly available solutions.

Extranet VPNs between a company and its strategic partners, customers, and suppliers require an open, standards-based solution to ensure interoperability with the various solutions that the business partners might implement. The accepted standard for Internet-based VPNs is the Internet Protocol Security (IPsec) standard, although provider-based MPLS VPN solutions are also unfolding. Some comprehensive VPN service offerings leverage both IPsec and MPLS for an integrated service provider solution that offers strong authentication and confidentiality via IPsec for sensitive data while using MPLS for broader connectivity. Issues of authentication via certificates in extranet connections are also an area of focus due to the need for a third-party Certificate Authority (CA). A CA issues these digitally signed, digital certificates to users within a public key infrastructure (PKI) that binds their identity to the certificate and to a public key listed in the certificate. A PKI consists of all the services that are used to issue, distribute, validate, and revoke public key certificates. These topics are covered in detail in Chapter 12.

Some of the largest and best-known examples of VPNs and extranets are offered by ANXeBusiness.[3] Originally, the Automotive Network Exchange (ANX) was organized and managed by the Automotive Industry Action Group (AIAG), but it is now a wholly owned subsidiary of Science Applications International Corporation (SAIC), one of the largest technology research and engineering companies worldwide. A penetrating look into ANXeBusiness beyond their start in the automotive industry offers some valuable insight into business-to-business (B2B) solutions using a wide range of industry standard technologies such as IPsec and Secure Sockets Layer (SSL) for communications security, LDAP-based directory services, and X.509-based PKI.

VPN Features—A Business Perspective

To achieve the goal of providing secure connectivity over a shared infrastructure, a VPN solution must offer some essential elements. Any organization looking to deploy a VPN system needs to be aware of these services. A VPN solution is only a piece of the overall corporate-security architecture, which should be driven by the corporate-wide information security policy. Understanding the features of VPNs will enable management and IT personal to select the appropriate solution that satisfies the business requirements while being in full compliance with the corporate-security policies.

[3]ANXeBusiness at **http://www.anx.com**. The first step in developing a VPN system is to understand the various types of VPNs as well as the purpose for which these solutions were designed. Looking at the features of VPNs to get a comprehensive view of the underlying technologies and deciding on the correct deployment strategy for your organization are the next steps in the process.

Security

One of the primary purposes of VPNs is to ensure that business critical traffic remains confidential via security mechanisms such as tunneling, encryption, key management, traffic separation, packet authentication, user authentication, and access control. Security is the foundation of VPN technology, which we will discuss at greater length later in the chapter, but it is critical to understand what is being secured with a VPN. Security functions are applied to data transmissions as these packets of information traverse the network. Security is only offered between the endpoints of the established tunnels in order to get packets from point A to point B safely. All of the security protocols and mechanisms are designed for this purpose.

Reliability

Organizations are looking to use VPN technology as an enabling strategy to provide access to enterprise resources in order to increase opportunities and revenues while lowering the costs of providing connectivity. To satisfy the predictable and extremely high service availability that is required in today's competitive business market, we must focus on two different components: hardware and software-communications services.

Using standard, proven platforms is a must for any medium to large-scale VPN deployment. Raw throughput, host or gateway encryption/decryption speed, simultaneous-supported tunnels, and product performance are all critical elements in the platform. High availability (HA) services are also critical because they satisfy some businesses' need to remain online and operational nearly non-stop. To this end, creating redundancy at the hardware and software levels provides for the automatic recovery of failed devices with limited interruption of service. Reliability of transmissions is still a concern of the Internet; many organizations are looking to include regional private networks as part of the solution in deploying VPNs. This may include provider-based private networks such as xDSL networks or provider-based MPLS solutions.

Manageability

Manageability is essential for cost-effective provisioning to enforce both security and Quality of Service (QoS) policies. Management systems need to quickly roll out new services and support QoS via Service Level Agreements (SLAs). The VPN solution should offer a comprehensive management platform that enables easy development and distribution of security policies, while offering complete accounting, auditing, and logging functionality. The management of your VPN solution is a critical piece of the infrastructure and should offer security administrators the ability to monitor both gateway and client VPN devices for any breaches, potential intrusions, and other security-related events. The monitoring of your VPN solution is paramount to maintaining a secure corporate security solution and adds to the overall security of the network environment. The management of security for VPNs is fairly straightforward, especially for authentication of users and access to network resources in accordance with the security policy. However, an understanding of tunnel management and the associated algorithms and key management to authenticate security gateways and remote hosts on the VPN is required. This is an important part of VPN management, which will be discussed later in this chapter.

It is also critical for any VPN solution to centrally control the security policies for both clients and gateways. This security-policy enforcement is especially important for the management and security of remote VPN clients. Centrally controlling client configurations means having the capability to audit the remote system, disable features like split tunneling, or query the network adapters on the remote system. Without this functionality, users could simply tie the Internet into your corporate network, using the remote client as the gateway, and security administrators would have no way of knowing this was happening.

Scalability

Scalability is a critical piece of a VPN solution, which must be able to adapt to the changing bandwidth and connectivity needs in a very dynamic market, accommodating for unplanned growth. In planning for growth, it is critical to select a product that offers support for the increasing number of users and faster performance in an upgradeable or modular-product line. Scalable solutions enable growth as the business grows and eliminates the need for forklift upgrades that have relatively high associated costs.

The choice of authentication methods for user and tunnel authentication can also impact the scalability of the solution. Shared-secret authentication is not a scalable solution. Other authentication systems such as certificates or token cards and other legacy systems may have increased associated costs that may hinder scalability. The issue of gateway performance is a critical factor in choosing a solution. Dedicated VPN-hardware solutions typically offer greater performance and scalability than software or integrated software and hardware solutions. Dedicated hardware typically offers accelerated-cryptographic processes built into the hardware solution, which are limited in the standard Intel or SPARC platforms, which results in better performance and a higher number of supported simultaneous tunnels; this translates to fewer gateway systems to deploy and manage.

Usability

For a VPN solution to be successful, the end users of the system should be able to seamlessly use the services provided. The building and tearing down of tunnels should be effectively transparent to end users, with the exception of authentication requests. The bottom line in this area is that if your end users (the support of which is the main reason for implementing this technology) can't use the technology without significant effort, then your deployment of a VPN solution will most likely result in failure.

Interoperability

Interoperability is important to purchasers because they need to know if a product from one manufacturer will work with a product from a different manufacturer. One size does not fit all when the big picture scenario comes into play. The Virtual Private Network Consortium (VPNC) is an organization that conducts conformance and interoperability testing of VPN products and is a good source of information on these issues. If your business is planning extranet connectivity with partners, then interoperability will be a major concern. Forging ahead with standards-based protocols like IPsec has greatly helped in this area, but different vendor implementations of the standards' specifications can still create major headaches.

Issues of interoperability are incredibly tricky and have posed a number of problems. As an example, two different vendor gateways may create an IPsec tunnel between the endpoints when vendor one initiates a connection, but fails in creating the tunnel if vendor two is the initiator. Another known issue is that two products that may fully interoperate with each other today could fail tomorrow due to a necessary upgrade in one of the gateway products. Focusing on interoperability issues will enhance the organization's ability to enable new forms of electronic commerce in the future and continue to capitalize on the cost advantages of VPNs as well as protect investment.

Quality of Service

Quality of Service (QoS) ensures prioritization of mission-critical or delay-sensitive traffic and manages congestion across varying bandwidth rates. QoS policies work by assigning a specific protocol, or applying a designated communication priority that either must be met or will be met to the best of the ability of the systems and networks that service the given protocol or application. QoS types of functions are queuing, network-congestion avoidance, traffic shaping, packet classification, and VPN-routing services. Network performance and VPN technology are inextricably interlinked. If VPN tunnels are to be transparent to the end users, they cannot act as a bottleneck in the connection.

However, because VPN links may not have the same allocated bandwidth found on your local area network (LAN), some focus must be placed on the performance of the links for remote users and other sites. Provider service and QoS is becoming increasingly critical with the deployment of technologies like Voice over IP (VoIP) and multimedia services. Obtaining a Service Level Agreement (SLA) with your provider can address the issues of QoS. A SLA can cover areas of installation, network availability, outage notification, latency, and packet loss, with latency defined as the average round-trip transmission on the provider network. SLAs for international connections may differ in the latency guarantees from the provider, with around 80ms transmissions domestically compared to around 120ms internationally.

Multiprotocol Support

Protocol support is an issue that may be of concern when dealing with legacy systems. Although a majority of organizations and the Internet operate on the IP protocol, other protocols may be in use on your network such as Novell Netware's Internetwork Packet Exchange (IPX). If the IPX protocol, for example, is in popular use within your corporate network, this can be a problem when a VPN solution that is IPsec based is implemented because IPsec is designed for encapsulating only IP packets and does not tunnel non-IP packets. However, vendor implementations of IPsec (Cisco VPN5000) are available that do tunnel other protocols within IP such as IPX and Microsoft NetBIOS by using IP header extensions. As long as the tunnel endpoints that establish and terminate the tunnel are IP, you can tunnel just about any protocol over the tunnel connection, making IPsec a viable multiprotocol solution after all. The Point-to-Point Tunneling Protocol (PPTP) and Layer 2 Tunneling Protocol (L2TP) have native multiprotocol support in their tunnels, but may not scale to the needs of a large enterprise VPN solution or offer the necessary security. If this is the case, you may have to include upgrading these non-IP-based services to run on IP in order to deploy an effective VPN system that will offer access to all the necessary corporate resources.

VPN Technology

During this time, when the Internet provides essential communication among millions of people and is being increasingly used as a tool for anything from secure commerce and payments to private communications and password protection, security becomes a tremendously important issue. Cryptography is one of the essential aspects of secure communications. Although cryptography is not itself sufficient for providing this security, it is one of the key components, and gaining an understanding of these systems and protocols is a cornerstone to the successful deployment of a VPN solution. In this section, we will look at some of the cryptographic processes and other systems employed for security within VPN technologies. Because this area of technology is so vast, we will focus on what the technologies are and how they apply to VPN systems. We will not address cryptanalysis, crypto history, or the like. Interested readers can look at the reference section for more detailed and comprehensive coverage of these other areas.

Cryptography

Cryptography is the science of writing in secret code, it has been around for centuries. In data and telecommunications, cryptography is necessary when communicating over any un-trusted medium, which includes just about any network, particularly the Internet. Within the context of this communication, specific security requirements are necessary as discussed earlier: authentication, privacy, integrity, and non-repudiation. These show us that cryptography can be used for authentication in addition to data protection. Generally speaking, three forms of cryptographic schemes are available to accomplish this security, as shown in Figure 7-1: secret key (or symmetric) cryptography, public key (or asymmetric) cryptography, and hash functions. In the first two cases, the initial unencrypted data is referred to as plaintext, which is encrypted into ciphertext and usually decrypted back into usable plaintext.

Secret Key Cryptography

Secret key cryptography uses a single key for both encryption and decryption. Because the same key is used for both functions, secret key crypto is also called symmetric encryption. The main problem with this technology

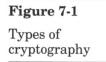

Figure 7-1

Types of cryptography

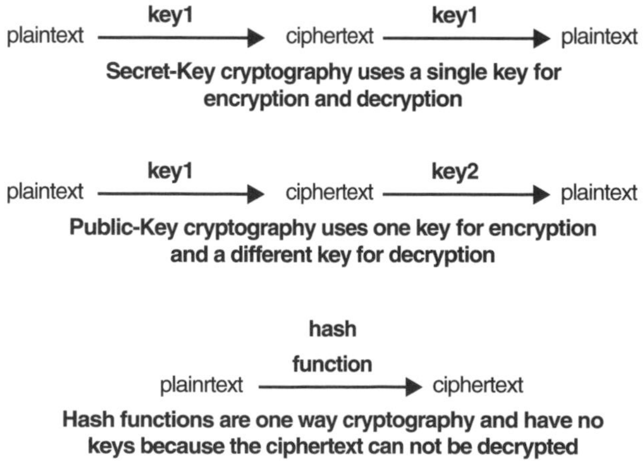

is the distribution of the key, which creates serious scalability issues. The most common secret-key schemes used today are the Data Encryption Standard (DES), designed by IBM in the 1970s, and Triple-DES (3DES) introduced in the late 1970s, early 1980s. 3DES became more prominent in 1998 after DES was hacked, yielding pressure from cryptography advocates on the U.S. government to raise export restrictions in place. A number of other secret key crypto algorithms are offered in VPN solutions.

- CAST
- International Data Encryption Algorithm (IDEA)
- Rivest Cipher 2 (RC2)
- RC4
- RC5
- Blowfish
- Twofish
- Advanced Encryption Standard (AES)

Public Key Cryptography

Public key cryptography (PKC) uses one key for encryption and another for decryption. Generic PKC employs two keys that are mathematically related although knowledge of one key does not allow someone to easily determine the other key. One key is used to encrypt the plaintext and the other key is used to decrypt the ciphertext, which is why this approach is also called asymmetric cryptography. In this system, one of the keys is designated as the public key and may be advertised as widely as the owner wants. The other key is designated as the private key and is never revealed to another party. Sending messages under this scheme is straightforward. The sender, for example, encrypts some information using the intended receiver's public key; the receiver decrypts the ciphertext using his or her own private key. This method could also be used in both directions at the same time. For example, the sender could encrypt the plaintext first with his or her own private key and then encrypt again with the receiver's public key; the latter scheme might be used where it is important that the sender cannot deny sending the message (non-repudiation). The following are widely used public key crypto algorithms used in VPN technologies:.

- RSA
- Diffie-Hellman

- Digital Signature Algorithm (DSA), which was part of the National Institute of Standards and Technology (NIST) proposed Digital Signature Standard (DSS)

RSA has been the mainstay in public key systems for over two decades, but other systems such as Elliptical Curve Cryptography (ECC) offer an alternative. ECC is exciting because of the potential to provide similar levels of security compared to RSA but with significantly reduced key sizes, presumably offering faster processing, and lower demands on memory and bandwidth, which are critical when moving into the space of mobile VPN solutions.

Hash Functions

Hash functions are also called message digests and one-way encryption. They are algorithms that transform plaintext mathematically so that the contents and length of the plaintext are not recoverable from the ciphertext. Hash algorithms in VPNs are typically used to provide a digital fingerprint for authentication of data transmissions. Hash functions are also commonly employed by many operating systems to encrypt passwords. The most common hash functions used for commercial applications today are the family of message digest (MD) algorithms (MD2, MD4, MD5) and the Secure Hash Algorithm (SHA). Another cryptographic algorithm called HMAC (for hash-based message authentication code) is available that is used with MD or SHA for improved authentication. This was developed due to susceptibility in keyed MD5 to collision attacks, where a matching hash value can be computed for two different messages.

Choosing Cryptography

Although we are not even scratching the surface in our discussion of cryptography, you may be asking why do we need so many complicated encryption technologies? Each of these schemes is best suited for specific applications when implemented in VPN systems. Secret keys are great for message encryption, public keys are best for key exchanges for secret key systems and non-repudiation, and hash functions are well designed for ensuring data integrity. Public key cryptography could also be used for message encryption, but because secret key cryptography offers significantly faster processing for this, public keys are not employed for this function.

When selecting the appropriate algorithms, it is important to consider certain issues that arise with key lengths and choosing public or private algorithms. With regard to key lengths, you should first determine the sensitivity of your data and how long it will be sensitive and need protection. Then select encryption algorithms and key lengths that will take longer to break than the length of time the data will be sensitive. If you submit to Moore's Law that computing power doubles every 18 months, you can begin to understand the need to address concerns of key lengths for data privacy as they relate to the dynamic changes in computer system power that is used to crack these keys and comprise your data. For an in-depth analysis of key lengths and the strength they provide in securing your data, review Chapter 7 of *Applied Cryptography* by Bruce Schneier (2nd edition, John Wiley & Sons, Inc., 1996).

The issues associated with public and private code are simple to address. Most experienced security engineers will demand open-source code for anything related to security. Because security has little to do with functionality, no amount of beta testing can uncover security flaws, leaving the evaluation of code in cryptographic algorithms or security protocols as the only means to accomplish this. The only really effective way of achieving this type of evaluation is by allowing the experts in the security community around the world to evaluate the code in an open-source environment. This is a proven methodology as seen in a variety of programs and protocols that have never been broken such as PGP, SSL, S/MIME, IPsec, and SSH. The bottom line is that when choosing a VPN solution, make sure it incorporates the use of public algorithms and not proprietary solutions. As we can see, many cryptographic technologies are involved in creating secure communications, and many of these technologies are employed in the various protocols and systems designed for VPNs.

Authentication Systems

As we start distributing data through the use of VPN technology, we realize the need for authentication. It is a vital part of a VPN security structure to reliably authenticate users, services, and networks to control access to your organization's resources. These systems offer different authentication processes and purposes than the cryptographic algorithms MD and SHA. These authentication systems are based on one or more of the following attributes: something you know (passwords), something you have (token card) or something you are (fingerprints or retinal scans). It's generally agreed upon in the security industry that simple authentication using only a single method is not adequate protection. It is typically recommended that strong authentication that utilizes at least two of the authentication methods be used. Authentication will be required at several levels.

First, it is required that each VPN endpoint authenticate with the other VPN device that it is communicating with. This requires that device A and device B have properly exchanged information (passwords, keys, certificates, and so on) to authenticate before they begin the encryption/decryption or authentication/verification of communications. This is authenticating the tunnel. Second, it may be necessary (as in the case of the remote laptop users) to follow up with user authentication to ensure that the person in possession of the device is who he or she claims to be. This can be in the form of simple passwords, one-time passwords (S/Key), password systems using Terminal Access Controller Access Control System (TACACS), Remote Authentication Dial-In User Service (RADIUS), hardware-based tokens (token cards, smart cards, PC cards), or biometric IDs (fingerprint, voice print, retinal scan). These authentication methods provide an extra measure of protection to mitigate the risks of lost or stolen devices. Some of these systems also offer authorization and accounting, which are typically required as part of the management capabilities of the overall VPN system. In designing the authentication portion of your solution, you can combine some of the authentication systems, such as using tokens with a RADIUS system to improve the strength of authentication.

The technologies we've discussed surrounding encryption, authentication, and key cryptographic systems are all used by the security services of a public key infrastructure (PKI) that offers key generation and distribution mechanisms, which can be critical to the deployment of a VPN system. A PKI enables an organization to use keys and digital certificates, which are electronic objects used to issue and validate public keys, as well as manage these keys, certificates, and security policies. Although secret key encryption is easier and faster, the management of secret keys in a scaling network environment is problematic. Public key systems offer a solution to key management as well as advantages in creating digital signatures. Whether your company serves as its own Certificate Authority (CA) or uses a third-party CA (which is typically necessary when creating extranets or any external B2B communications), some form of a PKI may be required when deploying your VPN solution. The topic of certificates, key distribution, certificate revocation, and certificate authorities is covered at great length in Chapter 12 of this book.

Tunneling and Security Protocols

The primary component of a VPN is security. Different protocols and technologies are available to achieve the desired security measures, but the focus of this section will be on the three widely used protocols: IPsec, PPTP, and L2TP. Additionally, other tunneling protocols such as SSH and Socks v5 offer application layer tunnels as well as various implementations of tunnels (cascaded tunnels, nested tunnels, or end-to-end tunnels) that may be required in your deployment based upon the requirements of your VPN solution.

The Socks v5 protocol offers an application layer VPN by providing desktop-to-server authentication and encryption. Although Socks v5 is a viable open Internet-standards protocol for a VPN solution, it is does not have the market share or focus of the many VPN solution providers that offer OSI Layer 2 (link) and Layer 3 (network) solutions. SSH is also a widely used application layer tunneling protocol that uses a public key cryptographic system to ensure security and is freely available by means of the OpenSSH initiatives. The SSH protocol suite offers a secure replacement for Telnet, rlogin, FTP, and other programs in addition to tunneling capabilities. Although these application-tunneling protocols offer exceptional security, they are not widely deployed in corporate-wide strategic VPN solutions, but are often deployed as a tactical solution to satisfy more specific security concerns.

Each of these three VPN protocols provides different levels of security and ease of deployment; however, the standardization process has made the IP Security Protocol (IPsec) and the Layer 2 Tunneling Protocol (L2TP) the protocols of choice although the Point-to-Point Tunneling Protocol (PPTP) is the most widely used for remote access connections mainly because of its integration in the Microsoft operating systems. All three protocols support tunneling, but PPTP and L2TP are strictly tunneling protocols. The tunneling mechanisms differ in terms of what is done to the data for encryption and authentication, the OSI layer they operate at, and the headers that describe the data transmission and packet handling. PPTP, L2TP, and Cisco's Layer 2 Forwarding Protocol (L2F) are all designed to work at Layer 2 of the OSI model. IPsec is the only protocol engineered for Layer 3, or the network layer of the OSI model. As the industry emerging standard in VPN solutions, IPsec has become the protocol of choice to build the best VPN system because it offers strong security, encryption, authentication, and key management. IPsec is designed to handle only IP packets. When dealing with VPNs in a multiprotocol non-IP network environment,

PPTP or L2TP may be more suitable. When developing your VPN solution, consider the strengths and weaknesses of each protocol and how the protocol will work in your business environment.

Each of the VPN protocols or protocol suites specify their own allowed algorithms for data encryption. We briefly discussed many of these cryptographic functions earlier, but we will not go into any great lengths about each of the algorithms available. Once again, you can reference many available cryptographic materials for all the in-depth mathematical details. Instead, we will concern ourselves with learning what each technology is designed to do, and focus on some of the security concerns with the individual protocols, which will help you in deciding the appropriate technology to deploy for your business.

PPTP

Driven at the onset by the increasing numbers in the mobile workforce, the Point-to-Point Tunneling Protocol (PPTP) was developed by the PPTP Forum consisting of the following organizations: Ascend Communications, Microsoft Corporation, 3Com/Primary Access, ECI Telematics, and U.S. Robotics. With Microsoft's market share in the PC operating system market coupled with their support of PPTP on the NT server platform version 4.0 and above, and the offering of a free PPTP client in their desktop operating systems, PPTP has become the most widely used protocol for creating dial-in remote access VPNs. It is important to realize that Microsoft has implemented their own version of the IETF PPTP standard, developed out of the vender consortium; although their version of PPTP is not standardized, it is the de facto standard for PPTP deployments. Most vendor products use Microsoft's version of the protocol. The PPTP protocol was designed for secure-remote access client connections and did not support network-to-network tunneling until the release of Routing and Remote Access Server (RRAS) for NT 4.0 in 1997. Due to the lack of key management controls in the PPTP architecture, authentication and encryption are controlled via Compression Control Protocol (CCP), Challenge Handshake Authentication Protocol (CHAP), or other Point-to-Point Protocol (PPP) extensions or enhancements that rely on secret passwords. For that reason, PPTP is not a very good choice in creating medium- or large-scale VPN networks that offer site-to-site connectivity. Instead, PPTP is best suited for remote access connections.

The PPTP protocol was designed to allow the PPP, which is the most commonly used protocol for dial-up access to the Internet, to be tunneled through an IP network in a client-server architecture to offer VPN support for these existing dial-access solutions. The PPTP protocol enables functions of the existing Network Access Servers (NAS), used to terminate PPP connections, to be separated using the client-server design. Call control and management of the connection is done by the client and server endpoints. PPTP has two parallel components: a control connection between the client and server over TCP and an IP tunnel used to transport the Generic Routing Encapsulation (GRE) PPP packets for user sessions. Working at Layer 2 of the OSI model, PPTP encapsulates the PPP packets using a modified version of GRE, which gives PPTP the capability to handle any supported network layer protocol, such as IP, IPX, and NetBEUI.

It's clear that PPTP is best suited for remote access VPNs, but questions about the security provided by the widely used Microsoft implementation of PPTP have been raised and addressed by industry security experts. In a paper from Counterpane Systems, a full analysis is done on the security of the Microsoft implementation of PPTP, which shows how to break both the challenge/response authentication protocol (Microsoft CHAP) and the RC4-based encryption protocol (MPPE), as well as how to attack the control channel in Microsoft's implementation.[4] Microsoft has countered with security updates to the protocol to address some of the concerns, but it is still recommended that the Microsoft PPTP protocol not be used in VPN systems that are deployed in order to protect sensitive data. PPTP may be an appropriate and simpler solution to deploy in smaller organizations that may only need a limited regional VPN, supporting small numbers of mobile workers.

When deploying a PPTP solution of any size, as with other tunneling protocols, you must be aware of access restrictions for mobile workers based on their connection into the Internet. The PPTP protocol uses GRE, which initiates a connection to a PPTP server or gateway device on TCP port 1723. This can create a problem for any mobile workers attempting to connect to your corporate network from within another corporate local area network (LAN), where those user connections will most likely pass through a firewall where the GRE service may not be permitted. This is not the case when dialing into any service provider Point of Presence where this network service is not filtered.

---

[4]Bruce Schneier and Mudge, *Cryptanalysis of Microsoft's Point-to-Point Tunneling Protocol* (PPTP): Counterpane Systems, 1998.

L2TP

The Layer 2 Tunneling Protocol (L2TP), defined in RFC2661, is a protocol for tunneling PPP sessions over various network types. The IETF working group has joined the PPTP group efforts with Cisco's Layer 2 Forwarding Protocol's (L2F's) initiatives to develop L2TP. The L2TP protocol is the successor to PPTP and L2F, and is being defined within the IETF's standards committees. The developmental efforts associated with this protocol, therefore, do not focus completely on the Windows NT platform as PPTP had. Because L2TP has not yet seen wide deployment in replacing PPTP, we will not focus on the protocol. According to Infonetics Research, an average of 80 percent of remote-access workers are using PPTP clients for VPNs, with 13 percent using IPsec clients in the U.S. in the year 2000, with the movement in the market toward increased IPsec implementations. If you are interested in L2TP, you can reference the IETF Web site for any associated RFCs.

IPsec

The Internet and the TCP/IP protocol suite were not built with security in mind and were never initially intended for the commercial-grade financial transactions that they are now used for. In response to this issue, the IETF formed the IP Security Protocol Working Group, which in turn developed the only Layer 3 IP Security protocol (IPsec). The first protocols comprising IPsec, for authentication and encryption of IP datagrams, were published by the IETF back in 1995, which laid out the IPsec architecture that uses a number of standardized cryptographic technologies. IPsec is not a single protocol, but a suite of protocols that provide a mechanism to maintain data integrity, authentication, and privacy for IP. Although intended primarily for IP version 6 (IPv6), IPsec is also employed in the currently used IP version 4 (IPv4). Three main components form the building blocks of the IPsec protocol suite:

- **Authentication Header (AH)** For packet authentication
- **Encapsulating Security Payload (ESP)** For packet encryption and/or authentication
- **Security Associations (SA)** Defines the security policy to be used in managing the secure communication between two nodes

AH/ESP The IP Authentication Header (AH) provides a mechanism for data integrity and data-origin authentication for IP packets using the hashing algorithms HMAC with MD5 or HMAC with SHA-1. Use of the IP AH is indicated with the value 51 in the IPv4 Protocol field or IPv6 Next Header field in the IP packet header. This can be useful information when doing data-packet analysis during a testing phase of your implementation or when creating filters through existing firewalls during the deployment phase. The need for the latter, of course, depends on the VPN architecture designed.

The IP Encapsulating Security Payload (ESP) provides message integrity and privacy mechanisms. As in AH, ESP uses HMAC with MD5 or SHA-1 authentication; privacy is provided using DES-CBC encryption. Use of the IP ESP format is indicated by placing the value 50 in the IPv4 Protocol field or IPv6 Next Header field in the IP packet header.

The IPsec authentication scheme for both AH and ESP uses the HMAC authentication code, which uses a shared secret key between two parties, rather than public key methods for message authentication. The generic HMAC procedure can be used with just about any hash algorithm although IPsec specifies support for at least MD5 and SHA-1 because of their widespread use. In HMAC, both parties share a secret key. The secret key is employed with the hash algorithm in a way that provides mutual authentication, but at the same time, prevents the key from being transmitted on the line. IPsec key-management procedures will be used to manage key exchange between the two parties via Security Associations.

Security Associations Before two parties can exchange secure data that is authenticated and encrypted, those parties need to agree on which algorithms will be used, how the key exchange will take place, how often keys will need to change, and then actually exchange the keys. All of these values are packaged together in a Security Association (SA) to facilitate secure communication between two nodes that are central to the IPsec Protocol. Authentication and confidentiality using AH or ESP use SAs; a primary role of IPsec key exchange is to establish and maintain SAs. SAs are logical, uniquely defined and unidirectional, or one-way connections between two communicating IP endpoints that provide security services to the traffic it carries using either AH or ESP procedures. The endpoints of the tunnel and can be an IP host or IP security gateway, which is a VPN-enabled network device. Providing security to the more typical scenario of two-way (bi-directional) communication between two endpoints requires the establishment of two SAs (one in each direction).

Two types of SAs are defined in IPsec, regardless of whether AH or ESP is employed. A transport mode SA is a security association between two hosts that provide the authentication and/or encryption service to the higher layer protocol. Only IPsec hosts support this mode of operation. A tunnel mode SA is a security association applied to an IP tunnel. In this mode, an IP header specifies the IPsec destination and an encapsulated IP header specifies the destination for the IP packet. Both hosts and security gateways support this mode of operation and it is considered the more secure of the two.

Before we understand the importance of SAs, we should first understand how we establish them. These tasks can be accomplished in one of two ways. The simplest form of SA and key management is manual management. In this method, a security administer manually configures each system with the key and SA management data necessary for secure communication with other systems. This was the method used by product vendors and the S/WAN (secure WAN) initiative to do almost all interoperability testing of IPsec products until the end of 1997. Manual techniques are practical for small, reasonably static environments, but they do not scale well due to the nature of shared-key setups. For a successful deployment of IPsec, however, a scalable, automated SA and key management scheme is necessary. Several protocols have been defined for these functions.

- The Internet Security Association and Key Management Protocol (ISAKMP) defines procedures and packet formats to establish, negotiate, modify, and delete security associations. It also provides the framework for exchanging information about authentication and key management, but it is completely separate from key exchange.
- The Oakley Key Determination Protocol (OAKLEY) describes a scheme by which two authenticated parties can exchange key information. OAKLEY uses the Diffie-Hellman key exchange algorithm.
- The Internet Key Exchange (IKE) algorithm is the default automated key management protocol for IPsec, which is the result of combining both ISAKMP and Oakley protocols.

Key exchange is closely related to the management of security associations (SAs). When you need to create an SA, you need to exchange keys, and IKE is the framework that wraps all the required pieces together and delivers them as an integrated package.

IPsec Concerns Although IPsec is probably the best solution currently available for VPN implementations and the solution being reviewed or deployed by large enterprises and ISPs, it is not without fault. Issues that deal with Extended Authentication, NAT, and interoperability surround IPsec implementations. ISP support and overall complexity of the IPsec Protocol standard are also of concern for some security practitioners. Perhaps this raises concerns about the security actually implemented by IPsec. Let's take a look at some of these concerns.

Authentication is required in building IPsec tunnels where IKE is the standard method using either pre-shared keys or stronger authentication via public key cryptography (raw keys or embedded in X.509 digital certificates). In small deployments, key pairs and certificates can be configured manually, but in larger VPNs, a PKI can be used to manage certificate enrollment, distribution, and verification. To date, few companies have a PKI system in place for such authentication and instead, would like to integrate this into legacy-authentication systems, primarily RADIUS, but also TACACS+, two-factor tokens like RSA SecurID, and one-time passwords. The issue here is that none of these legacy methods are directly compatible with standard IKE because it provides mutual two-way device-level authentication and methods like RADIUS provide one-way user-level authentication. The open-ended interaction of these authentication systems is not supported in the IKE standard so the IETF responded back in 1997 with XAUTH and later in 1998 with Hybrid Authentication to address this issue.

To better understand the issues, let's examine XAUTH, which inserts a new exchange in the middle of IKE after device-level authentication (phase one). With XAUTH, an IPsec gateway can prompt a client for extended authentication in the form of a username and password, for example. If the client's credentials are approved, phase two of the tunnel setup continues. All of the legacy user authentication systems are supported by XAUTH (CHAP, RADIUS, TACACS+, two-factor token authentication (SecurID, Defender), one-time passwords, and S/Key); however, issues surround XAUTH as it is vulnerable to man-in-the-middle attacks, among other things. Because of this, an enhancement to XAUTH was developed called Hybrid Authentication, which offers strong authentication and addresses concerns found in XAUTH. With both Hybrid and vanilla XAUTH, the open-ended exchange between IKE phases can inhibit gateway-client interoperability with products that do not support XAUTH. This means that if you are going to use legacy-authentication systems, it may be necessary to use one vendor for the complete solution due to the interoperability issues. The IP Security Remote Access Group (IPSRA) is addressing issues of user authentication in the IPsec protocol in an attempt to standardize this process.

The issue with using NAT and IPsec is that NAT changes IP header information, which causes failures in the various protocols employed for IP security within the IPsec framework. Of course, this depends on your implementation and where NAT is being done in the end-to-end tunnel communication, but in any case, it is something to be aware of in deployment. Using the AH protocol with NAT can fail because changing the IP headers causes a violation in AH. Failure can also occur when using the ESP protocol with NAT port translation in IPsec transport mode because the algorithms of ESP protect the port numbers.

The IETF is working to standardize the encapsulation of IPsec in User Datagram Protocol (UDP) to address these issues of NAT and IPsec operability. Vendors like Cisco/Compatible Systems have already implemented IPsec clients that use the IKE standardized UDP port 500 to allow IPsec packets to pass through a NAT process without issue.

Cooperation of your service provider can be important in successful IPsec remote-access deployment. Some ISPs have implemented filters blocking IPsec protocols (such as 500/udp (ISAKMP/IKE), AH Protocol 51, and ESP Protocol 50), effectively shutting down client VPN access. Some ISPs have initiated higher rates for these "business class" services in an attempt to gain higher revenues for increased bandwidth usage that the IPsec protocol causes. In deciding on what providers you will use, make sure that your agreement includes provisioning for IPsec traffic.

Issues with the IPsec protocol can be reviewed in the complete analysis by the Counterpane team.[5] Much of the concern derives from the results of developing cryptographic protocols by committee, where the issues of complexity creep into the final outcome, creating security issues. If the IPsec protocol were streamlined to support only the necessary algorithms to offer a secure protocol, it would be far better than the results we've seen to date.

If you are planning a global VPN solution that provides the best offered security, supports both network-to-network and client-to-network tunnels while still complying with any national restrictions on key strengths, then

[5]Ferguson, Neils and Bruce Schneier. A *Cryptographic Analysis of IPsec*: Couterpane Systems, 1998.

the options and flexibility of IPsec are a must, regardless of the issues with the protocol. You will see all of the technologies we have discussed within the VPN products on the market and will need to understand them especially when you are in the testing and implementing phases of your deployment. Gaining an understanding of all of these technologies and the protocols involved in creating VPNs will enable you to make the best choices when designing and implementing a solution.

VPN Solutions

VPNs are not just encrypted tunnels, but encompass an entire spectrum of features and technologies as discussed in this chapter: access control, authentication, encryption, tunneling, routing, filtering, high availability, QoS, and management. For a list of supported features by many of the major vendors in the VPN market, you can review the Virtual Private Network Consortium's Web site at **http://www.vpnc.org**.

The following listings are intended to give you an idea of the products available that incorporate combinations of the technologies we've discussed to offer VPN solutions to customers. Before the implementation of any solution, you should always go through an evaluation period with at least two products that appear to fit your requirements. Then test them thoroughly, making sure that all the security concerns and functionality of the entire system meet the needs of the business and conform to the company-wide security policies. Be aware that all vendors implement these technologies in different ways, and even protocol standards such as L2TP or IPsec are left somewhat open to interpretation upon vendor implementation. Many different VPN vendor solutions are available. When making the decision, it is helpful to realize that these systems fall into four general categories:

- VPN-dedicated hardware
- VPN-enable hardware and software firewalls
- VPN software
- VPN-service providers

The dedicated hardware solutions offer low-end, mid-range, and high-end solutions based primarily on the number of simultaneous connections as well as dedicated VPN-router solutions. Service providers that offer

VPN services generally purchase high-end dedicated hardware solutions because those are the systems that provide the best throughput performance and high availability.

Managed IP VPN service offerings have really taken off over the last two years. ISPs are looking to gain revenue by productizing value-added IP services like VPNs. If your organization wants to reap the benefits and cost savings of VPN technology but doesn't have the IT resources or capital to buy and deploy a traditional VPN system, then using ISP-based VPN services may be the way to go. Telecommunications providers are deploying improved global VPN solutions for customers, often trying to leverage ATM and frame-relay connections. Some of the global VPN carriers include Global One, Sprint, WorldCom (UUnet), and AT&T. Some of the most ubiquitous global VPN-service providers, including Equant and Infonet, primarily own nodes and switches in hundreds of countries and territories and base their business on managing that huge network. Fiberlink Communications Inc. offers services through established partnerships with other service providers in more than 150 countries and 8,000 points of presence. This type of anywhere access will enable companies to extend their existing networks to company sites and partners via the VPN by buying an access link to the nearest switch. Provider-based VPNs are truly coming of age and may be a viable solution to the VPN needs of your business.

Analysis of Case Study #1—Corporate

The MCC corporation has some interesting challenges that can be addressed by implementing VPNs. We have discussed some of the foundations of this technology, so now let's take a look at a few ways that we can use these technologies to resolve some of the business requirements for MCC. Realize that VPNs can be implemented in many possible ways and we will only discuss a few of them in this chapter and address some of the issues you will need to be aware of. Before we discuss designs, we will briefly mention some basic processes in successfully implementing any technology.

Once your company decides that a VPN solution is needed to meet a set of business requirements, the first step is to address and document what the business requirements are for this technology. This should be done in coordination with the company department responsible for corporate-security policies. With that document, you can begin conducting vendor evaluations and testing to determine what product will best meet your documented set of requirements. This phase is usually just a proof of concept and should be done with at least two to three vendors. Upon selecting the best product for your needs, you can deploy a pilot in which a small segment of your user base will test the solution in a production environment; in the case of site-to-site connections, you may develop a migration plan for network segments to move over in a stepped approach. If this phase proves successful, you can move on to a full-scale deployment taking into consideration all the issues of integrating the solution into the existing network architecture, monitoring, managing, logging, supporting, and backend-systems integration. MCC will be offering its employees and clients a variety of client-access technology options that will need to be supported (cable modems, xDSL, dial-up, wireless), so testing the client VPN software with each of these connection types is necessary. On that note, be aware that different service providers may incorporate additional desktop software in their access solutions, so you may want to have a corporate standard that states that users and clients can gain VPN access to MCC if they use one from a list of the selected pre-approved service providers that MCC technical staff has tested with the VPN solution.

In addition, regional private-broadband access will be offered to high-end users because of the increase in QoS that may be mandatory for business groups such as investment banking. As stated before, a VPN solution is only part of the overall corporate-wide security program and should be fully integrated into existing processes and systems so that it becomes an enabling technology for your business. Let's take a look at what VPNs can do for MCC.

Many possible solutions for remote VPN access are available such as PPTP or L2TP compulsory or voluntary tunnels and a host of hybrid solutions combining the various protocols and technologies (such as, L2TP using IPsec for data security). We won't discuss this in detail, but compulsory or mandatory tunnels are created automatically without any action from the end user; voluntary tunnels are created at the request of the user. We will consider a pure IPsec-based remote access solution over Internet-based connections and private broadband provider networks, implementing dedicated VPN hardware because it offers the best performance and scalability that is needed to accommodate MCC's large corporate- and client-user base. We're choosing IPsec because it offers the best flexibility and security for MCC's extremely sensitive applications, data, and diverse remote-user groups. It is an established IETF standards-based protocol that is becoming the deployed standard for secure remote access in the industry. You can refer to the MCC network diagram in Figure 7-2 as we discuss this solution.

Issues of design and deployment are typically worked out in the pilot phase of the project. Let's say in MCC's case that our pilot was run in the North America region. Of course, we will need to perform the same gateway and client-deployment tasks in our European site, so let's consider what these tasks are. The first task is the placement of the gateways in the corporate network, which will be wherever the service provider link comes into your organization or is extended internally to your perimeter network architecture. We won't discuss the variety of perimeter network designs, but let's talk about the placement of your hardware-based VPN gateway in the existing network.

One concern to be aware of in the design and deployment of a VPN solution is that of the crypto conundrum. The security that encryption technologies offer to your data transmissions can also create security holes in your network if they are not carefully addressed. The reason is that your border-guard security devices, such as firewalls, cannot scan encrypted traffic of any kind and anti-virus software; therefore, you are potentially allowing unauthorized traffic into your organization. This is a concern that will be addressed in the design phase of your solution; it is handled by addressing both client security and gateway placement. In building the VPN architecture, one way to address this issue is to make sure that all encrypted tunnels are terminated outside or at your security gateways, thus allowing the unencrypted traffic to be processed by the policies enforced by your existing security devices. Because we're not running a VPN gateway on our existing firewall, our design will place the VPN gateway parallel to the existing firewall gateway that services Internet traffic. This will enable MCC to segment VPN traffic from Internet-based traffic via routing protocols. The following lists the different placement alternatives for a hardware-based solution, all of which have different benefits and concerns.

- Outside the firewall
- Inside the firewall
- Parallel with the firewall
- Single interface configuration

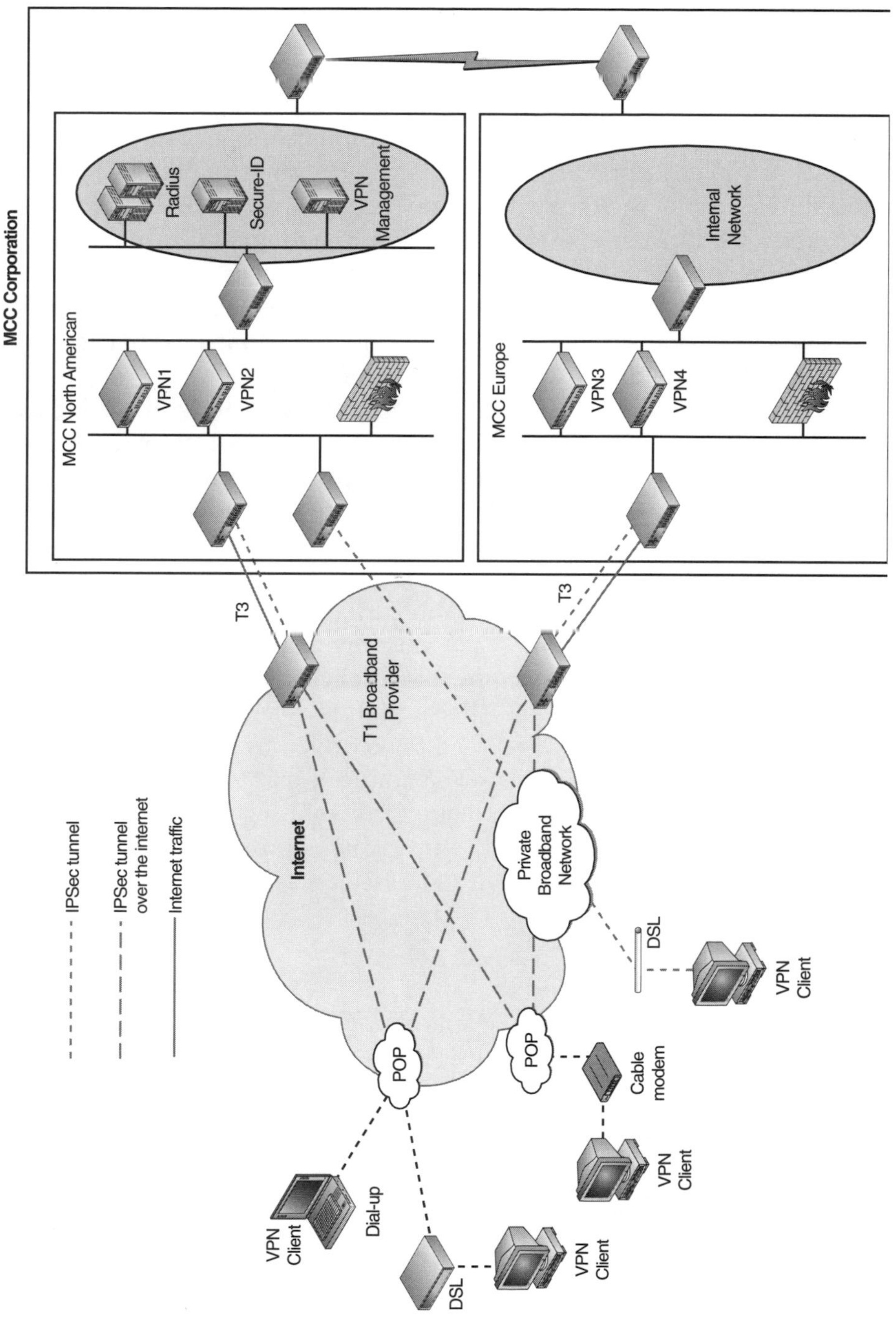

Figure 7-2 MCC remote access

When dealing with perimeter networks and securing traffic in any design, you need to focus on routing issues, and have an understanding of the protocols used for the VPN communications that you are attempting to process. Table 7-1 shows some of the protocols and port numbers to be aware of when directing or filtering traffic in the edge network. For example, if you place your VPN gateway inside the firewall gateway, you will need to configure the firewall to pass the appropriate VPN traffic. When directing traffic from your external router, you may want to make packet-forwarding decisions based on protocol information as well as IP addressing. Note that other MCC network traffic, such as IPX, will be tunneled within IP and transmitted over the network, being unencrypted at the far end and then forwarded to the final destination.

Parallel placement of the VPN gateway makes the issue of routing a bit more involved. Isolating the perimeter network using internal and external routers offers the best solution to this problem, making sure that all VPN traffic is passed through the VPN gateway based on the address pools configured for the remote VPN clients or the gateway's external IP address. This type of design gives MCC the best possible control over the traffic in the perimeter network. You can additionally deploy a firewall gateway on the inside of the VPN gateway to process the unencrypted packets against your deployed security policies. This will fully segment your Internet VPN traffic and offer a high level of security to MCC, but again the level of security will need to be driven by the security requirements set forth for the business. For financial institutions or other organizations where security is paramount, this solution of segmenting traffic and processing the internal VPN data streams through a firewall is usually a requirement. Once we have addressed these issues, we need to make

Table 7-1

Tunneling Protocols

Protocol	IP Protocol	Transport	Port Number
IKE	IP 17	UDP	500
ESP	IP 50		
AH	IP 51		
L2TP	IP 17	UDP	1701
PPTP	IP 6	TCP	1723
GRE/PPTP data	IP 47		

sure that the gateways are fully integrated into the backend systems; this means connectivity to authentication servers (RADIUS, SecurID), networks and network services (NTP, DNS, WINS, syslog, SNMP), and the VPN gateway-management system.

After we have fully integrated and tested the gateway system functionality including some client connections, we can concentrate on the larger client issues. There are a number of concerns here to be aware of including remote-access methods, client-software deployment, policy distribution, strong authentication, tunnel establishment, and client support and usability.

The success in deploying any technology typically lies in the end user's response to it. In the case of implementing VPNs, it is best to minimize the interaction the user needs to have with the system, while offering end-to-end secure access to the resources they require. Client software needs to be installed on each remote-access system in order to establish the IPsec link back to the VPN gateway. Standardization of corporate-supported desktops is typically a good practice in a large organization and offers a simpler process to testing VPN-client solutions. The installation of this software for MCC will either be done by the IT support group on a system-by-system basis or via a standardized system-build script. Each vendor implements the client-software solution in a different way and a serious, in-depth evaluation of the client software should be done in the testing phase. This is the piece of the solution that your end users will experience, and it will have critical impact on the success of the VPN deployment. Define how the IPsec tunnel is built and what user input is required. IPsec tunnels are established between peers using Internet Key Exchange (IKE) and Security Associations (SAs). The protocol specifies a two-phased negotiation to accomplish this. We have talked in some detail about the IPsec protocol, but what we are concerned with at this point is the user interaction required to successfully establish this secure link. IKE phase one or Main Mode (MM) has three steps to the exchange. The third step is authentication of the peers to establish an IKE SA. This authentication can be accomplished via pre-shared keys or digital certificates. We won't consider pre-shared keys because as stated, they don't scale at all. It is possible to use the same pre-shared key and a generic identity so that all users could authenticate phase one using the same key. Although this has been done in some larger-scale deployments, it is not the best secure solution, and it requires the user to input the shared key. Instead, we will use digital certificates. Most hardware VPN solutions offer an internal Certificate Authority (CA) implementation as part of the gateway product that can then be used to generate and issue standard ISO X.509v3 certificates. Although this can be used to authenticate phase-one negotiations without user intervention, you should be aware that these CAs do not offer a full-scale PKI solution, and certificate distribution is generally a manual process. If MCC wants other vendors to accept their certificates, they may need at least some certificates from an external CA. For our deployment, we will use this method for phase one to limit user input required. The critical authentication will come from user input during phase two of the IKE negotiation where we establish the IPsec SA. We will implement strong authentication using token cards such as SecurID. If you are currently using RADIUS in an existing RAS (remote access service) environment, you can simply add the correct RADIUS attributes necessary to support authentication requests from the VPN gateway without having to make any changes to your infrastructure. Using an existing system like RADIUS, that may be in place in your organization, can ease the VPN deployment efforts. If strong authentication is required (SecurID), it can be phased in later by issuing token cards to end users and configuring RADIUS pass-through authentication to an RSA ACE server as you migrate to token-based access. Using token cards offers a single-user authentication request that is required to successfully build the IPsec tunnel and authenticate the user to the corporate network. With this method, we can be sure that users are who they claim to be and that all traffic traversing the Internet will be secured. Of course, this does not account for token card and pin sharing between people. Once the tunnel is built, the user can begin to access the corporate resources that they have permission to via the access security policies in place. Access to these systems may require additional authentication criteria that the user will need to supply, such as an NT domain login ID and password.

You need to watch out for a few other items in client functionality. If MCC has a requirement for login and logout scripts to update corporate desktops, it is critical to test the VPN client to ensure that the IPsec tunnel remains established throughout the duration of the connection. Additionally, it is important to verify support for network authentication (NT 2000 domain-authentication support). Market leading company Checkpoint Software does not support W2K domain login, but claims they will support this functionality in version 5 of their VPN-1 software. Some of the other user concerns that MCC will need to focus on are the support of the technology and the central management of the client-security policies.

From a security-management perspective, it is critical to be able to enforce the policies on the remote-access devices from a central system, whether it is a management system or the gateway device. Remote-client policy enforcement and verification of remote-system configurations such as additional network adapters installed should be criteria in permitting the establishment of an IPsec tunnel. This is the only way that MCC can, to a reasonable degree, ensure the security of the overall VPN solution and scale the system as dictated by the growth of the business.

The complete remote access VPN we have discussed for MCC could also support other tunneling connections such as PPTP, L2TP, or site-to-site connections. MCC has additional requirements for site-to-site connectivity with different financial institutions to support a new investment banking application called FinApp. Let's take a look at what VPNs can offer to address this business requirement.

Analysis of Case Study #2—FinApp

Traditionally, financial institutions create network connectivity with business partners or customers over point-to-point links or frame relay that directly connects the two organizations. These links can be extremely expensive; therefore, a VPN solution may prove to be a huge cost saver. For critical, time-sensitive market-financial data feeds, reliability and availability are a must. In order for MCC to offer its business partners the options of a site-to-site VPN solution to access FinApp, the system must be dependable and able to handle large amounts of throughput. Another area of concern is QoS over the Internet, seeing as the Internet is still considered a best try connection. These issues can be addressed through regional dedicated service provider networks and SLAs with the providers. The FinApp systems are hosted at co-location facilities in three different geographical regions. MCC can offer site-to-site VPN solutions for its clients connecting to one of these three locations. Figure 7-3 diagrams the MCC deployment of this VPN solution in one of the three regions, which will be replicated in the other two regions. One of our biggest concerns in this implementation is no downtime, or at a minimum, no downtime during the financial market operational hours.

Solutions like that of Nokia's Cryptocluster offer IP clustering (Nokia-patented technology), where a number of VPN gateways can function as a

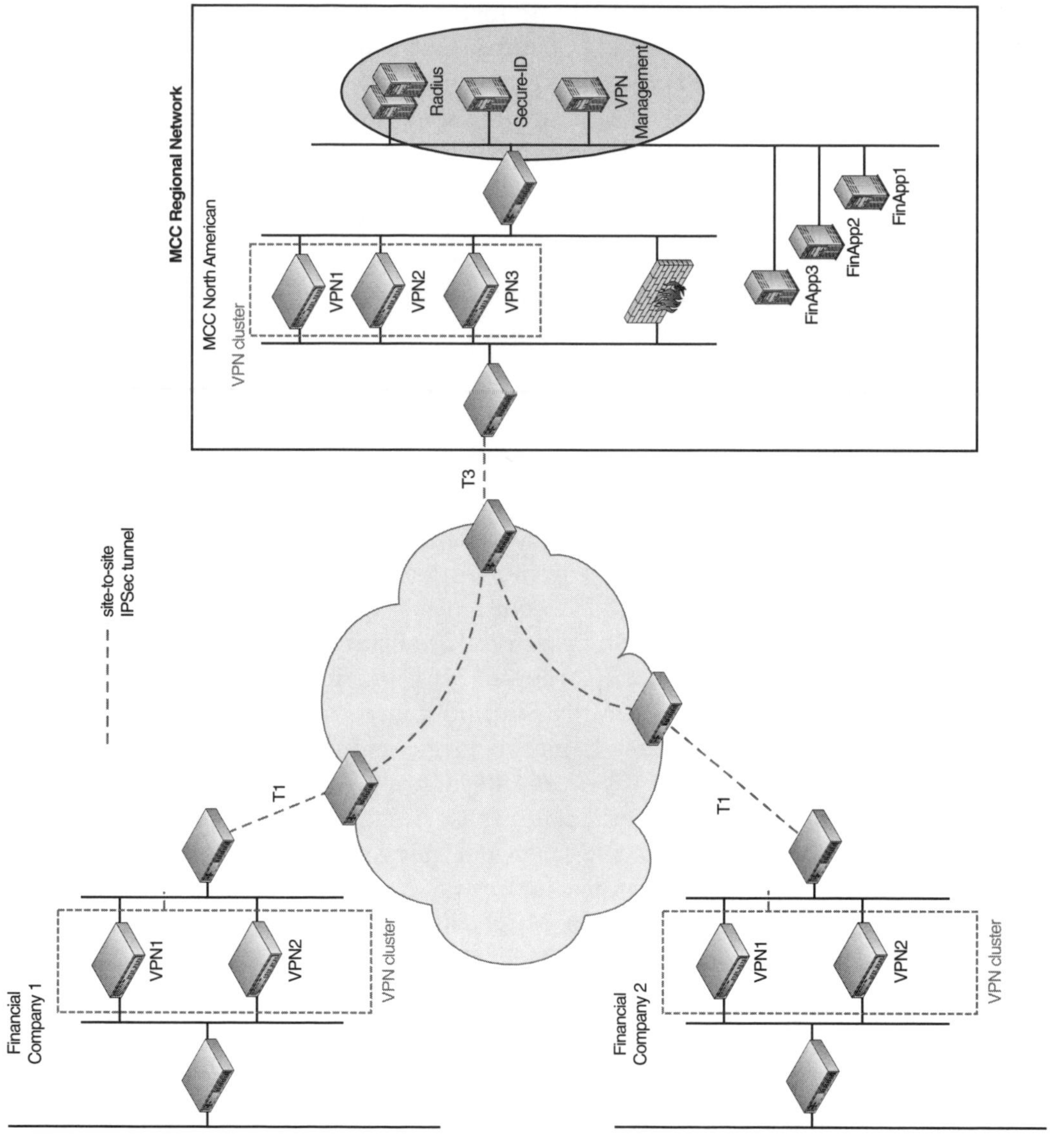

Figure 7-3 MCC regional extranet network

single gateway, which enables greater throughput via dynamic load balancing and redundancy with active session fail-over, eliminating the single point of fail-over issue. The deployment of the VPN gateway systems for MCC would be three separate hubs and spoke topologies supporting each of the three regions, with the MCC locations as the hub and the number of clients as the spokes. We would need to define the IKE and IPsec policies to be enforced in creating the IPsec tunnels according to the security polices set. The configuration of the gateway endpoints would be done centrally at MCC via the policy-management system. The remote-gateway systems would then be shipped to the client. Once the Internet links were installed and the IP networks were defined, the secure link can be established and all traffic from the client-financial institution destined for the FinApp system would be routed over this secured IPsec tunnel. Many of the other issues of integrating the VPN system that were discussed in the remote access solution will need to be applied here as well. This solution allows MCC to offer alternative access to the FinApp system to their clients without making any compromises in security and performance. If MCC decides that they do not have the internal resources required to manage this service, it is an option to evaluate different VPN service provider solutions. Issues of QoS, SLAs, and even the ability for MCC staff to have access to monitoring and some management capabilities can all be negotiated in the contract with the service providers who offer various value-added IP services like managed VPNs.

Analysis of Case Study #3—HealthApp

One of MCC's initiatives is to convert their existing dial-up access to their Health Application to a more universal, secure Web-access solution. The most common method of securing this type of data in transmission from a Web browser interface is to use the Secure Sockets Layer (SSL) to encrypt the data streams over the network from the client to the destination Web server. MCC could consider a variety of VPN solutions to secure these transmissions, but SSL is probably an adequate end-to-end solution for secure transmission. Issues of authentication may need to be addressed before deployment, but these concerns are not in the realm of VPNs and will be better addressed in other areas of security.

Conclusion

Although we have covered a wide range of VPN technologies and issues, other growing areas of focus and various initiatives are currently happening in the VPN space. VPN security for wireless communications is a rapidly growing market because of the demands for more corporate data and resources from the increasingly large mobile workforce. Wireless VPN technologies from companies such as Certicom, F-Secure, and Nortel are already being offered, but standardization of devices and protocols has yet to come. S/WAN (secure wide area network) was an initiative to promote the widespread deployment of Internet-based VPNs, and although it is no longer actively going on, related projects such as Linux Free S/WAN and the Virtual Private Network Consortium (VPNC) do actively support the standardization, development, and deployment efforts of VPNs. Service providers implementing MPLS VPN solutions are addressing areas of reliability and QoS. Although we will not be covering these topics here, it is important to recognize that all of these efforts will help support and grow the VPN technology that we will all come to use in the future.

VPN solutions have been around for years now, and the market is rapidly growing. According to Infonetics Research, organizations of all sizes throughout the world plan to deploy VPNs by the year 2002, with worldwide expenditures on VPNs growing from $205 million in 1997, to an estimated $12 billion by 2002. International Data Corp. (IDC) predicts the total worldwide IP VPN services market will grow from $2 billion today to $17.6 billion by 2004. These numbers may sound too optimistic, but some analysts predict an even more lucrative market. Whatever the numbers may be, it is easy to see the increasing interests of organizations in VPN technology.

Many different options and technologies are available within VPN solutions, but choosing standards-based, proven technology is the direction to take. A VPN design needs to not only secure data streams in transport, address bandwidth and latency requirements of your business applications and incorporate capacity planning, but you will also need to consider how the solution will integrate with the rest of your security and network-management systems. The right VPN for your network will depend on the number of users and sites you will support, as well as the type of applications your business requires. The combination of VPN hardware and software, if properly configured and deployed, will provide MCC or any organization with a secure, reliable, high-performance security solution that scales as requirements change. It is easy to implement and maintain, and it may even help you sleep better at night.

References

ANXeBusiness at **http://www.anx.com**

Electronic Frontier Foundation. *Cracking DES: Secrets of Encryption Research, Wiretap Politics & Chip Design*. Sebastopol (CA): O'Reilly & Associates, 1998.

Ford, W. and M.S. Baum. *Secure Electronic Commerce: Building the Infrastructure for Digital Signatures and Encryption*, 2 Ed. Englewood Cliffs (NJ): Prentice Hall, 2001.

Ferguson, Neils and Bruce Schneier. *A Cryptographic Analysis of IPsec*: Couterpane Internet Security, Inc., 1998.

Grant, G.L. *Understanding Digital Signatures: Establishing Trust over the Internet and Other Networks*. New York: Computing McGraw-Hill, 1997.

Kaufman, C., R. Perlman, and M. Speciner. *Network Security: Private Communication in a Public World*. Englewood Cliffs (NJ): Prentice Hall, 1995.

Kahn, David. *The Codebreakers —The Story of Secret Writing:* Simon & Schuster, 1996.

Kosiur, Dave. *Building and Managing Virtual Private Networks*: John Wiley & Sons, 1998.

Schneier, B. *Applied Cryptography*, 2nd edition. New York: John Wiley & Sons, 1996.

——-. *Secrets & Lies: Digital Security in a Networked World*. New York: John Wiley & Sons, 2000.

CHAPTER 8

Wireless Security

Wireless access to data is a field that will see explosive growth over the next several years. The demand has existed for many years already. Workers in virtually every industry often require access to their company's network without being tethered to their desks by an array of wires. Medical personnel, for example, have had to resort to paper copies of medical reports and documented procedures, which must then be transcribed to an electronic format simply because wireless capabilities have not been implemented for them. Many other forms of business also have the demand yet continue on without wireless capabilities. Warehouse and store shelf inventories are recorded multiple times: first on paper out on the floor, and then again in the back office to update the electronic database. Stockbrokers have relied on paper transactions to conduct business. When working in an environment in which a wired infrastructure does not exist, corporate trainers and executives have had to rely on slides and single-distribution point electronic training and presentations. Employees from virtually every walk of life have relied on wireless technologies to maintain contact with their business partners, but many have not had concurrent access to e-mail and corporate databases while doing so.

The market demands described are now being met with various degrees of maturity. In most cases, the process began with proprietary implementations. These implementations still exist and continue to be the market leaders in some technologies. However, both formal and de facto standards have developed in the past few years; as the standards have matured, the manufacturers' focus has moved to the development of products that adhere to the standard. These standards have sped adoption, driven down prices, and have also extended the market to the convenience users: those users who simply want to be able to move about an office environment with a laptop, handheld, or other digital communications device, while maintaining network connectivity.

This chapter will address the differences between wireless and wired communications and provide a security overview of the leading emerging wireless technologies. The focus of this chapter will be on the three leading standards-based implementations: Bluetooth, the Wireless Application Protocol (WAP), and the 802.11b wireless local area network (LAN) standard. This chapter will also discuss select proprietary implementations that specifically address security. Although these technologies and implementations are vendor-specific at the time of this writing, they represent best-practice solutions to address the gaps in the existing standards. This chapter will focus on the design, deployment, and use of these wireless technologies. A brief overview of each of these technologies will also be included to provide the framework over which the security implementations will be addressed.

How Is Wireless Different?

Although wireless telecommunications devices have certain specific limitations (which this chapter will cover), for the most part, standard security practices still apply. Principles such as authentication, authorization, and accounting (system and network monitoring and management) are just as relevant to the wireless world as they are to more traditional, wired communications methods. Many of the concepts concerning design and deployment guidelines in the other sections of this book apply equally to wireless communications devices; however, wireless communications differ from their wired counterparts in certain areas. This chapter will address each difference and provide the reader with a good understanding of the security implications associated with this technology.

Physical Security

Physical security is of paramount concern in the discussion of wireless communications. The types of devices that organizations are enabling for wireless data communications are mobile by definition. This increases their risk of theft because they are most commonly used outside of the physical perimeter that the organization can secure. Although existing safeguards are available for these devices, the safeguards were engineered based on minimal information protection requirements. Simply put, the type of data that was previously stored on devices such as cell phones was not considered to be at sensitive classification levels.

Wireless data devices can now store corporate information such as e-mail, snapshots of databases, and price lists, as well as sensitive client data, such as patient medical records. If a device containing possibly confidential corporate or client data is stolen, the thief now has exclusive access to the device for a potentially unlimited period of time. This makes it possible for the thief to systematically break down the security of the device to get at the protected data.

The significance of this to a corporation depends on the classification of the data that is stored on the device. A traditional cellular phone or personal digital assistant (PDA), for example, may contain a personal phone book or contacts database, which may reveal to an attacker the direct phone numbers, e-mail addresses, and postal addresses of specific individuals or partner businesses. This in itself is not especially threatening, yet a greater risk exists in the financial risk of unauthorized calls being placed before the phone or wireless PDA can be disabled.

At the midpoint in the spectrum of risk are the personal information manager (PIM) devices, typically running the Palm or Microsoft PocketPC operating systems or a device-specific operating system such as the Research in Motion (RIM) text pagers. These devices usually contain message storage capabilities and can often contain small snapshots of databases, patient medical records, and other sensitive data. The laptop computer is at the high-end of the spectrum with respect to device sensitivity. In many cases, local instances of corporate databases are stored on the laptop's hard drive in addition to offline storage of e-mail, business plans, and other potentially sensitive documents.

Moving forward, wireless technology will increase both the amount of data that can be stored on the devices and the type of access that these devices employ to access the corporate network. Cell phones will store corporate e-mail, light versions of databases, and even documents. In addition, they will have remote access into the corporate network. Laptops that use current wireless communications protocols can access corporate networks without requiring physical access to the network, due to the extended range of wireless LANs and wireless modems. These risks do not mean that these technologies should not be utilized, but rather that their unique physical security requirements need to be addressed. Laptop locks, and now PDA locks, address the basic physical security requirements needed to lower the risk of theft of the devices. User authentication and encryption of the data on the device can be used to restrict access to the data if the device is stolen. It is important to realize that physical security requirements for wireless devices will increase in importance as the technologies discussed in this chapter gain wider acceptance and use.

Device Limitations

Current wireless devices have many limitations that have a potential impact on the security of the data stored on them and on the communications link that they establish. Presently, wireless devices such as personal digital assistants (PDA) and mobile phones suffer from the following limitations, as compared to personal computers:

- Battery life
- Small displays
- Limited/different input methods (touch screen versus keyboard)
- Reduced bandwidth on communications link
- Reduced memory capacity
- Slower CPU processing speeds

The issues are approximately listed in the order from least to most significant concerning their impact on security. Although a small display has an impact on the applications that will run on the device, it obviously has very little impact on connection security. The unpredictable latency and the absence of a guarantee of the packet sequence affect encryption methods (a topic that this chapter will discuss later). The most significant device limitations include reduced memory and the slow processing power of mobile devices because these factors can make the encryption of data, for example, a less attractive option.

Bluetooth

Bluetooth is a communications protocol designed for use in personal area networks (PANs) and for other uses that require short-range communications. The initial Bluetooth specification defines a device communications range of 10 meters. It is a protocol that will primarily be used to expand remote communications capabilities and eliminate the need for cables. It provides physical as well as link-layer connectivity to the network. Several well-known protocols provide upper-layer application support. These include the Wireless Application Protocol (WAP), the Point-to-Point Protocol (PPP), and IP (TCP/UDP). The Bluetooth Special Interest Group (SIG) has defined a number of usage models for the Bluetooth protocol. By indicating potential applications for the protocol, these usage models provide insight into the levels of security that are required for the protocol. Published usage models include

- **Internet bridge** In this model, a PC uses a mobile phone as a method for accessing the Internet. The PC communicates with the mobile device using the Bluetooth protocol; the mobile phone in turn dials the Internet in the same manner that a modem cabled to the PC would do. The Bluetooth protocol in this usage model supports PPP, which in turn can transport IP packets.
- **Synchronization** The focus of this usage model is to create a PAN for the purpose of synchronizing e-mail, calendar, and contact data, which is typical of personal information management (PIM) applications and devices.
- **Three-in-one phone** This usage model is for devices that will function as (1) cordless phones, connecting to the public switched telephone network, (2) intercom phones for device-to-device communications, and (3) cellular phones connecting to the public cellular infrastructure as a regular cell phone.

These are just three of the usage models developed for the Bluetooth protocol. The usage models vary greatly, and each potentially dictates a different information security approach. This variation in security requirements is built into the Bluetooth protocol.

Bluetooth Security

The Bluetooth specification provides three levels of security: non-secure, service-level, and secure. The security levels dictate the point at which security is implemented. In non-secure mode, devices do not initiate security measures. This may be helpful in a small number of usage models, where security will never be required. Secure mode always implements security, prior to any link-level connectivity. Within the scope of Bluetooth devices, this is excessive in most current usage models. Future models will lead to the development of devices that function in roles that will require an "always-on" security model.

The most common deployment of Bluetooth devices is with service-enforced security, known as Mode 2 security. Service-enforced security enables the requirement of security to be established on an application-by-application basis. This mode recognizes the fact that existing devices will function in a variety of roles for the user. During a business card exchange using the vCard application/functionality, it would be inappropriate for the devices to be forced to implement security. These same devices, however, could be used for e-commerce applications in an untrusted environment—a usage model for which security would be appropriate. The following section will focus on Mode 2 security in Bluetooth security.

Bluetooth security is implemented at the link layer. It is based on the concept of a trusted device. A device attempting to establish a link with another will either be considered a trusted device or an untrusted device by the second. If the first device is considered trusted, then the second device automatically grants link-layer access to the first. If not, then the first device is considered to be untrusted, which invokes a more granular, service-based authentication and authorization mechanism.

At this point, the service can require one of three security levels: authentication and authorization, authentication, or no authentication. This security model enables services with differing security requirements to coexist on the same device. Access to a vCard application for the exchange of contact information could be defined as a service that does not require authentication or authorization. The same device could also support file transfer or database transaction services, which would most likely require both authentication and authorization. The Bluetooth security model contains provisions that when setting up a link with an untrusted device, granting access to one service does not automatically grant access to any other services. It also does not automatically change the status of the foreign device (the device will still be considered untrusted for future link establishments).

The Bluetooth security model defines the functions that the mobile devices provide as services. When implementing Mode 2 security, the access controls to the device are based on the service that the remote device is attempting to access. If the remote device is trusted, then no access controls are required. In the event that the remote device is not trusted or is unknown (which Bluetooth considers to be untrusted), the device can require several levels of access control. The base level is authorization. As with wired security, authorization provides the baseline of access control. Authentication identifies whether or not the remote device is allowed to access the service running on the local device. At a more basic level, however, by determining the identity of the remote device, the security mechanisms built into this model can then determine what level of access the remote device is entitled to on the local device within the given service. This is known as authorization. As a result, authorization always requires authentication as a first step.

The last element of security that can be implemented before access is granted to the service is encryption. When encryption is required for a service, it is established at the link layer before the local device grants access to the service. By default, authentication and authorization are required for incoming connections, and authentication is required for outgoing connections (to verify the true identity of the device that the service is running on). Figure 8-1 illustrates the flow of security within the Bluetooth solution.

As previously stated, it is the device, not the user, that is trusted in the Bluetooth security model. The authentication model for Bluetooth is based on a shared key. When two Bluetooth devices communicate for the first time, the user of each device will be prompted and indicate whether the other device is trusted or not. This establishes the relationship between the two devices for future communication. The establishment of trust must occur during this initial connection because the Bluetooth security model does not enable user intervention (a username/password check) during subsequent connection requests. Conceptually, this is not unlike the model that is implemented for most wireless devices today: a mobile phone must authenticate with the network when it places a call, but it is the device, not the user, that is authenticated. Although the user can require authentication before access is granted to the device, that access control is implemented for the device, not for the network.

Figure 8-1

Generalized Bluetooth security flow

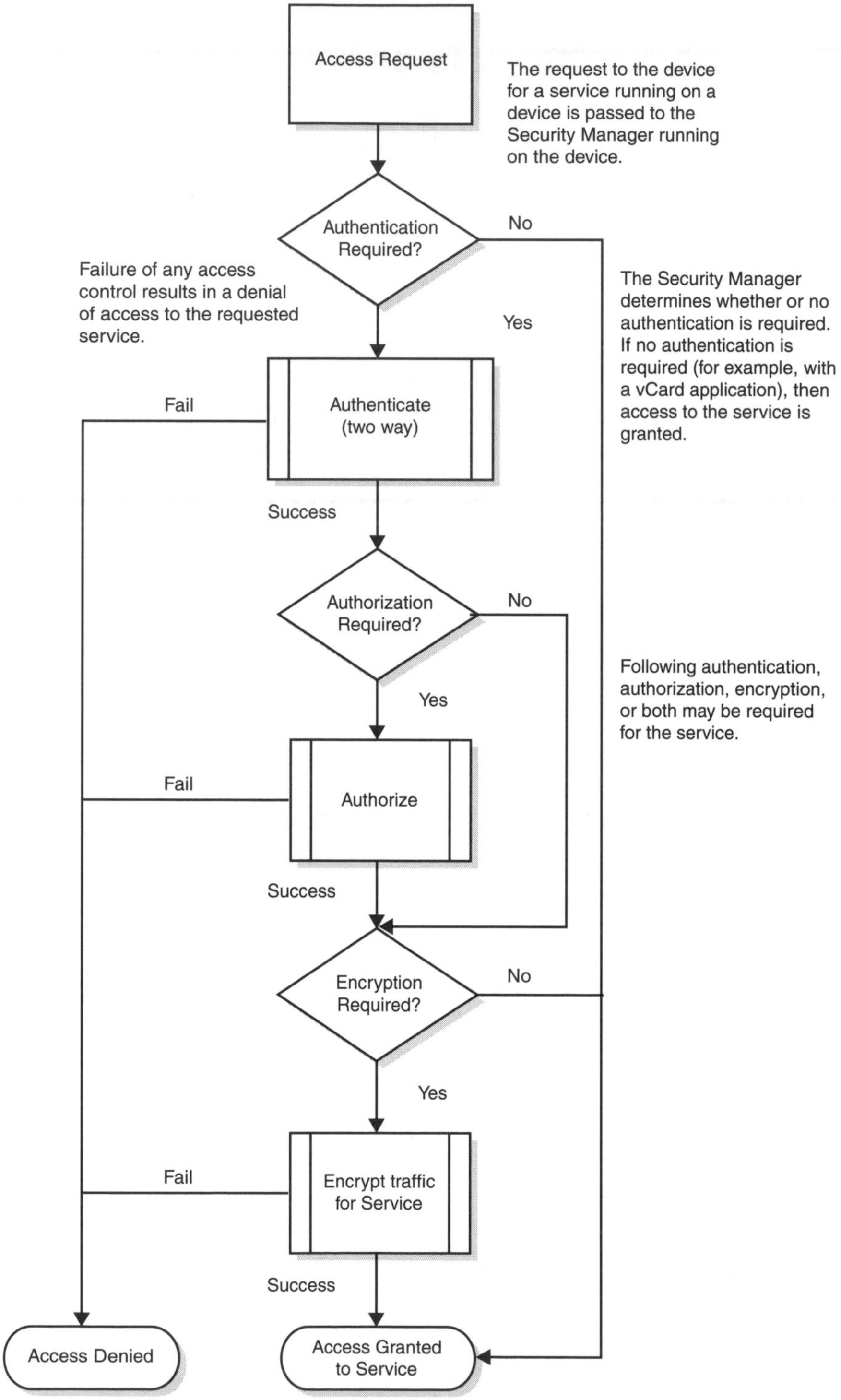
Access Request
The request to the device for a service running on a device is passed to the Security Manager running on the device.
Authentication Required?
No
Yes
Failure of any access control results in a denial of access to the requested service.
The Security Manager determines whether or no authentication is required. If no authentication is required (for example, with a vCard application), then access to the service is granted.
Fail
Authenticate (two way)
Success
Authorization Required?
No
Yes
Following authentication, authorization, encryption, or both may be required for the service.
Fail
Authorize
Success
Encryption Required?
No
Yes
Fail
Encrypt traffic for Service
Success
Access Denied
Access Granted to Service

This security model is acceptable when only one service is available on the network. Until recently, the mobile network provided only one service: voice communication. In the future, mobile devices will increasingly use either mobile networks that support both voice and data or use multiple networks, depending on the use of the device at that moment. Emerging mobile networks using different technologies—the Global System for Mobile Communications (GSM), Cellular Digital Packet Data (CDPD), and Code Division Multiple Access (CDMA)—will provide access to voice and a variety of data services. These networks are adopting new security models, recognizing that the information passing over them is increasingly sensitive as wireless devices are made to serve new purposes. Scanners could be used in the past to eavesdrop on cellular network transmissions. CDPD networks use encryption with session-based keys to deter the casual eavesdropper, recognizing the potential sensitivity of the data packets. Bluetooth security provides a similar level of encryption, which will deter the casual attacker. In both cases, the physical and link levels for communication provide for device-based authentication, privacy, and data integrity through encryption.

Safeguarding Bluetooth

Although Bluetooth security can deter the casual attacker, the security professional must realize that this technology has limitations. The limitations in securing Bluetooth devices should not prevent the security practitioner from considering the technology altogether, but certain precautions should be taken. The primary limitation in Bluetooth's security implementation is that it is the device, not the user, that is trusted.

Bluetooth was not designed as an end-to-end security solution. It was designed to provide security only at the link level. This limitation simply means that if Bluetooth is used to provide link-layer connectivity and greater security is required, then upper-layer security (usually provided by the application) will be required.

Another limitation of the Bluetooth protocol is actually a limitation of the devices that Bluetooth was designed for. The reduced processing capacity and limited memory of the devices intended for Bluetooth means that a security check cannot be performed on every packet. For this reason, security checks are implemented only at connection setup and for connection-oriented traffic. If connectionless traffic is required or if security checks are required in addition to connection setup, then the upper-level application must be made to implement additional checks.

Upper-layer applications can include either the security implemented within the Wireless Application Protocol or security measures must be built into the given application that uses this technology.

When considering the degree of security that should be required by Bluetooth, two additional pieces of information should be considered. First, what is the data that is to be secured? Is it public, proprietary, confidential, or restricted? Chapter 3 of this book covers Information Classification (IC) and defines the criteria for each level of classification. If the data that Bluetooth is protecting is public, then fewer resources should be expended in safeguarding it. Bluetooth is simply the transport in this case; it does not change the IC level.

Second, to what degrees do the upper-layer applications and protocols protect the data? If Bluetooth is the transport for restricted information, what are the safeguards (encryption, non-repudiation, or authentication) that are in place within the upper-layer protocols and the application? Examine the entire packet when assessing the overall strength of security. Bluetooth can authenticate the device but cannot authenticate the user of the device. If this is a requirement of the data passed across the link, then Bluetooth security should be combined with additional upper-layer security mechanisms that authenticate the user. Bluetooth security has some limitations, but when combined with other security measures commonly taken with sensitive information, it provides solid mechanisms for securing the link between devices.

Wireless Application Protocol (WAP)

WAP is a protocol that has been optimized for mobile devices. These optimizations mainly address the limitations discussed earlier in this chapter. WAP is an open standard and makes use of existing standards where possible. This reuse extends, as well as works to adapt to, the standards for wireless communications. It is necessary to examine the security implications of these adaptations. For example, if an existing encryption algorithm is optimized for wireless communications, does this weaken the strength of the algorithm?

One primary concept that the WAP specification has adopted is the concept of layering the protocol. Layering is the concept of breaking up the entire communication process into discreet pieces. Each of these pieces handles a specific function. The standard for layering TCP/IP in wired communications is the Open Standard Interface (OSI) model. Layers in the OSI model handle functions such as physically transmitting the communications on the cable or fiber (the physical layer), providing a source and a destination address that is unique worldwide (the network layer), and formatting the communications for the application (the presentation layer). The most important facet of the layered approach is that each layer provides a standard, known interface to the layers that surround it. This permits the layers to evolve over time without compromising compatibility with the other layers.

The WAP specification defines protocols at the application, session, and transport layers. The application layer addresses the applications that the user employs and the scripting that increases the functionality of the applications. The session layer manages the connection for the user. The transport layer receives the communication from one of several types of wireless networks, secures it, and delivers it in a formatted manner.

The upper layers of the protocol stack are modeled on the Web protocols HTTP 1.1, scripting languages, and markup languages. External applications can interface with the stack anywhere above the transport layer. One layer is dedicated to security. This security layer will be discussed in further detail later in the chapter. Figure 8-2 illustrates the WAP protocol architecture.

Wireless device users do not use their devices in the same way that wired device users use theirs. This is not due to security reasons, but because of device limitations. The small display and limitations in network throughput have led to different usage models for wireless devices. Wireless users are less likely to surf content on their provider's network. Usage models favor more streamlined applications that require limited or predictable input, that are custom designed for reduced displays, and that consume a limited amount of bandwidth. These tend to be more business-oriented in nature: text e-mail/short messaging, stock trading, and database queries and transactions.

From a security perspective, the policies and procedures in place for wired network traffic apply to wireless traffic as well. The data must be safeguarded to the same degree that a wired connection is protected. It is important for the security practitioner, who is familiar with existing data security standards, to understand the differences between the wireless standards and the standards for the wireless protocols. WAP version 1.1 is currently deployed. Version 1.2 is soon to be deployed, with devices shipping to consumers in 2001.

Figure 8-2
WAP protocol architecture

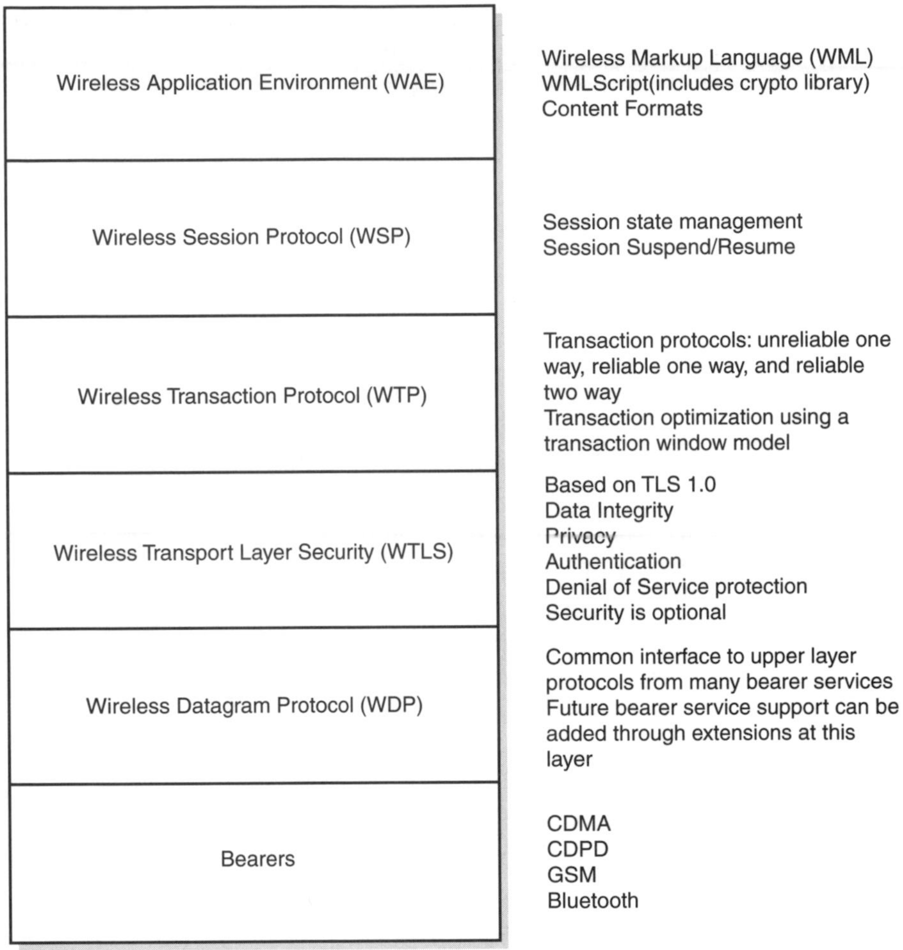

Most WAP-capable devices are phones; however, other types of devices also support WAP. WAP browsers are available for the Palm VII, PocketPC, and even certain Research in Motion (RIM) platforms. Although these devices have capabilities beyond that of WAP, an organization standardizing on WAP for wireless communications could then tailor its wireless application development to just the WAP interface (the Wireless Markup Language). Security will be improving as the WAP standards develop, so this option may provide a universal solution that prevents splintering in wireless application development. Following the discussion of WAP security and safeguarding WAP-based communication, the following section will describe some of the proprietary solutions that are available to further secure wireless communication.

WAP Security

Security is optional in the Wireless Application Protocol. In the WAP specification, security is provided through the Wireless Transport Layer Security (WTLS) layer, which operates directly on top of the transport protocol layer. The goals of the WTLS specification are to provide authentication, privacy, and data integrity through the use of certificates and encryption. Although it is based on the IETF Transport Layer Security (TLS) 1.0 specification, (the successor to Secure Sockets Layer [SSL]), it is optimized for the previously discussed limitations of wireless networks. WTLS specifically addresses limited storage/memory capacity, low bandwidth, low-processing capabilities, and long/unpredictable latency.

Many emerging applications that run on mobile devices contain sensitive data. Although many mobile network operators encrypt their traffic, this encryption is not consistent and end-to-end security cannot be guaranteed. WTLS provides end-to-end security between the protocol endpoints. In the case of WAP, the protocol endpoints are the mobile device and the WAP gateway. If the protocol endpoints can be trusted, then the connection can be secured. Note that WAP by itself cannot provide full end-to-end security. As with Bluetooth, if end-to-end security is required, an upper-layer application or protocol is required.

The WTLS sets up the security parameters during a handshake process with a server. It is during this handshake that the client and the server agree on the requirements for authentication and encryption, the encryption method to be used, the certificates that the client will accept, and any other non-default parameters. These parameters are passed initially in the direction of the client to the server. The server then has the option of responding with acceptable parameters and can request authentication from the client.

In most cases, because of the limitations of the mobile device, the client will only be able to use a small number of encryption mechanisms and may only accept certain types of certificates. The server, due to its greater processing power, storage capabilities, and memory, is expected to be able to accommodate a number of different parameters that could be passed to it from a variety of different clients. Either the client or the server can terminate a connection during the handshake phase if the other passes to it a parameter that is not acceptable, either because it is not supported or because it does not meet a minimum-security requirement.

Currently, the three modes of security in the WTLS are

- **Class 1** Anonymous authentication
- **Class 2** Server authentication
- **Class 3** Two-way (client and server) authentication

As mentioned in the previous section, authentication is performed using certificates. X.509v3, X9.68 (X9.68 is still being developed as of the WAP-199-WTLS specification drafting), and WTLS certificates are widely supported. The request for security comes in the client "Hello" message, which initiates the handshake. The server responds by sending its certificate. The certificate includes the following (any values listed are the values defined in the WAP-199-WTLS specification):

- **Certificate version** Value=1
- **Signature algorithm** The algorithm used to sign the certificate
- **Issuer: Note** This must be a Certificate Authority (CA) that the client trusts
- **Valid not before** Beginning of the validity period for the certificate, in UNIX 32-bit format
- **Valid not after** End of the validity period for the certificate, in UNIX 32-bit format
- **Subject** Owner of the public key
- **Public key type** Algorithm of the public key
- **Parameter specifier** Any parameters relevant for the public key
- **Public key**

To optimize the network bandwidth and processing capabilities on the client, the server can send only its certificate, signed by the CA's private key. Although this scenario requires the client to trust the CA, it prevents the entire key chain from being sent over the link. If the server authenticates with the client, it may then require authentication from the client (Class 3). When this request is made, the client responds with its certificate (if it has one), with a blank certificate (if it does not have one), or an alert message that ends the handshake. Following this, the master secret, which will be used to encrypt all application traffic, is exchanged using the Rivest-Shamir-Adelman (RSA), Diffie-Hellman, or elliptic curve Diffie-Hellman algorithms.

Privacy and data integrity are enforced using encryption and Message Authentication Codes (MAC). Both of these parameters are negotiated during the handshake process—the client sends a list of supported encryption algorithms and MAC algorithms. The first combination on the list is the client's first choice. The server will decide on the combination; it should be implemented to use the highest available choice that both the client and server support. If it cannot find an acceptable combination, then the handshake process fails. WAP relies on existing encryption algorithms such as DES, 3DES, RC5, and IDEA. These are block cipher algorithms that encrypt data. Data integrity through the use of MAC is implemented using well-known algorithms that include SHA and MD5. For performance reasons, the WAP standard also enables the use of the SHA_XOR_40 algorithm, which is optimized for use in devices with limited processing power.

Safeguarding WAP

The protocols used in implementing security in the WTLS, although streamlined for performance reasons, are a solid solution to the problem of security. Most of the security risks associated with WAP are due to implementing the architecture in an unsecure manner. The greatest security risk that exists when deploying applications that use the Wireless Application Protocol is the well-documented "Gap in WAP." The problem arises on the WAP gateway because the encryption and privacy within the WTLS exists only between the protocol endpoints, not the endpoints of the application. In the typical WAP gateway deployment, data is encrypted using WTLS from the handheld/wireless device to the WAP gateway. At the WAP gateway, the data must be unencrypted and then re-encrypted, typically using SSL. The vulnerability lies in that the data sits in an unencrypted form on the WAP gateway in memory during this process. Additionally, the wireless device in the WAP security model authenticates, through digital certificates, the WAP gateway, not the end application server.

When the technology was in its earliest stages, wireless carriers provided the WAP gateway on their networks. After receipt on the gateway, the traffic was sent via a virtual private network (VPN) or using SSL to the enterprise/service provider's network. This early model relied upon the physical and logical security enforced by the service provider to protect the data as it was decrypted and re-encrypted prior to forwarding. As e-commerce applications become more critical to organizations and as the data that passes across wireless links becomes more sensitive, organizations must take end-to-end ownership of the security responsibilities for wireless communications. Figure 8-3 shows many possible implementations of mobile communications across wireless wide area networks (WANs).

The figure shows many potential variations in deployments. Initial deployments terminate security at intermediate gateways, such as the WAP gateway in the mobile network. More secure deployments move the WAP gateway into an area of organizational control. Alongside the WAP deployment, device-specific implementations, such as those for Palm, PocketPC, and RIM, are included. These solutions will be discussed later in the chapter and are included here for comparative purposes.

When planning a WAP-based architecture, an organization should place the WAP gateway in a trusted environment. For most organizations, this means placing the WAP gateway inside of a firewall, either in a Demilitarized Zone (DMZ)/perimeter network or on the corporate LAN. In some cases, it is possible to put the WAP gateway directly on the Web server. This significantly reduces the risk brought on by the insecurities of the WAP gateway. The degree to which the security of the server can be assured will be the driving factor in the security classification levels of the data that organizations can wireless-enable.

Outside of the WAP specification, additional safeguards are available that can further protect the link. Most of these solutions are proprietary in nature and are implemented with customer front ends (WAP browsers on the wireless device) and customized extensions on the back end. Lessons learned from these implementations and ongoing work in the WAP standards will ultimately improve the security of implementations even further.

What Else Is Available?

When properly implemented, WAP provides many mechanisms for authentication, privacy, and data integrity. For organizations that require an even greater degree of security, alternatives and extensions are available to provide improvements over the existing WAP standards. These solutions are usually tied to a single vendor or a single platform. These can provide an advantage to an organization that only intends to deploy

Figure 8-3

Mobile application deployment architecture

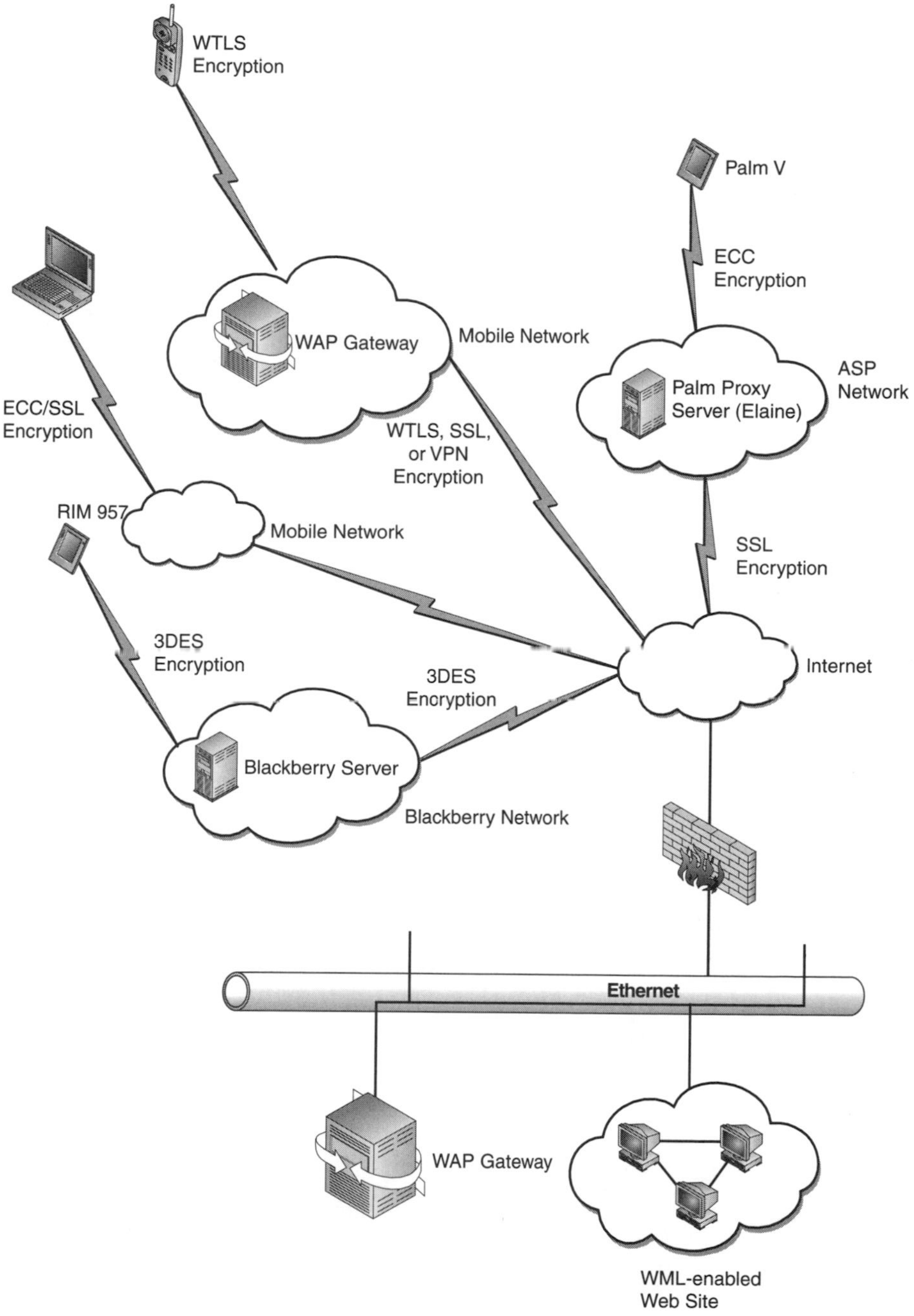

the supported platforms. The market has recognized certain limitations in the security of existing protocols; these products address those limitations. The primary areas that are addressed are authentication, end-to-end security, and gateway replacements.

The type of mobile device will determine what safeguards are available. The PocketPC platform includes native support for 128-bit encryption and due to its support of SSL, provides a well-known standard that organizations can develop for. Organizations interested in deploying mobile applications on the Palm platform have the option to write custom applications. Access to the custom applications is made available to the mobile devices via Palm Query Application (PQA). The PQA represents the client-access portion of these applications developed specifically for mobile usage.

To minimize the bandwidth used on communications links, the applications are broken down into a query portion and a response portion. The query portion of the application enables the client with the PQA loaded to send only the data required to make the request to the end application. The end application sends only the response, minimizing the amount of data that must flow across the communications channel. An additional advantage to this model, from the security perspective, is that an organization can integrate native authentication mechanisms into the application.

Improving Authentication

Keeping in mind that one of the greatest problems with the security of mobile communications is that wireless networks authenticate the device (not the network), a best-practices model for increasing security is to insist on two-factor authentication for mobile users. Two-factor authentication forces the user to authenticate using two different forms of authentication. Traditional forms of authentication include one or more of what you know, which is an authentication mechanism that is usually implemented through the use of passwords; what you have, which is implemented using token technology; and who you are, which is implemented by using biometrics.

Several proprietary implementations now enable the integration of token technology into mobile devices. Among these solutions is the integration of RSA's SecureID, which many organizations have already implemented for remote access. Regardless of the vendor, if token technology has been implemented by an organization, a solution may be available for your wireless platforms.

Improving End-to-End Security

End-to-end security eliminates the Gap in WAP. One solution to address end-to-end security is to implement a VPN for mobile devices. Certicom is one vendor that has released VPN software for mobile device connectivity. Although a VPN solution may not be relevant to all mobile platforms, it represents a strong security solution for encryption and data integrity and can increase the strength of authentication. When selecting a VPN solution for mobile devices, the same criteria that are used for wired clients should be examined for wireless clients.

Another alternative, which does not have the same degree of overhead, is to encrypt the data above the WTLS layer. This is implemented through WML scripting and in currently available implementations, it can both authenticate the user and encrypt all data. These advantages enable authentication not only at the WAP gateway, but also at the origin server.

Gateway Replacements

As previously mentioned, PocketPC, RIM, and Palm platforms can communicate through the use of the Wireless Application Protocol. Although this can help an organization that is interested in deploying a single wireless protocol across multiple devices, it is by no means the only alternative available. Because of the greater processing power and memory/storage capabilities on these devices, stronger methods of authentication and encryption are available. As an example, native support for SSL is built into the PocketPC platform. Palm devices can utilize numerous encryption algorithms to include ECC and DESX. In the case of the Palm platform, traffic is encrypted using ECC between the PDA and the Palm Proxy Server and is then re-encrypted using SSL between the Proxy Server and the host application server. These solutions provide greater levels of security, but in most cases they are platform-dependant. For the organization that requires these levels of security, however, they provide a superior option to WAP.

Wireless Local Area Networks (WLANs)

A wireless local area network (WLAN) is an extension of an existing wired local area network (LAN) using radio waves instead of copper cables or fiber optics to carry data. Through the use of radio communication, data can be transmitted over short range at high-transmission rates to devices equipped with radio receivers and transmitters. This enables the device to participate in the local area network as if it were another wired device. This chapter will explore several usage models for WLANs in various environments.

The most important thing to consider when planning for the security of a WLAN is that the data using the WLAN as a transport is most likely the same data that is protected by the wired corporate security infrastructure. The same level of information protection should be applied; although in the case of WLANs, additional challenges exist that make this more difficult. Figure 8-4 shows typical wireless LAN deployment.

Figure 8-4

Typical wireless LAN deployment

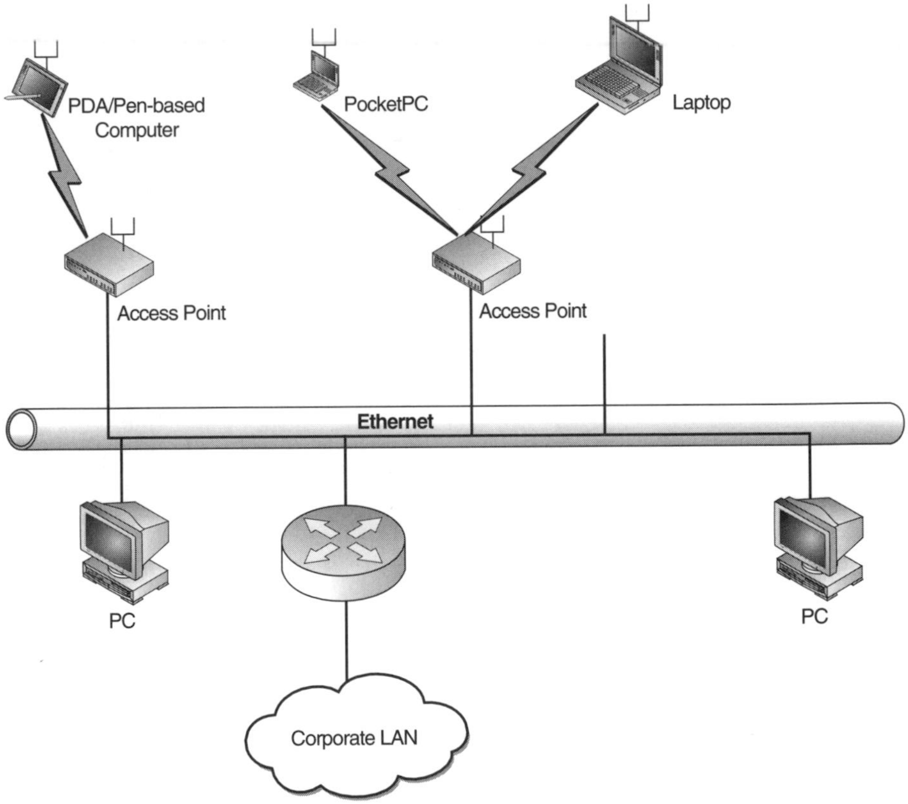

Wireless LANs have two primary components: the wireless network interface card (NIC) in the remote device and the wireless Access Point. Wireless LANs operate by transmitting in the unlicensed 2.4-GHz range. Eleven channels are allocated by the 802.11b standard (the current Institute of Electrical and Electronics Engineers [IEEE] wireless LAN standard), which are listed in Table 8-1. Due to the wavelength width of the transmission, the United States has three non-overlapping channels: 1, 6, and 11.

Table 8-1

802.11b DSSS Frequencies

Channel	Starting Frequency US (FCC)	Starting Frequency Europe (ETSI)	Starting Frequency Japan
1	2412	----	----
2	2417	----	----
3	2422	2422	----
4	2427	2427	----
5	2432	2432	----
6	2437	2437	----
7	2442	2442	----
8	2447	2447	----
9	2452	2452	----
10	2457	2457	----
11	2462	2462	----
12	----	----	2484

In addition to the channel that wireless LANs operate on, the traffic can further be segmented by the use of the Extended Service Set ID (ESSID, also referred to as the SSID). The ESSID can equate to the name of the network—it is a shared, cleartext name between the Access Point and the wireless LAN adapter. If the ESSID of the LAN adapter and the Access Point are the same, then the LAN adapter is allowed to associate with the Access Point and use it as a method of bridging to the wired LAN.

It has parallels to the Microsoft Windows workgroup name in the systems arena and a virtual local area network (VLAN) in the wired, networked arena; the EESID does not implement any real security, although it does segment traffic. From the operating perspective, once a client has associated with an Access Point, it is treated by the wired infrastructure like any other wired client, with normal access to network resources.

Wireless LAN Security

Security in wireless LANs is addressed primarily through the use of Wired Equivalent Privacy (WEP). WEP uses a 24-bit Initialization Vector (IV) with a 104-bit key in its strongest form to encrypt network traffic that is passed back and forth between the protocol endpoints, typically the Access Point and the remote wireless device. Traffic is unencrypted before being passed on to the LAN. This ensures that wireless users will be able to access LAN resources in the same way as wired users.

In most implementations, the WEP key is set manually on both the client and the Access Point. The WEP key is typically set by a user who enters hexadecimal or ASCII characters, which are then used to generate the actual key. The same WEP key is shared among all devices in the network, although most implementations enable more than one WEP key (typically four) to be stored and used on the client.

Access Points from most major vendors can be configured to enable only encrypted traffic on the wireless segment. When this is implemented, an Access Point will not enable a client device to associate with it. The end result in this case is that the client will not be allowed to transmit packets to or through the Access Point using network addressing. In other words, the client will not be able to ping, Telnet, or make any other type of upper-layer connection to the Access Point or anything else on the network, even though the client device is in the correct IP subnet, operating on the same channel/frequency, and using the correct ESSID. Most Access Points can also be configured with MAC address filtering. With this in place, the MAC addresses of all trusted client devices can be manually entered into the Access Point, at which point the Access Point will only enable association attempts from those MAC addresses.

The primary vulnerability associated with wireless LANs concerns the extension of the corporate network. One of the primary usage models for wireless LANs is to extend the wired infrastructure to areas that it could not otherwise reach. The problem with this usage is that the corporate

LAN could easily be extended beyond the physical security perimeter. The typical transmission range of wireless LANs using the 802.11b standard is approximately 200 feet. Most vendors advertise 11 Mb/sec at 100 feet, but with a line of sight, 11 Mb/sec is easily achievable at much longer ranges. Additionally, an Access Point can drop its transmission rate on a client-by-client basis to achieve greater range.

Due to the variable range and transmission rates, it is not possible to accurately define the external perimeter of the wireless LAN. The wireless LAN could extend outside of the physical building or into an office space of another corporation. The security vulnerability in this case is essentially that an attacker/intruder could avoid the physical security access controls that a corporation has in place simply by sitting outside of the company gates (or perimeter of physical control) or in an adjacent office, and capture or observe network traffic or possibly even gain access to the network itself.

Recently, vulnerabilities in the methods that WEP uses to safeguard data have been published. This chapter will cover the vulnerabilities in general terms for the purpose of identifying the implementation methods that can lead to a potentially insecure implementation. Most of the vulnerabilities that have been identified to date are mathematical or hypothetical, due to the expense and resources that would be required to compromise the protocol. Although WEP uses standard methods of safeguarding data, the method by which those standards were implemented has led to the vulnerabilities.

As previously mentioned, WEP uses a 104-bit key and a 24-bit IV. WEP uses the RC4 stream cipher to encrypt packets. RC4 is used to encrypt the entire packet with the exception of the IV (which must be passed in clear text and is changed with every packet). The IV and the key (entered by the user) are combined to generate a different key stream for each packet. Due to the size of the key, it is not feasible to attack each packet with brute force. The size of the IV, however, is rather small: 24 bits. This means that the entire IV space has only 16,777,216 possible values. Using this as the attack point, the IVs wrap many packets after this, and the same IV/key combination is used to encrypt a second packet. This collision in the IV space means that the contents of packets encrypted with the same IV could be determined if some portion or all of one of those packets is known. The greater the number of IV collisions, the easier it is to determine the contents of all packets sharing that IV. Because the IV is transmitted in cleartext, it is trivial to determine whether or not the IVs match.

Note that this method of determining packet contents relies on the plaintext contents of a portion or all of a packet (eventually over 16 million packets) being known. One can determine the plaintext contents of a packet through many ways, such as relying on the predictability of IP packets (most header contents are predictable), or by injecting known plaintext traffic from the wired infrastructure and then monitoring the encrypted contents.

Safeguarding Wireless LANs

Several levels of security can be implemented to safeguard the wireless LAN. The level of security that is implemented should match the security requirements of the wired LAN and the data that passes over it. Most wireless LAN implementations treat the wireless user as a regular LAN user, and most current wireless LAN devices run the same network applications as wired devices. The same principles that apply to identifying the IC levels of network traffic passing over Bluetooth links or WAP connections apply to wireless LAN connections. The two primary security safeguards that should be considered when implementing wireless LANs are the degree of control that is required in identifying the remote user and the degree to which the network traffic must be safeguarded. These security requirements are addressed by different mechanisms by wireless LANs, although some overlap occurs.

If the intent is to validate the identity of the remote device that is attempting the connection, then several measures can be employed. Obviously, the remote device will need to operate on the same channel and will have to use the correct ESSID in order to form the necessary association. These two control mechanisms were not designed for security, but were implemented to satisfy traffic management and user segmentation requirements.

With only a small number of channels operating at a known set of frequencies, determining the channel that a wireless LAN is operating on would be simple. The ESSID must be transmitted in the clear, so any device capable of sniffing or monitoring the wireless network would be able to determine the ESSID, once again with little difficulty. MAC address filtering is an effective method of determining which devices can participate in the wireless LAN. By filtering at this layer, a specific list of unique devices that have access to the LAN can be identified.

The downside to this is scalability/maintenance. In most current implementations, the filters are stored on the Access Points themselves. Large wireless deployments could have hundreds or even thousands of Access Points. Although configurations can be replicated from one access point to another and scripting is possible to update configurations as new devices are added to the client base, realize that a substantial planning effort is required to correctly implement this in a large enterprise.

If the intent of the security policy is to safeguard the contents of the data on the network, then WEP should be used. At the most basic level, only traffic encrypted with WEP should be allowed on the wireless LAN. Note that in most commercial implementations, this is not the default. This configuration is performed on the Access Point. All Access Points must be configured identically because a client can attempt to associate with more than one Access Point and will continue to attempt to associate with it until the client succeeds.

The industry is increasingly treating wireless users as remote access users. This is being done to address both the authentication and encryption security requirements and is improving the capabilities of both. The improvements in security address the fact that connection setup is conceptually similar for remote access (traditional dial-in) users and wireless users alike. Similar types of authentication mechanisms are now being developed for wireless that historically provided security to wired networks. For example, a proprietary implementation now exists that enables users to authenticate using extensions to the PPP protocol (Extensible Authentication Protocol [EAP]), which enable temporary connections to be set up between the remote device and the Access Point (which under this model plays the role of the access server). The remote device undergoes authentication steps where credentials are verified, typically consisting of a username and password combination that the Access Point forwards to an authentication server. If the credentials are correct, the user is allowed to join the network and is subsequently given a session-based WEP key unique to both that user and that session.

This is an improvement for both authentication and encryption. With regards to authentication, this security model now authenticates the user, not the device. It represents a break from traditional wireless authentication and provides a track for future improvements to include biometric or token-based authentication methods. It improves encryption through the use of a session-based key. When the WEP key is changed with every login (for the typical user, this is once per day) and the WEP key is unique to the individual, then the chances of an IV collision are very low. In addition, even if an IV collision occurs, the information gained is good only for the duration of the session. The IV can be reused in the next session because in a new session the WEP key will be different, generating a different keystream. This model could be extended as performance improves, with a refresh of the session as often as necessary to generate the required level of security.

Until these technologies advance, one method to address WLAN security is to use the same methods used to address any other user accessing the corporate network from a location that cannot be physically secured. The best existing model for this is a remote access model. The existing solution of putting wireless users behind a firewall and limiting access is one possibility. In most cases, however, because of the data that users must pass over the wireless link (common LAN traffic), this is not a practical solution that increases security in a measurable way.

A far better method is to make sure that the user of the wireless device is allowed to use the device and gain access to the network. Token-based or two-factor authentication methods can ride easily on top of existing technologies such as VPNs. This solution, although cumbersome to implement for what many consider to be LAN users, does address the dual problems of authenticating the user and safeguarding the data as it traverses the wireless link.

Analysis of Case Study #1—Corporate

The MCC corporate case study exemplifies the typical usage models for organizations of any size that have recognized the productivity potential of wireless-enabling their applications. The greatest security risk, mentioned numerous times throughout this chapter, is a two-fold physical security risk: the security of the mobile device itself and the fact that the extension of the network using wireless technology means that physical security and control of that portion of the network cannot be guaranteed. The different major wireless technologies (Bluetooth, WAP, and 802.11b wireless LANs) have devised various methods to secure the physical link in a way that is optimized for the devices that the technologies run on. The critical issue for the MCC is whether or not these methods are sufficient to safeguard the MCC's data and potential backdoor entry points into the corporate network.

The MCC will make certain security-related decisions as they evaluate wireless technologies, which will focus on three questions: 1) should the MCC implement this technology, 2) should the implementation be proprietary or standards-based, and finally, 3) should the implementation be in-house, or outsourced to a wireless application service provider (WASP)? There is no single correct answer to any of the above questions; they are implementation-specific and should be made on an organization-by-organization basis.

The MCC has analyzed its corporate functions to determine which wireless technologies provide a fit with regards to usage models and security. The following sections describe the technological factors that the MCC considered and the standards that the MCC has established for the implementation of each technology. In general, selecting the wireless technologies that fit each function was a matter of analyzing usage models. Bluetooth technologies are targeted at short-range communications. Implementing this technology will allow the MCC's users to "extend their desktops," both logically and physically. The MCC has adopted the model of treating WAP users as remote access users from the security standpoint, and an initial implementation is targeting the applications that remote users have the greatest need for. These applications include access to e-mail/calendaring and sales information.

The most widespread wireless technology deployment, however, is with wireless LANs (WLAN). From the application standpoint, the MCC's goal is to open all LAN resources to WLAN users. Table 8-2 is a summary of corporate electronic communications, initially identified in Chapter 1, and the wireless technologies that the MCC has chosen to deploy for each technology. In the sections below, there will be an analysis of specific wireless implementations.

Physical and Logical Security

The MCC has requirements for physical and logical security as they relate to the devices themselves. These requirements will drive vendor and device selection, as well as how the devices are distributed, maintained, and controlled. The first requirement is that the device itself can be physically secured in some manner. The MCC has defined this requirement for any device that can contain information that it considers to be of a classification level of Internal or higher. The focus of this requirement is on the personal digital assistant (PDA) and PocketPC type of device. These

Table 8-2

Corporate Application and Functional Wireless Breakdown

Corporate Function	Purpose	Wireless Components
Electronic mail, Calendaring	Collaboration	Bluetooth, WAP, WLAN
Corporate directory	Locate user's contact information	Bluetooth, WAP, WLAN
Internet connectivity	Research	WLAN
Sales contact information (existing customer base and prospective clients)	Sales forecasting, accounting, and legal departments	WAP
Marketing database	Repository for marketing research and engineering requests	WLAN
Engineering network and systems	Repository for hardware and software designs of MCC products	WLAN
Legal and HR network and systems	Hold and process employee and legal information	WLAN
Technical support (help desk)	Support the internal MCC staff	Bluetooth, WAP, WLAN
ERP systems	Supports many LOBs	WAP, WLAN
Remote access and control (Citrix)	All users to connect securely to the Intranet	WAP, WLAN
Intranet applications	Supports many LOBs	WAP, WLAN

devices contain increasingly sensitive information as they gain database connectivity, increased storage, and advancing document capabilities. Devices such as these can be secured using physical device locks similar to the devices used to secure laptops.

The second requirement is that, if physical control of the device is lost, access control mechanisms must be available for the information or data stored on the device. As a minimum requirement, this should consist of a

Barnes & Noble Booksellers
4140 W Jefferson Blvd. Bldg J
Ft. Wayne IN 46804
219 432-3343 12-06-01 S02036 R011

Caffe Latte Grande	3.10
0765547201	
SUB TOTAL	3.10
SALES TAX	.19
TOTAL	**3.29**
AMOUNT TENDERED	
CASH	**5.00**
TOTAL PAYMENT	5.00
CHANGE	1.71

SALES TAX ANALYSIS

CODE	RATE	TAXABLE	TAX
LOCAL	6.000%	3.10	.19

Thank you for Shopping at
Barnes & Noble Booksellers
Shop online 24 hours a day www.bn.com
#37105 12-06-01 09:17A dh

Booksellers Since 1873

Full refund issued for new and unread books and unopened music within 30 days with a receipt from any Barnes & Noble store.

Store Credit issued for new and unread books and unopened music after 30 days or without a sales receipt. Credit issued at lowest sale price.

We gladly accept returns of new and unread books and unopened music from bn.com with a bn.com receipt for store credit at the bn.com price.

Full refund issued for new and unread books and unopened music within 30 days with a receipt from any Barnes & Noble store.

Store Credit issued for new and unread books and unopened music after 30 days or without a sales receipt. Credit issued at lowest sale price.

We gladly accept returns of new and unread books and unopened music from bn.com with a bn.com receipt for store credit at the bn.com price.

Full refund issued for new and unread books and unopened music within password that controls access to the device prior to use and a second layer of security that enables specific applications or files to be secured.

The last requirement for logical security of the device is the capability to revoke any trusted designations that the device may have been granted in the event of device compromise. As mentioned earlier in this chapter, the primary authentication model for mobile devices is that the network trusts the device, not the user. The MCC has determined that the device must be able to be declared either unknown or untrusted (depending on the implementation). This process can be implemented using methods such as the revocation of digital certificates or by tagging the device identifier in device databases.

Bluetooth Implementation

The MCC is examining potential opportunities for a Bluetooth implementation within specific departmental areas of their corporate network. If the technology is found to be secure enough to meet corporate security policy, the MCC plans to implement Bluetooth in areas that align with standard implementation models/Bluetooth profiles. The primary profile that the MCC is focusing on is the creation of a personal area network (PAN) at the user level for device synchronization: primarily calendar, e-mail, and contact information. They have also recognized that a second potential opportunity exists to implement Bluetooth as a transport for either a three-in-one phone or the "ultimate headset." These usage models target the capability of Bluetooth to carry voice in addition to data while giving the user population an increased ability to move limited distances from the wired base station.

The MCC has focused on Bluetooth Mode 2 security-enabled devices. Mode 2 enables security to be established on an application basis. An analysis of the marketplace reveals that although only a small number of devices and applications are currently tailored to the Bluetooth architecture, initial applications will have varying security requirements. The MCC plans to take advantage of the vCard application and wants to implement this with minimal security for ease of use. Because individual contact information is classified as public information, no access control mechanisms are required.

The MCC also plans on implementing PANs using Bluetooth to ease device synchronization. Thus, a user with a Bluetooth-enabled mobile phone, PDA, laptop, and bridge to their PC can seamlessly synchronize mail, contact, and calendar data. Some of this information is considered to be proprietary by the organization; e-mail regularly contains internal and confidential information and some contact information, such as the corporate phone directory, which is considered internal. The MCC has published a policy that calls for users to designate only their own devices as trusted devices for Bluetooth connections. These devices are allowed to synchronize seamlessly. All other devices, such as those of coworkers, customers, and competitors, are considered untrusted.

The MCC also considers Bluetooth to be of benefit to technical support personnel working in call centers such as the help desk and the Network Operations Center (NOC). These individuals often have the need to move limited distances from their desks when working to resolve problems with co-workers. These individuals often use headsets but are limited due to the cumbersome nature of the cables required to maintain connectivity. From the security point of view, the ultimate headset usage model meets corporate security guidelines. The Bluetooth protocol has the capability to encrypt traffic sent across the link. Additionally, for power consumption reasons, it has self-tuning output levels; the devices will only transmit with the power level required to maintain connectivity. This is in contrast to other technologies, which transmit at a constant power level, regardless of whether or not this is required.

Wireless Application Protocol Implementation

A broad range of applications exist that the MCC has identified for wireless connectivity using the Wireless Application Protocol. The three primary applications targeted for initial deployment are "e-mail anywhere, anytime," access to the corporate Intranet, and sales access to contact information and forecasts. The corporate Intranet will include an interface to access the MCC's NOC trouble ticket system, which will enable detailed remote problem diagnosis. The MCC has decided that due to the various security classification levels of information that can traverse the WAP physical link, especially when accessing corporate e-mail, WAP users are to be treated as remote access users to the corporate network. Recognizing that WAP authenticates the device, not the user, the MCC has implemented security access controls at multiple layers for WAP users.

The first step in the process is that the MCC has taken steps to secure the Gap in WAP: the WAP gateway. The MCC's WAP gateway is located in one of the organization's DMZs. The firewalls and filtering routers that protect the WAP gateway permit only WTLS-encrypted traffic on the ports that the protocol needs. In addition, to prevent against possible compromise from internal users, only select addresses and protocols are allowed access to the gateway. This is in line with the configuration standards applied for access to other such devices protected by the corporate perimeter security infrastructure. This creates a secure environment for the decryption and re-encryption that takes place on the gateway. Within the security capabilities of the Wireless Application Protocol, the MCC has selected a vendor that supports implementing WTLS as a mechanism for securing the link.

Because of the IC levels of the data that will potentially pass over this link, the MCC has selected a vendor that can provide a Class 2 security implementation. Class 2 security provides mandatory certificates from the server side of the transaction. Additionally, it provides support for certificates, encryption, and Message Authentication Codes.

The MCC has determined that this alone does not provide adequate authentication or non-repudiation for the transactions that will take place across the link. The MCC has implemented an access control system that requires two-factor authentication for WAP users. Because this capability is not built into the Wireless Application Protocol, it is implemented as a proprietary solution using a vendor that supports this method of end-to-end authentication. The implementation details of this system emulate the mechanisms and policies employed for remote access users. Because of limited displays and data entry capabilities of the devices that communicate over the wireless network, this adds a burden at the user interface level. This is identified as an acceptable burden to bear in order to protect the MCC's information assets.

Wireless LAN Implementation

The MCC has decided to extend the traditional, wired LANs by adding a wireless LAN infrastructure in their corporate locations. All corporate information assets are available over the LAN. Prior to wireless technologies, the user of the information had to be at a fixed, wired workstation. Collaboration and data exchange at meetings was limited, due to the costs involved with cabling shared areas (conference rooms, shared areas, corporate cafeterias, and the headquarter's auditorium). By moving forward with a wireless LAN implementation, the MCC was able to provide an instant network in these locations at a fraction of the cost. Recognizing again that the organization could no longer define the physical boundaries of the network, the MCC took steps to secure the link and enforce the required level of security in order to protect its information assets.

The MCC determined that WLAN users, although not considered remote access users, could not be given access to the network in exactly the same manner as wired LAN users. Both the device and the user would have to be authenticated and the MCC would implement WEP to encrypt all network traffic between the WLAN protocol endpoints. The MCC first selected a vendor that could satisfy the requirements of authenticating both the device and the user. The MCC then developed a configuration standard for their wireless Access Points to enforce the policy stated above. The policy included the following elements:

- *Disable the Broadcast ESSID permissions on the Access Points.* This prevented a user with a blank ESSID configured on his or her mobile device from associating with the Access Point.
- *Require WEP.* This involved disabling the functionality on the Access Point that allowed mixed cells and unencrypted cells. Mixed cells are Access Points that could communicate with some clients using encryption and others without encryption.
- *Use a proprietary vendor solution to perform user authentication.* In their initial implementation, the WEP standards had the effect of only authenticating the device. Because the WEP keys were traditionally entered into the client configuration, a compromise of the device also meant a compromise of the WEP key. User authentication was performed against a database; if a wireless user left the organization, it was simply a matter of disabling the user account to also disable WLAN access. The mechanism that the MCC employed used user authentication as a method of distributing the WEP key. This means that the WEP key was unique to the user and unique to the login: a session-based WEP key. This significantly reduced the inherent risks in the WEP design.

It should be noted that WEP encrypts traffic only between the protocol endpoints. Traffic is unencrypted on the Access Point and sent over the LAN like any other traffic from a wired user. The MCC enforces the same standard for information safeguarding for WLAN users as they do for wired LAN users. This is transparent to the WLAN user and the WLAN protocols. If an application normally encrypts traffic prior to sending it on to the LAN, then the application will encrypt it normally when operating in a WLAN environment as well. The traffic will then additionally be encrypted using WEP.

Analysis of Case Study #2—FinApp

The MCC is approaching a wireless deployment of the FinApp with caution. Due to the regulations of the industry and complemented by policies internal to the MCC, any wireless deployment of the FinApp will need the maximum levels of confidentiality, data integrity, and authentication. The same levels of protection afforded by wired connectivity must be available for any connection coming over wireless links. The topic of personal area networks, implemented with Bluetooth, is not relevant to the discussion of the FinApp deployment. Similarly, no additional measures need to be implemented in the wireless local area networks (WLANs). The MCC has already carefully considered the necessary security measures for this type of network. Employees accessing the FinApp via WLANs are already safeguarded appropriately. The focus of the security assessment for wireless deployment of the FinApp will be on securing the communication link across the wireless wide area network (WWAN).

The MCC will be taking a two-phase approach to implementing wireless access to the FinApp. The first phase will provide access to PDAs, specifically the Palm platform, through a Palm Query Application (PQA) over a virtual private network (VPN). This was selected because this platform is robust enough to handle the additional security required for the FinApp. The second phase of the rollout will open access for the FinApp to a potentially larger range of devices and will target a more standards-based deployment.

Phase 1: Palm Pilot

The first phase of the rollout is a deployment of proprietary, "best of breed" components. Due to the early emergence of applications oriented to the Palm platform, the widespread deployment of Palm Pilots, and the security features and capabilities available for the platform, the MCC chose the Palm V handheld device as the wireless platform slated for FinApp development. The critical facets that the MCC considered when planning for the rollout of the FinApp to wireless users were the distribution of the PQA file to users, the authentication of users, and the method of securing the data as it passed through the wireless network. To address the security requirements for both of these issues, the MCC will rely on both traditional and newly available technologies.

The Palm Pilot running a PQA was an appropriate choice to initially deploy the FinApp because the transactional nature of the FinApp lent itself to the development of a query-response application for wireless connectivity. By developing a query-response application, FinApp could determine exactly what authentication would be required to access the application, as well as a high degree of control over what data (and also what Information Classification levels) could pass over the wireless links. The first step in the process will be the distribution of the PQA to clients.

For this, two methods of distribution are available. Both of the distribution methods are out-of-band, in that they do not use the wireless network as a distribution mechanism. The first mechanism is through a download from a secure company Web site. The Web site performs checks to identify the user to the degree that they are authorized full access to their account. After performing the checks, the user is able to register for and download the PQA file from a secured Web site (via SSL). The user can then install the PQA on the device.

The second method also relies on a traditional method of delivery. After being successfully identified, the client requests the PQA. The PQA is then digitally signed and sent to the client, who unpacks the signed PQA file, verifying the signature of the MCC in the process. In this manner, the authenticity of the PQA file can be verified and its integrity is assured. Because the PQA file only directs the user to the MCC Web site, where authentication and authorization are then handled, it could be distributed freely throughout the public domain without risk to corporate assets. It is important, however, that the PQA file be digitally signed by the MCC to ensure its authenticity and integrity (freedom from viruses and so on) upon receipt by the user.

To address the issue of user authentication, the MCC is leveraging its existing token technologies by extending it to the wireless platform. Once again, the PDA platform provides a more robust set of solutions with regard to token technology. These technologies are emerging in de facto standards for other wireless devices, but in an initial deployment, the MCC is using established, third-party applications to support strong (two-factor) authentication.

An additional requirement for wireless access to the FinApp is an IPSec VPN between the wireless client device and the MCC's corporate VPN concentrator. The implementation of a VPN between the endpoints of the connection enables the end-to-end security and privacy that is not available in current standards-based implementations. Although the gateways and proxy mechanisms are considered secure for the majority of the MCC's data, the MCC determined that opening the FinApp to this environment was too great of a risk. For a VPN solution, the MCC has turned to a vendor that has a VPN client that runs on the Palm platform and is compatible with the MCC's gateway/concentrator. This saves the cost of having to purchase an additional infrastructure just to support wireless VPN access.

The minimum requirements for the VPN software included

- Support of Diffie-Hellman (DH) Group 7 (ECC) for the generation of IPSec SA keys, with an elliptic curve field size of 163 bits. This is strictly for performance reasons. Using DH Group 1 (768 bits) or DH Group 2 (1,024 bits) can cause the concentrator to time out (correctly, for security reasons) while waiting for a response from the wireless device. This is due to the high-processing requirements for these algorithms. ECC generates keys of equivalent encryption strength with much lower processing.
- Support for Triple-DES (3DES) for data encryption.
- Interoperability with the client and concentrator platforms.

Phase 2: WAP

The MCC is planning a WAP implementation of the FinApp as the overall wireless market matures. In addition to an established, stable Web-based interface for the FinApp, the company has established two additional pre-requisites prior to moving to a WAP solution:

- Widespread availability of clients that support the Class 3 security mode—client and server authentication through certificates
- Widespread deployment of WAP version 1.2 to overcome some of the security problems in WAP version 1.1

The MCC will use the same architecture that they have deployed in support of their own internal wireless remote access users, as discussed in the first case study. The WAP gateway will be located inside the enterprise security perimeter. Within the scope of the protocol standards, the use of client- and server-side certificates will provide a strong means of authentication across the physical link for the device. As is the case with the corporate deployment of WAP, the MCC will additionally require two-factor authentication (through the use of token technology), a proprietary mechanism. This is consistent with the model of authenticating remote access users. It is still the responsibility of the upper-layer application (FinApp) to provide additional security measures as required. This would include things such as authentication and authorization controls already in place for all other current users. At the link level, ECC will provide the required privacy for key exchange, known algorithms such as 3DES will be used for encryption, and the use of Message Authentication Code (MAC) inherent in Class 3 security will provide data integrity.

Analysis of Case Study #3—HealthApp

The MCC line of business (LOB) that has developed the HealthApp, an application that automates health care claims processing, will employ many of the standards developed to support wireless remote access, as discussed in Case Study #1, and a sensitive business-oriented application, as discussed in Case Study #2. The critical security issues from the wireless perspective are ensuring privacy across the wireless link and enforcing an effective authentication mechanism. The HealthApp does not require the same degree of non-repudiation as the FinApp.

As discussed in the introduction of the FinApp in Chapter 1, due to the volatility of the business and the legal requirements associated with the industry, establishing a mechanism for non-repudiation is essential with the FinApp. Although the implementation of wireless wide area network (WWAN) access to the HealthApp includes measures to ensure data integrity and provides a certain degree of non-repudiation, the focus is on other aspects of security.

As is the case with FinApp, the security measures implemented for personal area networks and wireless local area networks do not need to be changed for the use of the HealthApp. The security assessments for these applications, when run in these environments, were a consideration in the establishment of the policies for those environments.

As the MCC moves toward opening up access to the HealthApp to Internet users, they will open concurrent access to wireless users. The MCC will also be accessed from a variety of platforms using various mechanisms. The primary requirement for any platform prior to adoption is that it be able to support the security requirements established for other remote access connections to the application. For example, the end device and communication method must be able to support encryption equivalent to 128-bit SSL encryption.

Although this security stance is in line with the implementation established in the first case study, it deserves special attention for the HealthApp. It requires that the MCC take a close look at the devices that they will support for remote connectivity. In the case of the HealthApp, independent health care providers will be accessing the application. The MCC does not have control over the devices that the providers may purchase or have already purchased, but through the adoption and support of certain protocols, they can dictate the security of the connection. Because the MCC has previously established strong security in the form of 128-bit SSL encryption as a mechanism for ensuring privacy, inbound connections from PocketPC/Windows CE 3.0 devices will be permitted. Starting with Windows CE version 3.0, 128-bit encryption is possible.

The MCC has also established that in addition to the RSA and Diffie-Hellman algorithms for key exchange, 163-bit key ECC provides an acceptable level of encryption strength for key exchange. This opens access to the Palm platform, which uses both 163-bit ECC and 128-bit SSL encryption in the data path from the device to the corporate gateway. Additionally, the HealthApp will be open to internal users using the WAP standard.

To address authentication, the HealthApp must provide its own application layer authentication mechanism. This is due to the population of health care providers that will be accessing the device. Managing digital certificate authentication from the health care provider population is not a feasible measure at this time. Token technology is also not feasible (this was previously discussed with respect to the security infrastructure of the HealthApp). Wireless users to the HealthApp will have to adhere to the same authentication standard as remote access users (complex passwords, password aging, and so on). WAP users will authenticate using the same system as non-WAP users. As the protocol matures and clients increasingly become capable of supporting Class 3 security mode, the MCC will be able to move the authentication to client-side digital certificates. Although token technology is currently available to this set of the user population (internal users that utilize token technologies for other forms of remote access), it will not be implemented in the initial deployment of the HealthApp but will instead be integrated alongside digital certificates.

Conclusion

The wireless data industry is evolving on every front. Certain technologies, such as wireless LAN technologies, are standardized with respect to protocol definitions. The changes that are taking place in this industry are a maturation of the technologies. Recent changes have improved security by enabling the dynamic assignment of WEP keys. These changes are not currently standards-based but are on strong standards tracks. Other technologies are still in the early stages of development. The new and proposed Bluetooth and WAP protocol suites offer significant improvements to the security aspects of the protocols. The industry and protocol developers have recognized the potential commercial benefits of securing the protocols and are moving aggressively to close the existing gaps in security.

Two significant lessons can be learned from the analysis of wireless data security. First, the same principles that apply to wired data security apply to wireless security. The difference is the emphasis that must be placed on the different aspects of security. Because wireless networks are more vulnerable to data interception/monitoring, the privacy component of an organization's overall wireless security policy should be carefully considered. The same applies to authentication because many existing wireless authentication models rely on the trust of the device, not the user. Other components of an overall security policy, such as authorization or accounting, do not need to be much different for wireless or wired communication.

The second lesson from an assessment of wireless security is that it is a fluid topic. Change is constant, so it is important to continuously re-evaluate the technologies available. In some cases, an organization may make the assessment that certain wireless protocols may not provide the necessary level of security in their current release. By analyzing the development paths, however, an organization can begin to plan to deploy applications as the security improves.

Although this is the case with all technologies, the immature status of certain wireless technologies means that these changes will come at a faster pace than traditional technologies. Changes may also occur in more dramatic fashion; new vulnerabilities will be uncovered, and new features will be introduced that will significantly change the strength of wireless protocol security. By staying current with changes in wireless security protocols, a security practitioner will be able to best determine which technologies and features will provide secure, available wireless connectivity to their organization.

CHAPTER 9

Platform Hardening

When broken down to its simplest level, modern information-technology infrastructure is divided into two categories: networks and platforms. The routers, switches, load balancers, and fiber optics that provide a path for data to travel across the Internet and corporate networks all belong to the network category. Web pages, databases, and other types of applications, data, or software reside on platforms. The physical realities of technology require an intruder to travel through network resources, but the ultimate targets of most attacks are located on a platform.

Platform hardening involves a methodology used to analyze a host to determine its weaknesses and then integrate necessary changes that serve to protect the host and its applications from attack. This methodology helps examine the various components of an operating system (OS) and its associated applications to determine the most secure configuration. This configuration process includes the removal of unneeded services, software, and users from the system, along with tightening individual controls on OS utilities and software. The end result is a platform that takes an active role in its own security, instead of solely relying on an external-security mechanism.

The security industry has expended countless resources in the development of network-based defenses to discourage an intruder from using the network to reach their target. For most organizations, security relies on network obstacles like firewalls to block intruders at the perimeter. They build a hard shell around their critical resources, but leave themselves vulnerable when an intruder successfully defeats the perimeter.

Information-security paradigms employed by banks clearly illustrate why this security methodology is flawed. The average bank is ringed in layers of security. Access points like doors and windows utilize bars and strong locks. Door, window, and motion sensors provide a second layer of security that sounds an alert when these outer layers are defeated. Closed-circuit television cameras and roving guards add a third layer of defense to monitor authorized users who enter the bank.

With all of these security measures in place, does the bank choose to store money and valuables on publicly exposed tables or in unlocked drawers? Obviously, the answer is no; these critical items are stored in a massive safe with tons of steel and complex-locking mechanisms to keep them secure. If banks followed the common-security practices of most IT organizations, money might actually be stored in the middle of the room! Banks understand very clearly that a layered approach must be used to defend their critical resources.

Platform hardening is another information-security foundation that adds to a layered defense; in most cases, it is the final defense. An intruder that defeats perimeter-network defenses will find him or himself at the front door of a server or servers. In modern OSs, this front door can be comprised of many different services. These services could include remote access (Telnet or rlogin), e-mail (SMTP), file transfer (FTP or NFS), and monitoring (SNMP) to name just a few. Any of these services could contain bugs in their software that an intruder could exploit to gain unauthorized access to the host system. Additionally, an intruder might not even need to exploit software bugs if he uses known default-user accounts or passwords. Once on a host system, an intruder could continue the attack to elevate his access privileges on the system by exploiting countless weaknesses in software packages, system utilities, and even the OS kernel itself.

The obvious question is why would an organization build a host with so many vulnerabilities? This question has two answers. The most common answer stems from a general misunderstanding by the IT community of the design principles used by operating system manufacturers. Today, OS developers strive to make their software the most flexible and powerful in the market. To attain market penetration, an OS will ship with multiple capabilities that can be harnessed right out of the box. The increased emphasis on Internet capability means that OS distributions will, by default, provide Web, e-mail, file storage/transfer, and database services. In addition, to ensure smooth integration with existing systems, today's technologically bleeding-edge systems will still enable access to unsecured services with 1970's vintage! Average IT consumers will utilize one or two of these services, but will never deactivate the others, which unknowingly leaves themselves open to attack. The flexibility, which allows an OS to fill many roles in an enterprise, comes at the cost of security.

The second most common reason that hosts are left so vulnerable is due to misunderstanding feedback from security technology principles. To most, securing an infrastructure means erecting a firewall. "It's behind the firewall, so it's safe," is one of the most common phrases used by IT professionals. Rarely do intruders directly attack and penetrate the firewall itself, which is typically an extremely daunting task.

Firewalls simply control traffic. If a firewall is programmed to only allow Web traffic from the Internet to a Web server, then no other traffic will presumably get through. The firewall does not stop the intruder from attacking the Web server. In fact, it allows this to happen because the attack utilizes Web traffic as a vector. In reality, the firewall only acts like a funnel; the real defender is the Web-server software on the platform. If no security measures are in place to defend the Web server, then a successful attack against it neutralizes the firewall. A layered defense that includes platform hardening would not only defend the host, but also monitor it for intrusions and allow the organization to react and repel the attack.

It must be noted that this rule has one exception. OpenBSD is the closest to a secure out-of-the-box OS distribution available today. The OpenBSD project from Canada made security their primary goal in the development of the OS. OpenBSD, a descendant of the Berkeley Software Development (BSD) UNIX OS family, implements security by default methodology for all of its components. The development team spends most of its time combing through every line of code, from kernel to application, looking for bugs that could compromise system security. They also include pre-configured security tools like OpenSSH for remote access, ApacheSSL for secure Web-site hosting, OS- level firewall tools, and strong encryption libraries to support security in other applications. The focus on security has left little user-friendliness in this distribution. However, the developers have little interest in the desktop market or in achieving market penetration. They want a secure OS and have often rejected offers for commercial support.

As we will also see later in the chapter, platform hardening does not only involve technology. Business processes also steer the decisions used in the methodology. In many cases, security best practices will be superseded by business requirements through risk-acceptance processes. In this chapter, we will examine both platform-hardening strategy and practice building an understanding of this important security methodology.

Business Case, Costs, and Resource Requirements

Information security is just as important to an organization's risk management program as casualty and liability insurance. As with conventional insurance, information security practices are preventative measures that, although non-revenue producing, are business necessities. Information systems are no longer tools that assist the business process; they enable them. These systems must be properly protected to ensure business continuity. The legal system is also adapting itself to the problems inherent with the lack of proper security. Organizations will become liable when intruders leapfrog through them to damage others. Stakeholders in today's businesses know that the lack of best-practice security standards is just as bad as a warehouse without fire or theft protection.

We have already begun to lay out the business case for platform hardening. More layers of security translate to a higher probability of an organization surviving attack by intruders. Unless an organization is quite sophisticated, its firewalls and intrusion-detection systems will only face outward, leaving internal systems unprotected. Platform hardening leverages the security features of existing-operating platforms to add an internal layer of defense. This extracts added value from previous infrastructure investments.

Platform-hardening costs need to be broken into two categories; both are generally non-recurring. The first category includes the man-hours needed to analyze the current state of the infrastructure and determine how the project will be executed. Considerably more time will be required in a situation where existing platforms need hardening. In a large enterprise, with hundreds of platforms, labor resources will have to be redirected from other projects or outside consultants will be required.

In the second category, a smaller team can be dedicated to a situation where a hardened-standard build is going to be rolled out to replace existing platforms. This smaller team will develop the build, but the system manager will be tasked with the rollout, similar to other upgrade projects. In both cases, a larger up-front expenditure will be required to either bring the enterprise into compliance or internally develop a standard build.

Because most organizations do not have infinite resources to spend on security, it is rare for every platform to be hardened. Security budgets must also fund other programs such as policy development, awareness, firewalls, and encryption; therefore, it is important to decide which platforms would benefit the most from hardening and allocate resources to them. Every organization has different needs. Whereas one might decide to globally replace Telnet with SSH, another might expend the entire hardening budget on securing a few transactional systems. As with all security programs, risk analysis is the key factor in determining the specifics of a platform-hardening program.

Platform Anatomy

OS software is the soul of any computing platform. Whether the device is a thermostat or a supercomputer, the OS is what empowers the silicon chips to do their job. Because OSs must be able to provide a wide range of functions and services, they are comprised of many different subsystems. Although different platforms may have more or less capable components, all OSs can share a common set of functional subsystems. Each of these subsystems has potential areas of weakness that are addressed during the platform-hardening process.

- **Network** The outermost layer, or skin, of an OS is its network services. Network services provide the OS with a means to communicate electronically with other systems on a network. Because these services are the most exposed and visible to intruders, special care must be taken when securing them. Like the gates of a walled city, network services are usually the front line in OS defenses because they are the only way, other than using the system console, for an intruder to access a platform.
- **System software** An OS functions through dozens of smaller applications and utilities. Because many of these applications require very high system privilege, they become prime targets for attack.

Usually, this privilege is hidden from the user. Sometimes, the simplest system utility can contain bugs that when exploited, elevates the privilege of the user.

- **File system** Like an office's filing system, an OS stores and organizes its data with the file system component. The file system is responsible for keeping data safe through enforcement of file permissions, data access controls, and maintenance of file integrity. Improperly protected system-configuration files can lead to modification and destruction of these key elements.
- **User** The user subsystem is responsible for managing all aspects of user access to the platform including password storage, home directories, access controls, and security-privilege levels. The password store on a platform must be secured with strong encryption and inaccessible to unprivileged users. Outdated user accounts or accounts with weak passwords (such as children's names, birthdays, and so on) can be exploited, especially if manufacturer-default accounts are left active.
- **Physical** One of three sides of the information security triad is availability. A tightly hardened platform that sits under a desk, unprotected by backup power and HVAC is vulnerable to physical attack. Virtually every platform can be rebooted into a maintenance mode that would give an intruder access. Removable hard disks with highly sensitive data can be stolen from an unsecured cabinet. Platforms that can boot from a floppy disk are easily cracked open with any number of utilities.

Platform Hardening Approach

The goal of a platform-hardening project is threefold:

- Reduce the amount of unutilized software, services, and processes.
- Bring all software, service, and process configuration to their most secure state while continuing to provide access to resources.
- Minimize the information that a system reveals about its identity, services, and capabilities.

These goals might seem more in line with a performance-tuning project. However, although performance tuning streamlines a system for faster response, platform hardening streamlines a system to reduce the number of possible attack vectors. Intruders most often exploit buggy software to gain access to a system. An examination of the daily postings to the BUGTRAQ mailing list[1] will reveal that almost any software component from dir to complex encryption subroutines have the potential to malfunction and give an intruder unauthorized access. By reducing (where feasible) the number of extraneous software and service components, you are bolstering the platform's capability to resist attack.

As we have previously mentioned, most OS software and applications ship with default settings at the most unsecured levels to enable the most flexibility. Many times, these components have built-in security features that have the potential to improve overall platform security. For example, by default, Domain Name Services (DNS) are configured completely unsecured; they can be locked down with a few simple configuration changes. These changes make it harder for an attacker to steal, poison, and hijack this critical service while leaving authorized users unaffected. This is an extremely important piece of the platform-hardening triad.

Reducing and obfuscating the amount of information that a system reveals about its identity, services, and capabilities is the final goal of platform hardening. Just as bank robbers observe their target searching for a weakness, electronic intruders need to know something about their target in order to develop an assault strategy. Using readily available tools, attackers can fingerprint a platform to discover the hardware type and OS specifications. They can read service banners from Web and e-mail ports to reveal the service's software version and release. Finally, attackers can sometimes simply ask a system (Windows NT/2000 installations, for instance) for a list of its users and file shares. All of this reconnaissance information is compiled and used to develop the best mode of attack. None of this information is necessary for the operation of the platform and can therefore be safely hidden. Four phases are recommended to accomplish these goals and successfully harden a platform:

- Identify
- Assess
- Design
- Execute

[1] **http://www.securityfocus.com**

Identify

The first step in the process is to identify the purpose of the target system. Many times, technology upgrades replace existing platforms, but do not finish the process by decommissioning them due to ineffective system life cycle management. One of the most dangerous security threats to an enterprise comes from forgotten platforms that remain active. In more than one case, systems that were supposedly replaced are discovered to be alive and acting as a host for unauthorized activity. When hardening a platform, all assumptions must be erased and the following questions asked:

- Why was this platform built?
- Who is responsible for this platform?
- Does this system fulfill a business-related requirement?
- What services are required to satisfy this need?
- Who needs access to this system?
- What resources does this system need access to?

This list mirrors the type of requirements document that should have been compiled prior to the commissioning of the system. It acts as both a sanity check for the processes related to system life cycle and it defines a blueprint for the applications, services, and processes that the system must have.

Assess

Once system requirements are identified, the next step is to assess the system to determine if the actual implementation matches the initial set of requirements. This assessment does not have to use complicated methods and tools. A system operator can usually provide an inventory of the services, ports, applications, software versions, users, and processes. This simple list is usually enough to build a simple delta report. In most cases, the number of actual services will be much larger than those required. This information will act as a benchmark for the next phase.

Design

The design phase looks very similar to the define phase. Based on the requirements that we have defined for the system, we will design a strategy for implementing security in the five functional subsystems that we have already discussed. It is important to understand that at this point in the process we are not looking to design a detailed technical implementation. The strategy that we define will drive the technical changes in the next phase. This concept enables the process to work for any platform because it will hopefully follow the overall security strategy of the organization. The following questions must be asked of the five functional subsystems:

- **Network** How much network access will this system require to function properly? Do users require remote access to this system? Will this access originate from trusted or un-trusted parts of the network? Will the organization support the removal of all unencrypted access services? Should files from this system be shared with other systems? Will this system be remotely administered? Will a firewall or packet-filtering device protect the network access? If not, can we implement packet-filtering functions on the platform itself? If so, will the firewall support the expected throughput of the system?
- **System software** Does this system have the most recent corporate standard software release and patches? Do these software versions match the vendor-recommended security-patch levels? Are there major internal software packages that are not used and can be removed? Are menu/GUI-based administration programs used? Do critical software components log properly? Are these logs rotated/archived? Are standard images used to build new systems to maintain conformity?
- **File system** Is the file system local or are there remotely mounted volumes? Are these remote mounts using a secure protocol? Are the local volumes partitioned properly? Can logs outgrow their space and disable the system? Is OS-based encryption used to protect files? Are executables properly restricted? Is SUID[2] functionality limited to critical executables? Is the system properly backed up?

[2]SUID is a method of granting a system utility that requires elevated system privileges to complete a task (temporary elevated status) without passing this privilege onto the user.

- **Users** Which users require access to this system? Do they use strong passwords? Is password aging required? Are accounts stored and managed locally or through a common directory? Are user accounts regularly audited and re-certified? Who can create accounts? Can privileged functions be executed with role-based accounts? Is usage monitored? Are user paths and permissions set?
- **Physical** Is the system located in a secure data center? Is it connected to a secure power source? Is heating/cooling adequate? Is the system console secured in a locked cabinet? Does the console automatically log out after periods of inactivity?

The key to this phase is consistency. Although unanswered questions might highlight a weak or nonexistent security policy, the process should not stop because of this type of deficiency. The process will be successful as long as an organization has a strategy and rationale for the decisions it makes in the hardening process. Because platform hardening is only one layer in an information security plan, it must be uniform across all systems to ensure that security planners can integrate it with the other elements. If business requirements dictate that certain unsecured services run on platforms across the enterprise, planners will be able to add defensive capability to the firewalls and routers to protect this weakness.

It is vitally important to understand at this point that a system can be over-hardened. With enough work, any system can be stripped down to the absolute bare minimum to support a single function (like a dedicated firewall platform). Although this hardening produces an extremely secure platform, it leaves room for nothing else. If too many system utilities are removed, it might be impossible to run diagnostic checks or install software upgrades. Missing software libraries will make it impossible to add additional features and functions to the platform. Like most things, it is much easier to take away than to put back. Platform hardening succeeds when it brings a platform into line with industry best practice.

A good part of the time and resources dedicated to the design process must include testing. As with any technology upgrade, it is strongly recommended that any extensive hardening be done first in a lab environment. Legacy and internally developed applications are particularly vulnerable to breakage because documentation is usually weak and dependencies on other systems might not be understood. Most generic platforms that run simple Web or e-mail services have few internal dependencies that will be broken during hardening. Complexity increases when dealing with database or application servers, especially those developed internally. In many instances, older core-business applications that have been developed internally lacked the input of information security professionals during the development and deployment phases. The application developers might have tapped harmless software components that have no apparent function, yet are a requirement of the system. Application developers and system support personnel must be included in the design and testing processes to ensure that the process moves along smoothly. As we have already stated, information-security practices must support the business process, not impede it.

Execute

The execute phase is tackled by way of a two-pronged attack. The first prong addresses existing platforms. Significant challenges arise whenever changes need to be made to production systems. Management must allocate support personnel resources familiar with the target platform to be included in the testing phase to secure buy-in with the plan. Systems might require downtime and reboots as part of the hardening process. System managers might need some re-education to understand how to practice more secure maintenance. An integrated-project plan must address these issues to ensure a successful result.

The second prong of the attack addresses new platforms. New systems are ideal candidates for hardening because they can be designed with security improvements as part of the overall blueprint. One method of ensuring success in this area is the development of standard builds. A standard build is a cookie cutter image of a specific-system type that has all the features required to accomplish a specific goal. Organizations can develop profiles for desktops, Web servers, database systems, and every other type of platform that is used in the enterprise. These profiles specify the type of OS, patch levels, application software, and security settings. They are then handcrafted in the lab and imaged into a form that can be repeatedly reproduced. It lowers the time to production because all software and configurations are included in the image. The profiles and images must be updated as new patches and requirements, and software releases appear.

Standard builds can also be used to ease the hardening of existing systems. In many cases, a swap-out system can be implemented. With swap out, a standard build is imaged onto a comparable hardware platform. The configuration settings and data from the target system are implemented on the replacement system and the two units are swapped. In the final step, data is synchronized, resulting in a production platform that meets required operational goals, but in a secure way. The older unit can then be re-imaged to replace another production system, and the whole process repeats itself. The time and resources saved by using this method translates into a more efficient and effective security organization.

Practical Hardening Guidelines

Although this chapter is not a detailed technical guide to platform hardening, it is important to highlight the common weaknesses and compensating controls for some of the more popular OSs and platforms.

Ports and Processes

If you boil down all of the abstract layers of a platform with security in mind, you are left with the operating system, processes, and network ports. The OS provides a software interface to the hardware for processes, and processes open ports to the network. The quickest way to assess and lock down a platform is by looking at its process and port tables.

The netstat utility is a useful tool that lists the open TCP/IP network ports on a system, the de facto networking protocol for modern networks. Almost every UNIX and Windows platform ships with the netstat utility as part of its suite of networking software. With it, you can quickly assess the listening-network ports on the platform. These open ports are what intruders attempt to attack because they lead to the internals of the platform. Therefore, as part of platform hardening, we use netstat to identify extraneous ports that we can trace back to applications that can be removed or disabled (see Figure 9-1). Table 9-1 shows a list of standard ports that are commonly active on most out-of-the-box installations.

The process table also helps determine the current state of a platform. Every active software component on a platform must have an entry in some sort of process table. Because our goal is to identify and remove unnecessary processes and their related software, the process-table forms a roadmap for this task.

Figure 9-1

Sample output of netstat

```
netstat - na
Active Connections

Proto  Local Address          Foreign Address   State
TCP    0.0.0.0:23             0.0.0.0:0         LISTENING
TCP    0.0.0.0:111            0.0.0.0:0         LISTENING
TCP    0.0.0.0:135            0.0.0.0:0         LISTENING
TCP    0.0.0.0:445            0.0.0.0:0         LISTENING
TCP    0.0.0.0:769            0.0.0.0:0         LISTENING
TCP    0.0.0.0:1028           0.0.0.0:0         LISTENING
TCP    0.0.0.0:1039           0.0.0.0:0         LISTENING
TCP    0.0.0.0:1042           0.0.0.0:0         LISTENING
TCP    0.0.0.0:1047           0.0.0.0:0         LISTENING
TCP    0.0.0.0:1048           0.0.0.0:0         LISTENING
TCP    0.0.0.0:1748           0.0.0.0:0         LISTENING
TCP    0.0.0.0:2049           0.0.0.0:0         LISTENING
TCP    0.0.0.0:6677           0.0.0.0:0         LISTENING
TCP    1.0.0.1:139            0.0.0.0:0         LISTENING
TCP    169.124.170.101:139    0.0.0.0:0         LISTENING
```

Table 9-1

Some Common TCP/IP Ports

Port	Associated Application
21	FTP
23	Telnet
25	E-mail (SMTP)
53	DNS
80	Web server
111	RPC
139	NetBIOS (Windows file and printer sharing)

Shutting down and removing unnecessary applications in Windows NT/2000 is fairly simple. A graphic user interface (GUI) control panel configures each service and determines how it is started. It is a simple matter of running down the list and shutting down and disabling unnecessary services. Figure 9-2 illustrates the Windows 2000 services panel.

Disabling services on UNIX platforms can be more challenging. Depending on the distribution, services can be started automatically from a number of locations and at different times during the startup process. For each process to be started, a small shell script is built that takes

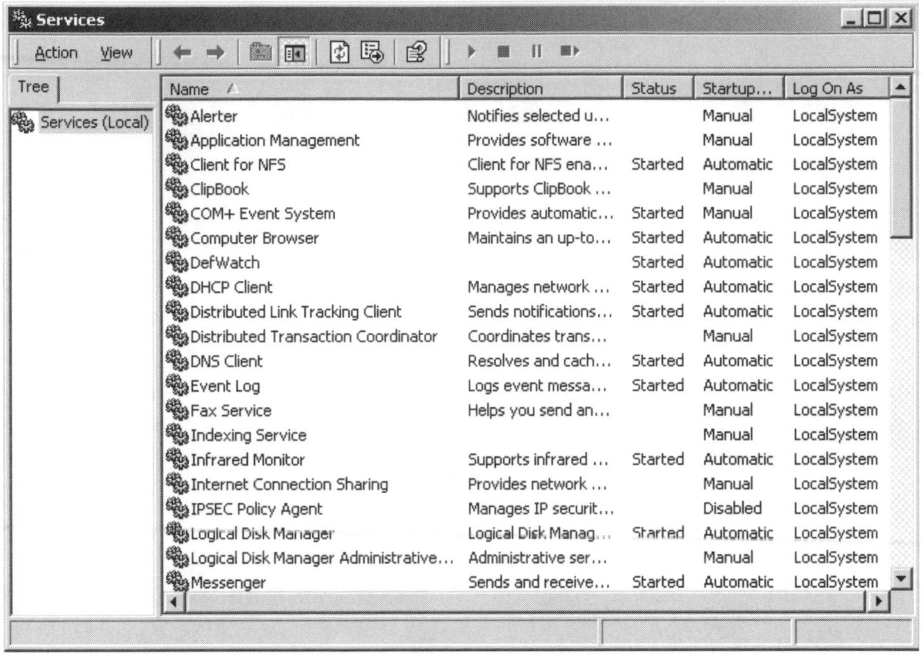

Figure 9-2
Windows 2000 services panel

parameters to determine whether to start or stop the process. The script then calls the application executable with the required parameters. A set of shell-script libraries are usually included with the OS, extending the startup script's functionality by adding routines that can gracefully stop the process. During startup, the OS calls these scripts in the order that they are required. During shutdown, the system sheds the processes in the same manner. During hardening, it is important to locate the startup scripts and properly disable unnecessary programs. Table 9-2 lists the startup file locations for some UNIX distributions.

Table 9-2
Startup File Locations for Some UNIX Distributions

Operating System	Startup Script Location
Solaris	/etc/init.d
Redhat and Caldera Linux	/etc/rc.d/init.d
FreeBSD	/etc/rc.init

Patching

All software contains bugs. Aggressive research by many camps in the information security community usually discovers these bugs, paving the way for security exploits. To repair these flaws, vendors release software patches. It is up to the IT and security groups to make sure that these patches are installed; without them, an organization is vulnerable to attacks. Professionals have little disagreement about this fact.

In organizations with strict change-control policies, timely patching can be a problem. Thorough testing of patches is a critical part of this process because vendors will sometimes introduce new problems by fixing old ones. This works well for patches that are not related to security bugs. However, the speed at which intruders seek out and exploit security vulnerabilities requires a fast-track process for security patches. Although six months might be a reasonable time frame for regular software patches and feature improvements, this time frame is disastrous for security. Organizations must be aware of security-patch releases and must be prepared to quickly act on them. A broken lock will not keep out intruders.

Password Stores and Strength

Vast improvements in computing platform speed and an increased interest and understanding of modern cryptosystems have created new challenges for platform security. UNIX systems have traditionally used some type of fast hashing to encrypt user passwords in storage. To allow lower privileged processes to use this password system, the password store requires global-read permissions, relying on encryption to protect it.

Table 9-3

Common patch systems

Operating System	Patch Type	Patching Method
Solaris	Individual or patch clusters	Pkgadd, installpatch
Linux (Redhat, Caldera)	Replacement package	RPM
FreeBSD	New source code	CVS and compile
Windows NT/2000	Hotfix or service pack	Self-installing
Netware	NLM	Patch utility

The strength of the passwords allowed on the system is another area where traditional UNIX systems are weak. Password strength is derived from both the number of characters used in the password and the degree of randomness used. As an example, "3Dg%de" is a much stronger password than "dog."

Faster computers and freely available password-cracking software have made these password stores increasingly vulnerable to offline attacks because virtually any user can gain access to the password ciphertext. Modern PCs have the horsepower required to brute-force crack these weak passwords.

UNIX systems have the capability to add layers of protection to the password stores; they just need to be configured to do it. Modern UNIX systems (and even some properly patched legacy systems) hide the password ciphertext from unprivileged users while still allowing them to access the authentication subsystem (called shadowing). They can also bar users from using easily-breakable dictionary words as passwords and force users to change their password on a regular basis. These are capabilities intrinsic to UNIX systems that are transparent to the user; they just need to be activated.

Windows NT/2000 also includes methods to protect the integrity of the local password store. Through the one-time use of the syskey command, the OS can be commanded to use a stronger level of encryption on the password store. Windows NT/2000 also has the capability to force users to use longer, more random passwords that change more frequently.

User Accounts

The user account identifies an entity (either application processes or humans) that needs to access a platform's resources. The OS ties the user account to its access control systems via permissions and privileges. Because user accounts are the legitimate mechanism of entry onto a system, intruders will often try to exploit weaknesses in user account management and access control. Why spend hours crafting a custom-buffer overflow attack, when you can simply log into a system as a legitimate user?

Weaknesses in user-account management come in five categories: weak passwords, manufacturer-default accounts, role-based accounts, corporate-default accounts, and abandoned accounts. In all cases, the goal of platform hardening is to reduce the number of user accounts to the absolute minimum required. The following list describes the five categories of weakness in user account management:

- We have already discussed in the previous section about addressing weak passwords.
- Manufacturer-default accounts are those that are set up by manufacturers for maintenance or for initial login to the platform during setup. Although less prevalent today, these accounts still exist on some older systems and can be extremely dangerous.
- Role-based accounts are dangerous because they do not allow for proper accountability. Instead of forcing users to log in using their own user IDs, role accounts are used by groups of people. Examples might include backup operators or Web-site administrators.
- Corporate-default accounts are accounts that are installed on platforms across the enterprise due to misuse of the standard-build process. These accounts are similar to role-based accounts in that they do not allow for proper accountability. However, they can be more dangerous because they allow users who would not otherwise be allowed to access the platform to log into it virtually anonymously.
- Abandoned accounts cause some of the worst problems because their existence ties into a dangerous lack of security procedures. Best practices dictate that users who are no longer authorized to access a resource or those who leave the organization have all of their accounts immediately suspended. Abandoned accounts are particularly vulnerable to internal attacks by co-workers and support personnel.

Another area of user-account management that needs to be addressed during platform hardening is user accounts used for running non-interactive processes like Web servers. By default, most of these processes run with Superuser privileges right out of the box. This means that any successful attacks against these processes yield system access with highly elevated privileges. Although critical system and kernel tasks need this higher access level, other applications do not. Special user accounts that have the exact access level required by the application can be created and configured to help protect the system against a successful exploit. These measures include locking the account's rights to remotely log in or obtain access to a shell prompt as well as limiting file access to its own files.

User Privilege

User privileges are one of the cornerstones of UNIX-system security. When implemented properly, user privileges assure that users have only the access they need to perform their tasks. The Superuser on a UNIX system is the one user account that has complete and unlimited access to the system resources. This account should be reserved for specific system-administration tasks that require high-level access, but system managers usually use it for their general day-to-day activities. Most UNIX systems do not provide an intermediate level of system privilege, so the Superuser privilege ends up being granted to far more users than necessary in order to complete required tasks. Because Superuser accounts can subvert and modify system-security functions, system managers increase their vulnerability to an attack every time they delegate this critical-access level. In addition, because only a single Superuser account is available, it is very difficult to track who uses it.

SUDO was designed to give system managers the ability to delegate Superuser access on a much more granular level. Each user can be assigned specific applications and functions that they are allowed to run as Superuser, without actually using the account. SUDO also enables detailed logging, so that any Superuser function run through SUDO can be tracked to a specific user. In practical application, using SUDO means that no one ever uses the Superuser account.

File System Security

On some occasions, a process requires temporarily elevated user privileges to complete a task. By setting the SUID flag on a program, a program gets these additional privileges without having to be granted full-time privileges at this higher level. This SUID flag is often overused and when combined with a defective-software package, a crashed program can lead to a user being granted full-time elevated system rights. An out-of-the-box UNIX system might have dozens of components with this flag set, but it usually only requires it on a few of them. Any capable system administrator can easily generate a report listing these files with a single line of commands. Another line of commands can remove these flags across the entire system, leaving only the required flag set. By stripping these flags away, you are adding another layer of armor to the system.

Remote Access Security

Telnet and rlogin are the most common methods of remote access used on UNIX systems. Neither of these systems use encryption to protect remote-access sessions. A passive network sniffing attack can watch every keystroke that a user types during a Telnet or rlogin session. Secure Shell (SSH) is a software package that is designed as a drop in for any UNIX or Windows NT/2000 system. It provides the same remote access functionality as Telnet and rlogin, but adds encryption. The package has become an industry standard for secure remote access with various configurable levels of encryption and access control.

Service Banners, OS Fingerprinting, and Disclaimer Screens

We have already mentioned that platform hardening attempts to reduce the amount of information that is leaked by a system. By default, services like e-mail and FTP display a banner when they are accessed describing their software version and platform type. Attackers use this information to determine if a platform has a service that is exploitable by reviewing any number of databases that contain exploit information on specific software versions and types. In fact, most amateur intruders will scan entire segments of the Internet looking for a specific version of a service they know they can exploit. This service information is completely unnecessary for the proper operation of the platform and can therefore be safely removed. By doing so, an attacker will have to attack a service blindly.

Another piece of information that is extremely useful to attackers is a platform's fingerprint. By using a special tool to query a system's network services, an intruder can match the results to a database of attributes and determine the type and version of the OS. Although this system is not 100 percent reliable, it does help focus an attacker's efforts because he or she can tailor the attacks to the weaknesses of the particular OS. On many OSs, this signature can be camouflaged to look like another OS or it can be obfuscated to not match any signature at all. As with service banners, making this modification does not affect the proper functioning of the platform, yet it does add considerable defensive capability to it.

Not all hardening methods are technical. Legal measures are a key component of information security. Wherever possible, legal notices warning against unauthorized access should be displayed. Notices can be displayed on the console, during logon, in periodic system-wide messages, and on the start screens of applications. Legal and human resource personnel should be consulted when crafting these warnings to ensure that they match company policy.

Hardening Tools

Just as the automobile industry transitioned to the assembly line to make manufacturing more efficient, the information-security community has begun projects to simplify the platform-hardening process. These projects attempt to automate the process of arming platforms by addressing the most common security issues. The tools are in various states of development and all carry caveats like the following for their use:

- It is *extremely important* to note that these tools are not one-stop solutions for hardening a platform. They merely help to identify and automate many of the more tedious hardening tasks.
- They *do not* compensate for a lack of good security practices like strong password enforcement, monitoring, or patching.
- They *do* help close down common vulnerabilities in an automated, efficient manner.

Titan[3]

Titan is by far the grandfather of all hardening scripts. Titan was developed by pioneers of information security Brad M. Powell, Dan Farmer, and Matthew Archibald. It is a series of very configurable scripts that provide the user with a great amount of flexibility in making low-level configuration changes on features like file permissions and home directories. It is written in shell script, which makes it very extensible because shells of the same type are designed to be compatible across any system. The authors developed Titan on Sun Solaris, but it also contains modules for FreeBSD and Linux.

[3]**http://www.fish.com/titan.**

Dozens of modules are written for Titan and each one affects a specific configuration change. The following is a sample of some of the modules included:

- Disable automounter.
- Configure the Solaris Basic Security Modules (BSM) to audit system events.
- Configure the Common Desktop Environment to ignore dangerous outside connections.
- Strengthen default permissions for all users at logon.
- Ensure that default-system accounts cannot be compromised.
- Remove unnecessary SUID configurations.
- Disable unrestricted trust relationships.

All of these modules are well documented and prompt the user with a simple description of the actions that they will take.

Bastille-Linux[4]

The Bastille-Linux project was born at the SANS 98 conference. Led by Jon Lasser, Ben Woodard, and a large group of contributors, the Bastille-Linux project is the first of its kind to focus specifically on Linux-platform hardening. The developers originally intended on building a secure Linux distribution, but that proved too difficult. The tool was then designed to help users of Linux lock down their existing systems without removing too much of the core flexibility enjoyed by Linux users. With the release of v1.2.0, the user can run the script in three ways. If run in interactive mode, the user is prompted with a detailed description of the intended modification before each action is taken. More advanced users can run the script in its fully automated mode. Finally, the latest version has a graphical user interface (GUI) that displays all possible actions and allows for quick configuration.

[4]**http://www.bastille-linux.org.**

JASS[5]

JASS, or Jumpstart Architecture and Security Scripts, is a package developed by Sun engineers to harden Solaris systems. It is particularly powerful in that it can be integrated with Sun's powerful Jumpstart system to deploy multitudes of standardized platforms in an automated manner. JASS adds to Jumpstart by running scripts during installation to harden the resulting platform. Like Titan, JASS breaks each security task into a simple script. JASS executes the appropriate scripts based on a profile that is created by the user.

YASSP[6]

YASSP, or Yet Another Solaris Security Package, is another package affiliated with SANS. YASSP is designed to run with the Solaris installation process. It aims to build platforms that face the Internet, but it can also be used for internal systems. Configuration of YASSP is done through the yasp.conf file. In this file, the user determines which files he or she wants YASSP to handle. This might include removing initialization files or adding files and directories that enhance basic security functions.

HardenNT[7]

HardenNT is one of many hardening scripts built for Microsoft Windows NT. It is designed to take advantage of the many poorly documented, yet extremely useful security features in NT 4.0. It is also compatible with Windows 2000.

---

[5] **http://www.sun.com/blueprints/tools.**

[6] **http://www.yassp.org.**

[7] **http://packetstorm.securify.com/filedesc/HardenNT-Source 20000917.zip.html.**

Case Study Overview

Our model corporate network spans the globe with thousands of platform and networking components. Dozens of different software and hardware vendors are represented throughout the enterprise. In this case, touching every platform would be an incredibly complicated task. The plan calls for two parallel efforts: one global and one local. In the global effort, the security team will develop a self-installing package for SSH, and system managers will be responsible for installing it. The effort will focus on replacing Telnet and rlogin with SSH using password authentication. Because SSH is designed as a drop-in replacement for Telnet, the challenges to its rollout will be more cultural than technical.

The second effort focuses on the infrastructure defined in Chapter 6. It is impossible to touch every platform in the organization. For each area of the infrastructure, the hardening effort will focus on the most critical weaknesses that are realistically addressable.

Analysis of Case Study #1—Corporate

The sheer size of the MCC organization makes it unfeasible to harden every platform to a high level of security. However, it is also undesirable to only touch parts of the infrastructure because that will still leave large security gaps. A balanced approach is needed. In this case, the decision was made to address the security issues that took the least amount of effort to fix, yet would still result in a significant overall improvement. System improvements were classified by the network-partitioning plan in Chapter 6, which defines three networks for each MCC site: user, server, vendor.

As with any large organization, the user workstations are the hardest to control. They lack strong physical security, and forcing users to lock their consoles when they leave their workstations is a continual challenge. Users are at constant risk to infection by viruses. Finally, the large number of systems poses a great challenge for the support groups to maintain current-patch levels. By installing virus-protection software that automatically updates its signatures, configuring screen savers to automatically lock after an idle period, and disabling the user's ability to make local-configuration changes, the organization is decreasing its exposure to internal attack.

The same limited approach is taken with servers. A security professional can spend significant amounts of time hardening individual server platforms, but that is not possible in this situation. In this case, efforts are focused on increasing accountability through removal of role accounts, increased logging, and the installation of SUDO. Unneeded legacy services are easily dealt with on UNIX platforms by adjusting the superdaemon configuration file (inetd.conf). On NT platforms, removing anonymous and NULL connection enumeration capability drastically decreases the amount of information leakage.

The PR department installed the Windows-based Internet kiosks provided to visitors for Internet access over the protests of the security group. To compensate, these systems will be fully customized via Windows profiles to remove all desktop functionality. A non-configurable version of the Web browser, with ActiveX and Java disabled, is the only usable component on the kiosk. In addition, the CDROM and floppy-disk drives are removed and the computer case is locked in a cabinet. Table 9-4 summarizes this hardening plan.

Analysis of Case Study #2—FinApp

The critical nature of the FinApp requires a slightly modified focus. Because the presentation servers provide an interface to sensitive financial data and transaction information, they must be locked down tighter. In addition, audit requirements from government financial regulatory organizations require that the audit servers must have added protection. For this reason, more resources are focused on these machines and less on the backend systems. Although this decision puts more pressure on the firewalls that separate the segments, it still does not totally rely on them, enabling the system to still maintain a layered approach. Table 9-5 summarizes this hardening plan.

Analysis of Case Study #3—HealthApp

Like the FinApp, the HealthApp requires a different approach. In this case, the parts of the system that store the customer's confidential medical data require more hardening. In the FinApp, the customer provides

Table 9-4
MCC hardening plan

Partition	Hardening Control
User (employee workstations)	■ Patch OS and applications ■ Install and update virus protection ■ Install locking screen saver ■ Install logon banner ■ Limit local administrative access
Server (all)	■ Patch OS and applications ■ Remove role accounts ■ Increase logging granularity ■ Add logon banner
Server (UNIX)	■ Sanitize inted.conf ■ Disable RPC where unnecessary ■ Install SUDO ■ Remove X-window software ■ Strip SETUID bits where not required[8]
Server (NT)	■ Install virus protection ■ Unbind NetBIOS from TCP/IP ■ Disable anonymous and NULL connections (where possible)
Vendor (Windows-based Internet kiosk)	■ Use windows policy manager to remove desktop components (Start button, control panel, network neighborhood, disk drives)

data to the system through the presentation segment, whereas in the HealthApp, the customer is accessing data that is stored and collected by the provider. The platforms that store the medical information must be able to protect its integrity and confidentiality through encryption. The platforms must also enforce tight access controls to ensure that administrators cannot access data outside of their scope. For this reason, more emphasis is placed on these systems. Table 9-6 summarizes this hardening plan.

[8]SETUI D bits cannot be indiscriminately removed because certain system commands such as lp(1) require the bit to be set.

Table 9-5

FinApp hardening plan

Partition	Hardening Control
Presentation (UNIX), Audit (UNIX)	■ Patch OS and applications ■ Add logon banner ■ Remove role accounts ■ Increase logging granularity ■ Sanitize inted.conf ■ Disable all services except for FinApp application ■ Install SUDO ■ Remove X-window software ■ Strip SUID bits where not required
Presentation (NT), Audit (NT)	■ Install virus protection ■ Unbind NetBIOS from TCP/IP ■ Disable anonymous and NULL connections ■ Set strong file permissions ■ Rename administrator account ■ Use syskey to encrypt password store
Middle Tier (All), Data(All)	■ Patch OS and Applications ■ Remove role accounts ■ Increase logging granularity ■ Add logon banner

Conclusion

The average auto consumer would be quite surprised if all base-model SUVs came with a winch, snow plow, super-duty engine, GPS, refrigerator, seats for 20, bulletproof glass, puncture-proof tires, water cooler, four cell phones, a backup generator, and front- and rear-deck flood lighting. They would have to strip off most of these features just to make the vehicle useful for everyday driving. When it comes to network infrastructure, the opposite seems to exist. OSs continue to ship with large feature sets enabled by default, yet little is done to strip off the unnecessary parts. In this chapter, we have examined the practical application of platform hardening. In a perfect world, this chapter would have guided the reader to harden every platform to its highest level of security. In fact, many organizations do choose to focus their efforts on building single-use security platforms. Instead, this chapter guides the reader to a more realistic goal of deriving the most value from platform hardening across the entire enterprise.

Table 9-6

HealthApp hardening plan

Partition	Hardening Component
Public	■ Patch OS and applications ■ Harden Web Server(s) ■ Remove role accounts ■ Increase logging granularity ■ Add logon banner
Application (UNIX), Administration (UNIX)	■ Patch OS and applications ■ Add logon banner ■ Remove role accounts ■ Increase logging granularity ■ Sanitize inted.conf ■ Disable all services except for FinApp application ■ Install SUDO ■ Remove X-window software ■ Strip SUID bits where not required ■ Data encryption ■ Strong authentication
Application (NT), Administration (NT)	■ Install virus protection ■ Unbind NetBIOS from TCP/IP ■ Disable anonymous and NULL connections ■ Set strong file permissions ■ Rename administrator account ■ Use syskey to encrypt password store
Development	■ OS and application patches ■ Virus scanning software

CHAPTER 10

Intrusion Detection Systems

The book *Firewalls and Internet Security—Repelling the Wiley Hacker*, written by Bill Cheswick and Steve M. Bellovin, is considered to be one of the most authoritative early sources of information on network firewalls and is a great read on the topic of network intrusions. It includes many details of attack and defense techniques as well as case studies of attacks against AT&T. In one such case, an administrator noticed that a computer user who was unlikely to use the system outside of normal business hours was logged in late one night. After a substantial analysis, it was determined that the user account had been compromised and that the intruders involved had widespread access to telephone control systems. It ultimately took more than a year for AT&T to finally dislodge the intruders. As a result of this and similar incidents, AT&T began a major effort to improve intrusion-detection technologies within their networks.

The incident with AT&T is an unfortunate example of how many organizations learn about the benefits of intrusion detection the hard way. However, AT&T had the unique benefit of having a staff of highly skilled system administrators and researchers who were available to assist in isolating the cause of the problem by using existing tools as well as building custom tools where needed. These tools were used to perform a detailed analysis of the situation as it evolved using a researcher's eye for details. As the intimate details of existing network weaknesses were learned, system patches and more tools were developed and applied to ensure that future incidences of the same nature would not be successful. At the end of it all, a great text was written about the whole experience. Not many organizations can claim to be able to dedicate resources or talents to such an arduous and painstaking task on a regular or even an ad hoc basis. In a sense, this is the primary driver for the existence of automated intrusion detection systems (IDSs).

Many people can benefit from deploying automated IDSs within an organization's security architecture. Some of these benefits include increased audit trails as well as possible real-time response to detected network intrusion attempts. However, without a proper understanding of existing IDSs and the proper preparation for their introduction into the security architecture, the initial visible impact will not likely be one of better visibility into an organization's security posture or more effective automated responses to potential security events; rather, a potentially negative operational impact involved with processing the extra audit trails during active investigations for detected events will occur. Many of these audit trails may initially turn out to be false leads. This chapter will provide the necessary building blocks, if not the necessary details, for effectively and properly selecting, deploying, and integrating IDSs into an organization's overall security architecture. To that end, this chapter presents a survey of current IDSs, the near future focus of research and advances in IDSs, the commonly accepted uses of intrusion detection (ID) within security architectures, and the impacts of deploying IDSs within an organization. The chapter closes with a few case studies for real world examples of effective IDS deployment.

Basic Intrusion Detection Terminology

Intrusion detection (ID) is the process of monitoring the events occurring in a computer system or network and analyzing them for signs of intrusions. An *intrusion* can be defined as any set of actions that attempts to compromise the integrity, confidentiality, or availability of a resource. IDSs are software or hardware products that automate this monitoring and analysis process.

A *firewall* is a system designed to prevent unauthorized access to or from a different parts of a network architecture. Firewalls can be implemented in hardware and software, or a combination of both. Several types of firewall techniques are available: packet filter, application gateway, circuit-level gateway, and proxy server. In practice, many firewalls use two or more of these techniques in concert. A firewall is generally considered a first line of defense in protecting private systems or information.

The following terms are taken primarily from the draft submitted to the Internet Engineering Task Force (IETF) on February 20, 2001. This draft was created by the Intrusion Detection Exchange Format Working Group (IDWG) whose charter defines data formats (such as the Intrusion Detection Message Exchange Format [IDMEF]) and exchange procedures (such as the Intrusion Alert Protocol [IAP] and Intrusion Detection Exchange Protocol [IDXP]) for sharing information of interest to ID and response systems, and to the management systems that may need to interact with them.

- **Data source** The raw source of information that an iIDS uses to detect unauthorized or undesired activity. These can be system audit logs, raw network traffic, or information on the integrity of computing system storage such as file system or memory cryptographic checksums.
- **Activity** Refers to elements of data source or occurrences within the data source that are identified to be of interest to the operator.
- **Operator** The person who is the primary user of the IDS manager.
- **Manager** The ID component or process from which the operator manages the various components of the ID system. The primary components of an IDS are the sensor and the analyzer.
- **Sensor** The ID component that collects data from the data source and forwards the events to the analyzer.
- **Events** The occurrences in the data source that are detected by the sensor. Events may result in an IDMEF alert being transmitted. For example, a sensor detecting *N* failed logins in *T* seconds might forward a brute-force login event to the analyzer.
- **Analyzer** The ID component or process that analyzes the data collected by the sensor for signs of unauthorized or undesired activity or for events that might be of interest to the security administrator. In many existing IDSs, the sensor and the analyzer are part of the same component.
- **Administrator** The person with the overall responsibility of setting the Security Policy (SP) of the organization. Thus, the administrator is responsible for decisions about deploying and configuring the IDS. This may or may not be the same person as the operator of the IDS.

- **Alert** A message from an analyzer to a manager that an event of interest has been detected. An alert typically contains information about the unusual activity that was detected, as well as the specifics of the occurrence.
- **Notification** The method by which the IDS manager makes the operator aware of the alert occurrence and thus the event. In many IDSs, this is done via the display of a colored icon on the IDS manager screen, the transmission of an e-mail or pager message, or the transmission of a Simple Network Management Protocol (SNMP) trap, although other notification techniques may also used.

Figure 10-1 shows the relationship among different IDS components.

Intrusion Detection Systems and Firewalls

Though they both relate to network security, an IDS differs from a firewall in that a firewall is primarily utilized as a traffic-filtering device, whereas an IDS is primarily utilized as a traffic-auditing device. An IDS looks for certain traffic patterns, or activity, that have been determined as anomalous or possibly malicious—in other words, an event. These traffic pat-

Figure 10-1

Relationship of different IDS components

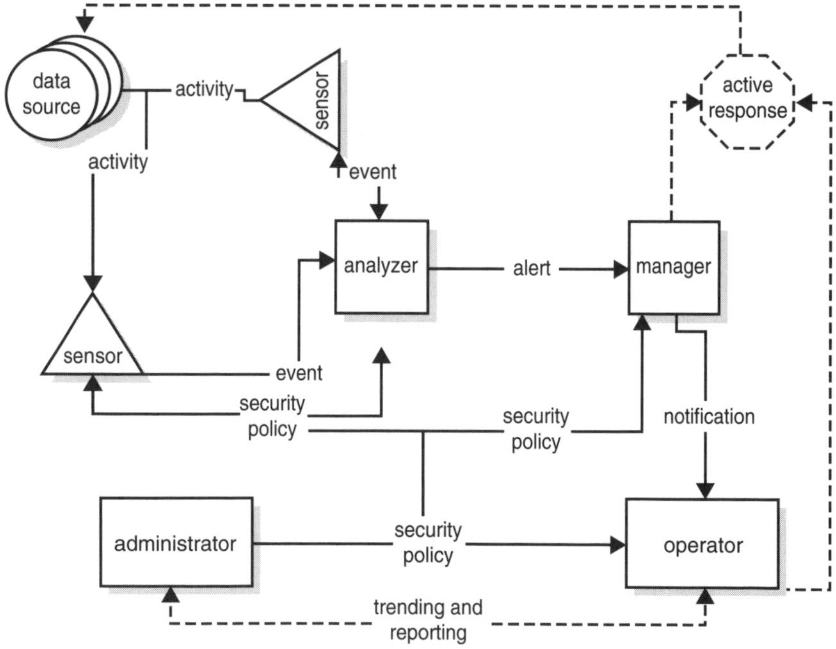

terns can be determined manually during configuration, automatically as part of an initial learning process, or a combination of the two. A firewall is designed to limit the access between networks in order to prevent intrusions. Generally a firewall is not designed to provide detailed notification of attacks or provide comprehensive detection of all possibly attacks or anomalous network activity. An IDS evaluates a suspected event as it takes place or after it has taken place, creates a detailed audit trail in one or more secured locations, signals an alarm or notification, and/or possibly automatically takes action to secure the protected networks. An IDS can also be setup to watch for attacks or events that originate from within an organization's network. This protects the organization from the possible legal punitive actions initiated as a result of attacks from inside the organization.

Another common way to think about the differences between firewalls and IDSs is that a firewall can be looked at as a safe protecting your valued assets. In such a situation, an IDS would be analogous to surveillance cameras, alarms, and associated motion sensors monitoring the area immediately around and even inside the safe. Figure 10-2 illustrates this example.

Just as a firewall does not generally have the ID capabilities of an IDS, an IDS does not generally have the firewalling capabilities of a firewall. Another important differentiator between the two technologies is that most firewalls are designed to fail in a closed mode (or closed-failure) in the event that the firewall has a critical system failure, thereby locking down access to the internal, sensitive parts of a network. Most IDS critical failures are open-failures, which means that the IDS engines are no longer processing the network patterns, but they are also not aversely affecting (nor securing) the monitored network. The two technologies are very complementary and are generally deployed in unison to achieve the maximum level of security.

A Brief History of Intrusion Detection

The system audit functions that are the core of the original vision for IDSs date back almost fifty years ago when research was done on how to use mainframe auditing and billing software to detect system misuse. However, the main part of the active IDS research field can still be said to be quite young with most work dating to the 1980s and 1990s. The seminal paper that is most often mentioned is James P. Anderson's technical report: *Computer Security Threat Monitoring and Surveillance*. Anderson

Figure 10-2

Firewall and IDS as safe and security camera

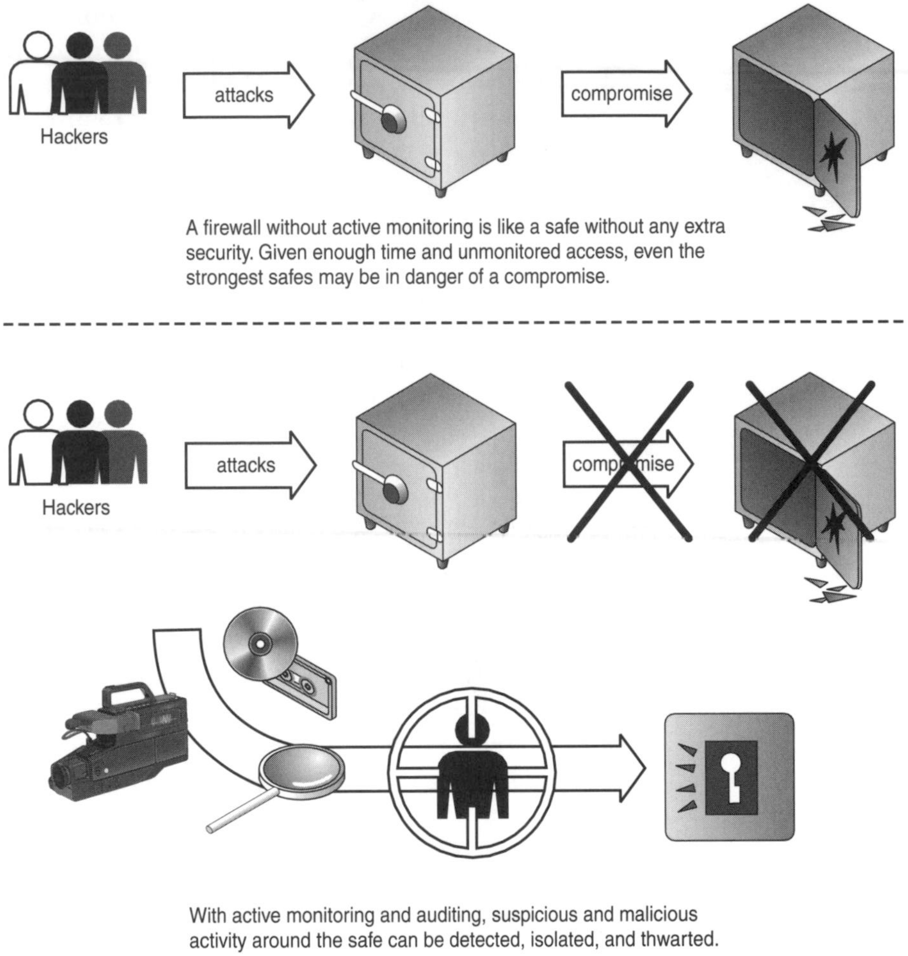
Hackers
attacks
compromise
A firewall without active monitoring is like a safe without any extra security. Given enough time and unmonitored access, even the strongest safes may be in danger of a compromise.
Hackers
attacks
compromise
With active monitoring and auditing, suspicious and malicious activity around the safe can be detected, isolated, and thwarted.

postulated that it was possible to distinguish between a masquerader and a legitimate user by identifying deviation from historically-tracked system usage. At that early point of research, available system auditing tools generally designed for accounting and billing purposes were the first to be examined and retooled for use in intrusion detection. By the late 1980s, two primary methods of intrusion detection were being researched: a) ID methods based on known attack signatures and audit trails from confirmed events of misuse, and b) ID methods based on the search for network activity that was anomalous to normal or historically observed traffic patterns. These two main distinctions remain today and are generally referred to as Misuse-Detection IDS (MD-IDS) and Anomaly-Detection IDS (AD-IDS) respectively.

Current IDS Landscape

Today, many academic research facilities around the globe are actively devoting resources to intrusion detection research, such as UC Davis Seclab, Purdue CERIAS/COAST, SRI, IBM Zurich GSAL, and MIT Lincoln Labs, to name a few. Many companies are also devoting resources to ID research, such as Internet Security Systems (ISS), Cisco Systems, Network Flight Recorder (NFR), Enterasys (Dragon), IBM, NetworkICE, Tripwire, SiliconDefense.com, Securityfocus.com, and so on.

The commercial research space has primarily, though not exclusively, been focused on signature or MD-IDS in the form of host-based IDS (H-IDS) and network-based IDS (N-IDS) systems. The academic and military research has focused on AD-IDS in the form of Distributed IDS and Autonomous Agents IDS. These different types of IDSs will be covered in more detailed in the IDS taxonomy section later in this chapter.

Future ID Landscape

The evolution of IDSs is an ongoing process with research being provided by groups in academia, the private sector, and even the government and military sector. There are two very promising areas of current research in IDSs and they are IDS Intercommunication with a standard taxonomy of events, and the merging of MD-IDS, AD-IDS, and other ID analysis methods. These two topics are covered in more detail in the following sections.

IDS Intercommunication with a Standard Taxonomy of Events

Although much has been learned from research-driven efforts in ID, the focus has primarily been on developing optimized computational techniques to detect intrusions. Less thought has generally been given to creating an overall operational view of anti-intrusion approaches to complement the intrusion detection. One of the primary limitations of modern commercial off-the-shelf (COTS) IDSs is this lack of seamless integration into large organizations' support infrastructure via existing Event Management Systems (EMS) in the areas of alarming and reporting.

A possible reason for this limitation is yet another well-known, but not uncommon, limitation usually found in scenarios involving rapidly evolving technologies driven by diverse vendor initiatives—the lack of interoperability between different IDSs developed by different vendors. It is likely that no major breakthrough has been achieved in the enterprise Security Event Management System (SEMS) space in the seamless integration of IDS due to this lack of standardization.

The area of standardized communications has experienced recent positive developments. The Intrusion Detection Working Group (IDWG) of the Internet Engineering Task Force (IETF) started from work originally pioneered by the Common Intrusion Detection Format (CIDF), and has progressed to the point of getting multiple-vendor support (ISS, Cisco Systems, and Snort, among others). They have also published a handful of RFC drafts on a common Intrusion Detection Message Exchange Format (IDMEF). If these are effectively implemented, they should provide better inter-IDS communications. In the area of event taxonomy, the Common Vulnerabilities and Exposures (CVE) project (see **http://cve.mitre.org**) has for the past several years accumulated a large database of vulnerabilities that are currently references in most modern IDSs alerts and are planned for use in proposed IDMEF.

The area of SEMS has also experienced some advancement achieved by EMS vendors (NetCool, eSentry, Tivoli, and so on) to improve an organization's Network Operations Center's (NOC) capability to effectively handle notification of security events from multiple vendors. For the majority of these systems, however, it's still primarily a case of data aggregation and manual filtering with no effective or smart automatic event correlation from distributed event sources. Again, it is possible that advances in this space depend on advances in the IDS intercommunication space and standard event taxonomy.

Some noteworthy recent developments have appeared in the private sector and in government NOCs' willingness to act as partners with other organizations in security incident handling. For example, as a part of its charter, the FBI's InfraGuard initiative has incentives to actively pursue cooperative engagements in the private sector to assist in handling security events. Securityfocus.com's ARIS service, CERT's Snort-based AirCERT, and the SANS Glocal Incident Analysis Center (GIAC) site are all examples of other third-party sites openly requesting that incidents be reported to them either automatically via available tools or manually.

For these recently developing initiatives to continue to succeed, they will need to push for a common standard for event communication and a common taxonomy of security events. This will in turn make IDS deployment for monitoring more effective and more robust within an organization.

Merging of MD-IDS, AD-IDS, and Other ID Analysis Methodologies

Because of the recent advances in IDS evasion and disruption tools (such as ADMmutate and stick) and the wide distribution of such tools via the Internet, modern developers of IDSs have been pushed further and further away from the classic distinctions of MD-IDS and AD-IDS as well as from monolithic systems to more distributed systems. For example, ADmutate is a toolkit that enables attackers to develop new polymorphic exploit code or to modify existing exploit code into a polymorphic form. In essence, this makes the bulk of IDS static signature databases obsolete. In other words, what ADMmutate can do for attacks can be loosely looked at as tunneling the attack via a mechanism that still achieves the intended results of exploitation of unauthorized resources. However, the exploit is morphed or changed in such a manner that it is never the same as far as the packets that are seen on the network and by an N-IDS. H-IDSs are not vulnerable to the current versions of the ADMmutate kit, but an H-IDS can still be easily overloaded with widely available IDS evasion tools such as *stick* and the more recent *snot*. In general, modern IDSs will increasingly perform both misuse detection based on signatures as well as anomaly detection based on established learning patterns and may do so with input from various data sources.

To put recent events in the IDS space into historical perspective with regards to the process of detection of computing systems resource abuse in general, some people in the computing risks field are calling the recent shifts in IDS detection engines away from purely MD-IDS (or signature-based ID) to a combination of MD-IDS and AD-IDS (or IDS using another form of software or programmed intelligence) somewhat analogous to what happened to virus detection engines back in the early 1990s when Dark Avenger released his MtE (or virus Mutation Engine) polymorphic virus engine. Sometime after the release of the MtE toolkit, virus detection engines based primarily on signatures were largely replaced by a combination of signature and algorithmic searches for patterns of viruses. The following is a quote from a paper by Tarkan Yetiser of VDS Advanced Research Group from back in 1992. This sounds quite similar to where IDS engines are going in modern times: "By implementing two algorithms and one scan string for the plain mutations, it is possible to recognize MtE-based viruses while keeping false positives to an acceptable level." By keeping false positives to an acceptable level, the IDS is more accurate and its notifications are more applicable to present conditions.

Benefits of IDSs

Consider the Weakest Link Principle of security: no security solution is stronger than the weakest component of that solution. In light of this principle, it can be seen that an IDS is not a panacea to network manager's problems; however, if properly configured, architected, and supported, it can be a powerful tool. As with all other security tools, a need still exists for a strong organizational SP document for proper enforcement. With those requirements in mind, the following is a short list of some of the benefits of integrating IDSs into a security infrastructure.

Detect Uncorrected or Uncorrectable Security Vulnerabilities

This is probably the primary reason most organizations cite for needing to deploy IDSs. It is almost common knowledge that dedicated attackers, using widely publicized techniques, can gain unauthorized access to many, if not most systems, especially those connected to public networks without any active systems monitoring. This type of unauthorized access or breach of confidentiality happens primarily due to known vulnerabilities in the systems that are not effectively corrected or in some cases cannot be fully corrected.

Table 10-1

Benefits of IDSs with Focus on Different Stages of ID Automation

Current State	Future Needs	Argument or Driver
Has no IDS	Automated ID	Detect uncorrected or uncorrectable security vulnerabilities
Has IDS	Surveillance	Detect vulnerability probes or preambles to attacks
Has surveillance	Improved surveillance	Avoid "Boiling Frog" Syndrome
Has improved surveillance	Publicized deterrents	Effective monitoring as a deterrent against probes and attacks
Has surveillance and deterrents	Improved risk management	Documentation of the existing threats
Has risk management	To prosecute incident/damage control	Detailed audit trail of actual intrusions

In an ideal world, commercial software vendors would minimize these vulnerabilities in their products, and every organization would diligently correct all reported vulnerabilities quickly and completely. However, in the real world, this seldom happens thanks in part to our reliance on commercial off-the-shelf software (COTS) where—because of market demands and other non-security-aware market drivers—new flaws and vulnerabilities are introduced on what seems to be a daily basis.

Given this state of affairs, intrusion detection can represent an excellent added approach to protecting an organization's network architecture. An IDS with the latest signatures can detect when an attacker has penetrated a system or is attempting to penetrate a system by exploiting an uncorrected or uncorrectable flaw. Furthermore, it can serve an important function in system protection by quickly bringing the fact that the system has been attacked to the attention of the proper administrators who can contain and recover any damage that results from the event.

Detect Vulnerability Probes: Preambles to Attacks

When adversaries attack a system, they typically do so in fairly predictable stages. The first stage of an attack is usually probing or examining a system or network, while searching for an optimal point of entry. In systems with no IDS, the attacker is generally free to thoroughly examine the system with no risk of discovery or retribution. Given this unfettered access, a determined attacker will eventually find a vulnerability in such a network and exploit it to gain entry to various systems.

The same network with an IDS monitoring its day-to-day operations presents a much more formidable challenge to that attacker. Although the attacker may probe the network for weaknesses, the IDS will observe these probes, identify them as suspicious activity, may actively block the attacker's access to the target system, and will send notifications to the IDS operators who can then take appropriate actions to block subsequent access by the attacker. In some cases where damages are incurred, legal action can be taken against the attacker. Even the presence of a reaction to the attacker's probing of the network will immediately elevate the level of risk that the attacker perceives from probing the organization, possibly discouraging further attempts to target the network.

Avoid "Boiling Frog" Syndrome

The "Boiling Frog" Syndrome refers to the concept that an average, healthy frog placed in a pan of cool water on a heat source will not detect a change in temperature as heat is slowly added to the water until it reaches its boiling point, killing the frog. A similar, healthy frog that is placed into an already boiling pan of water will quickly notice the extreme heat and immediately react by jumping away from the heat.

The U.S. Department of Defense (DoD) funded Information Warfare research shows that human operators in highly active NOCs may be prone to the "Boiling Frog" Syndrome. In one documented case, an experiment performed by the Defense Information Systems Agency (DISA) demonstrated that the threshold of human detection increases in response to a slowly increasing threat. In this particular experiment, DoD networks were subjected to low-level disruption at first, and the network disruption levels were slowly increased over time. Even though the levels of disruption eventually far exceeded levels at which human detection would normally take place, the attack was never noticed.

This and similar studies imply that relying largely on human operators for manual detection and analysis of network threats is not effective in this sort of highly active threat environment. The solution to the problem is to build effective multiple or tiered layers of IDSs and operators with automatic and manual feedback between layers. This ensures that the existing environment never reaches an unacceptable boiling point, thus making the whole monitoring mechanism ineffective.

Effective Monitoring as a Deterrent Against Probes and Attacks

One of the goals of computer security management or risks management is to affect the behavior of individuals (both internal and external) in a way that protects information systems from possible security problems. This is generally accomplished via instruction and training, but sometimes also by ostensible use of force. The effective deployment of intrusion detection systems and the strategic distribution of SP abuse trends as internal reports and as limited distribution external reports may further help organizations accomplish this goal by increasing the effective as well as the perceived likelihood of the discovery of probes or attacks against the organization's information systems. Just as the knowledge that security cameras and trained watchmen being deployed around the clock to monitor and analyze the physical security of a facility will generally help to deter most unsophisticated physical probes, a properly monitored and reactive IDS with strategically publicized feedback will also generally help to deter most unsophisticated network probes.

That said, some care must be taken to not cross the line of demonstrating proper security due diligence. If an organization's security system's strengths are publicized too widely, the cracking/hacking community may interpret this as bragging about an unbreakable system. Sophisticated and/or coordinated attacks on a network are generally perpetrated to achieve some predefined trophy and a very attractive trophy is one that is widely publicized as being unattainable or being very difficult to attain.

Documentation of the Existing Threats

When budgets are being established for network security, it is often helpful to substantiate claims that the network is likely to be attacked or is even currently under systematic attack. Furthermore, a detailed understanding of the frequency, nature, and characteristics of these attacks enables those persons responsible to understand what security measures are appropriate to more effectively and efficiently protect an organization's network.

IDSs generate detailed audit trails that can be used to verify, itemize, and characterize the threat from both outside and inside your organization's network. These audit trails assist people in making sound decisions regarding the allocation of computer security resources. Using IDSs in this manner is especially effective in a situation where managers (non-security managers, of course) mistakenly deny that anyone (outsider or insider) would be interested in breaking into their networks. The IDS-generated audit trails can, in such cases, be used as very effective, empirical data. This data provides the source and nature of existing and recorded attacks, enabling managers to make decisions regarding security strategy by demonstrated need, not guesswork.

Detailed Audit Trail of Actual Intrusions

Even in circumstances where IDSs are not able to repel or block attacks, they still collect relevant, detailed, and trustworthy information that can be used after the detection of a successful penetration. This detailed information can support incident handling and recovery efforts. Furthermore, this information can enable and support criminal or civil legal remedies under certain circumstances. Ultimately, such information can historically identify problem areas in the organization's security configuration or policy. This insight makes future reviews and recommendations for improvements more effective.

Existing Limitations of IDSs

Before continuing with a detailed analysis of the current state of IDSs, a separate overview of the existing limitations of IDSs is worthwhile. As discussed previously, ID is still an active area of research; much work is currently underway to improve the analysis engines, taxonomy or categorization of events, and the communications protocols used by modern and future IDSs. That said, the current state of IDSs has been discussed over recent years in online security forums, meetings of professional groups and conferences, and within the private sector in "around the water cooler" discussions. The effectiveness of current IDSs as viable and effective tools in modern network security architectures has been called into serious question over the last few years. The following section outlines some of the main threads of this discussion and offers insight into what ways and areas the security industry and academic community may be focusing on in an effort to overcome these currently perceived and demonstrated limitations.

Resource-Intensive

Oddly enough, one of the most obvious benefits of deploying IDSs is also one of the current main drawbacks. The amount of data collected and notifications generated by current IDSs may quickly overwhelm most organization's security operations, especially if the systems are deployed without

Table 10-2 Categories of Limitations of IDSs

Category	Description
Resource-intensive	Lack of incident handling, and lack of robust inter- and intra-IDS communications.
IDS evasions and disruption	Simple evasions: event signatures and anomalous patterns are usually a small subset of all traffic possible on a network. Complex evasions: fragmented IP packets, protocol tunneling, distributed/stealth attacks, and shell code mutation provide IDS evasion.
Complex networks	Modern complex network environments utilizing switching and many ingress/egress points make effective N-IDS placement challenging.
Base-rate fallacy limitation	The inability to suppress false alarms is the limiting factor for the performance of IDSs.

any customization based on the specific requirements of the monitored environment. Certain considerations should be taken into account before deploying and integrating IDSs into daily network management operations.

Most commercial IDSs do not currently perform automatic incident handling. Detailed forensics and analysis of events detected at particular IDS devices are still very resource-intensive, especially if no support forensics tools are developed or deployed along with the IDSs. Also, a wealth of attack signature information is available online. Most IDSs include extensive documentation on known signatures, but the IDS operators still have to make the final assessment on whether a given notification was a false lead (or false positive) or not.

Most commercial IDSs do not currently perform intercommunication between IDS devices. Most IDSs do not perform analysis on attacks distributed across an organization's networks because the individual IDS analysis engines do not talk to each other; rather, they talk to a manager or management console or tier of consoles, which generally only show a raw collection of the individual points and not an analysis of the overall security posture. Distributed IDSs (D-IDSs) have been developed and are being researched to confront this limitation, but these systems have another communication limitation listed in the next paragraph.

Most commercial IDSs do not currently perform intercommunication between IDS vendors. Many IDS tools and products are available, but unfortunately most of them have unique, non-standard, auditing or logging format. Though manual extrapolation can usually be made from one type of IDS to another during forensics or reporting, no uniform, widely supported event logging or event taxonomy or event communication format is currently available.

Despite these existing shortcomings, it should be noted, as was brought out in the "Future Trends" section of this chapter, that several groups and initiatives are actively working toward a standard model of event taxonomy (based on CVE), auditing/logging (based on IDMEF), and a communications protocol (based on IAP and IDXP). If successful and widely accepted, this work should enable the development of tools to alleviate, if not eliminate, these problems.

IDS Evasions and Disruptions

In the simple category of evasions, widely known attack signatures can be slightly modified to avoid detection by MD-IDS, thereby camouflaging the attack. In other words, MD-IDSs only detect known signatures.

Table 10-3

IDS Standards and Interoperability Research Groups

Group Name	Project WWW Site
CIDF	**http://www.gidos.org/**
IDWG	**http://www.ietf.org/internet-drafts/draft-ietf-idwg-requirements-05.txt**
CVE	**http://cve.mitre.org**
Snort/AirCERT	**http://www.cert.org/kb/aircert/motivation.html**
CERIAS/COAST	**http://www.cerias.purdue.edu/**

Signatures can be detected from various sources including active research forums where detailed exchanges on signature detection are carried out.

Another simple evasion technique is used by patient attackers who slightly modify traffic over time to keep attacks within AD-IDS detection parameters "flying under the radar". In other words, AD-IDS can't account for dynamic changes in networks so parameters must be set to allow some anomalous traffic, which borders on malicious (for example, internal high-range TCP port sweeps are often triggered from a Web server as they open TCP channels to client browsers).

Another simple IDS evasion technique utilizes the fact that IPv4 does not have strong source authentication in its network traffic. This basically means that an attacker or someone with malicious intent could easily spoof (or fake) the source of certain patterns of traffic to make it appear to come from somewhere else (for example, **http://www.whitehouse.gov**, **http://www.rootshell.com**, **http://www.insecure.org**, and so on). Using this technique is quite easy and it can be used to effectively mislead human investigative resources valid attacks to "fly under the radar."

These other classes of simple evasions usually involve a level of intended discretion or deception on the part of the attacker. For Denial of Service attacks (DoS), or Distributed DoS (DDoS) and the newer IDS-specific DoS attack such as the recently disclosed stick and snot, the intent is not to be discrete or deceive, but basically make accessible IDSs ineffective by flooding them with valid signature matches. The recent stick and snot tools basically take a popular IDS's (Snort's) attack signatures. From that recipe, they generate a large amount of network traffic resembling network attacks causing the receiving IDS to reach its threshold of monitoring capacity. Again, the attacker usually avoids direct detection by combining these attacks with a healthy dose of IP spoofing.

We have many recent examples in the class of complex evasions. For both types of IDSs, new, valid types of IP network traffic are making the job of ID more difficult. For example, UNICODE traffic (which may make non-kernel-based H-IDS ineffective) and IPSec/SSL encrypted traffic (which may make non-IPSec-aware N-IDS ineffective) are valid types of network traffic that can be used to easily evade detection by IDSs because they are encoded or encrypted and thus unrecognizable. UNICODE and IPSec are specific cases of protocol-tunneling evasion techniques. They are also additions to existing protocols that were designed to solve some existing security or application problems. However, when put to the wrong use, they can also be used to obfuscate malicious or suspicious traffic patterns.

A few older complex attacks or evasion techniques, such as Loki ICMP tunneling, can actually be used to tunnel all of IP into a single IP service (ICMP echo request/reply, DNS port 53, TCP port 80, and so on). In fact, some vendors have started emulating hackers by modifying their distributed client/server applications to communicate over well-known ports (such as Microsoft's DCOM) that can now be transported over the common HTTP port (TCP port 80). These types of attacks or evasions work by exploiting the bounds of what is acceptable on networks by exploring the limits and the edges of the definitions of IP and ICMP packets.

Then, some cases exist of innovations whose root design goal is to obfuscate malicious or suspicious traffic patterns. In early 2001 at the CanSecWest security conference in Vancouver, an advanced method for creating a polymorphic shell code for use in attacks (mostly buffer overflows) was released. The tools are not simple to use, but if widely distributed, they could invalidate most signature-based ID methods. The polymorphic code is basically a network vulnerability toolkit that can mask many of the known shell code buffer overflow attacks. This toolkit and its possible impact on the industry is being compared to the MtE (Mutate Engine) virus toolkit released by Dark Avenger in the early 1990s and its effect in the virus detection space. Namely, it creates less reliance on signature-based ID systems or MD-IDS.

Another type of complex evasion was brought to the forefront of security discussion by the publication of a paper written by Thomas Ptacek and Timothy Newsham covering packet fragmentation attacks. Their paper, titled *Insertion, Evasion, and Denial of Service: Eluding Network Intrusion Detection*, presented a thorough analysis of the state of IDSs in the late 1990s. In many ways, it opened the dialogue around the question, "Is intrusion detection dead?" Luckily for those responsible for security infrastructures, vendors and researchers alike took note of the very detailed analysis and used the work of Ptacek and Newsham and others to point the way for vendors to improve their systems' capabilities. Most vendor IDSs are now no longer vulnerable to many of the weaknesses pointed out in the paper.

Another weakness of modern commercial IDSs is Distributed Attacks andDistributed Stealth Attacks. As stated in the section on "Resource-Intensive" limitations of IDSs, most existing systems don't intercommunicate effectively. This limits their capability to detect a stealth attack coming into an organization with a multitude of ingress and egress points. Again, with the recent advances by the IDWG in specifying the Intrusion Detection Message Exchange Format (IDMEF) and the Intrusion Alert Protocol (IAP), the issue of lack of inter-IDS communication will hopefully be resolved.

The IDS space is still going through heavy rounds of research and many of these topics are active research areas that will see delivery into the commercial and real world space in short order. All of these weaknesses are pointing IDS design toward having a hybrid detection engine combining the best of signature (MD-IDS) and anomaly (AD-IDS) detection, better interoperability with existing SEMS, more interoperability between ID vendors and open standards of event taxonomy, and finally higher overall performance when running under conditions involving overutilized monitored network segments.

Complex Networks

Modern enterprise networking environments also add complexity to the question of the proper placement of IDSs, specifically network-based IDSs (N-IDSs). The modern large network is heavily switched. In this environment, packets are transmitted in such as way as to make it difficult, if not impossible, for N-IDSs to perform the needed analysis unassisted. This is because the N-IDS box needs to see all packets regardless of the endpoints of the communications and switched networks generally segregate packets forming channels for end-to-end communications at the physical layer.

A few options are available for properly deploying N-IDSs in such environments. These include using advanced switches with application or port replication abilities, such as Foundry and TopLayer switches, as well as using switch port physical and software taps such as the Shomiti taps (**http://www.shomiti.com/products/taps/index.html**) and Cisco SPAN settings on ports. In late 2000, Cisco systems also introduced modules for their 6000 series switches, which have the dedicated function of performing ID analysis. In some scenarios, it is possible to utilize a hub to aggregate traffic and to allow the IDS engine to capture all packets for analysis; however, this is generally not an optimal solution for modern enterprise network environments and has become less and less an acceptable practice.

Another aspect of modern networks that adds complexity to effective IDS design are modern networks with multiple egress and ingress points. Perimeters on modern large networks are blurring as high-performance networks bind organizations tighter to partners, clients, and providers. The evolving needs of modern e-commerce efficiencies—whether B2B, B2C, P2P, or any other current or future combination—dictate changes in network architectures. To be effective, the overall security designs need to keep up if not stay ahead of the game.

As vendors add more specialized and higher performance IDSs and security tools for deployment in modern enterprises to keep up with the evolution of enterprise network demands, it can easily be argued that the skills needed to properly design and support such architectures will become more and more specialized as well. Space will always be available for simple IDS deployment in most small- to medium-sized networks, but as the large networks become more tightly integrated with demands for higher performance and higher redundancy, the effective deployment of IDSs on a large scale will be a skill practically utilized by a subset of highly specialized security engineers utilizing industry best practices and established engineering design principles. In other words, that knowledge will not likely be something that someone could buy in a manual or a book.

Base-Rate Fallacy Limitation and False Positives

Even in a network with a fairly simple architecture, modern IDSs are hampered by what is known as the Base-Rate Fallacy limitation. Basically this statistical principle states that the inability to suppress false alarms is the limiting factor for the performance of all IDSs and not the ability to correctly detect a large number of incidences. In other words, it's not a matter of how many signatures an IDS system is reported to detect, but how well the system responds to false positives by not detecting them. True attacks are generally rare relative to the amount of traffic coming into a monitored network. The Base-Rate Fallacy limitation states that the more rare the event, the more accurate the test must be to be useful. This means that in most cases, modern IDSs without some regular customization unique to the site or active learning about normal network traffic parameters will not be accurate enough in testing for malicious or suspicious traffic. They will return more false positives than true positives.

Security Policy Documents and Acceptable Use Policies

An organization's SP, in essence, defines the details of what is permitted and what is denied within that organization's computer systems and networks. An SP is also a document that sets out rules and principles that affect the way an organization approaches problems. Ultimately, a SP is a document that exists to prevent the loss of an asset or a loss of that asset's value. A security breach can easily lead to such a loss, regardless of whether the security breach occurred as a result of an act of God, hardware or software error, or malicious action internal or external to the organization.

An Acceptable Use Policy (AUP), also known as Terms of Service (TOS), is a contract specifying what a subscriber can and cannot do while using an Internet Service Provider's (ISP's) service. It generally contains liability disclaimers, lists of actions or behavior that will result in the termination of a customer's account, definition of terms such as "unlimited use," billing policies, SPAM (or electronic junk mail) clauses, and so on.

The definitions of SP documents and AUPs are not strictly defined, but it is generally understood that an AUP is a (sanitized) subset of an SP that can be distributed not only internally, but also externally. The distribution of the AUP externally provides effective warnings against would-be attackers of the measures in place if not the actions that are likely to be taken in the event that a security incident is detected and damages are incurred. Please refer to Chapter 2 for a more detailed analysis of SPs, Standards, and Guidelines.

Taxonomy of IDSs

A current taxonomy of IDSs would be based primarily on two characteristics: the data source used by the IDS and the type of analysis engine used by the IDS. In the first grouping, there are two widely recognized characterizations of IDSs: IDS with host-based data sources and IDSs with network-based datasources. In the second grouping are also two widely recognized characterizations: IDSs with misuse detection analysis engines and IDSs with anomoly detection analysis engines. The two main groupings of IDSs and their respective subgroupings are discussed In more details in the following sections.

Classes of Events

It is sometimes, if not often, considered that intrusion techniques are advanced, and can only be done by elite and computer savvy individuals; this is often far from the truth and becoming more of a myth every day. In reality, anyone with even a basic understanding of computing has the ability to download an application off of the Internet and use it to cause serious damage to others. One of the greatest threats that modern networks may face is curious youth (script kiddies) who do not understand the implications of the command they just entered or the button they just pushed. The resources dedicated to pursuing script kiddies could also be used to investigate more advanced intrusions events.

The following list shows some of the more common classes of events detected and audited by IDSs:

- **Network scanners** These scanners are used primarily in detecting hosts. The pattern detected is generally flagged as a network sweep. Generally, the tools send an ICMP echo request packet to a host and check for a response. Stealth mode sweepers send other types of ICMP packets or TCP/UDP packets and analyze the results to see if the host responded.
- **Host scanners** These scanners are used primarily in detecting TCP services. Example tools are Nmap port scanner, Queso scanner, strobe, telnet to a port, and so on. Generally, a connection attempt is made for TCP or a packet is sent for UDP to a port and the results are analyzed to determine if a service was listening on the port.
- **Vulnerable services and exploits** These are used primarily to detect weaknesses in existing and publicly accessible services. Example probes are Cgi-bin phf scans, IIS vulnerability scans, IMAP vulnerability scans, and so on.

- **Trojans and rootkits** These are used primarily in establishing a beachhead on the host or to disrupt the host. Rootkits are generally used once a host is compromised to establish a means to regain access later or further open up existing access to the compromised host.
- **DoS attacks and distributed attacks** These attacks are used primarily to disrupt service provided by a host. Examples are resource-depleting worms and viruses, SYN Floods, WinNuke, and so on.

In addition to the scanners mentioned in this list, many commercial IDS vendors have "white hat" vulnerability scanners that can be used to measure an organization's susceptibility to known attacks. Examples of commercial scanners are the Nessus scanner (**http://www.nessus.org**), ISS (Internet, database, and system scanner), and Cisco Secure Scanner.

Classes of IDSs

Most IDSs can be classified in terms of three fundamental functional components: data sources, analysis techniques, and overall architecture.

Data Sources for IDSs

Data sources for IDSs are generally in one of two groups: host-based data sources and network-based data sources. The differences are covered in detail in the next sections.

Host as Data Sources Host-based intrusion detection (H-IDS) tools date back to the beginning of research into IDS and are still actively deployed and used in modern networks. Some older examples of H-IDS are file system integrity checkers, such as Tripwire, and system audit log checkers, such as Swatch, Logsurfer, Solaris BSM and post processing IDS, and custom mainframe applications built on top of system usage audit data collection tools.

Host data-sourced IDSs may monitor not only the system files and specific logs, but also other more dynamic parts of the host itself including login activity and application interaction with the operating system (OS). Examples of login activity monitors are ISS RealSecure Agent and Psionic PortSentry. Examples of root activity monitors are Psionic HostSentry and standard UNIX system accounting for root/admin activity or kernel state modifications. Kernel-based H-IDSs such as LIDS and Openwall for the Linux OS and Entercept 2.0 for Microsoft NT, Windows 2000, and Solaris platforms are also available. Kernel-based IDSs shield the system kernel from attacks by intercepting system calls from applications and processing them for suspicious or malicious content and then passing or alerting and logging the calls to the kernel. Figure 10-3 illustrates H-IDSs.

H-IDSs are good for deployment on servers that have encrypted communications channels to other servers or networks. H-IDSs are also good for servers that are deployed in a heavily switched network environment or a network with multiple ingress or egress points. Servers with many loosely qualified installed users or installed applications are also prime candidates for H-IDS.

An obvious problem with all H-IDSs is that you can't trust the audit trail from a compromised host. Using cryptography may alleviate the problem, but in general, if a host is compromised, it is safer to assume that all safeguards have also been compromised. Also, for some high activity networks with high network traffic saturation, the performance impact on

Figure 10-3
Host-based IDSs

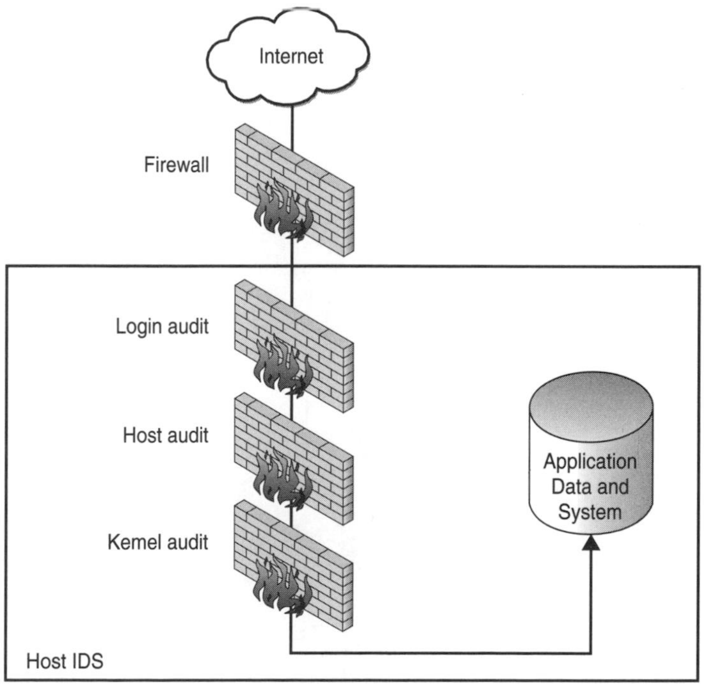

the monitored system may not be acceptable. Another problem with H-IDSs is the practicality of needing to deploy and manage the software on every desktop or server that needs to be monitored.

Network as Data Source In some ways, protocol analyzers or sniffers can be viewed as the original network-based auditors that would later evolve to network-based IDSs (N-IDSs). A protocol analyzer is a wiretap device that plugs into computer networks and eavesdrops on the network traffic. N-IDSs take that one step further by having the capability to validate the detected traffic as either normal or possibly malicious.

The common network security events best detected by an N-IDS are network sweeps (where a host pings several different hosts on a network), malformed packets attacks, fragmented packet attacks, and IP-spoofing attacks. N-IDS can generally be deployed in non-switched networks without affecting the flow of network traffic. N-IDS can also do content level checking similar to what is done with H-IDS. Examples of N-IDSs are NFR, Dragon, ISS, Snort, Bro, Cisco Secure IDS, and any IDS built using the libpcap library. Figure 10-4 illustrates N-IDSs.

The problem with N-IDSs is that in certain cases the passive network monitor can be defeated using evasion or disruption techniques such as those mentioned in earlier sections of this chapter. Also, some N-IDS may have performance problems with highly saturated, high-bandwidth networks. As stated earlier, the deployment of N-IDS on switched networks and networks using high amounts of end-to-end encryption may involve

Figure 10-4
Network-based IDSs

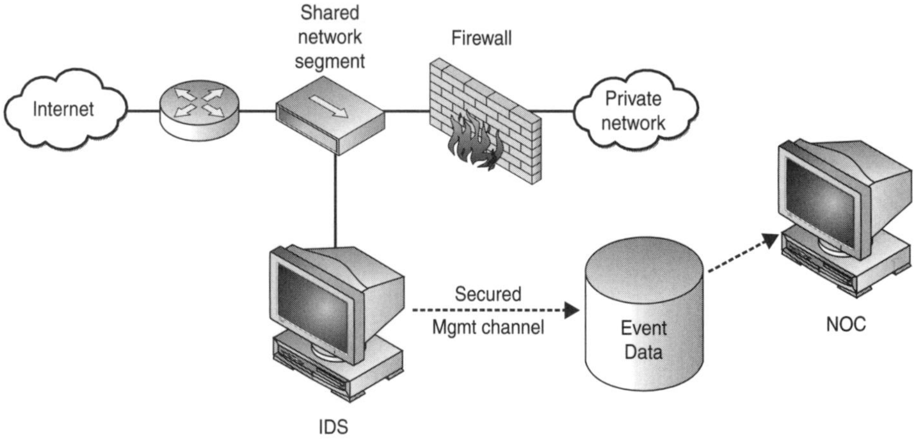

complex additions to the existing network environment or the distribution of decryption keys into the IDS infrastructure.

Detection Engine

Misuse Detection-Based Systems (MD-IDS) Misuse intrusion types of attacks are well-defined attacks conducted upon known weak points of a system. They can be detected by watching for certain actions being performed on certain objects. Misuse intrusions follow well-defined patterns that can usually be detected by doing pattern matching on collected audit-trails such as system C2 audit logs (which records events such as file accesses). For example, an attempt to create a setuid file can be caught by examining log messages resulting from system calls. An attempt to download an /etc/passwd file via the CGI interface to a Web site is another event that would be flagged for detection in an MD-IDS. This can be done using a pattern-matching approach explained in a paper titled *A Pattern-Matching Model for Misuse Intrusion Detection* by Eugene H. Spafford and Sandeep Kumar.

The MD-IDS engine may resemble that of a virus scanner. It is usually programmed with signature sets representing the types of connections and traffic that indicate a particular attack. These systems come generally come with a bundle of known signatures that a site can modify depending on site-specific needs. This limits the number of false positives, but usually does not completely eliminate them all. Like virus scanners, MD-IDSs cannot detect something that the network manager doesn't know about, which is generally the type of attack the network manager wants to detect the most. For an MD-IDS to be useful, its signature sets must be constantly updated. Even so, the network may still be vulnerable to ever-evolving new attacks.

One variant of the MD-IDS is the honeypot. A *honeypot* is designed to lure attackers away from real systems with apparently vulnerable decoys enabling the analysis of motives and techniques. The AT&T example cited at the beginning of this chapter involved the use of honeypots to learn about the attacker's motives and techniques. The problem with honeypots is that for most sites, it's not an acceptable risk to openly attract attackers to any part of their systems—not even those designed for attracting and close analysis.

Anomaly/AI/Expert Systems-Based Systems (AD-IDS) Anomaly intrusion types of attacks are based on observations of deviations from normal system usage patterns. They are detected by building up a profile of the system being monitored and detecting significant deviations from this profile. An AD-IDS learns what constitutes normal network traffic and develops sets of models that are updated over time. These models are applied against new traffic. Traffic that doesn't match the normal model is flagged as suspicious. Dorothy E. Denning proposed the classic model for anomaly detection in her paper *An Intrusion-Detection Model*.

These systems are attractive conceptually, but it is a genuinely hard problem to create a reliable model for normal traffic. No fixed patterns can be monitored for and so a more "fuzzy" approach must be taken. As networks grow, the mix of applications becomes so complex that traffic looks random. A patient hacker may even generate his or her own traffic to generate a distorted model of normal so that sooner or later, an attack may look normal and get past the IDS. On the other hand, if the IDS is set up with a narrow definition of normal, the system will generate large numbers of false positives, and the IDS will be ignored. Also, some AD-IDS algorithms are subject to state holding or other related state DoS attacks that disrupt the IDSs ability to monitor network traffic. Much research is still being done on AD-IDS. Some of the benefits of this research have found a way out of the research laboratories and into commercially available IDSs.

Overall Architecture

The overall architecture of modern IDSs falls into two types: monolithic or distributed. A distributed IDS is one that has distributed sensors and in most cases distributed analyzers. Sometimes the distributed analyzers even communicate with other analyzers to further fine-tune the correlation of events. A monolithic system is one where the sensor and analyzer are in a single unit and the analyzer generally only communicates back to the manager. Most commercial IDSs are of the monolithic variety.

The distributed IDS generally has a command and control hierarchy with the end goal of multi-sensor data fusion. An example of this is SRI's Emerald system. Another form of distributed IDS is the peer-to-peer architecture using autonomous agents. An example system is the CERIAS/COAST AAFID project. The problem with distributed IDSs is that the more intercommunication takes place, the higher the probability of impact on the network, and more importantly, the higher the probability of compromise or disruption of such communications by rogue elements. Also, truly distributed systems are still primarily used as research tools. Products for practical commercial deployment have not been developed and widely deployed successfully.

Case Study Overview

In this section, the knowledge of IDSs put forward in the previous section will be used in a case study. Each of the following case study analyses provides a brief summary of the issues pertaining to that particular case study. For more detailed description of the case studies, it is advised that the reader review them as originally detailed in Chapter 1 of this book prior to continuing.

MCC Corporation is supporting heterogeneous IDS solution deployed at several key points in the global network infrastructure. The individual case details will be explored in the following sections. Where possible, an OOB management network has been built to supply traffic back to MCC's Security-Network Operations Center (S-NOC) and to provide sensor time synchronization via NTP. If the details of the network site where the IDSs are deployed do not support or warrant a dedicated OOB management network, then host-to-host encryption such as SSH will be employed to create a secured, in-band management tunnel. The notifications and alert data for the remote sensors are carried over the available secured management channel back to the analysis center within the MCC's S-NOC. The S-NOC will be tiered into different response teams—the lower level taking more network centric and less detailed security-related events while the upper level focuses on very specific security events and less so on network-related incidences.

Analysis of Case Study #1—Corporate

The MCC corporate network is comprised of a mixture of Windows NT, Windows 2000, UNIX servers, and Novell file and print services. Network applications will consist of substantial amounts of PeopleSoft, Oracle, Novell NCP, Windows SMB, custom applications and standard TCP/IP applications such as, SSH, HTTP, HTTPS, and FTP.

To provide effective tiers of monitoring, the IDS notification and alerting schemes will be divided into three zones: first-level auditing, second-level auditing, and third-level auditing. Where appropriate, the division of schemes will be enforced using the specific vendor management tools and when those tools are not sufficient, in-house EMS tools will be used to collect the notifications and translate them into the appropriate schemes.

First-level Auditing

Because the corporate network fabric for MCC contains fairly well-defined applications but still requires a level of active auditing, a combination of static MD-IDS and AD-IDS will be deployed with settings set to alarm heavily on non-standard network traffic. At the network distribution layer, built-in IDS MD-IDS features such as Cisco 6000 Catalyst Intrusion Detection Modules with N-IDS built-in may be used. IOS-based ID will also be used in network segments where Cisco 6000 Catalyst switch modules cannot be deployed. The alarms and initial troubleshooting for these signatures will be passed to the first-level monitoring group within MCC's Security NOC.

Second-level Auditing

In areas requiring more visibility and quick and effective deployment of new signatures, the N-IDS Snort running on hardened Linux servers will be deployed. These IDSs provide rapid signature prototyping, but are not necessarily effective for high-utilization attack patterns or for attack signatures that require a great deal of detail in the signature. The notification for the first level will handle these events and where needed, it will escalate to second-level monitoring within the MCC Security NOC. The second-level monitoring group should be capable of performing forensics and fine-tuning the Snort signatures as needed.

Third-level Auditing

In areas of MCC's networks requiring the highest amount of monitoring, customizable H-IDS will be installed such as Dragon Squire H-IDS or NFR. Alarms and notifications for these sensors will be sent to the second-level monitoring group with possible escalation to the third-level monitoring group. The third-level monitoring group should be able to perform detailed forensics and fine-tune highly customizable IDS signatures as needed (see Figure 10-5).

For MCC's RAS via the high availability Internet, access point N-IDS will be deployed both in front of and behind the VPN termination point to enable the monitoring of attempted VPN architecture compromises as well as possible probes from a compromise of a VPN end point such as a

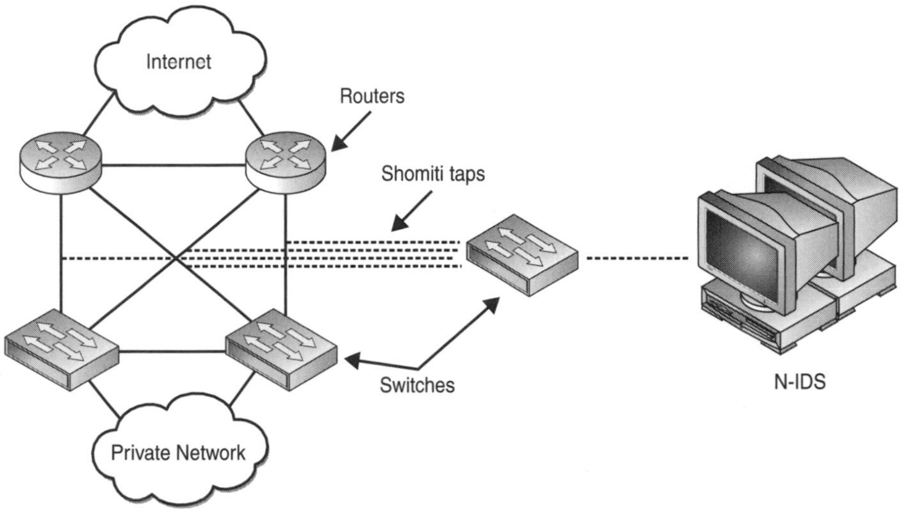

Figure 10-5
High-availability deploy of IDS sensors using Shomiti taps

roaming laptop. At the front of the VPN gateways, Shomiti taps will be utilized to capture packets from the existing switched architecture. If budget and project time scales permit, switches with port replication and application level switching capabilities such as TopLayer and Foundry will be used to replace existing switches. These switches will be configured so that data will be replicated to possibly multiple IDSs engines depending on the observed utilization of the existing architecture.

Analysis of Case Study #2—FinApp

FinApp is a TCP/IP-based application. The front-end application is written in XML. Middle-tier or middleware components provide business logic and transaction services. Back-end SQL database servers provide a data repository. A number of propriety market feeds provide data services to the middle-tier application servers.

Due to the customized and possibly changing nature of the applications and the associated network traffic protocols, combined with the complexity and tight integration of multiple networks with various threat models, the most customizable IDSs will be deployed to support the FinApp application. Using a combination of programmable H-IDS and N-IDS with the capability to intercommunicate and correlate some events, such as Dragon N-IDS and Dragon Squire H-IDS, security engineers within the second- and third-level monitoring group of the MCC can use their knowledge of the proper range of non-malicious traffic patterns to setup the proper policies and configurations on the H-IDS and N-IDS. This ensures proper enforcement of the SP.

To assist in rapid detection and prototype of new attack types, Snort devices will be deployed in combination with the N-IDSs and monitored by the first-level monitoring group. Events and notifications from the Snort engines will be resolved by the first-level monitoring group in collaboration with second-level engineers who will take the feedback if needed to verify the proper configuration of the highly customizable N-IDS and H-IDS.

Analysis of Case Study #3—HealthApp

To reduce cost and improve customer service, MCC is redesigning the health care claims processing structure for the HealthApp application. MCC is moving away from a costly managed dial solution to an Internet-based application utilizing end-to-end encryption to secure connections. The front end to HealthApp is Web-based and is written in HTML and Java script. Users communicate over 128-bit SSL. Application and back-end database components use a combination of OBDC and SQL to communicate with each other. All private information is stored in encrypted format within the databases.

Because this is a highly encrypted end-to-end application, an effective IDS design will have to include strong H-IDS, which can watch an end-server's system activity after it's been decrypted by the Web application for suspicious or malicious activity and report on such. Also, the possibility of deploying kernel-based intrusion detection will be reviewed in detail. Kernel-based IDSs have access to privileged OS calls and can verify the state of such calls to ensure that no malicious actions are being attempted. Alerts from H-IDSs and kernel-based H-IDSs will go to the second-level monitoring group, which will pursue resolution with the collaboration of the third-level monitoring group.

As an adjunct to the H-IDS and kernel H-IDS, AD-IDS will be deployed to monitor the encrypted traffic on the network for changes in traffic flows (volumes) over time and to alert to such cases. Alerts on traffic flow changes will be registered to the first-level monitoring group, which will

Figure 10-6
Kernel-based IDS example

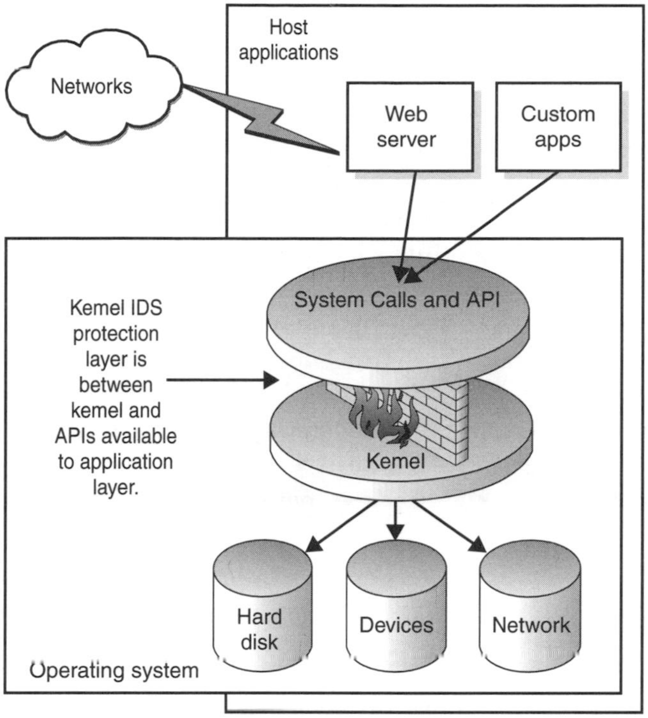

pursue resolution with collaboration from the second-level monitoring group (see Figure 10-6).

Conclusions

Some feel that the current status of IDS technology can be compared to that of firewalls a few years ago. Some others compare IDSs of recent years with the first virus-detection programs, with all the problems they used to have. Perhaps the solutions available on the market over the past years were immature. However, IDS principles are very much a reality today; this can't be argued away. Modern IDSs have rectified many of the initial problems and are heading strong into next generation improvements. The current devices are what is making IDS a reality today and are opening the path for the next generation improvements. These devices can be successfully deployed if properly planned, designed, and supported.

It should be noted that the optimization process of these systems or functions will be accelerated to an extent that is directly proportional to the international academic, industrial, and government research communities' commitment into studying and resolving the existing limitations as well as adding new functions. It should be considered that products such as those surveyed earlier will become at minimum reference points for functions built in some way into future security architecture because those functions (intrusion detection) are necessary and feasible. An organization committed to the optimum security for its networks now and in the future would do well to invest resources at this early stage of IDS development. Combined with an effective organizational SP document and a well-staffed Computer Incident Response Team (CIRT), an effective IDS deployment and understanding of current and future trends in IDS help to limit the chances that the organization learns about its existing security weaknesses or vulnerabilities the hard way.

In-Text References

Naji Habra, Baudouin Le Charlier, Abdelaziz Mounji, and Isabelle Mathieu. "Preliminary Report on Advanced Security Audit Trail Analysis on UNIX." Technical report. Institut D'Informatique, FUNDP. September 1994.

James P. Anderson. "Computer Security Threat Monitoring and Surveillance." Technical Report Contract 79F26400. James P. Anderson Co., Box 42, Fort Washington, PA, 19034, USA. February 26, revised April 15, 1980.

E. Sebring, E. Shellhouse, M. Hanna, and R. Whitehurst. "Expert Systems in Intrusion Detection: A Case Study," Proceedings of the 11th National Computer Security Conference. Washington DC. October 1988.

T. Lunt and R. Jagannathan. "A Prototype Real-Time Intrusion Detection Expert System," Proceedings of the 1987 IEEE Symposium on Security and Privacy. Oakland CA. April 1988.

Stefan Axelsson. "The Base-Rate Fallacy and its Implications for the Difficulty of Intrusion Detection," Department of Computer Engineering, Chalmers University of Technology, Göteborg, Sweden, May 1999.B.

Schneier, J. Kelsey. "Cryptographic Support for Secure Logs on Untrusted Machines," Proc. 7th USENIX Security Symposium, January 1998.

Dorothy E. Denning. "An Intrusion-Detection Model." *IEEE Transactions on Software Engineering*, 13(2): 222–232, February 1987.

Other References

S. Staniford-Chen, B. Tung, D. Schnackenberg. "The Common Intrusion Detection Framework (CIDF)," Information Survivability Workshop, Orlando, October 1998.

M. Wood. "Intrusion Detection Exchange Format Requirements," IETF Intrusion Detection Working Group Internet Draft, June 1999.

J. Balasubramaniyan, J. Garcia-Fernandez, E. H. Spafford, and D. Zamboni. "An Architecture for Intrusion Detection Using Autonomous Agents," Department of Computer Sciences, Purdue University; Coast TR 98-05; 1998.

S. A. Hofmeyr, S. Forrest, and P. D'haeseleer. "An Immunological Approach to Distributed Network Intrusion Detection," 1st International Workshop on the Recent Advances in Intrusion Detection, September 1998.

J. Riordan, B. Scheier. "Environmental Key Generation toward Clueless Agents," Mobile Agents and Security, G. Vigna, ed., Springer-Verlag, 1998, pp. 15–24.

T. Bass. "Multisensor Data Fusion for Next Generation Distributed Intrusion Detection Systems," Proc. Nat'l Symposium on Sensor and Data Fusion, Johns Hopkins University, Applied Physics Laboratory, May 1999.

T. Ptacek and T. Newsham. "Insertion, Evasion, and Denial of Service: Eluding Network Intrusion Detection," Secure Networks, Inc., January 1998.

V. Paxson. "Defending Against Network IDS Evasion," 2nd International Workshop on Recent Advances in Intrusion Detection, September 1999.

V. Paxson. "Bro: A System for Detecting Network Intruders in Real-Time," USENIX Security Symposium, 1998.

Sandeep Kumar and Eugene H. Spafford. "A Pattern-Matching model for Misuse Intrusion Detection," *Proceedings of the 17th National Computer Security Conference*, pages 11–21, October 1994.

B. Cheswick. "An Evening with Berferd in Which a Cracker is Lured, Endured, and Studied," Proc. Winter USENIX, San Francisco, 1992.

C. Ko, M. Ruschitzka, and K. Levitt. "Execution Monitoring of Security-Critical Programs in Distributed Systems: A Specification-Based Approach," Proceedings of the 1997 IEEE Symposium on Security and Privacy, pp. 134–144.

A. Ghosh, A. Schwartzbard, M. Schatz. "Learning Program Behavior Profiles for Intrusion Detection," USENIX Workshop on Intrusion Detection and Network Monitoring, April 1999.

Deception Toolkit, Fred Cohen & Associates, 1998.

Bill Cheswick and S.M. Bellovin. *Firewalls and Internet Security—Repelling the Wiley Hacker*, Addison-Wesley, 1994.

Sarah Gordon. "Inside the Mind of Dark Avenger", 1993 VFR Systems International, **http://www.research.ibm.com/antivirus/SciPapers/Gordon/Avenger.html**

Tarkan Yestiser. "Mutation Engine Report," 1992 VDS Advance Research Group, **http://vx.netlux.org/texts/html/mte.html**

CHAPTER 11

Application Security

Chapters 6 through 10 have focused on securing infrastructure components such as firewalls, virtual private networks (VPNs), intrusion detection systems (IDSs), and even wireless networks. With multiple connections of Internet, external business partners, and remote access traffic, traditional network and platform security controls do not provide the necessary granularity of access controls to sensitive resources. The infrastructure is not well suited to protect the inner application functionality and its data. Applications need to be able to ensure that they are used only for their intended purposes and only by the appropriate users. Application layer security is the enforcement of access control principles within the application to prevent and detect unauthorized access.

Numerous approaches can be used for implementing application layer security. Access control logic can be built directly into application during the development process, or a third-party product can be integrated to provide security transparently. Application layer security should not attempt to compensate for weak infrastructure controls; in fact, application layer controls should assume that infrastructure controls are in place.

The enforcement of the application access control can either be transparent to the application (for example, an access control filter applied to a Web server) or application-aware, using a reusable security Application

Program Interface (API) call within the application. This chapter will outline these options as well as other methodologies and approaches to achieving best practice application layer security.

Application Security Background

Application security controls and management rely on authentication, authorization, accounting, and administration, which are referred to as the four As. Any third-party product or in-house project that performs security within the application must support the four As.

Application security begins when a system or user needs to access an application or a function within the application. The first step in this process is identification and authentication; all application users must be properly identified before application access is permitted. This should not be confused with platform access (for example, NT login or UNIX login). Once the user is authenticated, the application must ensure that the user is authorized to access the various resources and functions within it. Authorization controls are used to restrict users to only the data and functions required. Authorization systems are intended to provide fine-grained access to internal application functionality. A number of different authorization systems will be discussed later in this chapter.

Accounting is the ability to record and monitor the access control processes. This includes successful and unsuccessful attempts. User accountability is accomplished by registering all the users' actions, such as successful and unsuccessful logins, access to protected resources, and administration changes.

Administration enables all the users, protected resources, and their relationships to be managed. Typically, this is done using a graphical user interface (GUI) that is Web-based or Windows-based. The storage of this information is typically in a database management system or a directory server.

Application Security Placement

Security architects who are responsible for enforcing access control must decide the best place to put this enforcement within the application process flow. The first large-scale computer applications were mainframe-based. The application consisted of a cursor-based terminal over a proprietary network (SNA). All the application security was performed on the mainframe. The terminal provided the input and output required by the given application. Next came client-server computing, which provided the capability to distribute the computing across multiple computers and provide a better user display. This also moved application enforcement from a centralized or monolithic to a distributed model. Mainframes are still being used, but middle-tier servers transparently access them. Client-server computing required that all the users have the specific client-side application loaded on their workstations. As far as access control enforcement placement, it could either occur within the application client software, on the application server side, or on the back-end mainframe. Lastly, most users have progressed to a universal client application referred to as a Web browser. The client-side application communicates with a Web server. The Web server in turn communicates with an application server, which queries a database or makes a mainframe request. From the user's perspective, he or she is just communicating with the Web server. See Figure 11-1 for clarification of these three scenarios.

Do's and Don'ts: *The best placement for any access control decision processing is as close to the data and resource as possible, and it should be performing the function on behalf of the user.*

Authorization Models

A number of different authorization models exist for controlling access to application resources. An *association* between a user and a resource is the basis for all authorization models. This can be a simple association such as an access control list (ACL) that defines which actions a user is permitted to perform on that resource. However, granting access on an individual basis can become cumbersome; most organizations use groups or roles for authorization. The *user's role* can be a one-to-one relationship or it can use a hierarchical approach. A *user's permission* (entitlement) is the intersection of a role and resource. The user's permission is associated with a user role and a resource type.

The converse of an ACL (users who have access to a resource) is a capability list. A *capability list* is a list of resources a user has access to. This

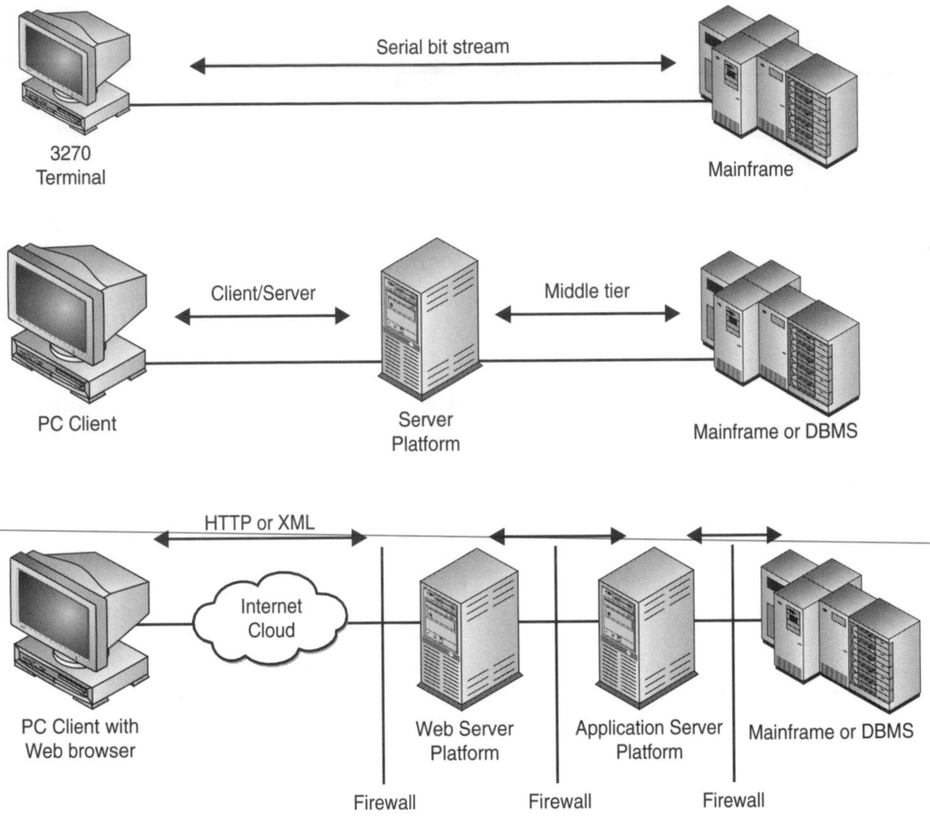

Figure 11-1
Application scenarios show the different levels of access control.

list could be created when the user is authenticated. It could then be passed to the resource in a secure fashion for access control, as opposed to the resource checking to see if the user has access (for example, querying a database).

Granting authorization by inheritance simplifies the administration by logically linking access to organizational structures (see Figure 11-2). To access a protected resource within this branch, you must be an employee of MCC as opposed to an Extranet partner. This employee would be in the Plastics Company rather than the consumer products company. He or she would be part of the Adhesive Polymer business unit in the Engineering division. This employee would be a senior tester within the Quality Assurance branch.

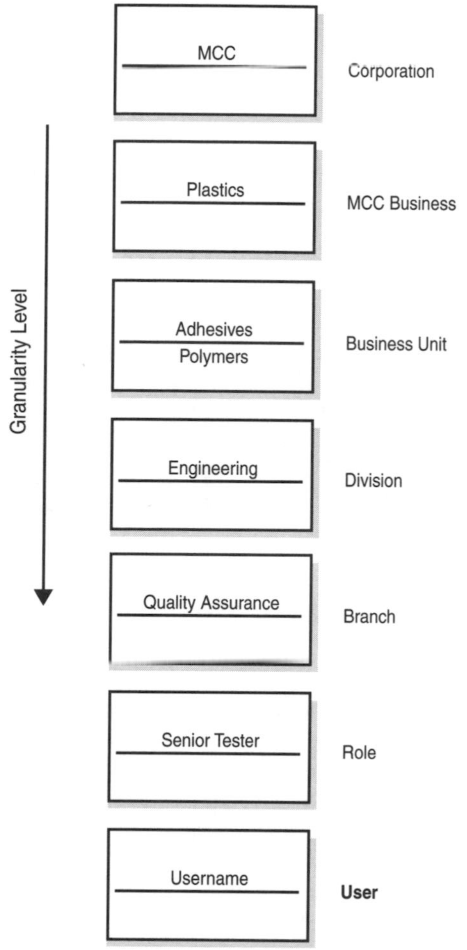

Figure 11-2

Example MCC hierarchical authorization model

When defining the various authorization models, the following terms defined in Table 11-1 will be used.

Associative Access Control

Most authorization decisions are based on a relationship with a given principal name and the operations that are allowed by the given user. This name could be part of a role (for example, a group) for a given job title within an organization. In most cases, access to resources is not performed

Table 11-1

Application Security Definitions

Authorization Term	Description
Application developer	An application developer works in unison with a security-aware application.
Application type	A grouping of resources by application (salary field, commissions, and bonus are all of the payroll application type).
Job title	A job title or job code is assigned to a user (many-to-one) relationship. A user can only have one job title, but many users can have the same job title.
Entitlement	An entitlement is a generic business policy rule that determines at run-time what privileges are necessary and sufficient for a given user and resource.
Location	A location is a set of users who are co-located geographically. Locations can failover to other locations.
Permission	A permission is an attribute given to the intersection of a role and resource that is associated with a given access (read, write, debit, credit, reconcile).
Principal	A principal is a user or a process that is requesting access to a resource.
Resource manager	A resource manager is the administrator of the resource who controls access to it using a standard access definition.
Resource type	A resource type is a grouping of resources by the set of permissions that are associated with each.
Resource	A resource is anything that access needs to be controlled (file, application, field, menu, transaction, account).
Role	A role consists of the authorities and responsibilities delegated to a user.

from a principal name but from a job title or role name. Associative access control mechanisms consist of resource ACLs or user capability lists (resources a user has access to). An ACL is associated with each resource, listing the individuals authorized to access the resource. Administration of resources down to the user level does not scale well. Most authorization models use the concept of roles (groups of users) versus individual access to resources. Conversely, a capability list consists of the resource(s) a role has access to.

To give a user (1) access to a resource (Server), the role (A) needs to be associated with the resource (Server), and the user needs to be associated with the role (A). To give another user (3) access to the same resource, the administrator needs to add the user to the role (A). See Figure 11-3.

Most authorization decisions within organizations are performed on behalf of the user or process. A more optimal approach is consolidating users into job categories (job titles). Examples of job titles are clerk, administrator, manager, director, and so on. This could be a one-to-one relationship or possibly many-to-many depending on the implementation. Resources can be grouped by type with each containing a common permission sequence (that is, a screen field would have different permissions than a transaction). Two choices are available when you describe these associations: 1) in a single level or flat name space or 2) in a hierarchical fashion. Administration of flat name space principals and resources is a complex endeavor. A hierarchical approach is easier to manage. An intermediary principal called a role is crucial to this hierarchical model. The role is associated with resources. Job titles have a one-to-many relationship with roles. This model enforces least privilege access. Access is given to a principal by assigning the job title with a given role.

Figure 11-3

Associative access model

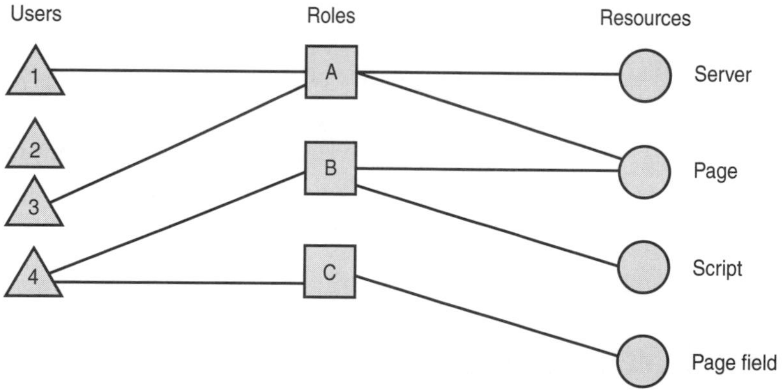

Entitlements

Once a user has been associated with a given role (job title) that has access to a protected resource, an *entitlement* is the specific business function that a user can perform on the resource. The most basic entitlements of most file systems are create, read, update, and delete, which are referred to as CRUD. The use of the entitlement depends on the application logic; for example, create could be used to write to the file system or create a file. The first authorization check confirms the existence of the user or group in the ACL (associative); the second check matches the function or action that the user is privileged to perform on the resource (for example, write, debit, and so on).

Logical Access Control

The last step in the authorization process is logical access control validation. Logical access control is based on the accumulation of a given action over a period of time (for example, thresholds, sequences, or some logical combination). It is assumed that an associative check will be performed before the logical check. For example, can the user perform the function? If so, how much can he or she trade in one day? This will enable organizations to limit the user's access based on necessary sequences to complete a transaction (such as bank authorization before purchase).

The closer the security check is to the business process, the harder it is to abstract the enforcement of the check. Logical access control requires application developers to apply security to their software in order to provide a finer, more granular access to corporate resources. The benefit of doing this is to provide application developers with a common authorization API that will enable them to achieve the same security level without writing security-specific software. This allows security-aware applications quicker time to market and the ease of maintenance.

Protected Resources

The enforcement of access control could happen at many points within an application infrastructure. An operating system controls access to the underlying file system, hardware devices (floppy, CDROM, Tape Backup), and network services. Application protection is from an invocation perspective only (can you start the application?). In most cases, users are not allowed to access (login into) server-type systems; they are just allowed to access the applications that are running under a system agent. This requires the application to control access to its own resources without relying on the operating system controls. Depending on the application, it can have its own privilege management system; for example, a transaction-based system might have a debit and query privilege.

Other types of resources that have protection mechanisms are database management systems (DBMS). These systems have the capability to protect access down to the record and table level. Many DBMS client-server-based applications utilize the DBMS security to enforce the proper level of access controls.

Authentication Schemes

The process of authentication is used to verify the claimed identity of a user (prove to the system that you are who you say you are). Depending on the system and the application, authenticators fall into four categories: something you know (passwords and PIN numbers), something you have (SmartCards and Digital Certificates), something you are (biometric identification systems such as fingerprinting, voice recognition, and retina scans), and where you are located (IP address). Depending on the level of control required (refer to Chapter 3), best practice authentication systems should combine two or more of the authentication categories.

One can prove the identity of a user to a given application or system through many ways. See Table 11-2 for a list of authentication schemes.

Single Sign-On

Single sign-on (SSO) is the capability to authenticate to a given system/application once and then all participating systems/applications will not require another authentication. This is typically a requirement of most large organizations with multiple systems that require separate authentication information in order to reduce help desk costs and improve the user experience.

Table 11-2

Protected Resource Authentication Schemes

Protected Resource	Something You Know	Something You Have	Something You Are	Your Location
Platform Host	Username/ password	Private Key-Smartcard, Security Token	Biometric (thumbprint, retina, or facial recognition)	Terminal ID or IP address
Network Operation System (Domain, File, and Print)	Username/ password	Private Key-Smartcard, Security Token	Biometric (thumbprint, retina, or facial recognition)	Time zone or location of the machine you're logging in from
Network Service (Web, FTP, Telnet)	Username/ password	Private Key-Smartcard, Security Token		IP address
Database Manage-ment System	Username/ password			IP address

Multiple techniques are available to provide user SSO. The major techniques are scripting, SSO-aware applications. Scripting stores all the authentication information in either a local storage area (for example, workstation hard disk) or on a directory server. Activation is either tied to a batch or Windows shortcut, or a more automated technique involving workstation interceptors or shim layer plug-ins. Workstation interceptors (for example, Passlogix, V-GO) store all the sensitive authentication information on servers. This provides centralized administration of this information. SSO-aware applications use a common login program. Microsoft Windows 2000 supports a Kerberos authentication protocol; every domain controller is a Kerberbos Distribution Center (KDC). The KDC is a trusted third party that vouches for the user's identity for each system the user is attempting to access. Each application has to be *kerberized* to take advantage of this underlying model. The MIT Kerberos distribution includes a standard replacement for the UNIX login program.

One of the drawbacks with scripting is the capability to synchronize passwords. If an application requires a password change, the centralized system must be notified, and vise versa, if the centralized application password changes, the application must be notified.

Do's and Don'ts: *In an SSO environment, special attention must be given to how access is granted (for example, weakest link in the chain).*

Do's and Don'ts: *SSO systems should use two-factor authentication for the initial access.*

One must consider many attributes (such as strong authentication, trusted repository, and secure communications) before deploying an SSO solution. Some organizations require that a higher level of authentication (for example, two factor) be used for SSO. Capturing all the passwords from an individual's heads and storing them in a single repository is a risky proposition. The capability to log into a single system and have access to all subsequent systems makes an auditor very uneasy. The repository must be able to protect itself from a mischievous administrator. Network access to the repository must be protected using a secure communications path (for example, secure socket layer [SSL] or virtual private network [VPN] technology).

The best most organizations can achieve is reduced sign-on. SSO has been an unattainable goal for the last 30 years. The best strategic solution is limited SSO.

Impersonation

Impersonation is the capability to pass your credentials to another process so the proper access control can be enforced. The application or Web server has to be client-aware to be able to pass client requests and security context to other server processes or to the operating system. Other server processes can then handle the request as if the original client made it. Most loosely coupled applications and Web servers do *not* provide impersonation. Therefore, client requests are de-coupled from the access control decision past the first-level server. For example, most Web-based transactions that utilize application and database servers perform the functions as a single user, typically with all privileges.

Security Repository

A *security repository* stores all the security-specific information about an organization. This is either a native directory server or a DBMS. Access to this information, as well as the communication path, must be controlled. DBMS are relational in nature; directory servers are more hierarchical (tree and branches). This makes administration and reporting challenging between each solution. Most IT professionals have automated DBMS reporting tools (for example, Crystal reports). Many auditors and data owners are interested in two questions: "Who has access to my resources?" and "How are the consumers of my resource accessing it (that is, normal access or fraud and abuse)?"

These questions are easily answered if the data is stored in a relational format. Automated reporting tools for the directory server are non-existent.

Authorization Namespace

A namespace has many definitions; in this case, *namespace* is a collection of names and attribute pairs that define the security repository. For example, all users must have a universal userID (UUID) that distinguishes them from within the organization. This userID could be unique within the whole organization or unique to a business unit or domain within the organization. This enables applications to find users, resource, roles, and so on.

An example of how to develop a namespace is detailed in the LDAPv3 Attribute Syntax Definitions document (RFC2252) and Distributed Computing Environment (DCE). A directory schema defines the namespace of the people, devices, organizations, and the attributes available to each entry. More importantly, a directory holds the userID, password, and protected resource information.

Transparent Application Security (Web)

Many organizations have many Web applications being developed within their business units. Web technology is providing a conduit into back-end corporate resources. Business units are busy developing secure Web-based applications to perform sensitive transactions like electronic commerce. Some of the existing Web applications, such as e-mail and access into back-end legacy systems, have some or no security. A myriad of Web servers (for example, Apache, IIS, Netscape) and application development techniques (CGI, active server pages, servlets, Common Object Request Broker Architecture [CORBA], Distributed Common Object Model [DCOM], and JAVA) are being utilized. This leading edge technology tends to leave security by the wayside.

Web server access controls are specific to Web servers. The interface between the Web server access controls and the application is nonexistent. Web application developers are developing security controls to meet their business unit security requirements (stovepipe). If the same user has access to different applications, no overlap occurs between the protection schemes and the administration. If a typical Web architecture is broken down into its functional components, an information security practitioner needs to answer the following questions: "Where should the access control mechanism be enforced?" and "Who is the access control decision being performed on behalf of?" See Figure 11-4 and Table 11-3.

Figure 11-4

Web access control points

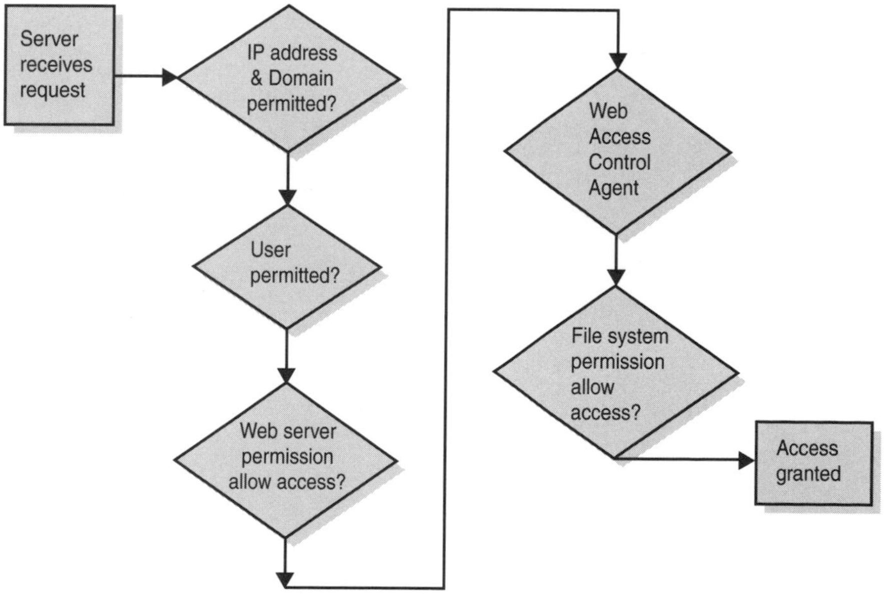

Table 11-3

Current Access Control Security Mechanisms

Security Mechanism Placement	Type of Security Mechanism	Discussion
Router	Network level	Routers have the capability to filter IP addressees. This enables you to limit lists of addresses attempting to access your site. The major drawback to this mechanism is that client firewalls and proxy servers use their address instead of the client's workstation. Another drawback is that routers do not support authentication, and they are very difficult to manage.
Firewall	Network and Application level	Firewalls can provide access control by IP address, Internet domain, and network service (such as HTTP or FTP). They can also provide user authentication using application proxies. The major drawback is that they only provide server-level access (not directory or page level). It is also hard to administer due to the application security needs affecting the overall network security policy.
Web Server	Network and Application level	A Web server can provide access control-based hostname, Internet domain, username/password (.htaccess), and certificates. The drawbacks will be covered in depth in a later section.
Application Server	Application level	An application server receives requests from the Web server. The application server usually provides username/password authentication and session timeouts. The drawback with this approach is that the administration is accomplished programmatically (no administration GUI is available).
DBMS	Application level	DBMS security protects tables based on access control lists. The user's authentication information must be passed from the Web server to the back-end DBMS. Administration is very complex and not scalable. The DBMS slows down considerably due to security checking.

Web Access Control Solution

The solution to this problem is to provide a heterogeneous Web access control system (hereafter referred to as WAC). It must support a variety of Web servers of choice (such as Apache, IIS, and Netscape) seamlessly. It must provide a centralized authentication, authorization, and distributed administration. It is a third-party product that provides SSO, centralized repository, reusable security policy (roles and resources), access reports, and monitoring.

Relatively speaking, this space has a limited amount of WAC products, but more are emerging everyday. The market leader is Netegrity Siteminder, followed by Entrust getAccess, Securant ClearTrust, and OpenNetwork Technologies DirectorySmart.

Web Server Integration

A *Web agent* is executable software that is integrated into the Web server network service and address space (server-side extension). The Web agent is executed every time the Web server responds to events during the processing of an HTTP request. This is referred to as *soft choke*—it can't be bypassed. This is analogous to a firewall, which is put inline between the Internet and the Intranet. Microsoft's Internet Information Server (IIS) Web agents use its Internet Server Application Program Interface (ISAPI). Netscape Enterprise Server Web agents use its Netscape Application Program Interface (NSAPI). The Apache server also supports custom modules for additional access control.

WAC Security Repository

Traditional Web server access controls use a file called .htaccess, which is stored in each directory that requires protection. The file contains the users or roles that have access to the specific page or directory it resides in. WAC security-related data is stored in a centralized repository (such as a directory server or relational DBMS). WAC products support relational DBMS (Oracle, Sybase, SqlServer). If your DBMS supports replication, you can take advantage of this independently of the WAC repository.

Access to these back-end repositories is provided using a Java Database connector or Microsoft's Open Database Connectivity (ODBC). Specific user information can be stored in a LDAP server or in an NT Domain. The front-end process to the repository is referred to as a Security (Entitlement/Registry) server. Whatever the back-end datastore is, it must be in a reportable format (see Figure 11-5).

WAC Scalability and High Availability

A security solution should not hinder the underlying business process. It may just slow it down. Most access controls systems first authenticate a user, then authorize each transaction. If the authentication system is unavailable, access is denied. If the authorization system has to perform a database lookup for each user action, it will impact the overall end-to-end flow.

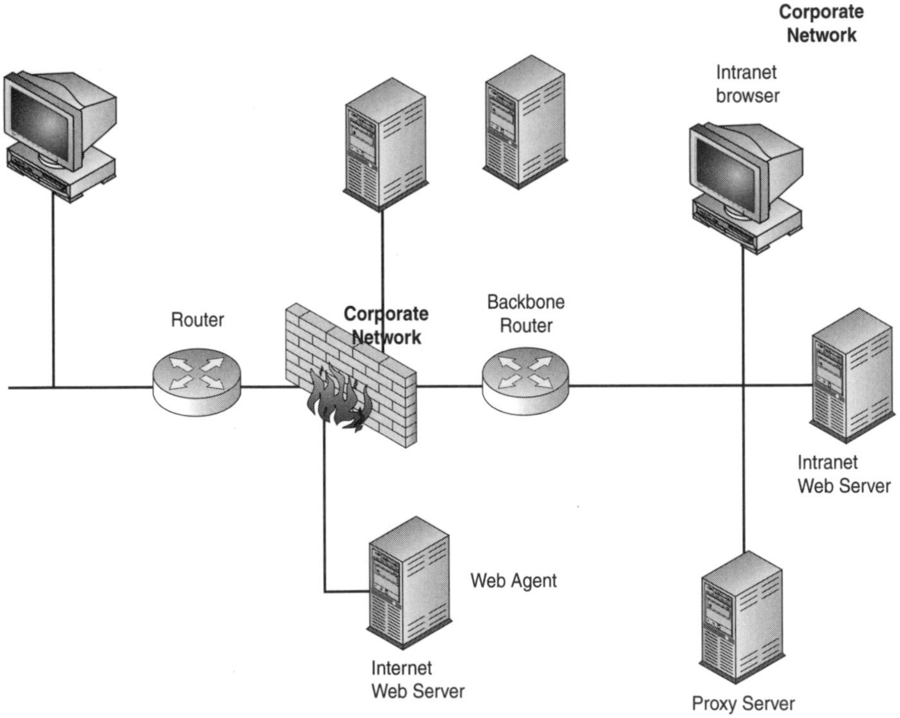

Figure 11-5

Traditional Web security control

Some techniques (such as redundancy, distribution, and caching) used to scale WAC are not unlike the rest of the application server industry. Most authentication protocols support redundant servers (if the first server is unavailable because of overload or system failure, it tries the next one in the list). The first server is the primary one that updates all the secondary servers when a change occurs (for example, PDC and BDC). The most prevalent distribution-computing environment is based on a common Object Request Broker (ORB). The ORB is responsible for locating and managing the interaction between clients and servers. The CORBA defines an architecture of interfaces and services that must be provided by the ORB. Lastly, the access server is responsible for communicating with the back-end WAC system. Authorization should be performed locally at each resource. Once authentication is completed, a capability list is sent down (cached) to the Web agent and enforced for every Web transaction.

WAC Password Management

WAC products provide a common access control mechanism across heterogeneous Web servers independent of the browser community. Typical Web server authentication is very weak (for example, no password management facilities are present like there are in domain access). One of the additional security features is an enhanced password management scheme (password expiration, length, and strength checks). Another feature not found in any Web server is failed password attempt checking (three failed password attempts will disable the account for a time period or lock it indefinitely).

If digital certificates are used as an authentication scheme, the Web server will verify that the requested certificate is signed by the proper authority (such as the Certificate Authority trust relation) and matches the certificate stored in the directory server. The last part of the certificate validation process is to check for revocation, which most Web servers and all Web browsers fail to provide. WAC can fill this void by providing a Certificate Revocation List (CRL) or making an Online Certificate Status Protocol (OCSP) query. WACs also provide the capability to check X.509 certificate extensions for more granular access to resources.

WAC Security Flow

The stateless nature of the Web negates any benefit provided by strong authentication schemes. Re-authenticating on every connection is unacceptable to the user community at large because it seriously degrades performance. WAC products use an access token, which is checked each time access control decisions need to be made. This token is kept in a user's browser cookie or within a hidden field in each user's HTML page. The construction of the access token is done in a secure fashion (encryption and/or digital signature) and varies among WAC vendors. This security information within the cookie is most likely authorization information (roles), timestamp, username, IP address, and a random number. The session key used to perform the cryptographic functions is only known to the WAC components. To impersonate an authorized user, the adversary would have the session key used to protect the token and spoof the source IP address. If the client's browser declines cookies, the user will have to authenticate for each request. Protection of the cookie over the medium should be ensured using SSL encryption, as this will prevent session hijacking.

Figure 11-6 depicts the WAC security flow between the browser, Web server, and all of the security architecture. The flow is as follows:

1. The Web browser selects a protected Web resource.
2. If user access has expired or it's the first time being used, then he or she will be redirected to the access server and asked to authenticate his- or herself. If the access token hasn't expired, then the user can skip to step 5.
3. The access server sends the user's credentials to the WAC repository/registry server.
4. If the authentication scheme requires an external authentication server, the request is forwarded.
5. If the authentication and authorization requests are valid, then access is granted.

Figure 11-6
WAC process flow

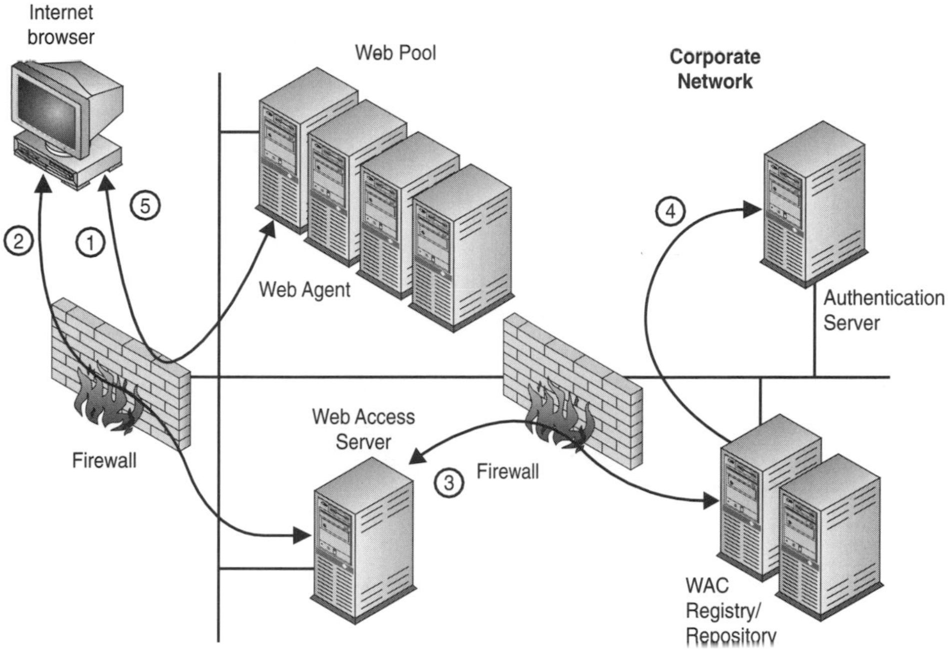

WAC Authentication Schemes

Basic authentication is the predominate scheme used by Web servers for anything from reading the *Wall Street Journal* to stock trades. A major drawback to the basic authentication scheme is that the password is sent in the clear (unencrypted) to the requesting server. HTTP 1.1 introduced digest authentication, which is based on a simple challenge-response paradigm using a random number (nonce value). The common key value (the user's password) is used as a seed of an MD5 hash. The user's password is never sent over the wire.

The goal of any enterprise access control system is to provide as few as possible authentication steps SSO. The problem with SSO is that all the software vendors that enforce access control need to adhere to some common security standard (such as DCE, DCOM, or CORBA). Some short-term solutions centralize authentication information, but not the application's state. WAC products support external authentication systems, such as RADIUS, NT Domain, popular security token, and certificates.

When a user comes to the system for the first time, he or she is presented with a login screen. If multiple authentication schemes are supported, the user has to choose which type he or she is going to use. The second page is a welcome page that displays the last successful and unsuccessful logins. This is to inform the user that somebody else was using his or her account. The last screen can be personalized depending on the user's profile. This profile contains the resources the user has access to, all the roles the user belongs to, and any other information necessary to make access decisions.

Another feature of WAC products is their capability to control session timeouts. One of the biggest desktop security concerns is inactivity timeouts. Once a user has been authenticated to the system and leaves his/her desktop unattended without logging off the system, the user is susceptible to an insider masquerading as him or her to the system.

Inline Application Security

The best way to perform access control within the application is to use a set of standard application programming interface (API) calls that carry out the security. The alternative to this is having developers be responsible for providing their own proper access control and monitoring security functions. This is prone to human error and very hard to administer. If access control is going to be provided explicitly in the application, the software logic and administration must be reusable.

Application Access Control Solution

Organizations are using two standard authorization APIs: the International Standards Organization (ISO) 10181-3 (Access Control Framework), and the Open Group Technical Standard C908 entitled "Authorization (azn) API". The ISO 10181 series is dedicated to developing security framework standards. This standard is under the JTC Information Technology committee, SC 27-IT Security Techniques, and is part of seven series of frameworks including authentication, non-repudiation, confidentiality, integrity, and security audit and alarms. The framework set is over 5 years old. The aznAPI was designed specifically for authorization functionality. It separates authorization from authentication. It supports authorization attribute types (for example, access identities, groups, roles, and clearances). It also audits (logs) all of its operations. The aznAPI conforms to the ISO Access Control Framework standard. See Table 11-4 for aznAPI function descriptions.

The azn_decision_access_allowed function takes a user's credentials (a username and a list of roles), the name of the protected resource, and the operation the user is trying to perform. The return value is the permission either permitted or not.

Table 11-4

AznAPI Function Descriptions

Interface Family Name Prefix	Interface Family Supported Functions
Azn_initialize	Initialize aznAPI implementation.
Azn_shutdown	Clean up aznAPI implementation in preparation for shutdown.
Azn_creds	Create, delete, modify, and combine credentials chains.
Azn_id	Build credentials chain based on authenticated identity produced by an authentication service.
Azn_decision	Make an access decision.
Azn_entitlement	Get access control policy information.
Azn_pac	Build credentials chain based on PAC produced by an authorization service.
Azn_error	Retrieve error information from status values returned by aznAPI functions.
Azn_authority	Discover authentication, authorization, and credentials, label, and pac mechanisms supported by aznAPI implementation.
Azn_attrlist	Create and delete attribute/value pair list.
Azn_release	Release data allocated by aznAPI implementation.

Administration

One of the biggest reasons to choose a third-party authorization product is the reduced administration cost. Most administration interfaces use a Web browser with a Java applet for a richer GUI. This enables security administrators to create users, roles, resources, and the associated relationships from a single source. A few third-party products enable the superuser to delegate administrators based on groups/domains (hierarchically). It is useful to large organizations, or Extranets, where distributing administration downward toward the business owner is beneficial. This approach will enforce accurate and uniform security policy across the organization.

Deploying a security system into an existing enterprise is not without its challenges. It requires a method to transition the existing legacy security system(s) to the new one. For instance, adding 1,000 users' entries with a GUI would take a man-month of time. Some third-party products offer an API that enables an intermediate-level programmer to automate the transition process (such as seeding the security repository). One can customize the login, welcome, and resource screens with this same API. It can also extend the product's functionality (such as password changes and username naming conventions). Some third-party products even support user self-registration. This is beneficial to service providers because it provides a timesaving effort over manually adding the users.

Reporting

Data/resource owners crave for detailed reports on who has/had access to their information. Audit departments require usage information for fraud and abuse analysis. Security departments collect security violation information, such as failed login attempts. Many easy-to-use tools are on the market for generating reports from a DBMS (such as Crystal reports). Because directory servers are still relatively new to the enterprise, a shortage of reporting tools exists. The marketing groups for trend analysis use page/site activity reports.

Analysis of Case Study #1—SSO

The MCC had an initiative to provide SSO to five applications. The applications are listed in Table 11-5. The solution they chose was a Windows interceptor product call Passlogix V-GO with a directory server back-end Novell Netware Directory Server (NDS). Anytime an application presents a login screen, the V-GO will intercept it, securely query the necessary information, and present it to the requesting application without user intervention. The user's login information is secured using cryptography and tight access controls within NDS. All the users are required to login into Novell before running any SSO-enabled application. The biggest security threat after the SSO deployment was users not locking their desktop when they were away from their desks.

Analysis of Case Study #2—FinApp

The FinApp application is a non-Web application requiring application level security. FinApp sends financial information using XML to its partners. It uses a set of proprietary API calls to perform the data transfers. All the Extranet partners use platform security (such as harden hosts

Table 11-5 SSO Application Breakdown

Corporate Application	Purpose	SSO Solution
Lotus Notes	Collaboration	Novell SSO with Passlogix V-GO
Internet connectivity proxy authentication	Research	Novell SSO with Passlogix V-GO
GoldMine	Sales forecasting, accounting, and legal departments	Passl Novell SSO with Passlogix V-GO
Oracle DBMS	Repository for marketing research and engineering requests	Novell SSO with Passlogix V-GO
WRQ Reflections	MainFrame Access TN3270 emulator	Novell SSO with Passlogix V-GO

with a product like eTrust's Access Control) and network security (such as firewalls and IDSs) mechanisms to protect themselves from each other.

The FinApp servers validate the incoming IP address of the initiating party before it accepts the connection. Authentication is accomplished using standard passwords. Because non-interactive users spawn a majority of the exchanges, user authentication is challenging. A user can perform five different functions within FinApp:

- Request a price quote.
- Send a positional message.
- Set a stock price.
- Buy stock.
- Clear stock trade.

Each user who has access to the FinApp will have one or more of these privileges to perform his or her jobs. The messages are formulated on a client-end system; this system uses the FinApp protocol to communicate with the proper FinApp server depending on its availability. This client-end system must be able to perform the following to formulate a FinApp request:

- Retrieve the user's password in a secure fashion.
- Fill in the required function (for example, set stock price).
- Format the message in XML.
- Call the underlying network transport (for example, middleware or TCP/IP).

User Administration is accomplished by procedural means (for example, phone call or Fax message). None of these transactions are totally automated. A human element is still required before any trade is cleared and money exchanged, so the security risk is not paramount.

Analysis of Case Study #3—HealthApp

HealthApp is a Web portal that has many Line of Business applications under development. The Web platforms vary between UNIX running Iplanet and Microsoft IIS Web servers. Fifteen distinct Web applications require protection. Because each individual application requires access controls, a single security solution is cost-effective. A Web SSO product was chosen that utilized a DBMS back-end instead of a directory server. A WAC filter (plug-in) will be added to the existing Web server logic that performs the access control across the different applications. Figure 11-7 depicts the layers within a Web server. The security architect deemed it necessary for five roles to be established for access to the 15 applications. It worked out that each role would have access to three HealthApp applications.

The WAC product enforces access to the individual HealthApp Web applications. When a HealthApp user accesses a protected area or the HealthApp home page for the first time or after the allotted timeout, the user is required to authenticate him- or herself using a username/password pair. If the user has access to the bookmarked page, he or she will be returned to that page and start the individual application. If the user

Figure 11-7

The layers within a Web server

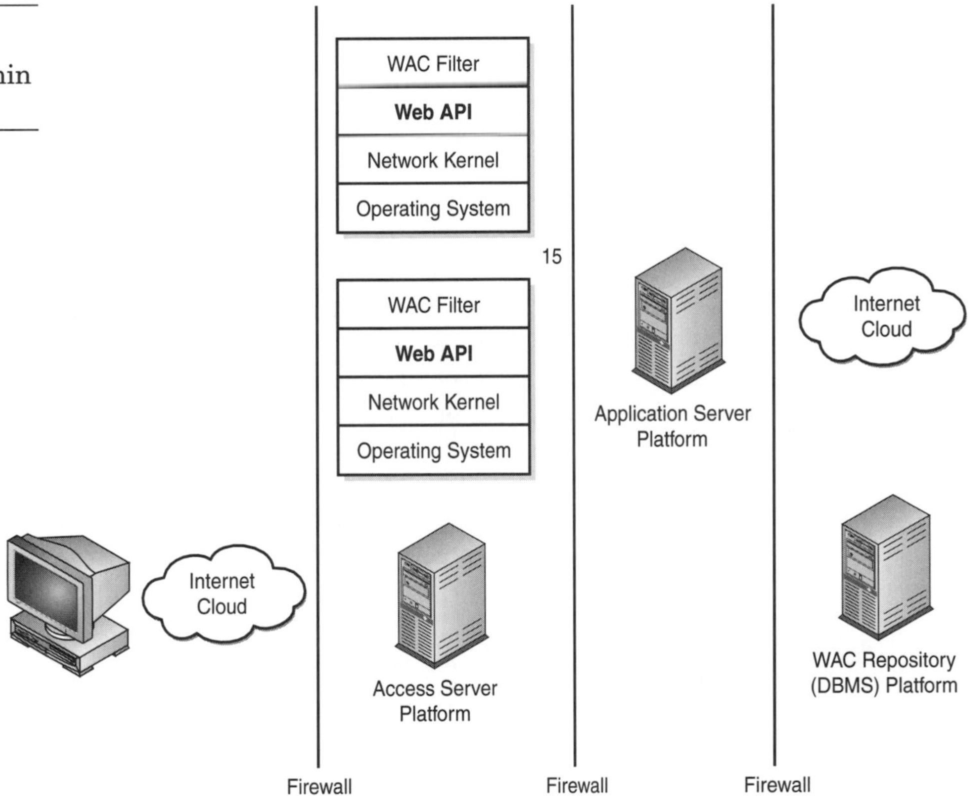

Table 11-6

HealthAPP WAC Configurations

WAC Configuration	Default	HealthApp Setting
Session timeout	12 hours	8 hours
Inactivity timeout	45 minutes	15 minutes
Failed password attempt before account disable	6	6
Time between three password failures	15 minutes	15 minutes
Password length	5 characters	6 characters
Password expiration	90 days	180 days
Password strength test	None	2 alphanumerics
Transport security	None	Secure Socket Layer

came through the home page and authenticated successfully, he or she will receive a list of authorized applications in the form of Web links. The security architect configured the WAC password management and timeout according to Table 11-6.

The HealthApp application developers are able to derive the username and roles from the HTTP header variables $HTTP-USER and $HTTP-ROLE. This will allow a more granular access within the application depending on the role. User-defined information is also available with the WAC repository. The requesting application is required to make a query to the repository with the username as a key.

User administration is delegated among the participating user organizations. The local administrator is capable of administrating users within their own organization. This administration includes adding, removing, and resetting user accounts, as well as adding users to a given set of roles. The roles to resource association are performed at the HealthApp headquarters.

Weekly and monthly reports are generated to the data owners of each application that contain the following:

- The number of access by application and user
- The number of failed login attempts

- The number of failed resource attempts
- A matrix of the given roles that have access to the given resource
- A matrix of users who belong to the particular roles

Conclusion

The majority of applications being developed are using three-tier architectures (Web server, Application server, and Database) on a variety of platforms (Solaris and Windows 2000). Many of these applications require access control. If the user is coming into a single site or multiple sites under the same auspices, the user should only have to be authenticated once. If all the access points could be directed to common entry point (not a single point due to high-availability concerns), then the access control consolidated.

References

Microsoft: Single Sign-On in Windows 2000 Networks

CHAPTER 12

PKI: Components and Applications

Public Key Infrastructure (PKI) is a collection of components and procedures that support the management of cryptographic keys through the use of digital certificates. PKI-enabled applications provide authentication, integrity of data, confidentiality, and non-repudiation security services. Several standards groups have emerged in the arena of PKI, but the Public Key Infrastructure, based on X.509 Working Group (PKIX) of the Internet Engineering Task Force (IETF), defines the most advanced and widespread specifications to date. The Public Key Cryptography Standards (PKCS), published by RSA Security Laboratories, have also been quite influential in advancing the adoption of PKI.

Public Key Infrastructures consist of several components. The most basic component of a PKI is the certificate. A certificate is issued to subjects and vouches for the identity of the subject. Subjects are usually people, but can be any end entity that needs to identify itself, such as a Web server or an application. A public/private key pair is associated with the certificate, which can be used to perform cryptographic operations. The following services are currently commercially available through the use of certificates and their associated key pairs:

- Web authentication and channel privacy
- Signed and encrypted messaging

- Signed transactions and form signing
- Network operating system, host, and mainframe authentication
- Remote access
- Virtual Private Networks
- File encryption
- Software code signing

Web Authentication and Channel Privacy By default, the Web is not a secure environment. All information is transferred in the clear and is prone to attack. In some cases (such as retrieving a recipe from a Web site), this is not a real problem; however, in other cases (such as performing a stock trade), security must be enhanced. Netscape's Secure Sockets Layer (SSL) and the IETF's Transport Layer Security (TLS) protocols are examples of mechanisms for establishing a secure channel between a client and a server. The SSL protocol will be described later in this chapter. Certificates are used to authenticate the communicating parties when establishing the secure channel. Once authenticated, these protocols use encryption keys to ensure confidentiality and message integrity between the two communicating parties. SSL 3.0 is the most widely used secure channel protocol in use today. TLS is also referred to as SSL 3.1, or the next version of SSL. The difference between TLS and SSL 3.0 are not dramatic, but the two protocols do not interoperate.

Signed and Encrypted Messaging E-mail is another ubiquitous technology that is not secured by default. Increasingly, organizations need a way to ensure that the information in e-mail is kept confidential and is not altered in transit (message integrity). Certificates and their associated keys can be used to encrypt and digitally sign e-mail messages. RSA Security originally published the S/MIME version 2 protocol to support this functionality. Soon thereafter, they released the specifications to the IETF, who then made several improvements and released S/MIME version 3. S/MIME, Secure Multi-Purpose Internet Mail Extensions, defines a MIME wrapper for digital signatures and one for encryption. S/MIME follows the syntax in PKCS #7, the Cryptographic Message Syntax Standard. Although other standards exist like PGP/MIME, S/MIME has become accepted as the industry standard method for securing e-mail and is supported by virtually all of the widely used commercial e-mail products.

Signed Transactions and Form Signing Digitally signing a transaction or form is similar in concept to using a *wet* signature. A digital signature can be used to legally bind the signer to the content of a contract or a transaction that has been initiated. In order to provide this functionality, users of the PKI must agree upon a set of strict policies and procedures.

Network Operating System, Host, and Mainframe Authentication Developers can PKI-enable systems thereby enabling certificates to be used as a method to authenticate end users. Potentially, certificate-based authentication can be used as a universal authentication mechanism to many different systems. This would eliminate the need to manage multiple username/password accounts for each user. In addition, the user need only authenticate once to access all desired applications.

Remote Access Many organizations have a distributed employee work force that requires remote access to corporate resources. Certificate-based authentication offers an alternative to username/password authentication. As mentioned previously, if developed, this method of authentication can be applied across different platforms providing a more streamlined solution. Additionally, using PKI to distribute certificates for authentication is a more scalable and secure solution than the standard username/password scenario.

Virtual Private Networks A Virtual Private Network (VPN) enables two parties to communicate securely over a public network. For example, an organization with a central office in New York and satellite offices across the U.S. could use a VPN over the Internet to establish secure communication between the central office and the branch offices. This is a secure method of communication that saves the organization the cost of leasing WAN lines for each satellite office. Certificates can be used to authenticate the end points in a VPN.

File Encryption Sharing files on a LAN has become a common task. Most LANs run TCP/IP and provide no encryption services. In most cases, permission lists protect access to files, but the process to apply and maintain these lists often breaks down. This can leave sensitive data out in the open for anyone in the organization to view (such as an employee list from the Human Resources department including salary information). PKI can be used to issue certificates that attest to the authenticity of their associated keys to encrypt sensitive data.

Software Code Signing As software is updated, it needs to be distributed. For example, Microsoft will often distribute patches to their software via the Web. This is an efficient method, but it presents some security risks. For example, it may be possible for the code to be altered with a virus. Software code signing enables developers to digitally sign code so that if it changes in any way, the receiver will be made aware of it.

The rest of this chapter is divided into three main sections. The first section introduces the reader to the concept and function of cryptography in modern-day computing systems. The next section defines the concepts and components that make up a PKI. Finally, the last section includes several case studies that are examined to demonstrate a Public Key Infrastructure in practice.

Cryptography

Cryptography is defined as the methods of making and using secret writing. Secret writing is necessary to keep messages private between two parties. One common though trivial example of cryptography is Pig Latin. Let's say Alice and Bob are at a party with a roomful of people and Alice wants to convey a private message to a Bob. The *plaintext* or *cleartext* message might read, "Meet me tomorrow at noon on Elm Street." If Alice were to write this down, anyone could intercept and read the message. To protect this message Alice uses a *cipher* to encrypt the message and create *ciphertext*. The ciphertext of this particular message would read, "Teema ema worromota taa noona noa Mlea teertsa." When Bob retrieves the message, he must use the appropriate cipher to decrypt the message and return it to its original state. Pig Latin relies on the secrecy of its encryption algorithm (cipher). In fact, the cipher is quite simple—reverse each word and add the letter *A* to the end of it. Modern day computer systems employ complex algorithms. The algorithms are publicly known. Keys are derived from the algorithm. It is these keys that actually perform the cryptographic operations. Keys must be made private, but the algorithms that produce them can be freely distributed. That is not to say that computers' ciphers are impenetrable. *Cryptanalysis* is the science of cracking algorithms—being able to decrypt a message without having the necessary key.

Thus far, cryptography has been explained in terms of confidentiality. Modern-day cryptography systems also offer the capability to preserve data integrity. Data integrity is the assurance that contents of a message have not changed since it was created. Additionally, cryptography can offer authentication by providing the knowledge of a message's origin. To provide these services, two types of key-based cryptography are used: symmetric and asymmetric.

Symmetric Key Cryptography

In symmetric key cryptography, both the sender and the receiver use the same key to perform encryption and decryption operations. For example, when Alice wants to send Bob a private message, she uses her copy of the key to encrypt her message. When Bob retrieves the message, he uses his copy of the key to decrypt the ciphertext back to plaintext. This type of cryptography is also commonly referred to as a *shared secret* key system. One of the most well known symmetric ciphers is the Data Encryption Standard (DES). DES was made a standard by the U.S. government in 1977. Today, due to its shorter key length (56-bit), DES is not considered highly secure. In response to this perception, the U.S. government set out to adopt a new symmetric key data encryption standard. On February 28, 2001, The National Institute of Standards and Technology (NIST) announced that a Draft Federal Information Processing Standard (FIPS) for the Advanced Encryption Standard (AES) is available for public review and comment. Numerous candidates were submitted to NIST for review. The Rijndael algorithm, written by Joan Daemen and Vincent Rijmen, was selected for its simplicity, performance, and cryptographic strength. Most computer systems and applications are not equipped to utilize the AES. For that reason, it will be some time until it sees widespread use. In the interim, DES and other symmetric key algorithms (RC4, Blowfish, and so on) will remain as the most commonly used symmetric key algorithms. Figure 12-1 illustrates symmetric key encryption.

Symmetric key cryptography is an efficient method for secure data transmission, but has its limitations. Most notably, it assumes that both Bob and Alice have a secure mechanism by which to exchange the shared secret (cryptography key). Perhaps Alice comes to New York once a month, and uses one of those trips to retrieve the key. However, what if Alice were not the only associate that Bob needed to communicate with in a secure fashion? For example, if Bob had 50 associates located around the world, it would become quite difficult for him to securely transfer the shared secret to all of these people. Further, Bob might want to use different

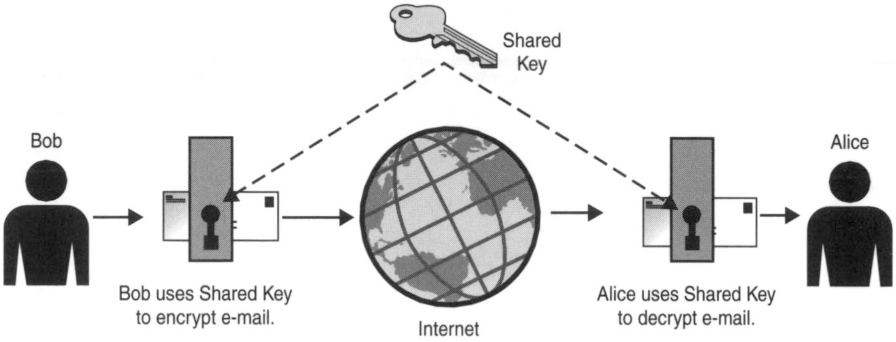
Shared
Key
Bob
Alice
Bob uses Shared Key
to encrypt e-mail.
Internet
Alice uses Shared Key
to decrypt e-mail.

Figure 12-1
Symmetric key encryption

shared secrets between different associates. That is to say, he might want to secure his conversation with Alice from conversations with other associates and vice versa. In this scenario, Bob would need a key for each individual that he wants to communicate with securely. Now he not only has to distribute these keys securely, but also has to manage their storage and use. Asymmetric cryptography addresses these concerns.

Asymmetric Key Cryptography

Asymmetric or public-key cryptography was invented and published by Whitfield Diffie and Martin Hellman when they introduced the Diffie-Hellman key exchange protocol. Diffe-Hellman is a key agreement protocol. Using DH, Alice and Bob possess both a public and a private key. Alice and Bob exchange their public keys. They then combine their own private key with the public key of the other party to create a new symmetric key that only the two of them know. The process has been greatly simplified for understanding, but the concept remains—this form of public-key cryptography provides a secure method for two parties to establish a shared secret. Shortly after the publication of Diffe-Hellman, Ron Rivest, Adi Shamir, and Leonard Adleman released the RSA public-key algorithm. Like Diffe-Hellman, RSA requires parties to have both a public and private key. RSA, however, does not create a shared secret. Rather, it can be used to directly encrypt and decrypt messages (see Figure 12-2). For example, if Alice wants to communicate a private message to Bob, she would use his public key to encrypt the message. Bob would then use his

Figure 12-2

Public-key encryption

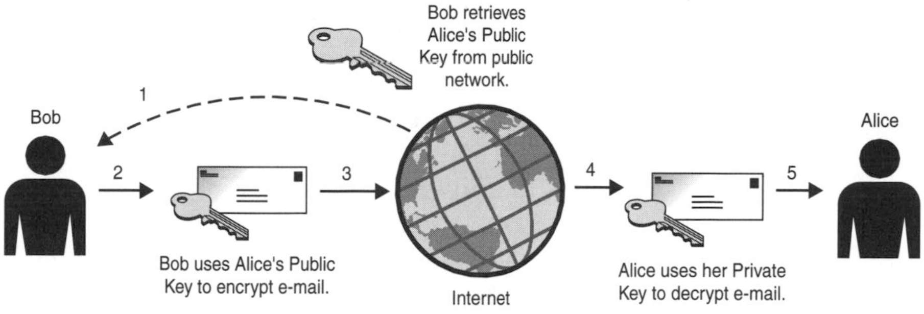

private key to decrypt the message. The public and private keys are mathematically related. Only the owner of the private key can decrypt a message that is encrypted with the associated public key. Because one key is public, algorithms such as RSA tend to rely on large keys to prevent effective cryptanalysis. Consequently, public-key cryptographic operations are generally slower than symmetric key operations. In reality, symmetric and asymmetric keys are often used in conjunction. Figure 12-3 illustrates symmetric and asymmetric keys in conjunction. In this scenario, public-key technology is used to securely transfer a symmetric key between two parties. For example, Bob would use Alice's public key to encrypt a shared secret. Alice would then use her associated private key to decrypt the secret. Bob and Alice can then use the shared secret to encrypt the remainder of their communication.

Figure 12-3

Symmetric key exchange with public-key encryption

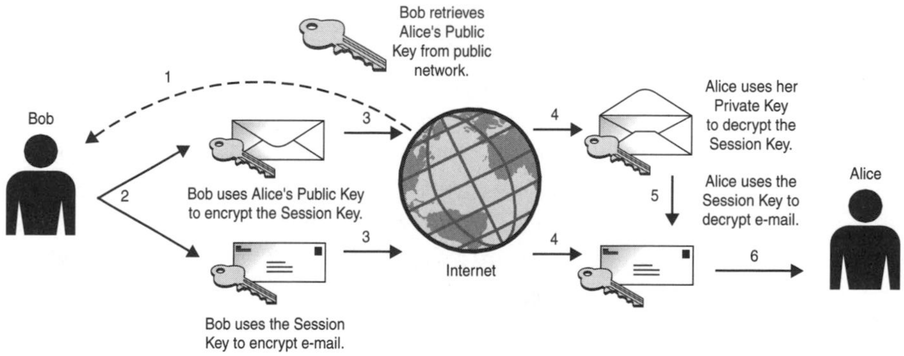

Digital Signatures

Up to now, only cryptographic algorithms that are used for encryption and decryption have been discussed. However, algorithms are available that are one way in nature. These algorithms take information and then scramble that information into an unreadable form often referred to as a *message digest* or *hash*. Mathematically, it is infeasible (nearly impossible within a useful amount of time) to reverse any information that has been transformed into a message digest. The algorithms that are used to create message digests are referred to as one-way hash algorithms. The terms hash and message digest are often used interchangeably. Common hash algorithms include SHA-1 and MD5.

Message digests are used to create digital signatures. To illustrate, we will once again return to Bob and Alice. In this scenario, Bob is sending a message to Alice. Alice wants to be able to confirm that Bob is the originator of the message and that the message has not been altered since its creation. The RSA digital signature algorithm works as follows. A hash algorithm is applied to the message that Bob is sending to Alice. Bob's private key is then used to encrypt the resulting message digest. The encrypted message digest is then attached to the original message and the entire payload is sent to Alice. When Alice receives the message, she takes the cleartext portion of the message and creates her own message digest, using the same algorithm that Bob used. Next, Alice uses Bob's public key to decrypt the message digest that was sent from Bob. Finally, the two message digests are compared. If they are identical, the digital signature is considered to be valid.

This process preserves the integrity of the message because if any part of the message were altered or corrupted during transit, the hashing algorithm that is run by Alice would produce a different message digest than the original. Authentication of origin is achieved because only the sender can create the message. That is, only the owner of the private key has the ability to create the original digital signature that is verifiable using the public key of that person. Because Bob is the owner of the private key, Alice can be sure the message came from him.

This description explains the process that occurs when using the RSA digital signature algorithm. The National Institute of Standards and Technology (NIST) developed the Digital Signature Standard (DSS), which defines the Digital Signature Algorithm (DSA). The process of how this algorithm works varies from the RSA implementation, but the functionality it provides (authentication of origin and data integrity) is the same. Figure 12-4 shows the digital signature.

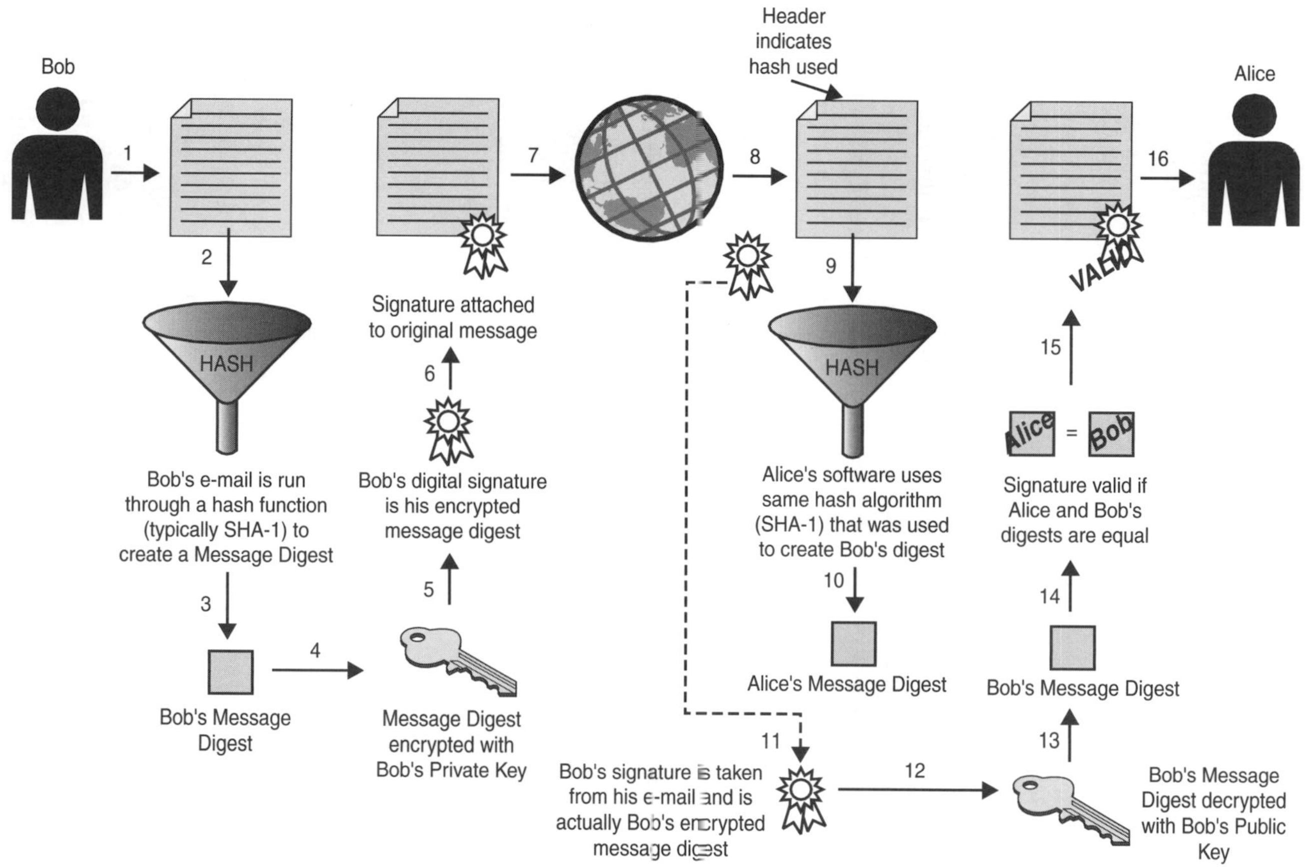

Figure 12-4 Digital signature

Strength of Cryptographic Algorithms

With enough time, money, and resources, virtually any cryptographic algorithm can be broken. That being said, some algorithms are stronger than others. Several factors contribute to the strength of a cryptographic algorithm. One of these factors is key size. A *key* can be defined as a value used by an algorithm to alter information. A *brute-force attack* attempts to use all possible keys with an algorithm. The longer the keys, the more difficult a brute-force attack becomes. With a 40-bit key, for example, it may be possible to crack an algorithm by a brute-force attack within a week's time, using a standard home computer. In a recent demonstration, DES was cracked with a brute-force attack in several months' time, using $200,000 worth of equipment. Today, 128-bit keys are seen as unbreakable by a brute-force attack, but as computational capability increases, even this size key may become vulnerable. Public-key algorithms need to be even longer because part of the key (the public half) is available to cryptanalysts. With this piece of the puzzle to analyze, the cryptanalyst may be able to derive the private key from the public key. This is different than a brute-force attack. Today, 1,024-bit RSA keys are deemed secure for the foreseeable future, whereas 2,048-bit keys are considered highly secure for some time to come.

It is important to remember that a cryptographic system is only effective in an overall security infrastructure. For example, a company may be using the strongest algorithms available, but security is still compromised if proper physical protections are not in place to protect the keys from theft. Table 12-1 describes several encryption algorithms.

Digital Certificates

Previously, it was stated that digital signatures offer authentication of the originating party. Alice, for example, could be sure that the message came from Bob because she has decrypted the message digest with Bob's public key. Only the associated private key could have encrypted the message digest, so it is therefore accepted that the message must have come from Bob. In fact, all that Alice really knows is that the owner of the public key, who in turn also owns the private key, has encrypted the message digest. If Alice has not verified that Bob is truly the owner of the public key, she cannot be sure that he is the person who sent the message. Alice could

Table 12-1 Table of Encryption Algorithms

Algorithm	Owner	Type	Key Length	Description
Diffie-Hellman	Introduced by Whitfield Diffie and Martin Hellman in '76	Asymmetric (Public Key)	Up to 1,024 bits	A means to securely exchange keys used to encrypt data.
DSS (Digital Signature Standard)	Created by NIST	Asymmetric (Public Key)	512 to 1,024 bits (DSA)	Signature-only algorithm endorsed by the U.S. DSS specifies DSA for digital signatures and SHA-1 for hashing.
RSA (Rivest-Shamir-Adleman)	Public domain, developed by Rivest, Shamir, and Adleman	Asymmetric (Public Key)	Up to 2,048 bits	Used for encryption and digital signatures.
MD2	Ron Rivest for RSA	Hash	16-byte digest length, 128-bit output	MD2 is a block message digest. RFC 1319.
MD4	Ron Rivest for RSA	Hash	16-byte digest length, 128-bit output	Message Digest 4 is an older hash algorithm with known flaws and is not recommended anymore. MD4 is a block message digest. RFC 1320.
MD5	Ron Rivest for RSA	Hash	16-byte digest length, 128-bit output	Message Digest Algorithm 5 is a block message digest. RFC 1321.
SHA-1	United States National Security Agency (NSA)	Hash	20-byte digest length, 160-bit output	Developed for the NSA by NIST. Stands for Secure Hash Algorithm. Currently considered the most secure hash algorithm. SHA-1 is a block message digest.
DES	Coppersmith, Feistel, Tuchmann, NSA	Symmetric	56-bit	DES' key length is too short to prevent brute-force attacks. DES is a block cipher.
DESede (Triple DES)	Diffie, Hellman, Tuckmann	Symmetric	112 or 168 bits (two to three 56-bit keys)	Uses up to three different DES keys. Triple DES is a block cipher.

(continued)

Table 12-1 Table of Encryption Algorithms *(continued)*

Algorithm	Owner	Type	Key Length	Description
Advanced Encryption Standard (AES)	NIST Standard using Daemen & Rijmen's Rijndeal algorithm	Symmetric	128, 192, and 256 bits (default 128)	DES replacement using Rijndael (Daemen & Rijmen). Announced by NIST in October 2000 as the algorithm to be used in AES.
Blowfish	Bruce Schneier	Symmetric	32 to 448 bits (multiple of 8, default 128)	Very complex, hard to break algorithm, but uses large memory space.
CAST-128	C. Adams & S. Tavres	Symmetric	40 to 128 bit (multiple of 8, default 128)	CAST-128 is a block cipher using 8-byte block size. RFC 2144.
CAST-256	C.Adams, H Heys, S Tavares, M. Wiener	Symmetric	128 to 256 bit (multiple of 32, default 128)	CAST-256 is a block cipher using 16-byte block size. RFC 2612.
IDEA	X. Lai & J. Massey	Symmetric	128-bit	Stands for The International Data Encryption Algorithm. It is faster and more secure than DES. IDEA is a block cipher used in PGP.
RC2	Ronald Rivest for RSA	Symmetric	0 to 1,024 bits (multiple of 8, default 128)	Stands for Ron's Code or Rivest's Cipher 2. RFC 2268. RC2 is a block cipher.
RC4	Ronald Rivest for RSA	Symmetric	8 to 2,048 bits (multiple of 8, default 128)	Stands for Ron's Code or Rivest's Cipher 4. RC4 is a stream cipher operating on data a bit at a time.
RC5	Ronald Rivest for RSA	Symmetric	0 to 65,536, (multiple of 8, default 128)	Stands for Ron's Code or Rivest's Cipher 5. RFC 2040. RC5 a block cipher.
RC6	Rivest, Robshaw, Sidney, and Yin for RSA	Symmetric	0 to 2,040, (multiple of 8, default 128)	Stands for Ron's Code or Rivest's Cipher 6. RC6 is a block cipher.

meet with Bob ahead of time to physically retrieve his public key, but this is no different than having to distribute a shared secret. Digital certificates address this problem. Simply defined, a digital certificate binds public-key values to subjects. That is to say, the certificate gives assurance that the public key being used is indeed owned by the entity claiming to own it. It is important to note that a subject is not limited to human users. Subjects can be hardware devices, computer applications, or anything that might make use of the associated private key. Certificates are issued by trusted third-party entities and therefore trust in certificates is implicit. For example, if Bob sends his certificate to Alice, he is in essence sending a copy of his public key. The public key is housed in a certificate. A third party issues the certificate vouching that Bob is the owner of the public key. Alice trusts this fact because she trusts the third party. In theory, digital certificates are similar to a passport. A governmental body issues passports. When traveling outside of one's own country, a passport is used as proof of identification. Other countries accept this as a valid form of identification because it is coming from a trusted source. Of course, a passport must have certain attributes to be deemed valid. The issuer of the passport and the name of the person who the passport is identifying must be listed. Additional information about the subject including a picture and signature are also included. Passports also include a validity period. Once a passport has expired, it is no longer deemed a valid form of identification. Finally, it is important for a passport to be tamperproof to avoid counterfeiting or masquerading.

Certificates share many of the same attributes as a passport and in effect serve a similar function in the electronic world. The ITU-T X.509 (formerly CCITT X.509) or ISO/IEC/ITU 9594-8 originally published the X.509 version 1 certificate standard in 1988. In 1993, the X.500 recommendations were revised. As part of this revision, additional fields were added to the X.509 certificate format creating version 2. Also in that year, the Internet Privacy Enhanced E-mail (PEM) group published specifications for a Public Key Infrastructure based on the X.509 version 1 certificate (RFC 1422). In response to the deficiencies discovered in the implementation of this standard, the ISO/IEC/ITU and ANSI X9 groups developed the X.509 version 3 certificate, which was standardized in June 1996. The PKIX working group has taken this standard and created an X.509 v3 profile for use on the Internet (RFC 2459, Internet X.509 Public Key Infrastructure Certificate and Certificate Revocation List Profile). An X.509 v3 certificate contains specific fields that contain information such as the certificate's issuer, subject, and validity period. Additionally, every certificate contains the subject's public key. This data structure does not truly become a certificate until a Certificate Authority (CA) digitally signs it. A Certificate Authority acts as the trusted third party. By digitally signing a subject's public key and related information, a CA gives assurance that the subject listed in the certificate is indeed the owner of the public key. Furthermore, the CA's digital signature creates a tamperproof entity. If someone tries to change the contents of a certificate, the digital signature becomes compromised, thus making others aware that it is no longer a valid statement of public-key binding. Table 12-2 defines a standard X.509 certificate format.

The following is an example of an X.509 v3 certificate:

```
Version: v3 (0x2)
      Serial Number: 5 (0x5)
      Signature Algorithm: PKCS #1 MD5 With RSA Encryption
Issuer: OU=INFOSEC Engineering Certificate Authority, O=Security,
C=US
```

Table 12-2

X.509 Certificate Contents

Version	Identifies the Version of X.509 Certificate
SerialNumber	Unique serial number used by CA to identify certificate.
Signature	Digital Signature Algorithm used by CA to sign certificate.
Issuer	Name of issuing authority.
Validity	A range of dates in which the certificate is valid.
Subject	Name of subject.
SubjectPublicKeyInfo	Public key of subject and algorithm used.
IssuerUniqueID	In most cases, this field is not used.
SubjectUniqueID	In most cases, this field is not used.
Extensions	Optional elements available in version 3 certificates.
Digital signature of CA below	
SignatureAlgorithm	Digital Signature Algorithm used by CA to sign certificate.
SignatureValue	The actual digital signature created by the CA.

```
Validity: Not Before: Tue May 6 13:02:09 1999
 Not After: Sun Nov 2 12:02:09 1999
Subject: CN=J.R. Carlucci, OU=Security Architect, O=Security, C=US
Subject Public Key Info: Algorithm: PKCS#1 RSA Encryption
 Public Key:
 Modulus:
00:ca:fb:f0:11:7a:f3:88:41:23:a9:f3:14:ef:91:16:c8:8bb7:75:19:91:01
:60:b8:93:bd:42:08:ae:7f:d1:cc:a9:1b:42:87:95:5b:76:c8:98:e0:83:0d:
c5:d9:c5:5d:96:b4:8b:cd:56:71:8a:4e:8f:9b:4f:98:01:ee:2d
 Public Exponent: 65537 (0x10001)
Extensions:
 Identifier: Certificate Type
 Critical: no
 Certified Usage:
 SSL Client
 Secure E-mail
 Identifier: Authority Key Identifier
 Critical: no
 Key Identifier: ae:21:86:de:0f:4f:90:80:e5:e7:22:1b:4c:77:bd:13:
76:10:60:ae
Signature:
 Algorithm: PKCS#1 RSA Encryption
 Signature:
52:f5:06:f3:82:22:ea:a9:c6:04:2c:79:53:df:f8:db:06:f6:7d:d5:13:d5:b
4:a6:17:e6:79:df:f1:d9:8d:ff:30:8c:38:5c:1a:e6:8e:15:38:2f:14:1f:85
:99:13:50:2d:89:c0:ec:08:35:24:30:c2:53:69:a7:8b:27:12:50:b8:25:06:
7f:75:8a:75:7e:1c:2e:32:dc
```

Certificate extensions are used to put additional information into the certificate beyond the basic fields described. A number of public extensions have been defined by the PKIX. Some of these extensions are commonly used and greatly enhance the functionality of a PKI. For example, the Certificate Revocation List (CRL) Distribution points extension gives the user or application reading the certificate information on where and how to obtain a CRL. A certificate is compared to a CRL to ensure that it has not been revoked. CRLs are discussed later in greater detail.

Extensions can be marked as critical or non-critical. If a critical extension is unrecognized by an application, the certificate is deemed invalid and cannot be used. Conversely, if a non-critical extension is not recognized, the certificate can still be used.

PKI Components

A Public Key Infrastructure (PKI) is put in place to issue, distribute, and manage the use of digital certificates. Several components are required in order for a PKI to complete these tasks. These components are

- Certificate Authorities (CAs)
- Registration Authorities (RAs)
- Certificate Management Protocols (CMPs)
- Certificate Revocation
- Certificate Repositories
- Time Stamp Authority (TSAs)

Certificate Authorities

Certificate Authorities act as trusted third parties in a Public Key Infrastructure (PKI). CAs issue certificates to subjects. A self-signed certificate identifies the CA itself. Thus, the CA is the initial point of trust. End entities must have a high level of trust in the Certificate Authority because they will in turn trust any subjects that the CA vouches for.

CAs are at the heart of a PKI and are responsible for performing several important tasks including certificate management (issuance, revocation, update, and renewal), certificate and CRL publication, and logging of events. Ultimately, these tasks are the responsibility of the CA; however, some functions may be delegated to other components within the PKI.

The primary function of a CA is to issue certificates. A subject is said to enroll for a certificate when a certificate request is made and then fulfilled by a CA. In some cases, a subject is requesting a certificate for the first time. In other cases, CAs fulfill requests to update or renew certificates. The exact steps involved during the certificate enrollment process vary depending on the subject, protocol, and vendor implementation, but the general process remains the same. First, the subject will generate a request for a certificate. In most cases, the subject will generate a public/private key pair, but in some instances, the CA will provide this functionality. This request will then be submitted to the CA where it will await approval. At this point, the CA must verify the identity of the requestor. Once verified, the CA can digitally sign the request thereby creating a valid digital certificate. Finally, the certificate is distributed so that it is accessible by the requestor. CAs also respond to certificate renewal requests. If a renewal request is generated prior to a certificate expiring, that certificate can be used to sign the request. This signature can be used as a way of identifying the subject of the request, thereby providing an automated method of verification.

Registration Authorities

In some implementations, CAs will delegate certain responsibilities to Registration Authorities (RAs). RFC 2510, Internet Public Key Infrastructure Certificate Management Protocols, states that the functions of an RA can include, "personal authentication, token distribution, revocation reporting, name assignment, key generation, archival of key pairs, et cetera." In most cases, RAs are used to verify the identity of a subject during the certificate enrollment process. For example, some Internet Service Providers (ISPs) offer PKI services to corporate customers. In this scenario, the ISP houses the CA and is ultimately responsible for issuing, renewing, and revoking certificates. The process of verification, however, is offloaded to the customer. The customer is responsible for administering its own RA. Clients of the customer request a certificate from the RA. At this point, the customer must verify the identity of the requestor. Once identity is confirmed, the request is sent to the ISP for fulfillment. This model assumes that the customer is more apt to verify the identity of the client. The decision to trust a subject and issue a certificate to that subject is up to the customer. Once that decision is made, it is the ISP's responsibility to issue a certificate in an efficient and secure manner. RAs may also be used in large corporate environments where a CA is centralized and corporate offices are dispersed. RAs could be used at local offices to receive certificate requests. Local administrators verify the identity of the requestors. Once the request is approved, it is sent to the CA for fulfillment.

Certificate Management Protocols

Several certificate management protocols define the specifics of certificate enrollment. In some cases, these protocols also help to define the certificate revocation processes. Some vendors append the functionality of these protocols even further by offering additional features such as key recovery and automated certificate renewal.

PKCS

The Public Key Cryptographic Standards (PKCS) are a set of standards protocols developed by RSA Security that define methods for securing information exchange. PKCS #1, #3, #5, #6, #7, #8, #9, #10, #11, #12, and #15 are published standards. PKCS #13 and #14 are proposed standards. PKCS #2 and #4 have been incorporated into PKCS #1. The following section briefly explains each Public Key Cryptographic Standard.

PKCS #1 addresses the implementation of public-key cryptography using the RSA algorithm.

PKCS #3 addresses how to establish secure communications using Diffie-Hellman.

PKCS #5 is a standard for password-based cryptography. Passwords can be a weak link in the security chain. They are a common mechanism needed to secure data or access secured data. Passwords are often based on what users can remember. PKCS #5 specifies how to make the password more secure by focusing on key derivation, encryption schemes, and message authentication schemes. Key derivation takes the password as a base key and derives another key from it. An encryption scheme can be used to also treat the password as a key for scrambling (encrypting) and unscrambling (decrypting) the message. PKCS #5 also discusses how a hash algorithm can be used with the password to make a hash value dependent on the password.

PKCS #6 is syntax that was intended to extend an X.509 certificate with a set of attributes to be able to certify other information about the entity whose public key is certified in the certificate. The same issuer that signed the X.509 certificate is the one that signs the extended certificate. This standard is no longer needed due to overlap with X.509 version 3.

PKCS #7, the Cryptographic Message Syntax, is another protocol that has become a de facto standard for certificate management. Simply put, PKCS #7 is used to protect messages with cryptography. It is most commonly used to secure communications between an RA and a CA. After retrieving a certificate request (which may be secured via SSL) and then verifying the identity of the requestor, the RA sends the request to a CA as a signed PKCS #7 message. In response, the CA issues the certificate and sends it back to the RA as a signed PKCS #7 message. PKCS #7 is also the underlying protocol used in the S/MIME secure e-mail protocol.

PKCS #8 specifies syntax for private-key information and encrypting private keys.

PKCS #9 defines attributes referenced in PKCS #6, #7, #8, and #10.

PKCS #10, Certification Request Syntax Standard, is one common protocol used in the certificate issuance process. PKCS #10 describes a specific syntax for certificate requests. The strength of PKCS #10 is in the simplicity of its format and the wide acceptance of its use. It has become a de facto standard that is supported by almost all applications and end entities. It is virtually a requirement for a CA to handle a PKCS #10 formatted certificate request. The main drawback of PKCS #10 is its limitation in scope. It merely defines the syntax for certificate requests. It does not provide any support for handling and securing the request process. In its simplest form, a PKCS #10 request can be generated on a client machine and then distributed to a CA by a secure, out-of-band means. This out-of-band method ensures that the request is not altered in transit. Remember, PKCS #10 does not protect a certificate request.

Often times, PKCS #10 is used in conjunction with the Secure Socket Layer (SSL) protocol to secure the certificate request in transit. SSL works in conjunction with the HTTP protocol, enabling a client and server to establish a secured session. The secured session is established by using a certificate to establish a symmetric key. Once the secured session is established, the client can send a PKCS #10 certificate request with assurance that it will not be altered in transit. When establishing the secured session, it is usually only the server that is authenticated (via its certificate). In most cases, a client who is requesting a certificate does not already have one to authenticate with. Thus, a mechanism must exist for a CA to verify the identity of the requesting client prior to issuing the certificate. The type of verification varies depending on the policy of the CA. One common method is for the CA to request an e-mail address from the client during the enrollment process. A message is sent to the client requesting a confirmation reply. Once the requestor replies to the CA, it will then issue the certificate. Higher levels of verification may be needed if an environment has more stringent security requirements.

PKCS #11 is a standard for cryptographic hardware tokens. PKCS #11 specifies a cryptographic token interface or Application Programming Interface (API) called *Cryptoki*. Cryptoki works between a PKCS #11 application and the hardware token such as a smart card. CryptoAPI (CAPI) is a competing standard for hardware tokens. The majority of hardware tokens available support both. A particular application will usually support just one of the standards. CAPI is backed more by Microsoft, whereas PKCS #11 is backed by Netscape among other products. Because most hardware tokens support a device like a smart card to be set up or formatted to support both standards, one API could be used to store a certificate on the card and the other API could be used to retrieve the certificate. The smart card middleware would need to have an interoperability layer that both libraries could run through. This way a Microsoft CA could issue a certificate to the smart card, but a Netscape Web browser could be read the certificate during a Web transaction.

PKCS #12 specifies a secure format for storing or transporting keys and certificates. This is necessary to prevent unauthorized access of confidential public-key files. Transporting a user's private key from his or her old computer to a new computer via a device like a floppy disk is a good application for this standard.

PKCS #13 is not available yet, but it will focus on encrypting and signing data using elliptic curve cryptography.

PKCS #14 is also not available, but will represent a standard for pseudo-random number generation.

PKCS #15 is a much-needed standard to enable different smart card-enabled applications and smart card vendors to store cryptographic tokens in a common format.

The PKCS have been instrumental in advancing the widespread use of PKI. PKCS #10 and PKCS #7 have become de facto standard for certificate request and reply messages. It is unlikely that they will be dismissed anytime soon. They are, however, limited in functionality. For example, these standards set no guidelines for the use and distribution of Certificate Revocation Lists (CRLs).

CMP

In 1999, the IETF approved RFC 2510, Internet Public Key Infrastructure Certificate Management Protocols, and RFC 2511, Internet Public Key Infrastructure Certificate Request Management Framework (CRMF). The PKIX working group has developed the Certificate Management Protocol (CMP) based on these standards. The CMP is an alternative method to PKCS of handling certificate request and response messages. Additionally, CMP supports a number of different certificate management functions including cross-certification request and response messages, revocation request and response messages, key recovery request and response message, and certificate and CRL distribution messages.

CMP is a complex and powerful protocol. Although many CA products support CMP, it is not yet widely supported by the applications and devices that interact with CAs.

Certificate Management Messages over Cryptographic Message Syntax (CMC)

As an alternative to CMP, the PKIX working group has published RFC 2797, Certificate Management Messages over CMS (CMC). This protocol supports the common practice of using PKCS #10 for certificate request messages and PKCS #7 for certificate response messages. In addition, CMC refers to RFC 2511 to support the more advanced certificate request format defined by CMP. The overall goal of this protocol is to offer advanced certificate management functionality while maintaining simplicity and support for the broad PKCS install base.

SCEP

Cisco Systems' developed the Simple Certificate Enrollment Protocol (SCEP) as a certificate enrollment protocol for network devices. It leverages PKCS #10 and PKCS #7 to support certificate request and response messages. In addition, SCEP supports CRL and certificate queries by network devices. Support for SCEP is widespread in CA products and Cisco devices. Network devices other than Cisco are also beginning to support this protocol. SCEP is not a complete certificate management protocol and has its limits, but it is the only viable alternative when deploying PKI with network devices.

Certificate Revocation

Certificate Revocation is required when a CA needs to invalidate a certificate prior to its expiration date. For example, an employee may be leaving a company. In this scenario, the organization may not want a former employee to be in possession of a valid certificate issued by its CA. Another example would be a user who has had his laptop stolen. If the private key that is associated with the user's certificate were on the laptop, then the person who stole the laptop could masquerade as that user. In order to prevent such situations, CAs need a way to both revoke certificates and notify end entities of revocations.

CRL

In the simplest terms, a Certificate Revocation List (CRL) is a listing of certificates that have been revoked. RFC 2459, Internet X.509 Public Key Infrastructure Certificate and CRL Profile, defines the format of an X.509 version 2 CRL. The data structure of a CRL is similar to a certificate. Table 12-3 lists the contents of X.509 CRL.

The following is an example of an X.509 v2 CRL:

```
Signature Algorithm: PKCS #1 MD5 With RSA Encryption
Issuer: OU=INFOSEC Engineering Certificate Authority, O=Security,
C=US
Issued: Tue Sep 6 07:02:09 1999
 Serial Number: 0x100B (4107)
 Issued: Tue Aug 23 16:29:55 1999
 Serial Number: 0x1005 (4101)
 Issued: Tue Aug 25 13:43:22 1999
 Serial Number: 0x1003 (4099)
 Issued: Tue Sep 1 09:13:34 1999
Signature:
 Algorithm: PKCS#1 RSA Encryption
 Signature:
52:f5:06:f3:82:22:ea:a9:c6:04:2c:79:53:df:f8:db:06:f6:7d:d5:13:d5:b
4:a6:17:e6:79:df:f1:d9:8d:ff:30:8c:38:5c:1a:e6:a1:27:8e:15:38:2f:14
:1f:85:99:13:50:2d:89:c0:ec:08:35:24:30:c2:53:69:a7
```

Each listed revocation includes the serial number of the certificate being revoked and the date of revocation. Extensions may also be listed

Table 12-3 X.509 CRL Contents

Version	Identifies the Version of the CRL
Signature	Digital Signature Algorithm used by CA to sign CRL
Issuer	Name of issuing authority
ThisUpdate	Issue date of the CRL
NextUpdate	Date by which the next CRL will be issued
RevokedCertificates	List of revoked certificates by serial number
crlExtensions	Optional elements available in version 2 CRLs
Digital signature of CA below	
SignatureAlgorithm	Digital Signature Algorithm used by CA to sign certificate
SignatureValue	The actual digital signature created by the CA

with each CRL (in addition to the extensions for the CRL data structure itself).

When a certificate is revoked, a CA adds that certificate to the revocation list. The issuing CA then digitally signs the data structure, thus creating a valid X.509 v2 CRL. In most cases, the CA publishes the CRL to a public repository where it can be retrieved by end entities (repositories are discussed in the next section). When receiving a certificate, end entities can retrieve the CRL and check whether or not the serial number of the certificate is on the CRL. If it is, the certificate is deemed revoked and will not be accepted by the end entity.

The biggest challenge when using CRLs is to limit the amount of time between when a certificate is revoked and when end entities are made aware of this revocation. For example, if a certificate is revoked, but CRLs are only published at daily intervals, then that certificate may still be used for an entire day after revocation. The publication interval can be increased, but most end entities tend to cache CRLs for pre-determined amount of times. Even if a new CRL is published, the end entity may not download it until its cache lifecycle has completed. In some cases, an end entity can be configured not to cache CRLs, but this option is not always available. Some CA implementations enable a CRL to be pushed to end entities each time a new revocation is made. This guarantees that end entities have the latest CRL, but it may not be feasible on a network with low bandwidth and large amounts of end entities. Further, some end entities do not support this function. Despite its drawbacks, CRLs are still the most popular method of certificate revocation checking in existence today. In many implementations, CRLs are an adequate form of revocation checking because a revocation is not required to be applied immediately.

OCSP

In some PKI deployments, a lag between certificate revocation and the practical application of that revocation is not acceptable. For example, a corporation that uses certificates to encrypt highly sensitive data (such as financial transactions) cannot allow a compromised certificate to be used for even an hour after it has been revoked. The Online Certificate Status Protocol (OCSP) is a real-time certificate revocation checking mechanism. An end entity sends a certificate status check to an OCSP responder (either a CA or a service delegated by the CA). The certificate is not accepted until the OCSP responder replies with a message either confirming or denying the revocation status of the certificate.

Real-time certificate revocation status checking has its advantages, but it adds some complexity as well. One of the strengths of CRLs is that they are digitally signed. They can be distributed as public entities. If they are tampered with, the digital signature will be compromised and they will not be accepted. With OCSP, messages between the end entity and OCSP responder must be secured.

OCSP is not yet in widespread use. Many CA products are beginning to support this protocol, but most clients and applications do not have support for OCSP.

Certificate Repositories

A Certificate Repository is used to store and distribute certificates and CRLs. In small implementations, a repository may not be necessary. Certificates and CRLs can be exchanged via e-mail. Indeed, this is a simple solution, but can become quite burdensome when dealing with thousands of certificates. Further, some end entities (such as routers) are not capable of retrieving certificates or CRLs in this manner. More commonly, certificates and CRLs are stored in a central repository that is accessible by all end entities and CAs alike.

Directory Services and LDAP

A Directory Service is an online repository that houses information about objects. Objects fit into an *object class* and each object class has specific *attributes* associated with it. For example, Alice might fit into the *People* object class. In turn, this object class may be associated with attributes such as height, weight, and e-mail address. The definition of a directory's object classes and their associated attributes is referred to as the directory's *schema*. RFC 2587, Internet X.509 Public Key Infrastructure LDAPv2 Schema, defines the object classes and attributes that are used in a PKI-enabled directory. In general, it defines object classes for certificates and CRLs and what the attributes of those classes are. The Lightweight Directory Access Protocol (LDAP) is used to access information in the directory. This is the protocol that is used to interact with the directory. For example, a client will use LDAP to query a directory for a certificate. The University of Michigan originally published LDAP as an alternative to the Directory Access Protocol (DAP). The X.500 directory standard defines DAP as the access protocol for X.500-compliant directory services. X.500 is the basis for most large directory services; however, DAP proved difficult to implement and was not widely deployed. LDAP proved to be much more efficient, and is now accepted as the industry standard for interacting with directory servers. With the use of LDAP, CAs can be configured to automatically publish certificates and CRLs to a directory. In addition, many end entities can be configured to automatically retrieve certificates and CRLs with the use of LDAP.

X.500 also defines naming conventions for objects within a hierarchical structure. Although many products are not completely X.500 compliant, most do support the naming conventions defined by X.500. In turn, certificates are often given a *distinguished name* to identify their location within a directory. In its simplest terms, a distinguished name is similar to a path in a file system. For example, a file named pkifaq.txt can be located on a disk drive by defining its path (c:\temp\pkidocs\pkifaq.txt). Temp and pkidocs are folders that one traverses to gain access to the pkifaq.txt file. Similarly, distinguished names are paths to objects in a directory server. For example, c=US; o=MyCompany; ou=Security; cn=John Smith defines a path to the John Smith object within a directory. Country (C), Organization (O), Organizational Unit (OU), and Common Name (CN) are naming attributes that define the containers and objects within a directory. In general, the CN naming attribute refers to actual objects, whereas the other naming attributes serve to define the path to those objects. When X.500 was originally published, a worldwide directory was envisioned (similar to DNS). For this reason, the X.509 v1 and v2 certificate standards only allowed for distinguished names. In fact, a worldwide directory did not emerge, and it is unlikely that one will. The X.509 v3 certificate standard introduced standards to provide alternate naming forms (e-mail, DNS) via certificate extensions (such as subjectAltName). Although alternate names are now available, it is important to be familiar with the distinguished name format as it is the primary name form that is used to identify subjects, certificate revocation lists, and certificate issuers.

FTP and HTTP

In RFC 2585, Internet X.509 Public Key Infrastructure Operation Protocols, FTP and HTTP define data types and naming conventions for the transfer of certificates and CRLs using FTP or HTTP. Indeed, an FTP server or Web server can be used as a repository in a PKI implementation. Practically, this is generally not supported. Most clients do not support certificate and CRL retrieval from an FTP or Web server. Further, most CAs do not have the capability to automate the publication of certificates or CRLs to an FTP or Web server. In almost all cases, a directory server is used as the repository and LDAP is used to access that directory server.

Time Stamp Authority

Using certificates to encrypt e-mails offers confidentiality. Digitally signing e-mail provides authentication of origin and data integrity. PKI can lso offer *non-repudation* services. To repudiate is to refuse to accept something or someone as true. Thus, if a PKI is said to offer non-repudiation, it removes the capability for a communicating party to repudiate a claim. For example, if Bob sends an e-mail to Alice, Alice cannot claim that she did not receive that e-mail. Further, she cannot claim that the information in the e-mail is different than the information Bob originally sent. In addition, non-repduation can flow in both directions. Bob cannot claim that he did not send the message. Further, he cannot claim that what he sent in the message is different than what Alice received.

To fully support non-repudiaton in e-mail applications, several additional components (beyond digital signatures) must be in place. First, some form of a digitally signed receipt must be available. For example, if Bob sends Alice a digitally signed e-mail, he cannot deny having sent it or the information therein. On the other hand, Alice can deny receiving the e-mail. To alleviate this issue, digitally signed receipts are implemented. In this example, Alice can be required to respond to Bob's message with a digitally signed receipt. She cannot generate a valid receipt unless Bob signed the original message and Alice as able to validate the signature. Now, non-repudiation is supported at both ends. S/MIME v3 supports the use of digitally signed receipts. One more component may be required to fully support non-repudiation: a time stamping service. In some cases, the time that a message is sent is crucial to supporting non-repudiation. Using the previous example, if Bob sends a message to Alice, she cannot deny having received it, but she can dispute the time in which it was received. If Bob is sending a message with time-sensitive information (such as a financial transaction), this can pose quite a challenge. For example, Alice could be required by contract to fulfill a financial transaction request within an hour of receiving an e-mail from Bob. If Alice can deny the time that she received an e-mail, then Bob would have no legal recourse if he were to lose money due to a transaction not being fulfilled in the allotted time. RFC 2001, The Internet X.509 Public Key Infrastructure Time Stamp Protocol (TSP), describes the use of a time stamping authority. Using a TSP, Bob can send the message hash and digital signature from his e-mail to a Time Stamping Authority (TSA). The TSA would then digitally sign Bob's request and return it to him. Bob can then store the TSA's response for later use. Obviously, Bob and Alice must agree to trust the TSA ahead of time. Now, if Alice tries to deny the time in which she received the e-mail, Bob has proof to refute her claim.

PKI Architectures

Thus far, the discussion of PKI components has focused on a single CA implementation. In fact, many CA products are capable of issuing hundreds of thousands of certificates. More often than not, however, large implementations involve multiple CAs.

Hierarchical Model

One approach is to create multiple CAs in a hierarchy. At the top of the hierarchy is the root CA. The root CA has a self-signed certificate. Subordinate CAs are below the root CA. The root CA issues certificates to subordinate CAs. An end entity can enroll for a certificate from a subordinate CA or the root CA. As long as the end entity trusts the root CA, it will also trust the subordinate CA. Many levels of subordinate CAs can be present if desired. Also, end entities can retrieve certificates from one subordinate CA but be at the same logical layer with another subordinate CA. Figure 12-5 shows the hierarchical model of the PKI architecture.

The strength of this model lies in its simplicity. The root CA is the end trust point. For example, if Alice has a certificate issued from Subordinate CA1 and Bob has a certificate issued from Subordinate CA3, they will both trust each other's certificates. This assumes that they both trust the root CA's certificate. In short, if a subject is configured to trust the root CA, then that subject will trust all entities under the root CA. This model provides great flexibility as subordinate CAs can be added as needed without interrupting services. The main drawback is that the root CA becomes a single point of failure. If the root CA were to become compromised, then all certificates in the hierarchy become invalidated. For this

Figure 12-5

PKI architecture: hierarchical model

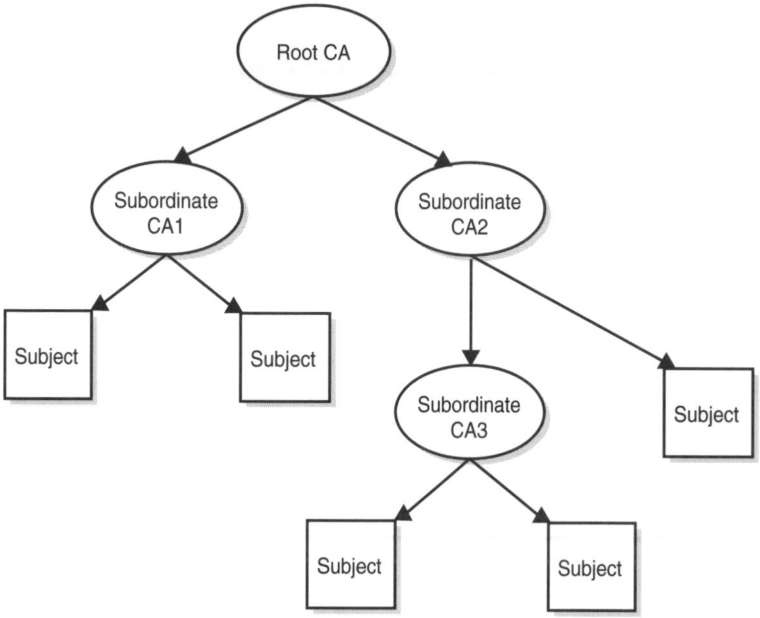

reason, the security of the root CA in this type of implementation is of the utmost importance. In many cases, the root CA is configured in such a manner that it only issues certificates to subordinate CAs. Additionally, the hardware for the root CA may be kept offline and be physically secured in a location separate from the rest of the network.

Subordinate CAs may be issued for several reasons. In some cases, multiple CAs may be installed to organize the types of certificates that are issued. For example, one CA might issue certificates that are used for secure e-mail, whereas another CA might issue certificates that are used for authentication. In other cases, multiple CAs may exist when multiple PKI implementations are present.

Cross-Certification

Cross-certification is the process whereby CAs certify each other in order to establish a lateral trusted relationship. This is a peer-to-peer model of trust. For example, CA1 and CA2 cross-certify each other. Once this trust is established, entities that trust CA1 will also trust CA2 and vice versa. Figure 12-6 illustrates a model of cross-certification in the PKI architecture.

Figure 12-6
PKI architecture: cross-certification model

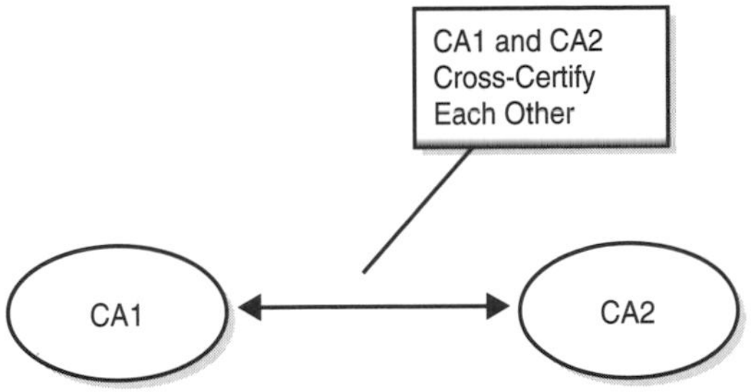

Cross-certification offers an easy way for separate PKI implementations to integrate with each other. For example, two organizations form a strategic partnership and they need to trust each other's certificates. In this scenario, the root CAs of each organization can simply cross-certify each other creating a trust among all entities in both companies.

Hybrid

The Hybrid model combines certificate hierarchies with cross-certification. For example, company A and company B may have existing certificate hierarchies in place. They may wish to cross-certify each other, but only at certain layers within the hierarchy. In fact, cross-certifications can be made between any two CAs within the two hierarchies. The trust that is established will only be between those two CAs and the entities that lie below those CAs. This is a very flexible model that enables organizations to establish trusts based on their business needs. Figure 12-7 shows the Hybrid model in the PKI architecture.

Certificate Policy and Certificate Practice Statements

RFC 2527, Internet X.509 Public Key Infrastructure Certificate Policy and Certificate Practices Framework, defines a certificate policy as "a named set of rules that indicates the applicability of a certificate to a particular community and/or class of application with common security requirements." More simply put, a certificate policy defines *what* a

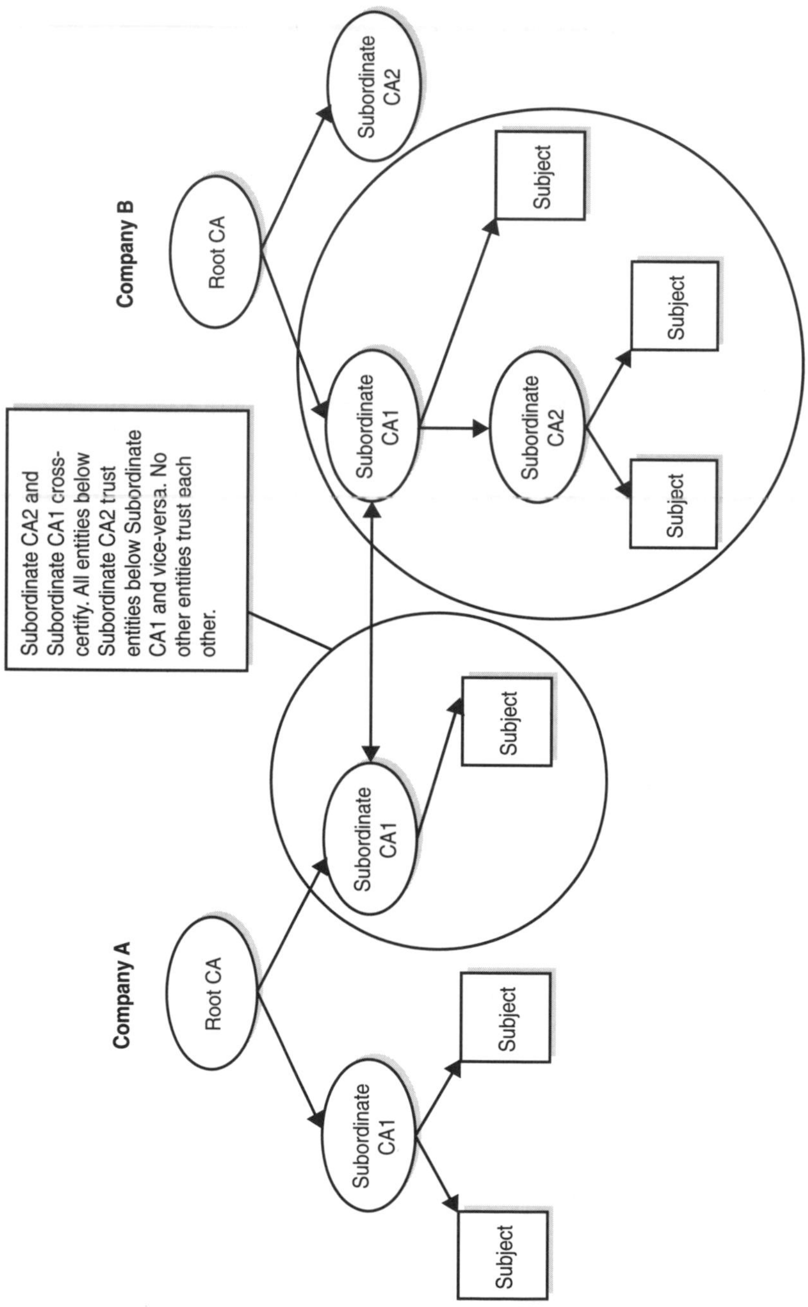

Figure 12-7 PKI architecture: Hybrid model

certificate can be used for. It is meant to be a high-level document that outlines what the CA and its associated components can be used for. For example, a certificate policy might state that the CA can be used to issue certificates for securing e-mail but not for digitally signing contracts. RFC 2527 defines a Certificate Practice Statement (CPS) as, "a statement of the practices which a certification authority employs in issuing certificates." More simply put, a CPS defines *how* a CA and its associated components implement the stated certificate policy. It is a detailed document that outlines the procedures used to enforce certificate policy. For example, a CPS might specifically define how to configure a CA in order to prevent it from issuing certificates for contract signing. A CA can have multiple Certificate Policies and/or multiple CPS documents associated with it. In general, this is avoided as it can add great complexity to an implementation.

RFC 2527 outlines specific section and sub-sections that are to be included in a CP and a CPS. The creation of a Certificate Policy and CPS should follow the guidelines set forth in RFC 2527. Further, creation of these documents should involve all interested parties including technologists, business executives, and legal advisors. It is also important for the Certificate Policy and CPS be made available to all end entities. This enables end entities to review these documents and make an informed decision on the level of trust that they choose to put in certificates issued by a particular CA. The X.509 v3 certificate format defines a certificate policy extension that indicates the certificate policies under which the certificate was issued. This extension, however, is not currently supported by many end entities. If this is the case, other methods must be in place that allow end entities access to a CAs CP and CPS. It is also important to review CP and CPS when entering into a trust relationship with a new CA. For example, if an organization were to establish a cross-certification relationship with another CA, it is imperative that the CP and CPS of the two organizations share similar security goals and procedures.

Analysis of Case Study #1—MCC: Corporate E-mail Encryption and Smart Card Solution

MCC requires that their employees have the ability to encrypt and sign e-mail messages. E-mail encryption prevents unauthorized users from viewing an e-mail message. Digital signatures enable the reader of an e-mail message to validate that it was actually written by the author indicated in the message.

The PKI products on the market differ greatly from one another in terms of features and capabilities. The following items need to be analyzed in order to identify the proper PKI solution to fit MCC's e-mail encryption and digital signature needs:

- Capability to back up and recover keys
- Capability for keys and certificates to be updated automatically
- Algorithms supported
- Capability to protect a user's private keys
- OS platforms
- Database compatibility
- Directory compatibility
- Messaging platforms
- Roaming capabilities

Some PKI products support one key pair, whereas others support two. A one key pair system, also called *public-key pair*, has a private key and public key. This is shown in Figure 12-8. A two key pair system has an encrypting key pair and a signing key pair. Encrypting key pairs have an

Figure 12-8
Public key pair

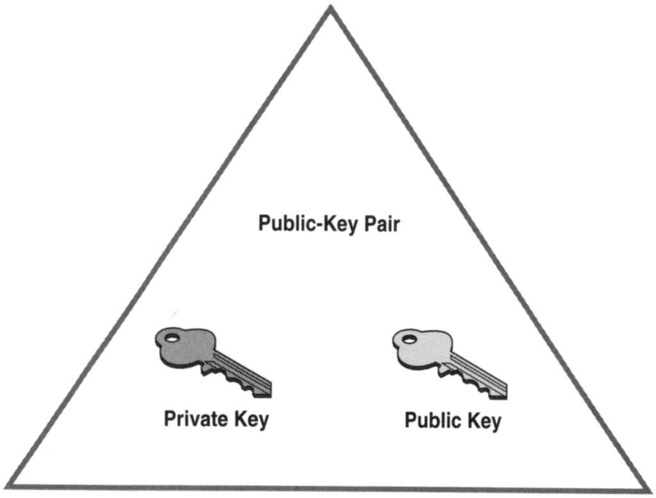

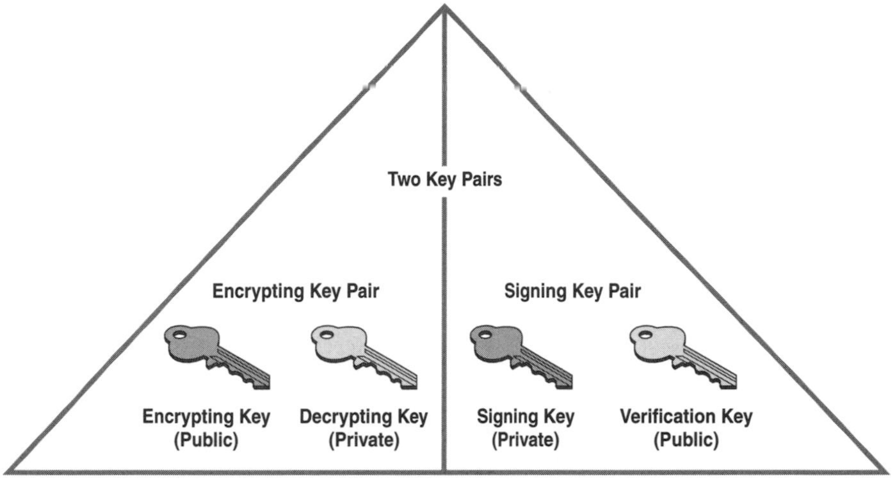

Figure 12-9
Two key pair

encrypting key and a decrypting key. Signing key pairs have a signing key and a verification key. Figure 12-9 illustrates a two key pair system.

Having two key pairs provides backup of the private key for decryption while supporting non-repudiation, key update, and the use of different encrypting and signing algorithms. Having access to a user's decryption key enables both the user and system administrator to be able to gain access to the user's data that was encrypted with the corresponding encrypting public key.

The inability to back up the user's signing key is one of the basic requirements to achieving non-repudiation because it's imperative to be able to show that only the owner of the signing key has had access to it—by having it backed up, there is a chance, however remote, that an administrator or outside intruder could access the signing key. Beyond this, it isn't necessary to back up a signing key. If it is lost or stolen, simply issue a new one. If someone other than the user had access to the user's signing private key, then that person would be able to digitally sign transactions as if he or she were the user. Key recovery is built into many PKI products and is necessary when a user forgets his or her password or is unable to access his or her keys for whatever reason (lost, stolen, or a broken hard drive, smart card, or floppy disk).

Key update is the process of generating completely new key pairs for a user, instead of just updating certificate lifetimes. Managing decryption key histories and destroying signing keys is an important part of key updates. An expiring encrypting public key is what triggers the update of encryption key pairs. An expiring signing private key is the trigger for updating signing key pairs. Having the key update process work automatically is a feature that can save administrators and users a lot of time.

After a user's private key or keys are generated by the PKI system, they are typically stored on the user's hard drive. Many PKI systems allow the private key to be stored on a smart card for enhanced protection of the key. Smart cards are miniature computers in the form of a chip with a gold foil on top and embedded into a credit card-like plastic card. The foil acts as the contact between the chip and the smart card reader. The smart card reader is connected to the computer and provides the connection to software installed on the computer. A user must know the smart card's PIN in order to be able to authenticate to the smart chip. Smart cards have the capability to generate the user's key on the card itself, never exposing it to those who may want to intercept it. The result is an extremely portable secure container for confidential files like private keys. Figure 12-10 depicts a typical smart card and some of its components as well as the power of those components.

Figure 12-10
Smart cards

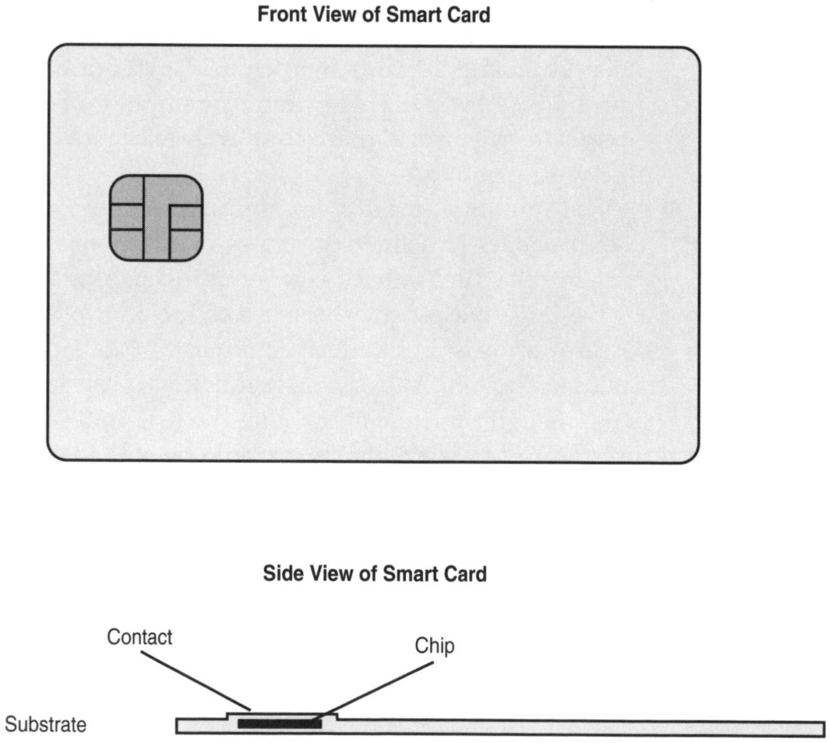

Incorporating PKI into an existing enterprise can be a complicated task. Additional servers and client software are often needed. PKI products differ in what OS platforms they will run on. PKI products also rely on databases and/or directories to house items such as Certificate Revocation Lists (CRL), public certificates, key histories, CA signing key pair, and general user identity information. It is necessary to find a product that is compatible with the messaging client and server applications used in the organization.

Business Need

MCC is interested in providing e-mail encryption and digital signature capabilities to all of its 10,000 employees. They are interested in the following features:

1. Provide for key recovery in case an employee leaves or can no longer access his or her encrypted messages. Provide separate keys for signing and encrypting, instead of one private key so as to promote strong non-repudiation.
2. Auto-renewal of certificates and keys.
3. Support for the latest algorithms.
4. Ability to use smart cards to store the private keys used for e-mail encryption and digital signatures.
5. Ability to run client components on Windows NT Workstation and Windows 2000 Professional.
6. Ability to run server components on Solaris.
7. Ability to integrate with Novell NDS eDirectory.
8. Ability to integrate with Microsoft Outlook and Exchange.
9. Ability for users to easily roam from workstation to workstation.

Solution

MCC has decided to use an Entrust/PKI solution comprising of the following modules:

1. Entrust/Authority
2. Entrust/RA
3. Entrust/Profile Server
4. Entrust/Entelligence
5. Entrust/Express

Entrust/Authority enables a Certificate Authority to issue and sign public-key certificates. Entrust/Authority provides users with two key pairs.

Entrust/RA provides a Registration Authority to register and manage user accounts. Some of the key user management features include key recovery and automatic key update and certificate renewal.

Entrust/Profile Server enables users to roam from workstation to workstation by housing user profiles in the directory instead of on the user's computer. Because the users will be using smart cards to store their major profile items, some roaming capability is available without this extra module. However, to make it possible to access all user profile items from any place in the enterprise, it is necessary to use the Entrust/Profile Server.

Entrust/Entelligence is the core client application that works with Entrust/PKI to transparently and automatically manage certificates, encryption, and digital signatures. Entrust/Entelligence enables the Entrust profile to be stored on a smart card. Entrust relies on the smart card vendor's Cryptoki API to be able to communicate with the smart card. The smart card must be formatted properly to work with Entrust. A typical smart card, set up for Entrust, will hold an RSA signing private key, an RSA decryption private key, several X.509 certificates, and application preferences.

Entrust/Express is the client e-mail plug-in that enables users to encrypt and digitally sign e-mail. Entrust/Express integrates with Microsoft Outlook. Express supports S/MIME and the following encryption algorithms:

- CAST (128-bit, 80-bit, 64-bit, 40-bit)
- DES

- Triple DES
- RC2 (128-bit, 40-bit)
- IDEA

Entrust/Express supports the following signing algorithms:

- SHA1-RSA
- MD5-RSA
- MD2-RSA
- SHA1-DSA
- SHA1-EC DSA

Implementation

Entrust/PKI will be implemented in a hierarchical design. The root CA will be kept offline for security purposes. Multiple subordinate CAs will be used for issuing all certificates; the root CA will sign their public keys.

MCC's NDS eDirectory schema will be extended to store users' public certificates and Certificate Revocation Lists (CRLs). Entrust and Novell support this application of their products and provide sufficient utilities and documentation to accomplish it.

In addition to a directory, a database to house the CA-signing key pair, user status information, and key pair history will be installed. Customers have the choice of using an Informix or Oracle database. The Informix database can be installed on Windows NT/2000, Solaris, HP-UX, and AIX. The Oracle database can be installed on Solaris. Solaris will be chosen due to MCC's preference toward this platform and because Oracle will be able to be used.

Entrust/RA, the interface used to add and manage users will be installed on all administrators' workstations in order to add and maintain users. The RA provides an interface to both the directory and database entries. Entries entered in local .INI files will point to the CA. Administrators will need to know the First Officer password to be able to view, add, or modify data. The RA provides remote access to the CA without the need to install any remote control software. Entrust/RA works the same on a workstation or on a server that contains other Entrust/PKI components.

Only the Entrust client applications necessary for e-mail encryption and digital signatures will be installed. Entrust/Entelligence and

Entrust/Express will be installed after Microsoft Outlook. Users will need to be educated on the new Express menu that will show up on their Microsoft Outlook menu bar. This will be how they will control which messages are signed and/or which are encrypted.

Entrust/PKI was chosen as a robust and very secure means of providing e-mail encryption and digital signatures to users of Microsoft Exchange and Outlook. The two key pair capability coupled with the key updating and recovery make this an easier system to administer as well. The support for smart cards adds an additional layer of security and strengthens the chance that the users' private keys will be protected.

Users will not have to learn a lot about this system to be able to sign and encrypt e-mail. However, care will need to be taken in designing the hierarchy of the Certificate Authorities, the directory integration, and the setup of the database.

Analysis of Case Study #2—FinApp: Certificate-Based IPSec Authentication for VPNs

By default, TCP/IP-based networks are inherently insecure. Data packets traverse the network in cleartext allowing anyone with Sniffer software to retrieve that data. The Internet Protocol Security (IPSec) is a set of protocols that is used to provide secure TCP/IP-based communications applied at the network layer. Two protocols are within IPSec: Authentication Header (AH) and Encapsulating Security Payload (ESP). AH offers authentication, whereas ESP offers both authentication and confidentiality. It is not required for both of these services to be taken advantage of. For example, on a Local Area Network (LAN), users may already be authenticated to the network by another service. In this scenario, IPSec may be used for encryption (confidentiality) but not for authentication.

IPSec is often employed when implementing Virtual Private Networks (VPNs). A VPN creates Local Area Network (LAN) functionality on a public network. In most cases, the public network is the Internet. For example, an organization may have a central office in New York with branch offices in California and Texas. Leased lines can be used to expand the Intranet infrastructure in New York to California and Texas, but this can be very expensive. An alternative is to create a *tunnel* to link California and Texas through the Internet. This tunnel is secured (in many cases with IPSec). In most scenarios, the users of this tunnel must be authenticated and all data that traverses the tunnel is encrypted. Thus, a Virtual Private Network is created over the public Internet.

RFC 2409, The Internet Key Exchange, defines several different methods of authentication when establishing a Security Association (SA). An SA is the basis for secure communication between two parties when using IPSec. Shared secrets represent one method of authentication offered by IKE. This is an effective mechanism, but shared secrets become difficult to distribute and administer as implementations grow in scale. Public-key cryptography without the use of certificates is also supported. This eases administration hassles, but is not as secure as using certificate-based authentication because no binding exists between subjects and their public keys.

For small implementations with basic security needs, shared secrets or public-key cryptography without certificates may be adequate, but for any large implementation requiring high security, the use of certificate-based authentication when initiating IPSec connections is recommended.

Business Need

The MCC financial data center will have many external trading institutions connecting to it to access the FinApp. The transactions that are carried out with FinApp will be encrypted and digitally signed with messaging middleware. Additional network layer security will be required for customers who connect to FinApp over public or shared leased lines. This will prevent third parties from connecting to FinApp over these leased or public lines.

Solution

Virtual Private Networks will be used to establish secure connections between the MCC financial data center and external trading institutions. IPSec will be used with the Authentication Header protocol to offer authentication of data packets. A Cisco router, which is capable of establishing VPN connections, will be located at the premises of each customer that signs up for FinApp. The MCC financial data center will house several large VPN devices, which are capable of handling thousands of simultaneous VPN connections from multiple customers. As more customers sign up for its service, MCC can expand by adding more VPN devices to handle the load.

External trading institutions will connect to FinApp services through their local router. The VPN will be established from the client's router to the MCC financial data center VPN device. When VPN tunnels are created, the client's router and the MCC financial data center VPN device will be required to perform certificate-based authentication. Once the initial authentication of the devices is complete, all packets that come from the router at the client end will be authenticated via IPSec AH. This type of VPN is often referred to as a router-to-router VPN because the connection is only secured between the routers. Responsibility for securing data that travels from the particular user utilizing the service and the router that connects to the service lies on the client. Figure 12-11 shows an example of VPN tunnels.

Figure 12-11
VPN tunnels

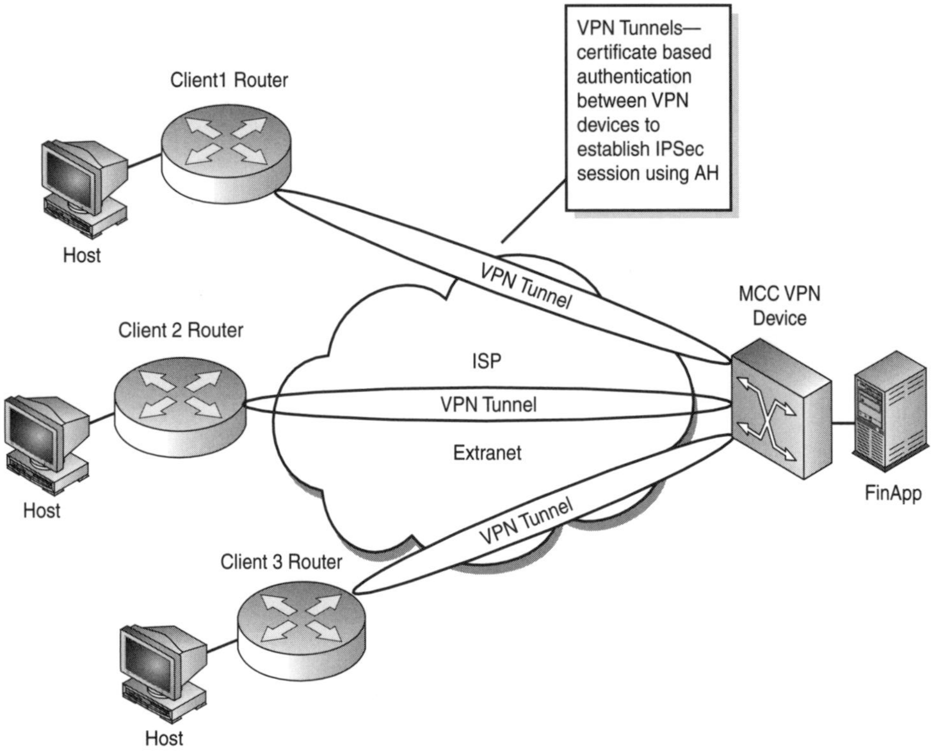

PKI will be implemented to support the issuance and management of certificates to the client routers and the MCC financial data center VPN devices. Devices will hold their own certificates and exchange them during the authentication process; however, CRLs will be stored on an LDAP-based directory. This PKI implementation has several requirements:

1. The Simple Certificate Enrollment Protocol (SCEP) must be supported. The majority of certificates will be issued to Cisco devices, which use this protocol for certificate and CRL request and response messages.
2. All PKI components must run on the Solaris Operating System. MCC prefers a UNIX-based operating system due to the reliability that is required of the FinApp.
3. The PKI must support third-party directory services. The directory servers will house CRLs, which must be made highly available. If a CRL cannot be retrieved, authentication will fail causing a Denial of Service (DoS).
4. All administration must be performed over a secure channel.
5. CAs must support Hardware Security Modules (HSMs) in accordance with the Federal Information Processing Standards Publications 140-1 Level 3 standard (FIPS PUB 140-1 Level 3) for the protection of private keys. HSMs are usually dedicated hardware devices that house the private keys of CAs.

Implementation

RSA Keon was chosen as the PKI product for implementation. RSA Keon houses an internal, secure LDAP-based directory server. In this implementation, however, Novell Directory Services (NDS) will be used as the repository for CRLs. NDS allows for multi-master replication, efficient convergence of information as it is replicated, and a transparent distributed database. These features will make it easier to create a high-availability LDAP-based directory server solution. In fact, CRL publication intervals will be set to 1 hour. If, however, a directory server is not available when a VPN device issues a query for a new CRL, authentication will fail and service will be denied.

A built-in Web server (Apache StrongHold) is also included with RSA Keon. It houses Web sites for administration and SCEP operations. The majority of administrative functions can be accessed via the Web interface. All communications between administrative stations and the Web interface are secured via SSL. Administrators will be issued certificates for authentication. In addition, administrators will be issued smart cards to store the certificates and private keys that are used when connecting to administrative Web pages. The SCEP Web site acts as a gateway between the VPN devices and the CA. It receives the requests from the VPN devices and then communicates with the CA to fulfill and respond to those requests. RAs are also available, but will not be used in this implementation as administration will be centralized.

RSA Keon enables services on the CA to be distributed on to different machines. The administrative and SCEP Web services will be run on different machines than the CA. In this configuration, all communication between the CA and off-loaded services are secured via SSL. The CA and administrative Web services will be attached to a dedicated management network. Only management stations from this network will be able to communicate with these services. Directory services and SCEP services will be accessible from both the management and production network (this is required as the VPN devices will need direct access to these services).

All CAs will have their private key stored on the nShield Hardware Security Module (HSM) from Cipher Corporation. The root CA will be used to issue certificates to the subordinate CA. The root CA will be stored offline, in a secured physical location separate from the subordinate CA. The subordinate CA will issue certificates to the VPN devices. The subordinate CA will be configured in a hardware cluster with a hot standby. This is intended to limit the downtime to the CA if any hardware component fails. Load balancers will be used to distribute load and provide redundancy for Directory Services, SCEP services, and administrative services (see Figure 12-12).

Subordinate CAs will issue certificates to VPN devices with a lifetime of one year. Prior to their expiration, VPN device certificates will be revoked, and a new certificate will be issued. SCEP does not support certificate renewal. Also, private keys for VPN devices will be stored in software. Revoking and reissuing certificates each year enhances security because the old private key becomes invalidated. It is important to note that all certificate requests must be generated from the VPN devices themselves. Some manual steps will need to be completed when requesting certificates from these devices. The root CA will issue three-year certificates to the subordinate CAs. The root CA will renew the subordinate CA certificates at two-year intervals. This will prevent a subordinate CA

Figure 12-12
PKI architecture

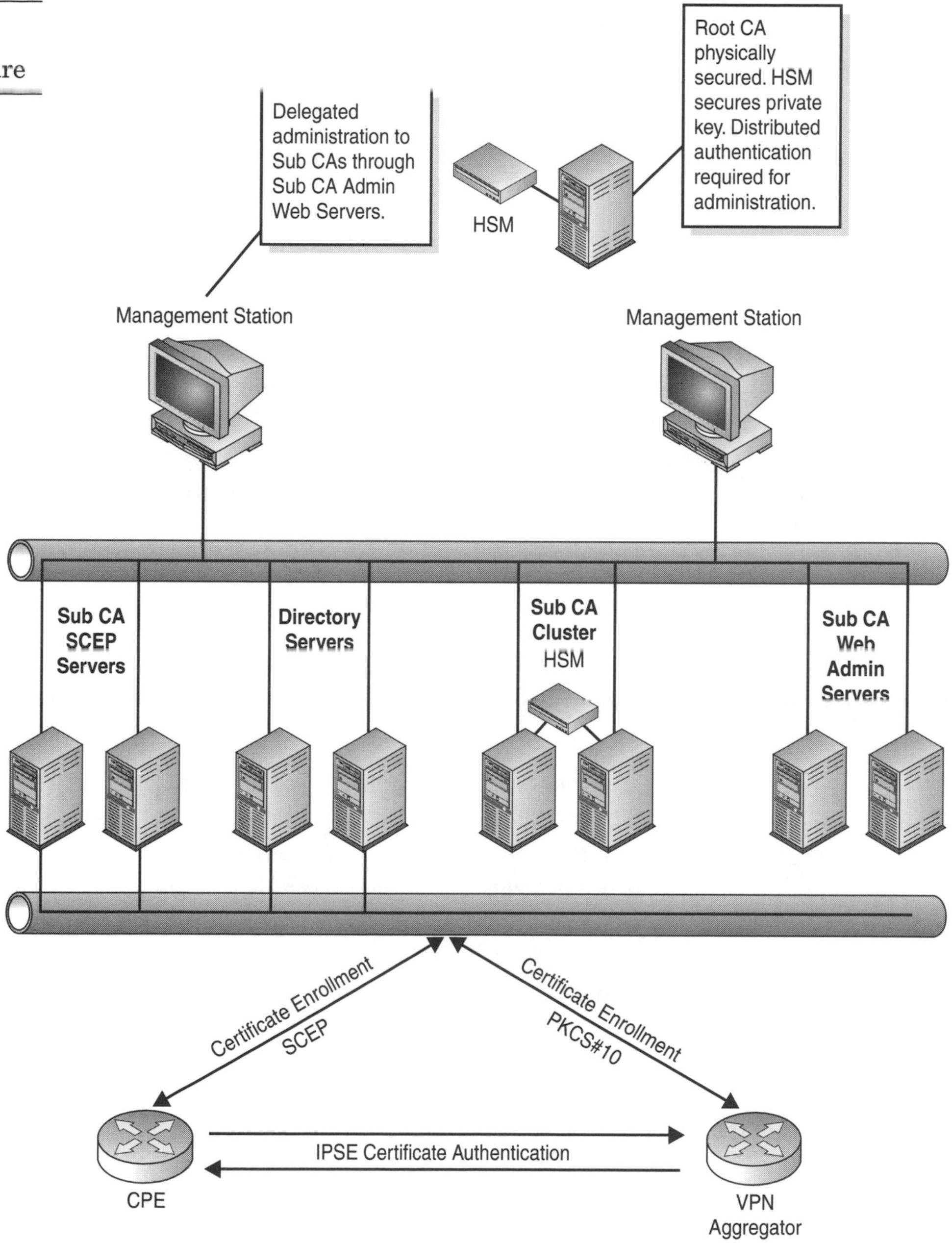

certificate from expiring prior to any VPN device certificates that it has issued. If this were to happen, VPN device certificates would become unwittingly invalidated prior to their expiration dates. Finally, the root CA certificate will have a 15-year lifetime. Renewing the root CA certificate will be an arduous task and options are limited by the PKI functionality of the VPN devices. In addition, the root CA will be offline and the private key will be protected with optimum security. The 15-year lifetime provides the flexibility of administration. If new developments arise providing an easier method for distributing a new root CA key, the 15-year lifetime does not preclude renewing the root CA certificate sooner.

VPNs offer a secure mechanism for communications over a public network. Certificate-based authentication for the end points in a VPN tunnel offers the highest level of security and the most scalable solution. The combination of RSA Keon Certificate Authority and Novell Directory Services fulfills the need of the MCC to authenticate all traffic that comes into its financial data center.

Analysis of Case Study #3—HealthApp: Web-Based Authentication

The 1990s saw the proliferation of the corporate network. Organizations began to see the value of sharing information. File and print sharing are now commonplace and seen as necessities to run an effective business. Corporate networks are a powerful method for sharing information within an organization, but do not scale well to business-to-business or business-to-customer relationships. In most cases, additional infrastructure is required, which can be a costly proposition. In recent years, organizations have looked to leverage the Internet as the network for external communications.

Web pages are the most common form of information sharing that occurs over the Internet. By default, Web pages house public information —no inherent security is present. Netscape's Secure Sockets Layer (SSL) and the IETF's Transport Layer Security (TLS) protocols are used to secure Web pages. Certificates can be used with these protocols for both client and server authentication. Server authentication using SSL is the most common implementation. The process works as follows: first, the user connects to a secure Web page: for example, **htttps://securewebpage.com** (notice the https as opposed to the usual http.) Next, a server certificate is presented to the client (Web browser). The client then validates this certificate (checks to make sure it is issued by a trusted CA, the date is valid, and so on). If the certificate is trusted, the Web browser generates a session key and encrypts that session key with the public key from the server's certificate and sends it back to the server. The server then decrypts the session key with its private key and all communication therein is secured with the session key. One common example of this exchange is a secure checkout page for an e-commerce Web site.

Business-to-business Web pages usually require mutual authentication. The process is quite similar to that described in the previous example. The only difference is that the client must present a valid certificate to the server before starting a session. This is because in most cases businesses want to restrict a service to known partners where sites that sell goods are offering a public service.

E-commerce Web sites often outsource their PKI to a company like VeriSign. In this scenario, VeriSign issues a certificate to the server hosting the Web pages. The root certificate for VeriSign is bundled as a standard feature with both Internet Explorer and Netscape Navigator. In this manner, anyone on the Internet with a standard browser can establish a secure channel with the Web site. Additionally, the administration and cost of deploying a PKI is avoided by the organization hosting the Web site.

Again, this is an effective strategy for a public service, but may not be desirable for a business with select relationships. For example, many organizations will want to dictate their own policies and procedures for PKI, which requires that they run the systems.

Business Need

MCC has a health insurance line of business (LOB) that is responsible for providing nationwide health care services. MCC is creating a Web-portal called HealthApp in order to automate and streamline business processes.

HealthApp members will use the Web site to access their statements and correlate payments with their policy coverage. Brokers will use the portal to retrieves quotes. Hospitals and physician's offices will be able to check the progress of claims and clear any submission errors.

PKI will be used to distribute and manage certificates to the Web servers housing HealthApp and the users accessing the Web site.

Solution

The HealthApp LOB will leverage MCC's existing Entrust implementation including the following components:

1. Entrust/Authority
2. Entrust/RA
3. Entrust/Profile Server

Entrust/Authority provides a Certificate Authority to issue and sign public-key certificates. Entrust/Authority provides users with two key pairs.

Entrust/RA provides a Registration Authority to register and manage user accounts. Some of the key user management features include key recovery and automatic key update and certificate renewal.

Entrust/Profile Server enables users to roam from workstation to workstation by housing user profiles in the directory instead of on the users' computer.

In addition to these components, Entrust/TruePass will also be utilized. This component will integrate with the HealthApp Web site to offer automated certificate services to users outside of the MCC organization.

Implementation

Entrust TruePass consists of a Java applet, a filter that resides on the Web server, and Java servlets that execute under a Java servlet engine. These services work in conjunction with the CA, Directory Server, Profile Server, and AutoRA. Entrust TruePass supports both Microsoft Internet Explorer and Netscape Navigator Web browsers. In addition, TruePass is compatible with both the Microsoft Internet Information Server and the Netscape Web Server.

The TruePass system consists of several Java servlets that provide advanced functionality beyond basic certificate-based authentication. For example, the authentication server module works in conjunction with the profile access module to securely transfer user profiles during the authentication sequence. Using profiles, certificate management (certificate renewal, key update, and so on) can be automated for external users in the same way it is for internal users. In addition, authentication can be mapped to back-end systems. During the authentication process, the user is issued a session cookie. This cookie houses the distinguished name of the authenticated user. Custom code will be written to map these cookies to user accounts in the back-end databases. This ensures that the HealthApp only allows users access to the functions that they are authorized to use.

The Web servers housing the HealthApp will be located on a De-militarized Zone (DMZ). It will communicate with the TruePass server on the Internal network through a firewall system. Users will be able to enroll for certificates through the HealthApp. Profiles will be created for users and stored on the MCC directory server. A new subordinate CA will be installed specifically to issue certificates to HealthApp users. This CA will have its own certificate policy and certificate practice statement (CPS), which will need to be observed by all business partners.

The Internet is a powerful tool that can be leveraged for business-to-business and business-to-customer relationships. The SSL and TLS protocols offer a mechanism for securing information exchange over the Internet. Certificates can be used to provide for basic authentication when initiating secure channels. By leveraging the existing Entrust infrastructure and using the Entrust TruePass system, both advanced certificate management functionality for external users and integration with back-end authentication is achieved.

Bibliography

Adams, C., and S. Farrell, Internet X.509 Public Key Infrastructure Certificate Management Protocols, RFC 2510, 1999.

Adams, C., P. Cain, D. Pinkas , and R. Zuccherato, *Internet X.509 Public Key Infrastructure Time Stamp Protocol (TSP),* work in progress, 2000.

Boeyen, S., T. Howes, and P. Richard, Internet X.509 Public Key Infrastructure LDAPv2 Schema, RFC 2587, 1999.

Chokani, S., and W. Ford, Internet X.509 Public Key Infrastructure Certificate Policy and Certification Practices Framework, RFC 2527, 1999.

Entrust Technologies, *Key Update and the Complete Story on the Need for Two Key Pairs*, August 2000.

Housley, R., W. Ford, W. Polk, and D. Solo, Internet X.509 Public Key Infrastructure Certificate and CRL Profile, RFC 2459, 1999.

Housley, R., and T. Polk, *Planning for PKI*, Wiley Computer Publishing, 2001.

Housley, R., and P. Hoffman, Internet X.509 Public Key Infrastructure Operational Protocols: FTP and HTTP, RFC 2585, 1999.

Kaliski, B., PKCS #10: Certification Request Syntax, Version 1.5, RFC 2314, 1998.

——, PKCS #7: Cryptographic Message Syntax, Version 1.5, RFC 2315, 1998.

Myers, M., C. Adams, D. Solo, and D. Kemp, Internet X.509 Certificate Request Message Format, RFC 2511, 1999.

Myers, M., X. Liu, J. Schaad, and J. Weinstein, Certificate Management Messages over CMS, RFC 2797, 2000.

Myers, M., R. Ankey, and C. Adams, *Online Certificate Status Protocol*, Version 2, work in progress, 2000.

Nourse, A., D. McGrew, C. Madson, X. Liu, *Cisco Systems' Simple Certificate Enrollment Protocol*, work in progress, 2001.

Olivia, C., Entrust Technologies, Entrust 5.0 Directory Requirements, January 2001.

Wagner, L., Novell Incorporated, Integrating Entrust 5 with NDS eDirectory, June 2000.

CHAPTER 13

Security Event Management and Consolidation

The expanding reach of corporate networks and data services has led to a proliferation of interconnectivity between organizations. Numerous links have been established between local corporate branches, business units, and often to external partners. Many organizations have also chosen to add Internet connectivity. The corporate enterprise is more externally connected than ever, whereas the amount of internal data and confidential systems expands. The importance of security in the corporate environment is paramount as the assets to be protected become exposed to a growing number of threats.

The continued addition of Internet connectivity and the resulting expansion of network reach raise the level of effort required to efficiently manage security events. The addition of external links has produced a flood of information to the enterprise-monitoring console. This makes the relatively straightforward operations that were possible when a limited number of links were in place impossible and also multiplies the security exposures present in a larger network. Information Technology (IT) managers need clear, concise views of enterprise security-related data in order to make appropriate decisions. For the IT department, creating effective reports often means dealing with an overload of security events and alarms from various devices.

The key to successful event handling and trouble-free operations is the ability to understand the network topology, include capable traffic analysis tools where logical, and log and alert suspicious event triggers to a capable monitoring system or intermediary system. Event sources and severity must be carefully scrutinized to ensure the data is relevant and reliable. Further, the monitoring system must be able to classify the various alerts into a usable report of system health, permitting a logical method for addressing critical events first, while classifying minor problems in a way that does not obfuscate underlying serious attacks.

Once pertinent security devices have been identified within an organization, event-related output can be aggregated, normalized, and correlated in such a fashion as to support a singular view of the enterprise from a security perspective. Such a perspective will enhance all security operations, both by reducing overall complexity and by eliminating any device-, subnet-, or geographic-specific bias toward security analysis.

Event Sources

The typical modern corporate network will include a significant number of internetworking devices (see Figure 13-1). In order to identify and understand potential data sources, it is important to build an asset list to include the various items as well as to classify the method of reporting capacity on capable devices. Depending on industry, specific connectivity requirements will expand the number of data sources, but the systems present in organizations will likely include

- Local LAN infrastructure gear at each office, consisting primarily of router-interconnected segments (including Asynchronous Transfer Mode [ATM], Fast Ethernet, Ethernet, Token Ring, and other topologies)
- Corporate WAN infrastructure connectivity for voice and/or data, via dedicated links or packet-switched networks
- Internet gateway connectivity for public data access
- Proprietary vendor connectivity as needs dictate (Bloomberg, Reuters, and so on)
- Supporting systems for functionality (UNIX and/or Windows based)

Figure 13-1

Security event sources

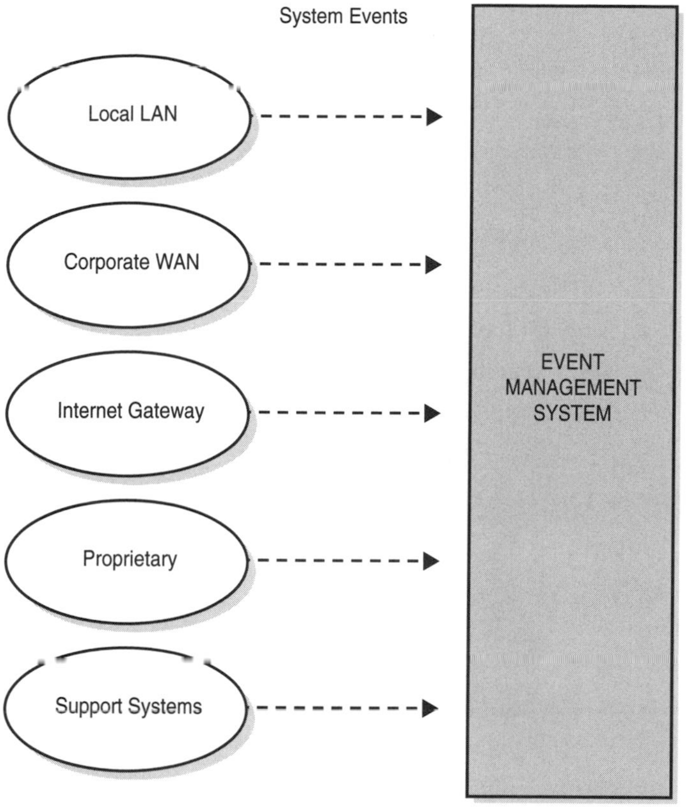

Many of these devices, regardless of vendor or model, support industry-standard event monitoring and alerting protocols. Although specific products differ in their implementation of reporting methods, a basic set of assumptions can be made about any modern infrastructure, security, or application tool. Event handling features based on the Simple Network Management Protocol (SNMP) have become universally accepted and key to the polling and status-reporting systems. Most commercially available systems will support one of the following reporting methods:

- SNMP-driven events (either trap updates or polled GET status monitoring)
- Application and OS event logging via Syslog or NT Event Log reported events

- Proprietary API-based reporting, custom console/terminal queries, and so on (such as Checkpoint LEA)

Product examples include

- Symantec Enterprise Security Manager
- Symantec Intruder Alert
- Network Flight Recorder (NFR) Network Intrusion Detection (NID)
- Cisco NetRanger Sensors
- Cisco PIX firewalls
- Cisco edge routers
- Cisco Secure Server
- Checkpoint firewalls

Intermediary systems that enable more granular event correlation and filtering include

- Cisco NetRanger Director
- Symantec Manager for ESM
- Symantec Manager for ITA

Enterprise Network Management Systems include

- Cabletron Spectrum Network Management System
- HP OpenView Network Node Manager

Event Protocols

Although numerous methods are available by which to gather systems information, the primary sources for security events can be categorized via generic models:

- Passive logging (UNIX syslog, NT EventLog, proprietary)
- Active polling (SNMP GET/query)
- Active alerting (SNMP trap/alert)
- Passive network/host monitoring (NFR NID, Cisco NetRanger)
- Active host vulnerability assessment (Symantec ESM)

Passive Logging—syslog

The UNIX syslog service receives messages from local or remote applications, and traditionally logs those messages to a local disk. The data connection is a stateless client/server communication, initiated by a suitable event and logged to the server where the UNIX syslog daemon runs as a User Datagram Protocol (UDP) service on port 514, and receives messages from devices. Syslog adds a time stamp (based on the receiving system's clock), the message-type keyword at the beginning of the message, a new line at the end of each message, and saves the output to a disk file or RAID system.

In the simplest scenario, this approach works well. Information is available for later review and auditing, and can be referred to in the event of a system breach that needs to be researched later. Unfortunately, syslog alone handles real-time events very poorly; no direct facility exists that permits intelligent event correlation and root-cause isolation.

Passive Logging—NT Event Log

The NT Event Log is the Microsoft equivalent of the UNIX syslog daemon. It receives and archives messages to each local machine, including System, Application, and Security logs. Each machine logs local events, and remote administrators with appropriate permissions may query systems for their log contents. The NT Event Log saves numerous variables with each message, including a date/time stamp, the source of the message (which application and which system), and the message contents.

Because the NT Event log is a local archive, this system is only useful on a single-user workstation. Numerous solutions, such as Event Log Monitor from TNT Software and Microsoft Resource Kit utilities like dumpel.exe, exist for consolidating the information to a central server. Responses to system events may be made based on general System or Application events, whereas Security events need to be closely monitored for change and/or unauthorized access.

Passive Logging—Proprietary

A number of products permit proprietary log generation and reporting. Along with vendor-independent protocols like SNMP, other vendor-specific standards have been introduced. Checkpoint-based firewalls are capable of reporting via LEA, a subset of the Checkpoint Open Platform for Security (OPSEC) protocols. Other systems may be capable of output in the form of comma-delimited text, bit-padded console output, and various non-structured output. In order to properly respond to security events, an Event Handler system must be chosen that is capable of classifying and categorizing events. Depending on your application, the data stream must be normalized to a format so that the Event Handler system may understand the dataset.

Active Polling—SNMP GET

A basic network feature is the Simple Network Management Protocol (SNMP). SNMP handles client/server connections via a system daemon. Queries are received via UDP to local port 161. Depending on the version of SNMP, supported devices permit levels of authentication and/or data encryption. SNMP organizes information in a tree structure known as a Management Information Base (MIB). The various vendor-supplied MIBs provide a volume of information about server health, interface up/down status, utilization statistics, and vendor-specific parameter values.

Because the SNMP design is based on remote query operation, it is well suited to event management. However, as numerous items are available to query, the key to successful use of SNMP as an event manager is the development of a baseline architecture view of behavior. This is because subsequent polls may show deviation from accepted levels that could be the first sign of an external attack.

Active Alerting—SNMP trap

Trap messages are a subset of SNMP that enable client-initiated notices sent to a remote server via UDP on port 162. These messages may be of an informative nature (line up/down on routers) or accounting related (user login information), which together provide a view into the remote system behavior.

Trap messages are sent by the initiating systems whenever required and provide a real-time notice of important events. Hacking attempts that yield a high number of inaccurate login attempts are quickly detected and a denial-of-service attack that attempts to flood an interface will activate a utilization trap. Other triggers may be set to generate Trap messages depending on the SNMP variable that is relevant to the environment.

The key issue with effective SNMP trap management involves the proper use of rules and policy so as to not allow an overload of messages as may often be caused by a link outage or similar event. Products like MicroMuse Netcool and E-Security's suite of tools offer intelligent, rule-based management and fault isolation based on SNMP trap analysis. Proper configuration of the management console is required to permit root-cause analysis of events otherwise a minor outage may overload the monitoring system and create spurious messages for support teams to track down.

Passive Network Host Monitoring

A number of solutions are available that permit the monitoring of IP-connected systems in order to detect and prevent against hacking attempts. When an intrusion detection system (IDS) is properly deployed, it can provide warnings via SNMP traps, indicating that a system is under attack, even if the system is not vulnerable to the specific attack. This warning can be used to alter the defensive posture of the installation to accomplish greater resistance to attack.

Once an information security technology is in place, it is necessary to monitor the system and to respond to the reported alerts. This means establishing roles and responsibilities for analyzing and acting on alerts, and monitoring the outcomes of both manual and automatic responses.

It is important to realize the IDS itself is a logical target for attack. Smart intruders who realize that an IDS has been deployed on a target network will likely attack the IDS first, by disabling it or forcing it to provide false information (distracting security personnel from the actual attack in progress).

Regular required activities include installing new signatures as they become available as well as installing periodic IDS upgrades. Sensor placement should be revisited periodically to ensure that system or network changes have not reduced the effectiveness of the IDS.

An IDS is only as good as the technology itself and the group that deployed it. It is critical to ensure that any IDS is deployed in a proper manner in order to see the network devices and potential traffic ingress points, while not being configured to generate excessive false-positive alerts to traffic.

Active Host Vulnerability Assessment

A number of products are available that permit host vulnerability assessment. Some products, like Symantec Enterprise Security Manager (ESM), load system agents that continually monitor system security parameters such as file permissions, user account security, audit parameters, and so on. Other products, such as Network Associates' Ballista product and Internet Security Systems' SAFESuite products, enable network-based host scanning and vulnerability assessment. Together these tools can be utilized to generate ad-hoc reports of system configuration and vulnerability areas.

Integration of host vulnerability assessment data into the event management infrastructure depends on the chosen software and output log format type. The use of additional information provides a security baseline on which subsequent events and trouble reports can be based, and is infinitely valuable when comparing anomalies to good system configurations.

Event Collection, Logical Grouping, and Classification

Once a collector is established as a central repository for central security event messages, it is necessary to further refine the data set in order to present it in a normalized manner. The key to successful event management is an understanding of which events to respond to and which to ignore. Also, important events must be presented in a manner that accurately identifies the

- Source
- Time

- Priority
- Type
- Variable value

Each of these variables must be consistent and traceable throughout the network otherwise the value of the data is degraded. In the event of an outage, this information should assist in any problem resolution or event classification.

The source of messages is quite obviously the first factor in identifying a message. Because some devices can have many source addresses, it is important to ensure that messages are sent out with consistent IP addresses or another unique identifier. This provides later grouping into logical entities and the association of relevant components with their components.

Time is a critical factor in the tracking of security events. Throughout the network, it is important to maintain consistency in time reporting, including compensation for time-zone information and appropriate padding for leap seconds. This time-source information can be synchronized via several time protocols—NTP being the most common—and received either from an external source such as a radio-clock or Global Positioning System (GPS) receiver, or if desired, an internal accurate authoritative time source such as a cesium time clock may be configured. Either solution will satisfy the demand for accurate time; the reliance on external sources is generally considerably less expensive than establishing an internal source, but is susceptible to minimal risk due to the time source being outside your organization's control.

Message priority can be set in accordance to business drivers and appropriate criticality for individual applications, and is often a multistep escalation pyramid, with only the most critical events being escalated to the top layer. A determination of what severity level to assign to events depends on both technical and business reasons, and must be decided on a case-by-case basis.

Message types are generally quite simple to determine and depend on event source. Alert messages are separate from simple notification messages; at the same time, use and accounting information should be classified differently from intruder notification alarms.

Variable values are the actual data that is contained in an event. Whether it is the details of an alert, the source of an intrusion attempt, the username that is being attempted without proper authorization, or any other content, the variables provide information that must be dealt with in an appropriate manner.

Logical Grouping and Classification

Security events and their classification are the first step to successful system operation. However, because the failure of one system component likely triggers multiple alerts, messages must be grouped in order to understand the actions that must be taken. Source components may be clustered by product, business group, or operations group responsible for that particular product. Regardless of chosen method, a clear understanding of the following must be present:

- The source that generated the events
- The product or service those events are associated with
- The likely cause of the events
- The operations process or course of action required to resolve the issue

SEM Project Planning and Initiation

Once a potential project has been identified, the recommended Security Event Management (SEM) architecture deployment methodology includes

- Project planning and initiation
- Security device inventory and assessment
- SEM requirements analysis
- SEM design phase
- SEM report and recommendations
- SEM build phase
- SEM documentation and knowledge transfer phase
- SEM conversion and turn-up phase
- SEM operational management, support, and maintenance

Project Planning and Initiation

Teams must meet to set goals and expectations, review documentation, detail future business and technical plans, and determine what the timeline for work will be. The first step to developing a thorough analysis and timeline for proper event handling involves some background research. A team leader, working with internal staff or a capable consulting organization, must define a clear goal and guidelines for the desired process. Internal documentation must be consulted, and in accordance with corporate policy and procedures, a formal project plan must be developed. This effort must include

- Timelines for review of existing documentation and infrastructure
- Plan for detailed network audit and analysis
- Listing of critical business goals and drivers for project
- Timeline for determining suitable vendors and technologies to complete project
- Dependencies on technology and staff resources required in order to complete the various tasks
- Estimated completion dates for the various system elements

Security Device Inventory and Assessment

After considering the various security options available for event handling, some fundamental options emerge. First, it is important to consider the event data sources. Even the most basic aspects of policy, operations, or functionality rely on the premise of inputs and outputs. Once properly monitored and tracked by devices, external security events generate alerts and log entries to a central console. Efficiently dealing with these events is critical to the successful operation of the enterprise. A formal process to consolidate the enterprise-monitoring systems and to clearly define the goals and ultimate deliverables of any project is the determining factor for success.

In order to identify the areas of concern, it is necessary to first confirm the system configuration and discover any undocumented features. This can be accomplished by referring to the existing topology documentation and by performing a thorough network survey to fill in any missing or outdated areas of information. Relevant work as part of performing this network survey will include the following:

- Current system configuration
- Determination of complete system inventory and elements to monitor
- Current technical and operational measures (if any) that monitor the system

Requirements Analysis

A determination of SEM goals and system design objectives must be made based on input factors from the client and end users who will be ultimately responsible for the system. Input must be solicited from all relevant business units and the operations staff, in accordance with industry guidelines and corporate business needs. These requirements may include

- Integration/segregation of the duties of the security function
- Devices to be included with/excluded from the SEM framework
- Physical security of SEM consoles and data stores
- Log/event rotation, archival, and handling
- Transmission method from security device to SEM framework (for example, encryption)
- Security device configuration and change management
- Escalation procedures and methods (for example, incident response plan) for a specific class of devices will be the deliverable of this phase.

SEM Design Phase

Any SEM endeavor requires a custom design based on the product environment and functionality requirements. Simple systems may require a straightforward trouble notification and resolution escalation, whereas complex corporate and three-tier component architectures have numerous dependencies on individual functionality. These factors must be taken into account when designing the escalation path for problem resolution in order to eliminate duplicate messages and trouble tickets that may be generated by outages.

Report and Recommendations

One likely step that will be encountered is the need to receive management approval for any build-out efforts. If necessary, an interim report may be generated, detailing the discovered requirements as well as the requisite SEM dependencies (see Figure 13-2). The proposal for requirements, solutions offerings, and potential timelines should be included as part of the report. Once management approval has been received for the SEM project effort, the build phase will begin.

Figure 13-2

SEM design report and recommendations

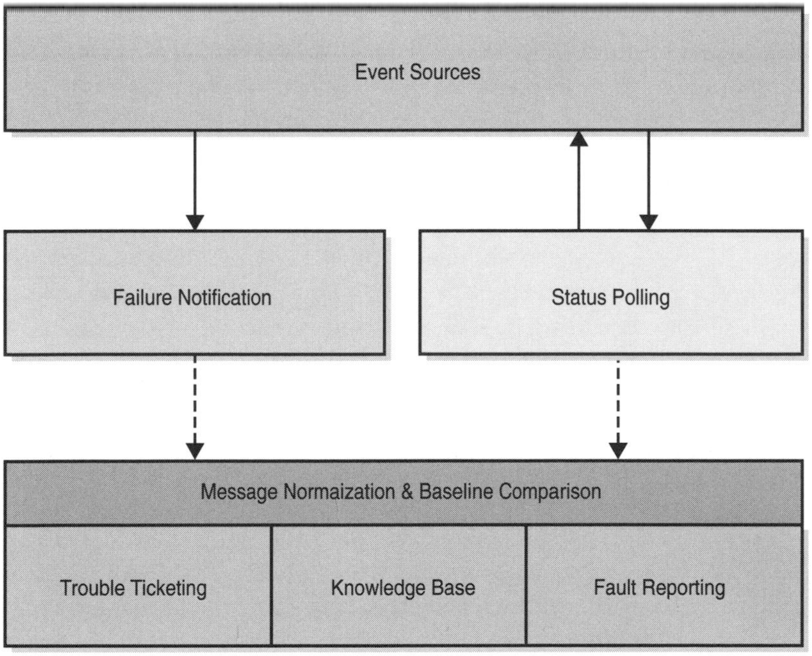

SEM Build Phase

This phase involves the actual system deployment. Whether the build out will be handled by an internal deployment group or by an external contractor, this is when the systems, consoles, and configuration required to make the system work are deployed. This involves complete system testing and the generation of baseline reports upon which to base future utilization comparisons.

SEM Documentation and Knowledge Transfer Phase

The proper operation of systems and processes needs to be documented throughout the SEM deployment. A set of documents presenting overall system design, purpose, and operations procedures must be created before being turned over to the operations team responsible for day-to-day system functionality. This ensures that the team is aware of system behavior and capabilities. Any specific considerations or exceptions to the documentation that may be decided at a later phase should be documented accordingly. At no point should the operation of the SEM system become out of sync with the documented design. This ensures that any anomalous behavior of the system itself is traceable and can be remedied.

SEM Conversion and Turn-Up Phase

The successful execution of a well-structured SEM project is dependent on numerous groups within an organization. A determination must be made regarding the scheduled migration of system elements, installation of new system components, and final operation of the complete new system. This will likely include the gradual migration of devices and systems based on various departmental or business unit schedules, with a master plan to be determined by the project manager in line with the SEM conversion schedule.

Any complete implementation of the SEM system should involve thorough system testing in order to ensure proper functionality. Simulated traffic patterns, system and device outages, as well as deliberate attacks made against the SEM system should generate expected results. This will ensure that in a production scenario all systems are properly functional. In the event the SEM system is consolidating previously disparate systems, it is important to confirm that the previous aggregate system capacity is not reduced, but rather that it efficiently summarizes and efficiently presents events generated previously by disconnected systems.

Ongoing Support, Enhancement, and Maintenance

As with any system, the product's life cycle will have many stages. Regular maintenance and attention to operations are required in order to keep the components running and the overall system conforming to the original business requirements. Regular necessary enhancements or changes to the configuration, in order to accommodate new business needs or to expand the scope and managed systems, will occur throughout the system life cycle. As new products become available for the management system, and as the equipment to be monitored is augmented by new gear, this will no doubt necessitate specific attention to system capacity and expansion.

These smaller projects will require careful attention and planning, but it is critical to note that any changes that are made to the system architecture must be thoroughly documented and integrated into the existing system architecture. By keeping a thorough documentation set of capacity, capabilities, and system function, any system changes or operations are made less challenging.

Analysis of Case Study #1—Corporate

The MCC corporate headquarters environment is a traditional corporate setting. Let us assume the MCC campus has a number of internetworking connections to business partners and to external vendors. Also, an Internet line is at the HQ facility and another MCC branch office (to which the corporate HQ is connected via the WAN) is also Internet attached. From the main MCC network, direct connections are outbound and are filtered by a Checkpoint firewall. Inbound connectivity is restricted solely to a Demilitarized Zone (DMZ), where a small Web server and mail server are attached. Assume that the corporate environment is running a RFC 1918 private internal network and their ISP has assigned a small public range of externally routable addresses to them. Two IP addresses out of this range are assigned to the Web and mail server and inbound connectivity is being translated on the firewall system.

Business Needs

MCC needs to ensure that the connectivity to the Internet and outside vendor networks does not subject them to hacking attempts or other malicious activity. Branch office WAN connectivity needs to be scrutinized closely in order to ensure that no branch office connectivity or dial up damages the network reliability. At the same time, these are critical networks and they must remain operational. MCC needs to be able to find problems when they occur and requires an affordable solution.

MCC is currently running HP OpenView and presently collecting minimal network statistics. They would like to

- Preserve existing investment in SEM software/hardware
- Expand the scope of the current monitoring to include all routers
- Understand business attack sources and likely actions
- Minimize downtime and/or data integrity loss

Solution

The relatively small size of the MCC environment makes it well suited for a small SEM setup (see Figure 13-3). It is unlikely that a complex system would need to be configured, assuming our company does not expect to increase the inbound connectivity permitted from external entities. Based on equipment documentation and site surveys, it is determined that

- Ten branch offices use a total of 50 routers.
- Each branch is connected to a primary frame relay line and a backup ISDN line.
- A total of three Internet-facing firewalls exist, two in the main office and one in a second branch office.
- Three internal addresses are mapped to externally accessible addresses. One services the mail server in the two connected branches and the other permits connectivity to the Web server in the corporate offices.
- Existing external-facing systems will have a host-based IDS software installed.
- Netcool will enable MCC to logically group alerts and take selective action.

- The existing devices will be configured to point SNMP traps to the Netcool system, determining when systems are performing beyond capacity, ISDN lines are brought up, and other system problems occur.

The Netcool installation will depend on the detailed MCC specifications, but will include provisions for determining product dependencies on vendor-line connectivity, Web server functionality, and mail system reliability.

Implementation

Rollout of the MCC Security Event Management infrastructure will be scheduled for off-hours maintenance changes to ensure that no interruption of production service occurs. Successful implementation will require configuring SNMP traps on the MCC routers. Users and system functionality should not be affected by the changes.

Figure 13-3

MCC corporate solution

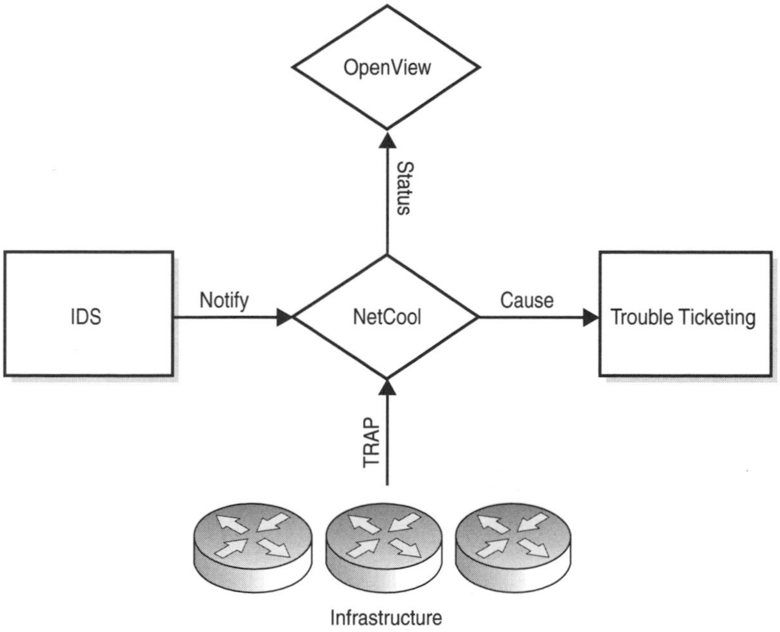

Operations

The SEM product will be turned over to the local MCC operations team for integration into the regular system documentation and operations.

Analysis of Case Study #2—FinApp

The FinApp product is an evolved market data financial application. Financial traders use it every day to monitor stocks, get news, and track their overall portfolio. It is currently deployed at a client site and needs to be carefully monitored for functionality and uptime as the application is critical.

Business Needs

FinApp is the key application of the customer's trading floor. Without it, no stock trading can be done during the course of the day; the customer's business is dead in the water. The application and the servers that support it must remain functional during the course of the trading day:

- Service Level Agreement (SLA) requirements permit no less than 99.99 percent uptime for services on the FinApp network.
- SLA requirements permit minimal (less than 50 ms) latency for transport on the FinApp network.
- Outages of the FinApp primary communications server must be resolved in 1 hour or less.

Solution

The reliability of the FinApp system relies on the effective operation of supporting infrastructure and components (see Figure 13-4). Based on equipment documentation and site surveys, it is determined that

- The primary office uses a total of three routers.
- The branch is connected to a primary T1 line, a backup T1 line, and a backup ISDN line.

- A total of two Internet-facing firewalls exist.
- Two internal addresses are mapped to externally accessible addresses. One services the mail server and the other permits connectivity to the Web server.
- Existing external-facing systems will have a host-based IDS software installed.
- Netcool will enable the FinApp customer to logically group alerts and take selective action.
- The existing devices will be configured to point SNMP traps to the Netcool system, determining when systems are performing beyond capacity, ISDN lines are brought up, and other system problems occur.
- OpenView will be used to monitor network problems and systems uptime issues that my come up during the course of the install.

Implementation

Rollout of the FinApp Security Event Management infrastructure will be scheduled for off-hours maintenance changes to ensure that no interruption of production service occurs. Successful implementation will require configuring SNMP traps on the MCC routers and FinApp communication servers. Users and system functionality should not be affected by the changes.

Figure 13-4

Services to add to FinApp market data

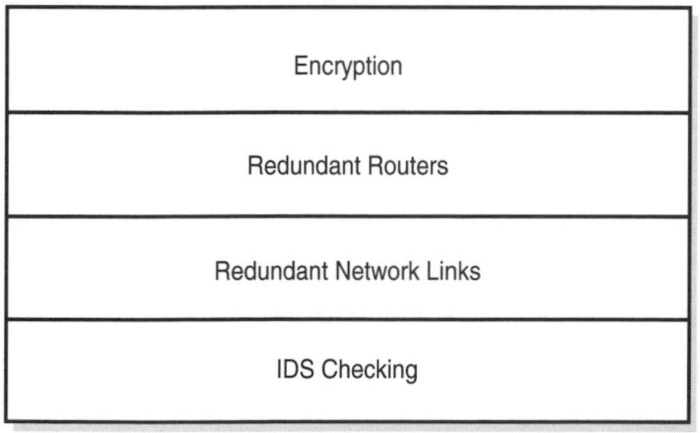

Operations

The SEM product will be turned over to the local FinApp operations team for integration into the regular system documentation and operations.

Analysis of Case Study #3—HealthApp

The HealthApp product is a Web-based front-end to a three-tier application. We'll assume it is currently being hosted in a Managed Service Provider (MSP) data center and used by many customers for their medical coverage information, appointment records, and so on. Data is proprietary and sensitive and must be handled in accordance with federal HIPAA regulations.

- Database systems response time must be under 2 seconds.
- SLA requirements permit no less that 99.99 percent uptime for services on the HealthApp network.
- SLA requirements permit minimal (less than 50 ms) latency for transport on the HealthApp network.
- Outages of the HealthApp primary communications server must be resolved in 1 hour or less.

Solution

Along with a series of other measures that should be employed to guarantee data integrity and encryption (see SSL certs and PKI solutions in Chapter 12), care must be taken to ensure that all systems are kept fully functional (see Figure 13-5):

- The data center uses numerous routers.
- The data center is connected to numerous OC-12 lines.
- Connectivity is split between the client facing (Web) layer and backend (DB/app) layers.
- Existing external-facing systems will have a host-based IDS software installed.

- Netcool will enable the HealthApp customer to logically group alerts and take selective action.
- The existing devices will be configured to point SNMP traps to the Netcool system, determining when systems are performing beyond capacity, ISDN lines are brought up, and other system problems occur.
- OpenView will be used to monitor network problems and systems uptime issues that my come up during the course of the install.

Implementation

Rollout of the HealthApp Security Event Management infrastructure will be scheduled for off-hours maintenance changes to ensure that no interruption of production service occurs. Successful implementation will require loading agents to monitor specific systems, configuring syslog and SNMP traps on the MCC routers and HealthApp servers. Users and system functionality should not be affected by the changes.

Operations

The SEM product will be turned over to the local HealthApp operations team for integration into the regular system documentation and operations.

Figure 13-5

Services to add to HealthApp Web

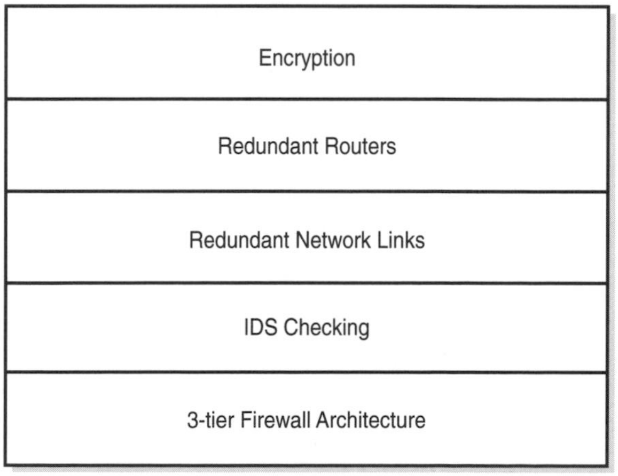

Conclusion

Technology offers numerous solutions for event management. Implementation of SEM systems requires an understanding of the system principles and the ability to vary the configuration as necessary in a client environment. Although the fundamental technology available is relatively straightforward and even simple, you can achieve similar goals innumerous ways; however, all require customer input and cooperation. Depending on business needs and technical requirements, it is possible to create a SEM solution to meet the challenges of the organization.

The use of technology alone is not sufficient to maintain network security and properly operate a production network. Once a solution is deployed, an organization needs to attract, train, and retain qualified technical staff to operate and maintain technologies. Only then can they ensure that the solution they have chosen will remain updated and supported adequately.

By utilizing all resources available, SEM solutions can be created to suit the requirements of the particular application or industry where they will be deployed.

CHAPTER 14

Security Management

What Is Security Management?

Months have been spent analyzing requirements, designing, and deploying the security architecture, but now what? Now it's time manage it all. Security management, basically, is the process of managing and maintaining security within the organization. Both design and deployment are relatively easy compared with managing and maintaining the security from a logistic perspective. Although design and deployment both have more definitive starting and finishing points, managing security, on the other hand, is a journey that has no true end point.

Why Is Security Management Important?

Security management has always been an important function within an organization. Now, with the ever-increasing risk associated with interconnections, the importance of good security management is paramount to an organization's ability to manage risk effectively and reduce it wherever possible. Internet, intranet, and extranet connections all add complexity, which in turn add to the inherent risk. Following industry best practices is the best way to mitigate risk. A few obvious side effects of best practices include quality of construction, scalability, portability, and ease of use. After the due diligence is invested in the design and build-out of the security infrastructure, don't handicap your design with faulty process. As the infrastructure is the machine, the security management is the oil—without adequate amounts of which the machine will fail. If the quality of your security management solution begins to falter, the security afforded by your infrastructure will also suffer. Determining the quality of your present-day security management practices is a natural first step and is the inherent purpose of this chapter. Upon determining where quality exists within your practices, you will inadvertently uncover where it does not exist.

The best technical security architecture can be designed and deployed, but without proper management and operations, it is of little use. Security management provides the necessary guidance and direction for the overall architecture and operations that govern the use of that architecture. This includes managing the policies and procedures, and managing the individual components within the architecture. Doing this enables the organization to stay on top of advances in technology that might affect how policy or procedures should be augmented.

Security management provides a framework for the change management and the incident management procedures typically followed by security staffers. Without proper change management, the systems can quickly become unstable. This instability can lead to downtime and can cost the organization a great deal of money in a short period of time. Lack of change management controls may also create a non-enviable environment where departmental teams enact changes without understanding the impact to other teams or the enterprise as a whole.

Incident management provides a framework for identifying, responding to, and reviewing security incidents. Without an enterprise-wide incident management process, incidents may be responded to inappropriately by the wrong group, by all groups, or altogether ignored. Support from all levels of the organization must therefore exist in order for your security management program to be successful. This support starts at the top of the organization with the support of the board of directors and the CEO, and continues down through management to the administrators and even down to each individual end user. As with management of the individual components in the security architecture, if one of these support levels does not exist, the security management process of the organization will not function properly. For this reason, not only must communication and common practices exist throughout the organization, but industry best practices should also be followed to guide the management of your security infrastructure.

Best Practices to Managing the Security Infrastructure

A core set of best practices should be applied across all components in the infrastructure. These best practices are detailed in the following section.

Secure It from the Start

Security is all too often an afterthought when setting up new networks and applications. This is not normally the case for a security system component, but it can be. Make sure security is implemented from the start with its own management in mind. Mismanagement of one small component in the security architecture can put the company at risk in potentially unforeseen ways. The most common analogy drawn to security is that of a chain of connected links—the strength of which is only as strong as the weakest link. By paying attention to detail and addressing even the most apparently insignificant architecture components, you increase the likelihood that your security infrastructure will achieve its design goal.

Administrators must have the ability to manage the elements within the architecture securely. This includes managing the devices via a secure interface through a secure channel such as Secure Socket Layer (SSL) or Secure Shell (SSH). Without an encrypted session, the entire security architecture could be compromised because an attacker could intercept passwords used to manage your devices. The use of strong authentication via certificates or tokens should also be used during the authentication sequence while managing the security infrastructure components. If usernames and passwords must be used in lieu of tokens or certificates, the passwords should be required to contain eight or more alphanumeric and special characters and expire after a predetermined number of days (this is typically 30–45 days). Requiring these constraints within your company reduces the likelihood that an attacker is able to guess a password, thereby circumventing much of the security your architecture is intended to provide. A password such as *ty!5^Wo1* would be far more difficult to guess than *bob*, for example. Corporations should also create accounts with varying degrees of administrative controls within a selected domain or domains. For example, a far greater number of security administrators who are able to enact user-level changes should be present than those administrators who are able to enact domain server level changes.

Separation of duties is another important factor in managing the security architecture. For example, the security administrators monitoring the intrusion detection system (IDS) should not be the same administrators managing the firewall. By creating an environment that utilizes specialized functions that protect device administration as well as software and hardware development efforts, and on that enacts a series of checks and balances to ensure these controls are functioning properly, no single user should be able to circumvent the security you have in place. Another example of separation of duties involves the auditing of the security architecture by an outside, unbiased, third party. A third party does not bring with it the same preconceived notions and knowledge. They provide an objective viewpoint that adds value to the security assessment process. They also generally have at their disposal the collective knowledge from numerous similar assessments and follow a battle-tested methodology that has been proven in both completeness and efficiency time and time again.

Understand and Enforce the Security Policies

Security analysts and administrators should not only understand and enforce the security policies, but they should also enhance the security awareness within the organization by helping others understand why the security policies and procedures are in place. People are more inclined to follow the policies and procedures if they know and understand the reasons behind them. In addition, security should become a part of the employee's job description. Not only should it be a part of existing job descriptions, it should also be incorporated into performance reviews. By incorporating security into the job description and performance reviews, the employees have a vested interest in managing and maintaining security in the organization. They will also tend to have a much better understanding of the importance security plays in their daily jobs.

Understanding and enforcing the policies is also critical when it comes to change management within the security infrastructure. For example, if someone requests the administrator to open up a port on the firewall for streaming media, how does he or she know if it should be allowed? It may be against a specific policy. Procedures should be in place to educate and inform the security administrators on the policies, standards, and guidelines within the organization. In addition, it should be clearly documented what the procedures are when a modification is in question as it relates to the security policy. As a part of the procedures, business requirements should also be assessed so the security does not cripple a business application. This involves a standard risk assessment to ensure that the security solution implemented provides the proper balance between security and usability.

Because the security administrators are on the front lines, they have a unique opportunity to see how security policies, standards, and guidelines are being received and followed. Part of their responsibility is to provide feedback on the policies, standards, and guidelines so they can be constantly improved. This may include better ways to enforce or communicate the policies, or it may be something as simple as a design change that can be fed back to the security architects, which will result in the reduction of risk.

Follow Defined Change Management Guidelines

Change management are two words most system and security administrators dread hearing. Most system administrators envision mainframes, control, filling out forms, and so on. They typically think of anything but system uptime and availability. Change management is the process of modifying equipment, systems, software, or procedures in a planned and authorized manner. This includes ensuring that a business purpose is behind the change request; the risks associated with the change are worth taking; and appropriate back-out procedures have been defined. Changes that are not executed properly can have major impacts on the business including financial impacts, customer impacts, and/or market loss.

If you look at the history of computing over the last 20 years, we have moved from a centralized mainframe environment, to a decentralized desktop environment, and now back to a more centralized mainframe-type environment with super fast servers with ultrahigh capacity and thinner client PCs and workstations. Somewhere between the mainframe-centric era and the desktop era, change management was put on the back burner. Now, we are coming full circle with change management as it plays an integral part of availability within (in particular) an e-commerce organization. Change management also plays a key role in the efficient management and operations of the security architecture.

Without change management, an organization can be a chaotic place to work. Human errors can result in a large number of system outages and downtime. With proper change management in place, many of these errors can be significantly reduced. Changes should follow a tightly controlled, repeatable process. Figure 14-1 shows the proper steps in the change management process.

Change control may include the alteration or installation of a firewall with applicable rule set, a router Access Control List (ACL) modification, or the addition of a new virtual private network (VPN) gateway. In fact, it does not need to be related to the security infrastructure at all. This process can be applied to all applications, networks, systems as well as procedures within your corporation. The following steps can be used to manage change control across the organization:

1. *Identify and document the change*. This step should include the type of equipment, system, or software to be modified. It should also include when the change will occur, how long the change will last, and who will perform the change.
2. *Document the business reason, or driver, behind the change*. Is this change in support of a new and critical business application, or is it to upgrade code on a firewall to fix an existing problem?
3. *Estimate the impact of the change and determine if the impact is acceptable*. Is this change likely to bring down the Internet connection for an extended period, or is it a change that the users and applications should not notice?
4. *Document accurate back-out procedures in the event that the change does not succeed.* In this situation, the affected changes can be safely removed, enabling you to revert to your previous operational configuration.
5. *Once the impact has been assessed and the change has been approved, the change should be communicated to all relevant parties.* Only then should the change be executed.

This may appear to be a lengthy process, but it does provide many benefits to the organization. By forcing the implementers to document and assess the impact of their changes, they think through the change more carefully. It also forces them to design and document a rollback plan ahead of time.

Figure 14-1

Change Management Process

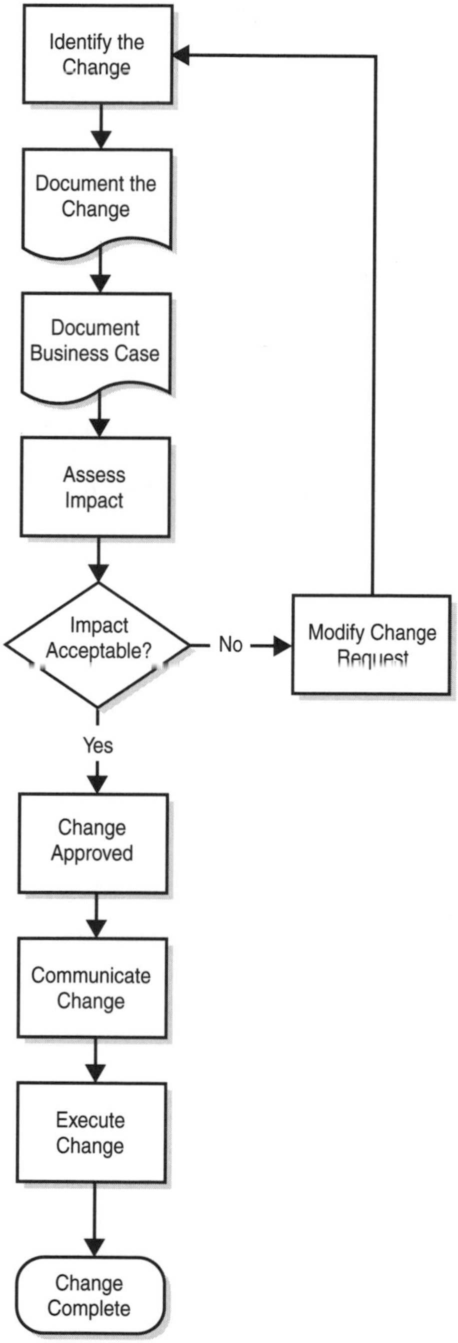

Monitor Information Sources

Keeping up with current issues in network and host security is one of the most important jobs of the security administrator. This should be a daily activity and not a weekly or monthly task. New vulnerabilities are found, documented, and posted to Web sites daily, if not hourly. With this in mind, it is imperative that the security analysts and administrators monitor ongoing threats, trends, and vulnerabilities. This enables them to react much faster and also gives them a more robust understanding of how to reduce risk associated with these vulnerabilities or even eliminate them altogether.

Web Sites

Security Web sites have the most up-to-date information on current security issues, vulnerabilities, patches, and solutions. Numerous Web sites exist for keeping track of security vulnerabilities. Table 14-1 lists some of the more popular information security Web sites that are focused on providing vulnerability updates and details.

Mailing Lists

Mailing lists are another great way to stay on top of security issues. Table 14-2 contains several of the more popular security mailing lists.

Trade Publications

Trade publications, although not the fasted way to stay on top of security issues, play an important role in keeping current on security issues. Trade

Table 14-1

Security Web Sites

http://www.securityfocus.com
http://www.securityportal.com
http://www.cert.org/
http://www.ciac.org/ciac/
http://www.sans.org
http://www.infosyssec.org/

Table 14-2
Mailing Lists

Mailing List List Name	To Join or for Further Information	Description
BUGTRAQ	Send e-mail to **LISTSERV @NETSPACE.ORG**. In the text of your message (not the subject line), write: subscribe bugtraq.	Provides detailed discussion and announcement of computer security vulnerabilities: what they are, how to exploit them, and how to fix them.
NTBugtraq	Send e-mail to **listserv @listserv.ntbugtraq . com.** In the text of your message (not the subject line), write: subscribe ntbugtraq.	Discussion of security exploits and security bugs in Windows NT and its related applications.
Firewalls	Send an e-mail to **majordomo @lists.gnac.net.** In the text of your message (not the subject line), write: subscribe firewalls.	Useful information regarding firewalls and how to implement and operate them securely.
Internet Security Systems X-Force	**http://xforce.iss.net/maillists/ index.php**	Various security mailing lists including: intrusion detection, network security assessments, NT security, and general security news, among others.
CERT (Computer Emergency Response Team) (CERT)	Send e-mail to **cert@cert.org** and, in the text of your message (not the subject line), write: I want to be on your mailing list.	CERT security vulnerabilities
CIAC-Bulletin: CIAC Information Bulletins and Advisory Notices	Send e-mail to **majordomo @tholia.llnl.gov** and, in the bodyBODY of your message, write: subscribe ciac-bulletin.	Contains important, time-critical computer security information.
Intrusion Detection Systems (IDS)	To join, send e-mail to **majordomo@uow.edu.au** and with the following in the body of the message, write: subscribe ids.	The list is a forum for discussions on topics related to development of IDSs.

publications will often go into more detail than a Web site and may include product comparisons, interviews, and case studies of real-world organizations and security issues. Refer to Table 14-3 for a list of security-related trade publications.

Books

Security-related books, such as the book you are currently reading, provide in-depth knowledge and references related to security issues and solutions. These books provide a common baseline of understanding so security practitioners can communicate on the same level. Although they provide in-depth knowledge and are great references, they should not be used to keep track of current vulnerabilities.

Table 14-4 lists some of the most widely read and referenced books in the information security field.

Table 14-3

Security Trade Publications

Security Trade Publications	Information	Description
Information Security Magazine	**http://www.infosecuritymag.com**	Monthly magazine focusing on information security and includes: security technology and trends, news, product reviews, and case studies.
SC Magazine	**http://www.scmagazine.com**	Dedicated to covering the world of information security, data protection, and disaster recovery.
Password	**http://www.issa.org/**	Bi-MBimonthly newsletter that provides Information Security Systems Association (ISSA) members with up-to-date industry information and association news.
Network Magazine	**http://www.networkmagazine.com**	Monthly magazine focused on security and networking and includes: product reviews, lab tests, and case studies.
Business Communications Review	**http://www.bcr.com/bcrmag**	In-depth analysis of networking technology, trends, management issues, pricing, and regulation.

Table 14-4 Security Books

Security Books	Author(s)	ISBN	Description
Security Architecture: Design, Deployment and Operations	Christopher M. King, Curtis E. Dalton, T. Ertem Osmanoglu	0072133856	Provides a step-by-step "thinking process" to solving complex information security problems. The focus is on design methodology, technology, and operational aspects.
Practical Unix & Internet Security, 2nd Edition	Simson Garfinkel, Gene Spafford	1565921488	Details the threats, system vulnerabilities, and countermeasures you can adopt to protect your UNIX system, network, and Internet connection.
Windows 2000 Security Handbook	Tom Sheldon	0072124334	How to safeguard Windows 2000 with IPSec, defend against hacking, spoofing, sniffing, and DDS attacks, and secure your network with firewalls, proxy servers, and VPNs.
Cisco Security Architectures	Gilbert Held, Kent Hundley	0071347089	Strong focus on how to use Cisco Access lists and the Cisco PIX Firewall.
Hacking Exposed, 2ndSecond Edition	Joel Scambray, Stuart McClure, George Kurtz	0072127481	A full disclosure book detailing system and network hacking.
Building Internet Firewalls, 2nd Edition	Elizabeth Zwicky, Simon Cooper, D. Brent Chapman	1565928717	A practical and detailed guide to building firewalls on the Internet.
Handbook of Information Security Management	Micki Krause (Editor), Harold F. Tipton (Editor)	0849398290	Case studies and analyses on how to protect systems and data using the latest tools. Also, it is one of the most important references used to prepare for the Certified Information Systems Security Professionals examination.
Computer Security Handbook	Arthur E. Hutt (Editor), Seymour Bosworth (Editor), Douglas B. Hoyt (Eeditor)	0471118540	Covers intentional and accidental dangers and threats to a corporation's computer systems and networks.

Procedural Management

Procedural management includes user administration, role-based administration, and security incident management. All these processes are manual in nature.

Account Management

Account management involves moves, adds, and changes of user and administrator accounts on the security infrastructure elements. Networks are very dynamic in nature. This applies to the systems as well as the users and administrators of those systems. Procedures should be documented to ensure the appropriate and authorized actions are taken when requesting, establishing, issuing, suspending, or closing user and administrator accounts.

Special care should be given to administrator accounts for those critical infrastructure components like firewalls and VPN concentrators. Account access should be limited to only a few administrators and those accounts should be closely monitored and maintained. The passwords should be changed on a periodic basis and the accounts should be configured with lockout periods for bad password attempts.

In addition, a periodic review of access rights should be instituted. This review should compare the existing accounts and their rights with the associated users and their roles. This accountability process will help reduce errors, misuse, and/or unauthorized activity.

Role-Based Administrative Functions

Appropriate roles and privileges should be set up within the security infrastructure components as well. Role-based administration enables specific rights to be configured depending on administrator requirements. For example, a firewall administrator may want to grant read-only privileges to senior analysts within a network operations center. Doing so would enable them to review the status of the firewall on a periodic basis to ensure it is operating correctly. This would also give the analysts the ability to troubleshoot the firewall in the event an application appears to be functioning incorrectly. Some suggested roles are defined in Table 14-5.

Table 14-5

Suggested Roles

Role	Description
Super Administrator	This administrator would have total control over both the operating system and the security component itself.
Administrator	This administrator would have access to the security component, but not access to the operating system itself.
Operator	This account would have only physical access (hands-on access) to the security component and would have the ability to monitor the operating system and provide tape changes for any backups that may need to be completed on the component.
NOC Analyst	This account would have read-only access to the element in order to troubleshoot the device.

Security Incident Management

So what do you do if you get hacked? How do you know if you have even been hacked? These are the questions that good security incident management will answer. Security incident management has three phases of security:

- *Identify the security incident(s).* This involves documentation of the incident.
- *Manage and recover from the security incident(s).* This involves informing the appropriate parties regarding the incident, correcting the immediate problem, and recovering from the incident.
- *Incident review and feedback.* This involves reviewing the incident and deciding what could have been done better and how the incident could be prevented next time.

Figure 14-2 details the security incident life cycle.

Identify the Security Incident

Identifying a security incident is the first step in the incident management process. But what defines a security incident in the first place? A security incident is defined as the act of violating an explicit or implied

Figure 14-2
Security Incident Lifecycle

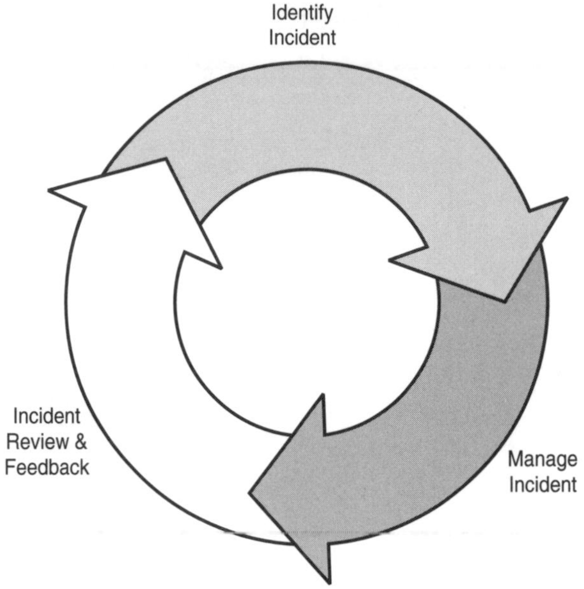

security policy. Obviously, in order to have a security incident, you must first have a policy that has been violated. Not only must you have a policy, but it must also be clearly understood.

Security incidents are identified and reported in four basic ways:

- Help desk
- IDS
- System logs
- Network element logs

The help desk generates security incidents in the form of trouble tickets. This may be something as simple as an end user reporting his or her laptop was stolen or it may be an e-mail administrator reporting that the latest variant of the ILOVEYOU VB script has just started bogging down the mail servers.

Many organizations find it difficult to manage security incidents. This is mainly due to the lack of documented procedures for handling various events. The logical place to document these incidents is in the organizational help desk system. If the help desk system is robust enough, this can provide proper tracking, reporting, and querying of events. Keep in mind, the events must be classified initially and provisions may need to be made in the help desk system to properly track these events.

Training help desk analysts to properly document and manage the incidents is another challenge facing organizations. This can be remedied by making security training a standard part of the new-hire orientation for help desk analysts as well a part of their ongoing training curriculum. The analysts will then be able to better identify, categorize, and prioritize security incidents.

Manage and Recover from the Incident

The second step in managing security incidents is to manage and recover from the incident. This involves informing the appropriate parties regarding the incident, correcting the immediate problem, and recovering from the incident. Depending on the severity of the incident, management may need to be notified immediately. This will depend on the written procedures defined for the organization. By informing management of the issue, it keeps them in the loop and helps them understand the issue better. Management may also assist in escalating the issue either internally or externally. Other groups within the organization may need to be notified as well. For example, if a security issue related to a new virus is found, it will be necessary to contact the e-mail administrators so they can take the appropriate action.

Incident Review and Feedback

The last phase of security incident management is the incident review and feedback phase. This phase enables all parties involved in the incident to recap what occurred during the incident, how it occurred, and how it can be prevented in the future. It also gives the security management team a chance to suggest changes that will improve the overall security posture of the organization. It is important to involve the appropriate parties to ensure that this post-mortem examination is accurate. The parties involved in this exercise should consist of a representative from the department or business line that owns and operates the application, a representative from the corporate information technology support team, a representative from the help desk support group, and a representative from the corporate information security team. Together, these parties will have the ability to discuss proper application operation and usage procedures, necessary network communications associated with the application, future developmental direction, and corporate information security restrictions or guidelines that both control and protect the application.

Component Management

Component management includes the mechanism and process by which each security infrastructure component is managed on a regular basis. These mechanisms and processes provide the administrator with the data that is required to perform his or her job well.

Logging Mechanisms

Centralized logging enables events from numerous elements to be consolidated into one or more locations. This makes the management and administration of the logs much easier. One of the challenges of log consolidation is encrypting the traffic from the element to the central repository. Some firewall vendors have created solutions that enable the messages to be encrypted in transit (such as Checkpoint LEA or RSA Keon).

Logging system messages is of primary importance for a number of reasons. Backup and archival of the logs to a central location is easier to manage because they are in one place. This scenario also provides better control over the log retention period, which should be specified in a policy. Further details on logging mechanisms can be found in Chapter 13.

Time Synchronization

Time synchronization is a critical element within the infrastructure. Time synchronization enables an organization to synchronize time to a highly accurate time reference. The Network Time Protocol (NTP) is the preferred method of synchronizing time across the organization. NTP is actually an Internet standard protocol used to communicate time updates between elements. An NTP client will request time from an NTP server and compare its current time against the reference server. It will then adjust its clock accordingly.

An NTP client could be an application server, database server, e-mail server, firewall, IDS, syslog server, router, and so on. The NTP server could be a UNIX server or Windows NT server running an NTP server process.

It may be configured to receive time updates from public NTP servers on the Internet. In mission-critical networks where time synchronization is crucial, it is considered best practice to set up an NTP reference device that receives updates via Global Positioning Satellites (GPS). This increases both reliability and security because the internal NTP servers are no longer relying on the single external source for time.

Having the correct time setting on all devices is important to ensure the accuracy of audit logs. Because these logs may be used during investigations as legal evidence or used in corporate disciplinary examinations, they should be as accurate as possible and synchronized across all provider elements (such as systems or devices that actually logged this data). If these logs are not accurate and appropriately synchronized among one another, correlating the logs becomes more difficult. In fact, poor time synchronization across these systems will also damage the credibility of this evidence when presented in a court of law.

It is the security administrator's job to ensure that the various elements are configured properly to use the NTP servers. This would include periodically checking the time on firewalls, routers, application servers, and so on.

Access Controls

Access controls have never been easy to manage. Part of the problem is the lack of centralized management tools for managing Access Control Lists (ACLs). ACLs provide the necessary control logic that either permits or denies traffic based upon communicating protocols, requested service ports to carry the traffic, and by user or process identification and authentication. One issue with the management of ACLs is simply implementing them correctly within the router, firewall, or other access control server. One simple mistake within a Cisco router, for example, can cause the access list to function incorrectly or not at all. One of the most common mistakes introduced when working with Cisco ACLs is incorrectly using the IP ACCESS-GROUP *nn* OUT or IP ACCESS-GROUP *nn* IN command on the interface. Just as common is the fact that many times ACLs are defined, but are never applied to an interface—therefore, they are not doing their job. If the access list is defined on the router but not applied to any interfaces, it is ineffectual. The danger is that a novice reviewing the Cisco configuration file may see the access list defined and incorrectly assume that it is functioning without verifying that it has been appropriately applied to the correct interface.

Do's and Don'ts: *Periodically check your ACLs to make sure they are accurate and applied to the proper interfaces.*

Often, the ACL is one of the first things to be removed when troubleshooting network connectivity or application issues. This may temporarily assist with troubleshooting, but what happens when the troubleshooting is over? It is imperative to periodically check access lists to ensure they are functioning correctly and have not been removed or tampered with.

Firewalls

Managing firewalls is no easy task. The firewall administrator faces many challenges when managing and operating firewalls dispersed throughout the organization. In recent years the interfaces have become user-friendlier, but managing multiple firewalls is still a difficult task.

One of the major tasks the firewall administrator faces is not even a complex technical issue. This is the issue of understanding a user's request to open the firewall (changing the firewall rule set). Often the user has only a vague idea of what needs to be accomplished.

Develop a firewall change request form and have the users fill it out and sign it before making the appropriate changes. Depending on the environment, it may be prudent to have the changes authorized. Also, follow existing change management procedures when modifying the firewall. This documents the change and makes it easier to troubleshoot should something break along the way. For more details on change management, review the previous section in this chapter.

Do's and Don'ts: *When making modifications to your firewall rule, set follow a change management process and have the user(s) fill out a firewall change request.*

The firewall change request form should include, at a minimum, the following information:

- Point of contact for the change
- Name of the project the change is associated with, including the project manager and one or more technical contacts who can answer details about the change

- Details about the application (application name, port number, port type, and so on), including how it authenticates users and manages access control in keeping with the organization's security policy
- List of IP addresses and network masks for both internal and external entities (servers, clients, client network, and so on)

The firewall management console must also be secured. This management console should be protected from both a network perspective (logical) and a physical perspective. If your firewall is managed via a general-purpose computer system acting as your management server, make sure the management server operating system is hardened and ensure that physical access to the server is highly restricted. Also, ensure that the management server is powered via UPS and placed in a controlled environment such as your Network Operations Center (NOC).

Firewall log analysis is another change associated with managing firewalls. The security administrator may elect to manage the logs via the provided firewall interface, but this can be cumbersome. If the firewall has a high volume of traffic and it is important to parse and report on the information, consider implementing a firewall log analysis and reporting product from one of the vendors listed in Table 14-6. These tools archive the log files into a database format and can be used to generate periodic or on-demand reports.

Restrict Physical Access

Make sure physical access is restricted to network elements. Are your wiring closets locked, or did you place key routers or switches in bathrooms? As with operating systems, if you lose physical access control to network elements, their security can easily be defeated. With physical access an attacker could pull the plug and create a quick and easy Denial of Service (DoS), copy the configuration after rebooting the device, or connect a packet sniffer and monitor sensitive traffic.

Table 14-6

Firewall Log Analysis and Reporting Products

Description	Security Web Site
WebTrends Firewall Suite	**http://www.webtrends.com**
Telemate.net NetSpective	**http://www.telemate.net**

Case Study Overview

The objectives of the following case study analyses are to apply the security management principles discussed in this chapter and offer a valid strategy for their deployment based upon industry best practices. Although each of the following case study analyses provides a summary of the issues pertaining to that case study, it is advised that the reader review the case studies originally detailed in Chapter 1 prior to continuing.

Analysis of Case Study #1—Corporate

MCC primarily employs Microsoft Windows NT Workstation as the predominant desktop operating system among its user population. File and print sharing is based upon Novell and most application servers are operated on either Sun Microsystems' Solaris platform or IBM's AIX UNIX operating system. Management has tagged e-mail as a critical application as both its messaging and attachments are key forms of communication within the company. Redundant Internet connections service access to the Web for both office-based and mobile employees who connect to the company by VPN access. Internet-facing systems have been segregated from Intranet-based systems by the establishment of a Demilitarized Zone (DMZ). Enterprise Resource Planning (ERP) applications such as SAP, Oracle, and PeopleSoft are in use.

From the case study analysis in Chapter 5 we learned that MCC would employ the use of strong authentication, encryption technology, and strict application controls. The strong authentication will be required for remote users accessing the corporate VPN gateways. Although soft tokens have been chosen over hard tokens due to cost reasons, a process will still need to be built in order to support the management and maintenance of this system. From a security operations perspective, the process will need to be documented starting with the user's request for access and ending with the turnover of the documentation to the end users. The steps will include the following:

1. The end user contacts help desk to request access to the VPN.
2. The end user is directed to an online, Web-based form to fill out for access.

3. The online form includes a review of the remote access security policy (the user must review and agree to this policy before the form is processed).
4. The access form is forwarded via e-mail to the user's manager for approval.
5. The manager forwards the request and approval onto the security administration team.
6. The security administration team verifies that capacity is available and configures new account.
7. Once the account is created, the end user is notified via e-mail.
8. The e-mail notification includes detailed instructions for configuration and access to the VPN.
9. The user is provided authentication information (if any additional is needed, such as an initial password) through an out-of-band mechanism, such as a telephone call.

The security operations teams will also document the specific client-side hardware and configuration parameters that will be accepted during the deployment process. One of the challenges of the security operations team will be to ensure that the requirement to disable split tunneling is adhered to. Split tunneling enables the user to connect back into the corporate MCC network, while still connecting to the Internet. This has obvious security implications and is against the MCC remote access policy. By using a VPN solution that does not provide split tunneling and by using the Microsoft SMS logs, the security of the VPN solution will be enhanced. The operations team will need to periodically review the Microsoft SMS logs and compare them with system configurations to ensure that the SMS system is truly disabling their login if it detects multiple adapters.

The security operations team will also need to manage and maintain the VPN devices. This will include the following:

- Ensure that the VPN devices are in a secure, controlled environment.
- Configure administrator accounts (including separate levels for super administrators vs. administrators who only have access to create new user accounts).
- Enforce strict password restrictions on accounts (both administrator accounts and user accounts).

- Configure Simple Network Management Protocol (SNMP) management on the VPN devices and make sure the network management stations at the NOC are monitoring them properly.
- Monitor security alerts and ensure that the code versions of the VPN devices are at the most recent level.

Password aging and complexity restrictions will be used to enhance the authentication of internal systems. Because the accounts that have not been changed after the 45-day cycle will be disabled and managerial approval will be required to reinstate such accounts, the security operations team will also need to create and manage the approval process and procedures for reinstating these accounts.

MCC has had several challenges dealing with system logs. One of the issues has been synchronizing time across the different platforms. This was necessary in order to correlate the logs across the organization. By designing a redundant NTP architecture that relies on GPS satellite receivers, they were able to create a reliable time infrastructure at a relatively low cost. This architecture has successfully created a reliable time service used by IDSs, firewalls, e-mail, network elements, file and print servers, and application servers.

Analysis of Case Study #2—FinApp

MCC has developed a financial application (FinAPP) that provides commodities futures to clients as well as post-trade statements and personal account information. The FinApp system not only requires strong security protection, but it must also be highly reliable and available. System downtime is reported to equal $500K per minute; hence, redundant network and application services have been deployed in its protection. The requirement to record all trades and provide non-repudiation to ensure identification for trading requests presents an interesting challenge to the security operations team.

Like Case Study #1, strong authentication via soft tokens will be used. Server-side SSL (128-bit) technology will be used to encrypt authenticated sessions using the Web user interface to the FinApp application, and application controls will restrict user access by both user account and group assignment creating separate containers of data for different access levels (for example, employees and institutional brokerage firms).

Security operations will need to monitor and maintain all firewalls and their associated rule sets. In addition, they will need to monitor and manage a network-based and host-based ID system that will monitor and report suspicious activity.

As in Case Study #1, the security operations team will be responsible for business continuity and disaster recovery. This will include creating the appropriate contingency and recovery plans.

Security event management and network management will be key elements in maintaining the availability of the FinApp application. The security team will develop policies and procedures that will identify the roles and responsibilities of operations and security staff. In addition, security incident and response procedures will be developed that will document the procedures used to identify, document, and respond to security incidents.

Analysis of Case Study #3—HealthApp

MCC has a health insurance line of business (LOB) that is responsible for providing nationwide health care services. An initiative to automate claims processing and broker quotes and to provide MCC members with online access to their statements is in place this year. The HealthApp Web-based portal provides its users with a content aggregation and delivery from a centralized point (one entry point for all the user base).

In order to provide the level of security demanded by this solution, HealthApp and its surrounding security infrastructure will be designed, deployed, and operated with HIPPA standards and guidelines in mind.

Strong authentication with tokens will not be used in this application due to the increased complexity. However, the system will utilize complex passwords that will change on a regular basis. In addition, server-side SSL (128-bit) will be used to encrypt data in transit between the Web application server and the user as well as ensure the integrity of the data delivered to the user's desktop. Because the passwords will be changed on a regular basis, the security operations staff will be ready to handle the increased workload once HealthApp is rolled out. They will also use a security question to verify the identity of a user when changing a password after a user has been locked out. This security question will be taken from the user's original access form and entered into an encrypted SQL database. The user will get to initially choose the security question (for example, "What is your childhood pet's name?" "What is your mother's maiden name?" and so on).

The HealthApp Web servers will exist in a DMZ behind a firewall. In addition, a network-based and host-based intrusion detection system will be deployed to report any intrusions. The security operations team will be responsible for managing and maintaining all of these systems to include

- Managing and maintaining administrator accounts on the firewalls and IDSs
- Managing and maintaining the rule sets on the firewalls
- Maintaining appropriate patch levels on the firewalls and IDSs
- Monitoring the IDS for security breaches and following the proper security incident processes

The security operations team will also be responsible for the following:

- Maintaining security patches on all devices (routers, switches, firewalls, application servers, database servers, and so on)
- Managing the data encryption schemes on the application and database servers
- Managing the business continuity and disaster recovery plans (including tape backup of the application and database servers as well as managing the off-site tape storage and rotation)

They will also document the roles and responsibilities of the network operations and security staff as well as the appropriate steps to follow in disaster recovery, security incident management, and change management.

Conclusion

Security management is a complex and never-ending task. It is also the most important aspect to maintaining an organization's security infrastructure and reducing the overall risk and exposure for the organization. Although future advancements in technology will continue to improve the overall landscape of security management, the human factor will remain an integral part of maintaining the organization's overall security posture.

References

Sniffing (network wiretap, sniffer) FAQ, by Robert Graham. **http://www.robertgraham.com/pubs/sniffing-faq.html**

CHAPTER 15

Validation and Maturity

The security architecture planning, deployment, and operational processes are at the end of their life cycle. The resilience of the security architecture to internal and external attackers needs to be validated. Technology is always changing; new applications are being developed, new platforms are being added into the Demilitarized Zone (DMZ), and additional ports are being punched in the firewall. The time to market for many applications is shortening due to competition. Software development life cycles are to the point where the testing and quality assurances are being overlooked. Many large organizations don't even have a complete inventory of machines, network devices, and applications running on the network, let alone the configuration of these components. Application exploits will continue to occur because security testing is not part of software quality assurance.

A security assessment validates that the security architecture meets or exceeds the security policies and the best business practices. One of the problems with typical security assessment findings is that they are often not applicable to the business impact. This chapter uses a concept called the security maturity model (SMM) to adequately measure a given criterion based on the best business practices in the industry and tie it back to the business. It also provides a methodology for improvement by including a list of deficiencies. The security maturity model will measure the three different parts of the MCC security architecture: the planning, the technology and configuration, and the operational processes. The physical security component of this analysis will not be covered in this chapter.

From a business standpoint, the most cost-effective solution provides the best security solution (best practice based on the particular industry). The security controls in any system should be commensurate with the business risks. However, the process to determine which security controls are appropriate and cost effective is quite often a complex and sometimes even subjective matter. One of the prime functions of security risk analysis is to put this process onto a more objective basis.

Risk Management

Risk management is the process of identifying, assessing, and mitigating risk. An organization has many individuals who are responsible for accepting the given risk for given applications. These individuals include the president, CFO, head of the business unit, and the information owner. The overall risk to an organization is dependent on the following attributes:

- The qualitative (effect of loss) and quantitative (monetary) value of the assets
- The likelihood of attack-based threats
- The business impact, if the threat is realized

The ability to associate a cost with an asset's value or to determine the Return On Investment (ROI) is often difficult. The converse of that is to justify the cost of the protection mechanisms. Classified national security information is valued as extremely sensitive. It's so sensitive that if it got in the wrong hands it could result in extreme damage to the national security of the U.S. The price the government is willing to spend to protect that information is typically much more than commercial-based organizations are willing to spend. This is because the cost of securing this data does not come from off the bottom line of the government's bottom line (the government is a not-for-profit business).

The direct quantitative costs include the replacement of damaged equipment, cost of restoring any backups, hard disks, and memory. The downtime suffered by the incident is measurable. Many financial trading systems have an associated cost of being offline (for example $100,000 per minute). Productivity can also be lost; if the e-mail or voice mail servers are down, most organizations' productivity will come to a standstill.

Qualitative costs can be more devastating to organizations than quantitative costs. If a retail Web site was broken into by a hacker and all of the client credit card numbers were stolen, this would seriously affect the site's reputation. In all likelihood, the site would be out of business within a short time (for example, CD Universe). If a state-run agency is operating an online business that requires a license (for example, life insurance) and the site shows a sign of negligence (no Internet firewall), then the state could take away the site's license. This could potentially put it out of business.

Do's and Don'ts: *A standard rule of thumb in the security industry is that the cost of the commercial security solution should never exceed more than 15 percent of the total system cost.*

Risks are assessed by examining the likelihood of a threat and vulnerability and by considering the potential impact of an unwanted incident. The threat level is determined by the incentive of the individual (typically thrill-seeking, espionage, or revenge) and his or her ability. Most insiders are not *that* capable to use automated hacker tools. They are, however, very familiar with the applications on the network. Typically, employees on their way out the door delete files or cause some physical damage. Some cases of logic bombs have been reported; these are software programs that once activated by a specific date, eat through files or reformat hard drives.

The vulnerability level is the inverse of the capability of the security architecture to protect an organization's assets (security controls). If the security controls are weak, then the exposure level will be high; this linked with opportunity can spell disaster. The likelihood of an exploit and vulnerability to the data/resource depend on the following attributes, which are difficult to predict:

- Assets value
- Attractiveness to adversaries
- The technology changes
- Network and processor speed
- Software exploits

The best way to describe threats and vulnerabilities is in terms of the business impact. In addition, the impact assessed for a particular risk also has an associated uncertainty as the unwanted incident may not turn out as expected. This impact could be on the specific line of business or the organization at large; it all depends on the level of exposure. All these factors may have a large amount of uncertainty as to the accuracy of the predictions associated with them. Planning and the justification of security can be very difficult. See Figure 15-1 for the risk assessment methodology.

Do's and Don'ts: *The security architecture should provide an acceptable level of risk for the organization to be successful.*

Figure 15-1

Risk assessment methodology

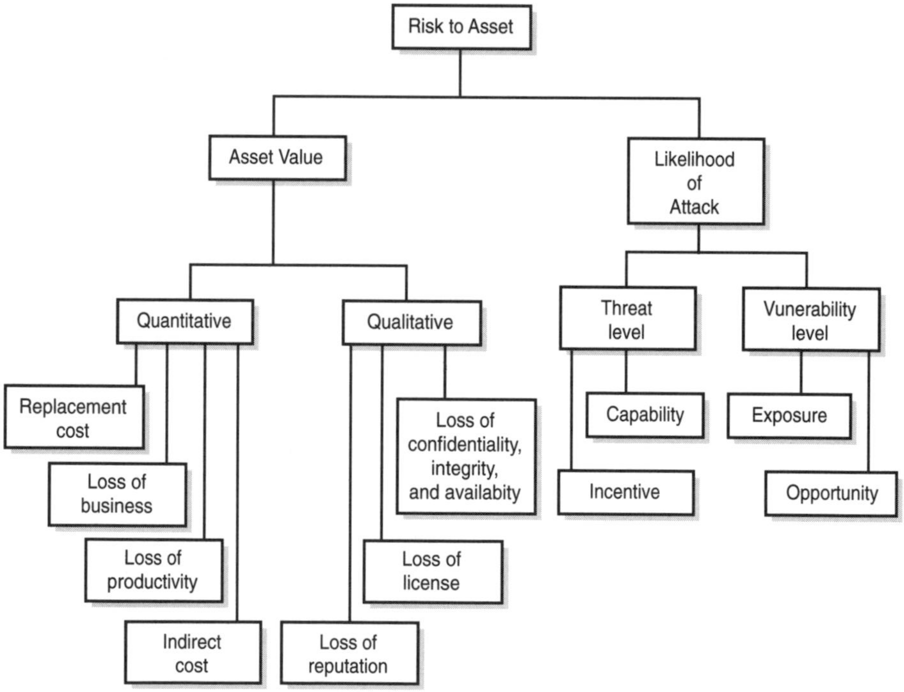

Security Maturity Model

The intent of a maturity model is to measure the capability and effectiveness of organization solutions (software, hardware, and system). In this case, the security assessment methodology is used to measure the MCC security architecture against the best practices in the industry. Three aspects will be analyzed: the planning, the technology and configuration, and the operational processes. The security planning includes security policies, standards, and guidelines, as well as the security requirements that are behind the components. The technology and configuration maturity level refers to the specific products that where chosen, the criteria, and their placement within the organization and product configuration. The operational processes include change management, alerting and monitoring, and security educational aspects. The background material for this section references some of the work in the Systems Security Engineering Capability Maturity Model (SSE-CMM) from the Software Engineering Institute (SEI) at Carnegie Mellon University.

Most organizations demand to know how their security solution stacks up to other vertical businesses' security solutions. Four capability levels are required to adequately rate the security architecture. These are listed in Table 15-1.

Table 15-1 Security Maturity Capability Levels

Security Maturity Capability Level	Description
Not effective (50 percent)	The overall security architecture is not addressing the corporate security policies, regulatory concerns, and best business practices.
Needs improvement (65 percent)	The security architecture is less than 35 percent effective.
Adequate (less than 85 percent)	The security architecture meets the overall goals put forth by the corporate security planning, deployment, and, configuration and process controls.
Excellent (over 100 percent)	The security architecture exceeds all the planning, deployment, and configuration and process controls.

Security Planning

All first-class security architectures are built from a solid plan. Chapters 2 through 5 of this book cover the typical security planning that go into building resilient security architectures. The planning documents must be well written and complete. Many organization security policies, standards, and guidelines suffer from the following problems:

- They are too old and therefore not applicable to today's applications. Policies should be updated yearly to keep up with the technological changes.
- The language is open to many interpretations. These documents have many users, such as developers, risk managers, and auditors. If the statements are too abstract, then the enforcement will be ineffective.
- Not enough detail is present. Many organizations' idea of a security policy is one of password management. The most common absent document of organizations' security policies is the information classification and access control planning document.
- The user needs to be aware of the existence of documentation. Some organizations keep the security-related documentation in a locked cabinet whereas others post theirs on an Intranet Web site. Anyone who is responsible for security at an organization (meaning everyone) should be aware of the policies. If an employee is unaware of the policy statement (for example, not viewing pornographic Web sites), he or she is not held liable if an incident occurs.

Technology and Configuration

Today, the market has a myriad of security vendors and products. No single product from a vendor provides a complete security solution. Many point solutions are available (such as firewalls, IDS, VPN, authentication servers, and so on) that solve a limited set of problems. The ability to properly choose the right set of products, place them correctly within the infrastructure, configure them properly, and support them is the goal of a security professional. Many individuals procure security equipment for the wrong reasons. For example, some people think that putting a firewall in front of a valuable asset will protect it. This is partially true from a network standpoint, but a firewall does not provide application and platform protection. Firewalls also do not provide useful intrusion detection information.

The proper configuration of security products is challenging. Out of the box, the default configuration of the product is to deny all access. Only explicitly allowed rules will pass traffic. The most challenging part of configuring a security device is to retain the knowledgeable staff that manages it. An example of determining the maturity level for an application is covered in the case studies at the end of the chapter.

Operational Processes

The operational processes include the necessary support and maintenance required by security components, change management, business continuity, security awareness training for users and security administrators, and security alerting and monitoring. The support and maintenance involved with security infrastructure components are analogous to the support required by mainframes and application servers. An agreed upon change management process that has a facility to roll back to a working revision must be present. This must work in concert with a business continuity plan.

Security equipment tends to generate an inordinate amount of logging information. Security equipment is complex to administer; one misconfiguration will prevent access to the network, application, or platform. Product training for multiple individuals is key to the success of any security architecture. Lastly, the ability to identify a security incident and react accordingly with an escalation procedure is paramount.

Technology is moving at a very fast pace. It is hard enough for members of the staff who have dedicated their careers to security, never mind the average employee. Security-aware employees are the key to an effective information security program. A good security awareness program uses a combination of the following media:

- Custom prepared newsletters
- Custom and commercially available video presentations
- Presentations
- Security Awareness Days
- Posters in common areas (lunch room and elevator lobby)

Every employee, from the CEO to the mailroom clerk, should receive this training. Because of this requirement, separate key messages should be targeted to specific audiences (system and security administrators, end users, and data owners).

Threats

A threat is any of the capabilities, intentions, and attack methods of adversaries to exploit or cause harm to information or a system. Threats are further defined as being passive (monitoring but no alteration of data) and active (deliberate alteration of information). The negative effect a threat can have on the secure operations of an information system is referred to as a threat consequence. Four common threat consequences are defined as follows:

- **Disclosure** If information or data is revealed to unauthorized persons (breach of confidentiality)
- **Deception** If corporate information is altered in an unauthorized manner (system or data integrity violation)
- **Disruption** If corporate resources are rendered unusable or unavailable to authorized users (denial of service)
- **Usurpation** If the corporate resources are misused by unauthorized persons (violation of authorization)

A threat action is the potential cause for a threat consequence. For example, an intruder penetrating a system's security perimeter may cause disclosure of proprietary information. In this case, the penetration represents a threat action that could result in the threat consequence of disclosure. Lastly, a threat agent is the source of actions, methods, or elements used to exploit vulnerability in an information system, operation, or facility (for example, a hostile outsider, authorized operator, natural disasters, human engineering, and so on).

Threat Agent Examples

Understanding the source of a threat is key to understanding how to reduce the likelihood that a particular threat may be realized. The following sub sections detail sources of threats that you should be familiar with.

Human Errors and Design Faults

The largest source of losses is unintentional human actions during operations. Some experts estimate that over one-half of the total financial and productivity losses in information systems are the result of human errors, as opposed to intentional and malicious acts. These errors include improperly installing and managing equipment or software, accidentally erasing files, updating the wrong file, transposing numbers, entering incorrect information in files, neglecting to change a password or back up a hard disk, and other acts that cause loss of information, interruptions, and so forth.

Many of these and other circumstances are arguably due to faults in design that do not prevent many common human errors (or other threats) from resulting in losses. An unusual, but legitimate, sequence of events also can reveal vulnerability in a system design. Such design errors may come with off-the-shelf software or hardware or may be built into the system by the network managers.

Insiders

Many violations of information safeguards are performed by trusted personnel who engage in unauthorized activities or activities that exceed their authority (abusing their access). Motives range from curiosity to spite to profit. The insiders may copy, steal, or sabotage information, yet their actions may remain undetected. The individuals can hold clearances or other authorizations, or may be able to disable network operations or otherwise violate safeguards through actions that require no special authorization. By most industry metrics, insiders perpetrate upwards of 70 to 80 percent of serious security violations.

Temporary Employees

Outside consultants, contractors, and temporary workers must be subject to the same basic information security requirements and have the same information security responsibilities as regular employees, but they may also be subject to additional restrictions. For example, the signing of an information security compliance agreement and receiving the proper security awareness training apply to both regular and temporary employees. In addition, temporary employees must be bound by specific agreements and have access only to the information and systems needed to perform their assignments.

Natural Disasters and Environmental Damage

Environmental extremes such as very high or very low temperatures, high humidity, windstorms, tornadoes, lightening, flooding, rain, fire, and earthquakes can destroy both the main information facilities as well as their backup systems. These issues are normally addressed by disaster recovery plans, which are outside the scope of this analysis.

Crackers, Hackers, and Other Intruders

A smaller but growing number of violations come from unauthorized *crackers* who may intrude for monetary gain, industrial secrets, or for the sheer challenge of breaking into or sabotaging a system. This group often employs sophisticated attacks and receives the most sensational treatment in the press. This group includes teenage hackers breaking into remote systems (such as workstations, servers, PBXs, and routers) as well as professional criminals, industrial espionage, organized crime, or foreign intelligence agencies.

Viruses and Other Malicious Software

Viruses, worms, Trojan horses, and other malicious software can enter a network through borrowed diskettes, prepackaged software, electronic mail, and connections to other networks. These hazards could also be a result of human error (negligence), insiders, or intruders.

Threat Scenarios and Countermeasures

The ability to apply countermeasures to avert the numerous threat scenarios that are possible first implies that you not only understand the source of the threat, but also how it functions to infiltrate your security architecture.

Social Engineering (System Administration Process)

A social engineering attack involves impersonating an employee with known authority, either in person (disguised) or by using an electronic means of communication (e-mail, fax, or the telephone). Examples of such attacks are

- An e-mail is sent by an attacker claiming to be the root of a system, informing all the users to change their passwords to an exposed password.
- An attacker places a phone call to the system administrator claiming to be a corporate executive who has lost the modem pool number and forgotten the password.
- A computer maintenance person falsifies a visit and is admitted into the computer room where he/she has access to the system console.
- Permanent storage media, such as hard disks and diskettes, containing confidential information may be discarded or improperly labeled and become available to unauthorized recipients pretending to collect the trash.

All of the four threat consequences are susceptible to these attacks.

Social engineering safeguards consist mostly of non-technical (procedural) means. Each of the following safeguards counters the corresponding aforementioned attack: 1) security awareness training for all corporate users, 2) security awareness training for all system administration personnel with well-documented procedures, handling, and reporting, and 3) security awareness training for personnel responsible for allowing outside visitors into restricted areas (such as assigned escorts).

Electronic Eavesdropping (Sniffing and Snooping)

The Internet protocol suite was not designed with security in mind. TELNET, FTP, SMTP, and other TCP/IP-based applications are susceptible to passive wire-tapping. User authentication information (such as username and password pairs) are easily sniffed off the network and used by outsiders to impersonate authorized employees. If an outsider gains physical access to a corporate facility by placing a portable computer with a cellular modem on the LAN or hub, all data traveling over the LAN and hub is susceptible to any threat consequence. In addition, if an outsider gains electronic access into a workstation running a server process with an attached modem, he/she could use this as an entry point into the corporate network. Any data that is transferred over the Internet is vulnerable to a disclosure threat. All of the four threat consequences are susceptible to these attacks.

Eavesdropping safeguards consist of authentication and encryption. One approach to provide strong authentication uses two-factor authentication. This is typically composed of a physical token that has encoded information about the user who is authorized to carry it and a user's personal identification number (PIN) and/or password. Encryption provides a safeguard against impersonation by protecting passwords and ID in transmission. Link encryption (SSL and Ipv6) provides protection of information while in transit between two systems that are directly connected by a physical or logical communications path (dedicated wire running between two systems or a virtual circuit in a circuit-switched communications system). Application encryption (Secure Telnet and FTP, S/MIME) provides protection of messages that are encrypted at the source and decrypted only at the destination. Digital signatures verify the authenticity of the sender and the integrity of the message in combination with hash algorithms.

Software Exploits

The two biggest software exploits to date are buffer overflow and denial of service attacks. A buffer overflow occurs when you write too much data, usually a string of characters, into a fixed length buffer. Insufficient bounds checking on the data buffer used for input allows the incoming variable to exceed the buffer size, overwriting the contents of memory beyond the end of the buffer. Typically, the system crashes due to a program trying to access an illegal addresses. However, it might be possible to craft a data string that, instead of creating detectable errors, causes particular system exploits desired by the attacker. The Carnegie Mellon Software Engineering Institute's Computer Emergency Response Team (CERT) has over 196 documented buffer overflow-related advisories: for example, Microsoft's Terminal server, Outlook Express, Internet Information Server, as well as well-known network services like Network Time Protocol (NTP) Sendmail, BIND, Secure Shell (SSH) v1.37, and Kerberos.

A denial of service (DoS) attack makes the target system's responsiveness slow to completely unavailable, preventing legitimate processing from occurring. This could come about for many reasons such as

- Programming mistakes that take 100 percent of Central Processing Unit (CPU) time.
- System memory usage may continually increase because of a memory leak.
- Malformed data requests such as Web requests or remote procedure calls (RPCs).
- Large packets such as e-mail addresses and Internet Control Message Protocol (ICMP) requests.
- Non-stop network traffic User Datagram Protocol (UDP) and ICMP (broadcast storms and network flooding).
- Forging routing information or unresponsive connection requests.
- Misconfigured wiring, power, router, platform, or application.

CERT has over 318 documented DoS type attacks on various application and platform operating systems. In most cases, the attacker has compromised the machine that is performing the attack. This makes it very difficult to prosecute the individual performing the attack.

Transitive Trust (Trusted Relationships Between Hosts)

Transitive trust delegates the trust relationship to a trusted intermediary. Once an outsider compromises a machine trusted by the intermediary, all other hosts or servers are easily compromised. Examples of such attacks are

- The misuse of an .rhosts file enables a compromised machine to attack any machine in the .rhosts file without passwords.
- If an outside user impersonates a network operating system user or server, all other servers that trust that particular user or server are vulnerable.
- A network of workstations share files via Network File System (NFS). If one of the client workstations is compromised, an attacker can create privileged executables on the file system server. Then the

attacker can log on the server as a normal user and execute the privileged commands.

All of the four threat consequences are susceptible to these attacks.

Transitive trust safeguards consist primarily of non-technical means. Most UNIX environments (non-DCE) offer *no* automated mechanisms for trust delegation. Therefore system administration personnel must take special care in mapping out relationships between hosts.

Data-Driven Attacks (Malicious Software)

Data-driven attacks result from malicious software embedded in data file formats (for example, postscript files, MS Word basic commands within documents, shell scripts, downloaded viruses, or malicious programs). Examples of such attacks are

- An attacker mails a postscript file with file operations that add the attacker's host identifier to the .rhosts file or opens an MS Word document with Word basic commands that can access any function in a Windows dynamic link library (DLL), including Winsock.dll.
- An attacker mails a postscript file that stays resident in a postscript-based fax server and then sends the attacker a copy of each fax that is transmitted and received.
- A user downloads shell scripts or malicious software off the Net that e-mails the victim's password file to the attacker and deletes all the victim's files.
- HTTP browsers can be employed to package malicious programs (Trojan horses): for example, "click on this icon to infect your machine."

All of the four threat consequences are susceptible to these attacks.

Denial of Service

DoS attacks do not exploit a software bug, but rather a shortcoming in the implementation of a particular protocol. These attacks disable computing platforms and network devices by interrupting and overloading particular network ports, applications (such as SMTP agents), and operating system kernels. Examples of some of these attacks are TCP SYN flooding, ICMP bombing, e-mail spamming, Web spoofing, the Ping o' Death, and Domain Name Service (DNS) hijacking. Most of these attacks can be avoided by keeping the computing platforms and network device software up to date. Some of these attacks require additional network-filtering systems such as network firewalls.

DNS Spoofing

The Domain Name System (DNS) is a distributed database that is used by TCP/IP applications to map between host names and IP addressees, and to provide e-mail routing information. If the binding process (mapping Internet address numbers to domain names) can be compromised, then the names cannot be trusted. The vulnerable points are a corrupted sender, a corrupted receiver, a corrupted intermediary, and an attack by a service provider. For example, if an attacker owns or compromises a DNS server and adds a host relation that is contained in a victim's .rhosts file, the attacker can simply log in to access the victim's host.

DNS attack safeguards consist of network firewalls and procedural means. The network firewall security mechanism relies on dual DNS servers, inside and outside (public) the corporate network. This would limit an attacker from knowing the IP addresses of the internal network's hosts and harden the internal DNS service. The Internet Engineering Task Force (IETF) is currently working on standard security mechanisms (authentication) to protect DNS. Procedural means of combating these attacks are to not rely on DNS for security-critical decisions.

Source Routing

Normally, IP routing is dynamic with each router making a decision about which hop to send the datagram to next. IP optionally allows the sender to specify the route. Strict source routing relies on the sender providing the *exact* path that the IP datagram must follow. Loose source routing relies on the sender providing a minimum list of IP addresses that the datagram must transverse. An attacker would first disable the victim's trusted host, spoof its IP address, and then use source routing to control the route to the attacked host. The victim's target host thinks the packets are coming from the victim's trusted host. Source-routing attack safeguards consist of network firewalls and router screening. Routers and firewalls can block source-routed packets into the corporate networks.

Insider Threat Scenarios

Insider threat scenarios consist of the aforementioned threat scenarios when perpetrated by insiders. Most computer security statistics show that insiders commit over 70 to 80 percent of all computer-related fraud. Insiders often have a motive to strike against a company, direct physical access to the computer and network, and familiarity with the resource access controls. The principal threat at the application level is the abuse/misuse of authority by authorized personnel. The network level threat is due to physical access to the LAN that provides insiders with the ability to view sensitive data traversing the network.

To combat insider threats, one has to employ some basic security concepts of separation of duties, least privilege, and individual accountability. Separation of duties is the practice of dividing the steps in a critical function (for example, approving monetary transactions, audit reviews, or wiretap approval) among different individuals. The least privilege principle is the practice of restricting a user's access to only those resources that are required in order for the user to perform his/her job. These resource access models might include file access (read, write, execute, or delete), or processing capability (ability to spawn or kill processes on a system) for example. Individual accountability consists of holding individuals responsible for their actions. Accountability is normally accomplished by identifying and authenticating users of the system and subsequently tracing actions on the system to the user who initiated them.

Security Assessment Methodology

The capability levels of the current security architecture will be assessed for three aspects of the security maturity model: the planning, deployment and configuration, and operational process. The first step in the methodology is the discovery phase. All the applicable documentation pertaining the security architecture must be reviewed. This includes security policies, standards, and guidelines; information classification and access control plans; and application security requirements. The overall infrastructure security design is also required. This will include the network partitioning design; the firewall rule set; the intrusion detection configuration; platform-hardening standards, the network, and the application server configurations.

The second step of the assessment phase is a manual inspection. The idea is to compare the documented architecture with the actual one. Typically, a difference appears between what is documented and what is deployed (the should verses the is). This effort can be accomplished using manual and automated methods. Network and platform discovery tools are available that can be executed on the inside of a network to map out all the network paths and detail the host operating system types and version number. The tool NetSleuth is an IP reachability analyzer that provides a detailed network inventory down to the port level. Tools like QUESO and NMAP have the capability to scan all the ports on a host and attempt to identify the type of device and version of software.

The next phase is a vulnerability test. This is a systematic review that determines the adequacy of security measures, identifies security deficiencies, and evaluates the effectiveness of existing and planned safeguards. The first step typically includes a network, platform, and application vulnerability test. The objective of a network vulnerability test (known as penetration [pen] testing) is to investigate the system from the attacker's perspective. This can occur from within an organization's Intranet (inside/out) or external from the Internet, or an Extranet partner inbound to the organization (outside/in). The tools used for pen testing are usually a mixture of commercial tools (such as ISS scanner and Cisco NetSonar) and publicly available tools (such as Nessus and NMAP). Pen test tools all work the same way. First they scan all the network ports on a given network component (for example, a firewall, router, VPN gateway, and platform). Once they detect an open port (one that will respond to the network request), they will try all the known exploits against that port (for example, buffer overflow in Microsoft IIS 5.0, Kerberos, SSH daemon, and Sun Solstice AdminSuite Daemon). Most of the commercial products are able to generate a detailed report of the well-known exploit categorized by the risk level (low, medium, and high) depending on the damage that could occur if the exploit were successful.

The second step in the vulnerability analysis is a platform scan. Platform scanning (or system scanning) verifies that the configuration is compliant with a given security policy. In addition, it detects any security vulnerabilities and misconfigurations (such as insecure file protections—registry or configuration directory) and exploitable network services (such as HTTP, FTP, DNS, SMTP, and so on). Once a secure build (refer to the discussion of platform hardening in Chapter 9) has been established, the system scanner will form a foundation (baseline). This baseline can be monitored at a scheduled time to detect any significant changes (for example, a home page was replaced with a file, defacing the Web site). The system scan will also check to see if the system is susceptible to any recent exploits.

The third step in the vulnerability analysis is an application scan. Application scanning tools are not as automated as network or platform tools; therefore, this is a manual process. The idea is to simulate how an attacker would try to misuse the application if he or she were an authorized user.

The last part of the security assessment is to validate the process portion of the security architecture. This consists of automated alerting facilities that rely on a human element. This is the same human element that is responsible for the configuration of all the security architecture components (firewalls, IDS, VPN, and so on). Many theories exist on how security controls are subverted. The most common is human error. Security controls, such as firewalls, rarely fail with an unconstrained filtering (totally open); the network device will not allow any traffic. The main cause of firewalls not operating in a secure fashion is misconfigurations and poor change management process. A typical situation of poor firewall change management procedure is as follows:

1. One of the firewall administrators gets an emergency call in the middle of the night because an application is failing due to the network.
2. The administrator opens up the rule set to see if the firewall is blocking the packets.
3. The application begins to work and the administrator falls back to sleep, forgetting the open rule set.
4. The enterprise gets broken into because the firewall is not performing any access controls.

During the vulnerability analysis test, the security architecture monitoring and alerting facilities should be at their busiest. The testing can be announced before hand to allow the security logs to be purged and to allocate the adequate disk space. Unannounced testing will measure the reaction time of the support staff to notice the increased system logs. It is useful to test the reaction time of Internet service providers, especially if they are responsible for managing the Internet firewall.

The results from the five vulnerability analysis steps are combined and analyzed in an overall risk analysis document. The amount of information produced by the five steps is overwhelming. Many of the automated tool vendors have a built-in report generator to categorize the exploit based on the damage it could cause. The risk analyses information has to then be applied to the business in terms of a business impact statement. For example, the administrator on the database management system (DBMS) server that contains all the product pricing information for all the clients has weak password controls. The case studies at the end of the chapter will provide examples of the aforementioned steps. Many security assessment reports fail to relate the risk analysis back to the business, thus the effort has little to no value (see Figure 15-2).

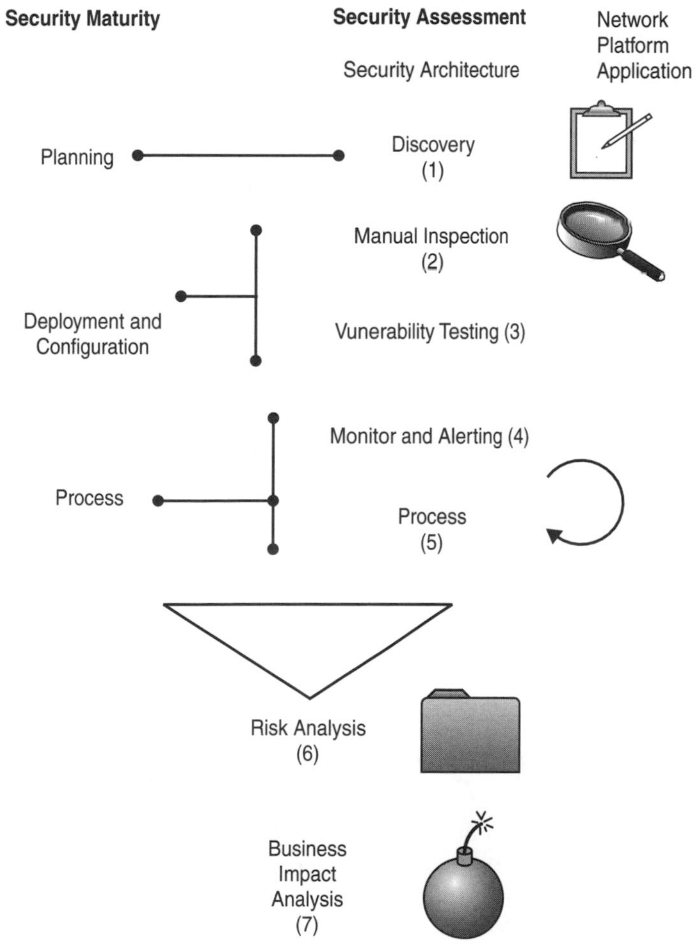

Figure 15-2

Many security assessment reports fail to relate the risk analysis back to the business.

Security Assessment Techniques

To properly perform a security assessment, one must understand the assessment techniques. These techniques test the resilience of the security architecture technology and configuration. The planning and process analysis is performed manually.

Network Security Assessment

The underlying internetworking protocol, TCP/IP, does not have any built-in security mechanisms. Therefore, the majority of network-based applications are insecure. The goal of a network security assessment is to ensure that all the possible network security exploits are closed. Most network security assessments are performed on the publicly accessible machines from an IP address on Internet (for example, the e-mail server, name server (DNS), Web server, FTP, and VPN gateway). Another variation in performing a network assessment is to be given the network topology, firewall rule set, and a list of publicly available servers and their types. Another variation is to do this completely blind like a hacker.

The first step in the network assessment is to understand the network topology. This is complicated if the firewall is blocking traceroute packets. Traceroute is used to map out network topologies. The second step is to acquire the names and IP addresses of the publicly accessible machines. This is easily accomplished using DNS and trying all of the public addresses registered at the American Registry for Internet Numbers (ARIN). The last step in the process is to port scan all the reachable hosts. A port is a term used in TCP/IP and UDP networks to identify an end point to a logical connection. The port number identifies what type of port it is; for example, port 80 is used for HTTP traffic. If a given port responds, then all the known exploits will be attempted. See Table 15-2 for different types of port scanning techniques.

Platform Security Assessment

A platform security assessment is intended to validate the platform configuration (the operating system is not vulnerable to known exploits and its file protection and configuration files are protected adequately). The only way to validate this is by executing a program on the platform itself.

Table 15-2

Port Scanning Techniques

Port Scanning Technique	Description
Vanilla TCP connect	This will open a connection to see if whichever port you are interested in is listening (no special privileges are needed on the attacking host). If the platform, firewall, or IDS is monitoring the packets, it's easy to detect the scanning of ports.
TCP SYN (half open)	This type of scanning does not complete the TCP 3-way handshake (SYN out, Ack back, and Rst out). In most cases, the monitoring will not catch this, but you do need root/admin privilege to control the low-level networking data.
TCP FIN, Xmas, or NULL (stealth) scanning	The TCP protocol specification (RFC 793) specifies that closed port must respond to reset (RST) packets. Using this feature you can detect which ports are open or closed without being detected. Microsoft networking stack will not respond to RST packets; this is another way to identify the type of platform on the network.
TCP FTP proxy (bounce attack) scanning	This technique enables you to use an FTP server to proxy (forward requests) connections into and organization. In other words, you can use an FTP typically located behind a firewall to scan addresses in the inside of the firewall.
TCP ACK and Window scanning	This technique uses an anomaly in some operating systems' networking kernels' TCP window-size reporting.
UDP raw ICMP port unreachable scanning	Many UDP services like SNMP, NFS, TFTP, and DNS are running on platforms. This method sends a zero-byte UDP packet to each port on the target machine. If an unreachable ICMP port is returned, then the port is closed;, otherwise it is assumed to be open.
Direct RPC scanning	This technique uses all the open TCP/UDP ports and floods them with SunRPC program NULL commands. If RPC is running on any of these ports, then the program and versions number will be sent to the attacking machine.
Remote OS identification by TCP/IP fingerprinting	The ability to identify the host operating system and version by its networking stack.

This program is sometimes called an agent because a centralized management program starts it. If the platform was properly hardened, then it will have a baseline configuration (a starting point to reference any changes). The first part of the assessment is to verify that the baseline configuration, operating system, and the network services (FTP, rlogin, Telnet, SSH, and so on) have not changed. One of the first tricks a hacker does is replace these files with hacked versions. These versions generally record the administrator passwords and forward them to the attacker over the Internet. If any of the files need to be patched or a service pack needs to be applied, the agent will notify the manager. The second test is to validate the administrator passwords. Most production machines do *not* allow application users to log into the platform. The users authenticate to the application running on the platform, *not* the platform itself. Another feature of these products is the capability to test the strength (for example, password length, composition, and dictionary attack) of the local passwords. Lastly, they lock down the audit subsystem; before the hacker is done, he or she tries to cover his or her tracks.

Do's and Don'ts: *The only way to adequately harden a platform is to do so with the application running; often you can harden a platform to a point where the application will not work.*

Database Security Assessment

Database packages are just as vulnerable to out-of-the-box exploits on operating systems. The database administrator (DBA) account is preset to a certain value as well as others. The default username and passwords need to be changed. The password must expire and the password strength must be able to pass the typical checks (for example, dictionary lookup, proper names, and blank passwords). The system privileges granted to the database tables can be baselined and verified so that they meet the security policy.

Do's and Don'ts: *Database security assessments always occur with internal assessments; direct access to the DBMS from an untrusted network must be available.*

Application Security Assessment

Performing an application security assessment is more of an art than using automated tools like network and platform scanning. The goal of a hacker is to gain system access to the application's platform and force the application to perform an action that the user is not authorized to do (absence of normalcy). Many Web-based applications developers use a Common Gateway Interface (CGI) to parse forms; an attacker can use many known exploits to gain access to a Web server platform using CGI exploits (for example, putting extraneous characters such as *:* and *&*).

The biggest risk of a poorly written application is to allow access to the platform it executes on. After an application is compromised, the security architecture must contain the attacker to the platform. Once a machine in the public layer is compromised, it can be used to attack the other machines. The most common method is to install a password sniffer on the compromised machine.

Analysis of Case Study #1—Corporate

MCC just contracted a third-party security group to perform an internal security assessment of the corporate office. The vendor performing the work had access to all the MCC security policies, standards, and guidelines. The vendor interviewed a cross-section of the data owners of some major MCC business units, the IT support contractor, and Extranet partners. Table 15-3 provides a summary of the detailed report findings.

Analysis of Case Study #2—FinApp

The FinApp performed a security assessment using the security maturity model. Table 15-4 shows the SMM on the FinApp planning phase, Table 15-5 shows the technology and configuration, and 15-6 shows the operational processes.

Table 15-3 MCC Security Assessment Findings

Threat	Business Impact	Probability	Countermeasure
Social engineering on the help desk with RAS password resets	All MCC's corporate information and resources could be vulnerable.	Medium: This is typically an easy way into an organization.	Better authentication challenge for password resets
Electronic impersonation due to the use of desktop modems	All MCC's corporate information and resources could be vulnerable.	Medium: The end user controls modem access control.	A centralized modem server or outsourced solution offers stronger authentication.
Software exploits	Few MCC's resources and information	Low	MCC has a secure build for desktops and servers; they also scan their DMZ server frequently.
Transitive trust between UNIX server	All MCC's resources and information	Low	MCC enforces the policy of no transitive trust between platforms.
Data driven	Many of MCC's resources and information	High: Due to WWW and Microsoft's openness between their apps and their operating system	MCC is lacking in virus protection software on the desktop and mail servers.
Denial of Service	All MCC's Internet and Extranet facing servers	Medium: Given the competitive PC networking software companies.	Firewalls cannot defend against DoS attacks.
DNS spoofing	All MCC's resources and information	Medium: Because of the lack of remote authentication devices.	An Internet draft of a secure version of DNS exists, but there is no commercial support for it is available yet.
Source routing	All MCC's resources and information	Low	Firewalls prevent this attack.
Insider threats	All MCC's resources and information	Medium: This threat is very hard to safeguard against.	Procure application that has built-in security. Least privileged, separation of duties, and user accountability must be practiced.

Table 15-4

SMM Planning

Item	Maturity Level	Description
Security policies, standards, and guidelines.	Excellent	The program, information/resource classification, standard access definition, password management, Internet usage, network security, desktop, server, and application security standards were complete and up to date.
Information classification	Adequate	The classification questionnaire was broken out by confidentiality, integrity, repudiation, and available for analyzing applications.
Risk assessment	Adequate	A risk associated with each type of information classification was well defined.
Access control plan	Adequate	The protection mechanism afforded to each type of information/resource classification type was completed for their existing production applications.

Analysis of Case Study #3—HealthApp

MCC just contracted a third-party security group to perform an external penetration test on the HealthApp perimeter. The vendor performing the test was given no prior information. Table 15-7 provides a summary of the detailed report findings by vulnerability. Note: a DoS test was not performed and the IP addresses listed in the table are fictitious.

Table 15-5

SMM—Technology and Configuration

Item	Maturity Level	Description
Three-tier perimeter	Excellent	Three distinct network partitions (public, application, and data layers).
Virtual Private Network gateways	Needs improvement	VPNs are using the public firewalls as the end point; a better solution is a dedicated VPN gateway.
Wireless 802.11b	Needs improvement	Many business units are utilizing this technology for office LANs. There are many security concerns are raised with the wired equivalency privacy (WEP) security.
Platform hardening	Adequate	All the platforms in the public, application, and data layers have been hardened. They also are scanned frequently for compliance.
Intrusion detection system	Not effective	No network or host-based IDS is present anywhere.
Application security	Adequate	FinApp uses a Web access control product that provides the internal application with access to a user's profile for more granular authorization.
Public-key infrastructure	Excellent	Digital certificate are used to sign sensitive transactions.

Table 15-6

SMM—Operational Process

Item	Maturity Level	Description
Security event management	Needs improvement	The events from firewalls are just being monitored. Applications and compliance monitoring are not included.
Security administration	Needs improvement	Log into the UNIX machines in the clear (no Secure Shell). Some of the developers have administrative access to production machines (separation of duty problem).
Security assessment	Needs improvement	The security infrastructure group has the perimeter assessed quarterly. No detailed security architecture has been performed.
Business continuity and disaster recovery	Needs improvement	The disaster recovery and business continuity plan are 3 years old and have never been tested successfully.

Table 15-7 The Detailed Report Findings by Vulnerability

Vulnerability	Severity	Hosts affected	Recommendations
SSHd version 1.3.7 (buffer flow)—the ability to execute command on the affected host.	High	12.39.100.10, 12.39.100.11, 12.39.100.12	Update to SSH version 2.
Public community name is equal to public. This would give an attacker the ability to change system information on network devices.	High	12.39.100.1	Use of a private community names.
IIS5.0 in IIS URL decoding routines—may allow remote attackers to view directory structures, view and delete files, execute arbitrary commands, and deny service to the server.	High	12.39.100.23–12.29.100.25	Apply patch that addresses Microsoft Security Bulletin MS01-026.
rwhod daemon is vulnerable to a buffer overflow—the capability to execute command on the affected host.	Medium	12.39.100.30	Most modern distributions of the affected systems include whod daemons that fix this buffer overflow. Sites that do not use the rwho services should disable this service by commenting it out of the inetd.conf file.
BIND servers can be remotely queried for their version.	Low	12.39.100.10	Refer to the documentation that accompanies BIND on the procedure for disabling the version feature.
Finger service.	Low	12.39.100.1	Disable finger or install a finger service or daemon that limits the type of information provided.

Conclusion

Risks are mitigated by the implementation of safeguards, which may address the threat, the vulnerability, the impact, or the risk itself. However, it is not feasible to mitigate 100 percent of all risks or completely mitigate all of any particular risk. Security assessments are snapshots in time of the state of the system architecture. They need to be performed when the security architecture changes and also periodically (for example, quarterly).

The best practices for the information security field are a collection of the finest solutions that other IT organizations are practicing. Many organizations are struggling with the same problems of securely sharing their data, performing high-value transactions with external parties, and ubiquitous access for their internal employees. It's very challenging to balance the business need and security effectiveness, strength, transparency, and monitoring.

References

Adams, C. and S. Farrell, Internet X.509 Public Key Infrastructure Certificate Management Protocols, RFC 2510, 1999.

ISO/IEC 13335 Information Technology—Security Techniques—Guidelines for the Management of IT Security—Part 1: Concepts and Models, Part 2: Managing and Planning, Part 3: Management Techniques, Part 4: Baseline Control, and Part 5: Safeguards for External Connections. An Introduction to Computer Security: The NIST Handbook, National Institute of Standards and Technology, Technology Administration, U.S. Department of Commerce, 1995.

Canadian Handbook on Information Technology Security MG-9, Communications Security Establishment, Government of Canada, 1998.

Information Security Management, British Standard 7799, British Standards Institute, U.K., 1998.

Systems Security Engineering—Capability Maturity Model, version 2, SSE-CMM Project, **http://www.sse-cmm.org**, 1999.

Index

A

E

J–K

L–M

N

O

P

Q–R

S

T

U

V

W–X

INTERNATIONAL CONTACT INFORMATION

AUSTRALIA
McGraw-Hill Book Company Australia Pty. Ltd.
TEL +61-2-9417-9899
FAX +61-2-9417-5687
http://www.mcgraw-hill.com.au
books-it_sydney@mcgraw-hill.com

CANADA
McGraw-Hill Ryerson Ltd.
TEL +905-430-5000
FAX +905-430-5020
http://www.mcgrawhill.ca

GREECE, MIDDLE EAST, NORTHERN AFRICA
McGraw-Hill Hellas
TEL +30-1-656-0990-3-4
FAX +30-1-654-5525

MEXICO (Also serving Latin America)
McGraw-Hill Interamericana Editores S.A. de C.V.
TEL +525-117-1583
FAX +525-117-1589
http://www.mcgraw-hill.com.mx
fernando_castellanos@mcgraw-hill.com

SINGAPORE (Serving Asia)
McGraw-Hill Book Company
TEL +65-863-1580
FAX +65-862-3354
http://www.mcgraw-hill.com.sg
mghasia@mcgraw-hill.com

SOUTH AFRICA
McGraw-Hill South Africa
TEL +27-11-622-7512
FAX +27-11-622-9045
robyn_swanepoel@mcgraw-hill.com

UNITED KINGDOM & EUROPE (Excluding Southern Europe)
McGraw-Hill Publishing Company
TEL +44-1-628-502500
FAX +44-1-628-770224
http://www.mcgraw-hill.co.uk
computing_neurope@mcgraw-hill.com

ALL OTHER INQUIRIES Contact:
Osborne/McGraw-Hill
TEL +1-510-549-6600
FAX +1-510-883-7600
http://www.osborne.com
omg_international@mcgraw-hill.com

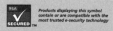

RSA SECURITY™

The Most Trusted Name in e-Security®

The Company

RSA Security Inc. is the most trusted name in e-Security, helping organizations build secure, trusted foundations for e-business through its two-factor authentication, encryption and public key management systems. RSA Security has the market reach, proven leadership and unrivaled technical and systems experience to address the changing security needs of e-business and bring trust to the new online economy.

A truly global company with more than 8,000 customers, RSA Security is renowned for providing technologies that help organizations conduct e-business with confidence. Headquartered in Bedford, Mass., and with offices around the world, RSA Security is a public company (NASDAQ: RSAS) with 2000 revenues of $280 million.

Our Markets and Products

With the proliferation of the Internet and revolutionary new e-business practices, there has never been a more critical need for sophisticated security technologies and solutions. Today, as public and private networks merge and organizations increasingly expand their businesses to the Internet, RSA Security's core offerings are continually evolving to address the critical need for e-Security. As the inventor of leading security technologies, RSA Security is focused on three core disciplines of e-Security, including:

Public Key Infrastructure RSA Keon® public key infrastructure (PKI) solutions are a family of interoperable, standards-based PKI software modules for managiang digital certificates and creating an environment for authenticated, private and legally binding electronic communications and transactions. RSA Keon software is designed to be easy to use and interoperable with other standards-based PKI solutions, and to feature enhanced security through its synergy with the RSA SecurID authentication and RSA BSAFE encryption product families.

Authentication RSA SecurID® systems are a leading solution for two-factor user authentication. RSA SecurID software is designed to protect valuable network resources by helping to ensure that only authorized users are granted access to e-mail, Web servers, intranets, extranets, network operating systems and other resources. The RSA SecurID family offers a wide range of easy-to-use authenticators, from time-synchronous tokens to smart cards, that help to create a strong barrier against unauthorized access, helping to safeguard network resources from potentially devastating accidental or malicious intrusion.

Encryption RSA BSAFE® software is embedded in today's most successful Internet applications, including Web browsers, wireless devices, commerce servers, e-mail systems and virtual private network products. Built to provide implementations of standards such as SSL, S/MIME, WTLS, IPSec and PKCS, RSA BSAFE products can save developers time and risk in their development schedules, and have the security that only comes from a decade of proven, robust performance.

Commitment to Interoperability

RSA Security's offerings represent a set of open, standards-based products and technologies that integrate easily into organizations' IT environments, with minimal modification to existing applications and network systems. These solutions and technologies are designed to help organizations deploy new applications securely, while maintaining corporate investments in existing infrastructure. In addition, the Company maintains active, strategic partnerships with other leading IT vendors to promote interoperability and enhanced functionality.

Strategic Partnerships

RSA Security has built its business through its commitment to interoperability. Today, through its various partnering programs, the Company has strategic relationships with hundreds of industry-leading companies—including 3COM, AOL/Netscape, Ascend, AT&T, Nortel Networks, Cisco Systems, Compaq, IBM, Oracle, Microsoft and Intel—who are delivering integrated, RSA Security technology in more than 1,000 products.

Customers

RSA Security customers span a wide range of industries, including an extensive presence in the e-commerce, banking, government, telecommunications, aerospace, university and healthcare arenas. Today, more that 9 million users across 7,000 organizations—including more than half of the Fortune 100—use RSA SecurID authentication products to protect corporate data. Additionally, more than 500 companies embed RSA BSAFE software in some 1,000 applications, with a combined distribution of approximately one billion units worldwide.

Worldwide Service and Support

RSA Security offers a full complement of world-class service and support offerings to ensure the success of each customer's project or deployment through a range of ongoing customer support and professional services including assessments, project consulting, implementation, education and training, and developer support. RSA Security's Technical Support organization is known for resolving requests in the shortest possible time, gaining customers' confidence and exceeding expectations.

Distribution

RSA Security has established a multi-channel distribution and sales network to serve the enterprise and data security markets. The Company sells and licenses its products directly to end users through its direct sales force and indirectly through an extensive network of OEMs, VARs and distributors. RSA Security supports its direct and indirect sales effort through strategic marketing relationships and programs.

Global Presence

RSA Security is a truly global e-Security provider with major offices in the US, United Kingdom, Singapore and Tokyo, and representation in nearly 50 countries with additional international expansion underway. The RSA SecurWorld channel program brings RSA Security's products to value-added resellers and distributors worldwide, including locations in Europe, the Middle East, Africa, the Americas and Asia-Pacific.

For more information about RSA Security, please visit us at **www.rsasecurity.com**.

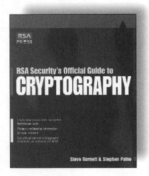

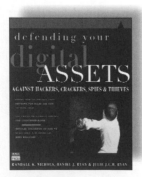